# The Ground You Stand Upon

*Life of a Skytrooper in Vietnam*

Joshua E. Bowe and Wilbur E. Bowe

Copyright © 2018 Joshua E. Bowe

IngramSpark Full-Color Hardcover ISBN: 978-0-692-14139-7 published June 2018, 2nd Edition ISBN: 978-0-578-54106-8 published July 2019, 3rd Edition published November 2019, 4th Edition ISBN: 979-8-218-28356-8 published September 2023, Barnes & Noble Press Full-Color Hardcover 4th Edition ISBN: 979-8-331-43216-4 published July 2024

KDP Black & White Paperback ISBN: 978-1-717-99437-0 published July 2018, 2nd Edition ISBN: 978-1-079-02638-2 published July 2019, 3rd Edition published November 2019, 4th Edition ISBN: 979-8-218-28372-8 published September 2023, IngramSpark Black & White Paperback 4th Edition ISBN: 979-8-218-47483-6 published July 2024, Barnes & Noble Press Black & White Paperback 4th Edition ISBN: 979-8-331-43211-9 published July 2024

E-Book ISBN: 978-0-692-11189-5, Kindle ASIN: B07DCJNN8X published May 2018, 2nd Edition published June 2019, 3rd Edition published November 2019, 4th Edition published September 2023

Audiobook ASIN: B07KFQ5W25, published November 2018

All rights reserved. No part of this book may be reproduced in any form or by any means, electronic, mechanical, photocopying, recording, or otherwise, without the author's written permission, except for a reviewer, who may quote a brief passage in a review.

The author does not claim copyright to the photos included in this work as they were obtained from various sources but requests that, if used, proper credit be given to the original owner, as noted in the caption. Unless otherwise indicated in the caption, all photos may be assumed to have been contributed by Wilbur Bowe or by the subject of the photo.

Every effort has been made to trace copyright holders and obtain their permission to use copyright material. The author apologizes for any errors or omissions and would be grateful if notified of any corrections that should be incorporated into future editions of this book.

The following permissions have been obtained:

"Letter by Richard Cantale" from *Dear America: Letters Home From Vietnam*, edited by Bernard Edelman. Copyright © 1985 by The Vietnam Veterans Memorial Commission. Used by permission of W.W. Norton & Company, Inc.

ASSOCIATED PRESS Photo 670211176, Catherine Leroy, photographer (photo of soldiers climbing down rope ladder from CH-47, Chapter 19)

Several articles from the 1st Air Cavalry Division's *Cavalair* newspaper appear reprinted in this book. The United States Army does not claim copyright on any of its material but does request that proper credit be attributed to all Army photos and articles.

To request permission to use any part of this work, email the publisher at: joshbowe@hotmail.com.

*It is a different type of war than we've ever fought. Even the weapons are new. Only the names of the fighting units are old. The 7th Cavalry, the 8th Cavalry... the 5th, the 12th, and the 9th. Regiments born and forged in the Indian wars that now ride into battle through the skies. It is a different type of country than we've ever fought in. Now flat and sunken with rice paddies, now rolling with hills and meadows, now mountainous and steep. It is hot, it is humid, it is thick with plants and vines. It is largely unpopulated, and in the military sense, it belongs to no one. Not to the Viet Cong who roam it, not to the South Vietnamese. It is no man's land. In Vietnam today, you will hold only the ground you stand upon.*

— John H. Secondari, *The Saga of Western Man*, 1965

For updates on my next book featuring war stories of veterans from the United States, Canada, the U.K., and Australia, serving in Vietnam, Iraq, and Afghanistan, please sign up at:

www.thegroundyoustandupon.org

www.facebook.com/thegroundyoustandupon.org

On our website and Facebook page, you can also find information on awards, editorial reviews, events, additional photos, videos, and order author-signed copies of this book.

Audio version narrated by Will Stauff available on Audible.

Submit additional information or corrections to:
joshbowe@hotmail.com

**7th Cavalry Regimental Crest**

We are the pride of the Army and a regiment of great renown, our name's on the pages of history, from sixty-six on down.

If you think we stop or falter while into the fray we're going, just watch the steps with our heads erect, while our band plays Garryowen.

In the Fighting Seventh's the place for me, it's the cream of all the Cavalry; no other regiment ever can claim its pride, honor, glory and undying fame.

We know no fear when stern duty calls us far away from home. Our country's flag shall safely o'er us wave, no matter where we roam.

Tis the gallant 7th Cavalry, it matters not where we are going. Such you'll surely say as we march away and our band plays Garryowen.

In the Fighting Seventh's the place for me, it's the cream of all the Cavalry; no other regiment ever can claim its pride, honor, glory and undying fame.

Then hurrah for our brave commanders! Who led us into the fight. We'll do or die in our country's cause, and battle for the right.

And when the war is o'er, and to our home we're going, just watch the step, with our heads erect, when our band plays Garryowen.

# Contents

Prologue ............................................................................... 7
1. The Letter ...................................................................... 12
2. Fort Carson ................................................................... 17
3. Army Life ...................................................................... 25
4. Airmobile ...................................................................... 42
5. Seasick .......................................................................... 61
6. Sorry About That .......................................................... 68
7. Into the Jungle .............................................................. 84
8. Air Assault .................................................................... 97
9. Life of a Skytrooper .................................................... 103
10. Search and Destroy .................................................... 115
11. The First to Fall ......................................................... 122
12. Deliver Us From Evil .................................................. 137
13. War Without Fronts ................................................... 147
14. Life and Death in the Jungle ..................................... 156
15. Valley 506 .................................................................. 170
16. Thanksgiving ............................................................. 180
17. The Best Day ............................................................. 190
18. The Outpost ............................................................... 201
19. Return to An Lao ....................................................... 211
20. LZ Santana ................................................................ 221
21. Hunter-Killers ............................................................ 230
22. Rumors ...................................................................... 233
23. R&R ........................................................................... 237
24. Beautiful Things ........................................................ 251
25. Unusual Load ............................................................ 261
26. Heart of Darkness ..................................................... 265
27. May 19th .................................................................... 273

| | |
|---|---|
| 28. Among Friends and Strangers | 285 |
| 29. The Final Patrol | 294 |
| 30. For What it Was | 304 |
| 31. Homecoming | 307 |
| Acknowledgments | 326 |
| Battle Maps | 330 |
| About the Authors | 335 |
| Bibliography | 336 |
| Glossary | 338 |
| Army Ranks | 342 |
| Units of the 1st Air Cavalry Division | 344 |

# Prologue

It is August 4th 2017 as I start to write this, fifty years to the day since my father returned home from the war. How do you write a story about something that happened over fifty years ago? I graduated only twenty-five years ago. All I remember is listening to some people talk and a nice lady in a maid outfit serving meatballs at my party afterward. Imagine trying to remember what happened on a particular day a half-century ago.

My dad remembers his best day, seeing Bob Hope's Christmas show at their base camp in An Khe. He remembers his worst day, Thanksgiving 1966. He remembers images, bits and pieces, friends made, and friends lost. Some of those images are grim. A dead soldier being carried down the hill on a stretcher, his arm sticking straight up in the air from rigor mortis, or their dead radio operator being loaded onto the chopper in the pouring rain. Others are happier. Vietnamese children holding their hands out and shouting, "G.I. numba one!" and "Give baby son chop, chop!" Others are simply foreboding. The San Francisco skyline disappearing into the mist as they sail to Vietnam, a column of infantrymen swallowed by darkness while taking their first steps into the jungle, or a disheveled, abandoned firebase that had been overrun by the enemy. Some are just oddities that stick in one's mind. A man in black pajamas running for his life through a flooded valley, or an unusually tall soldier standing atop a rice paddy dike amid a firefight, just looking around while everyone else takes cover in the muck below.

Starting out, I wanted to fill in the blank spaces between those images, documenting exactly where my dad and his friends were and what they did during their tour of duty. Useful information was scarce. Then I stumbled upon a map that showed the location of each battalion in the 1st Air Cavalry Division on October 4th 1966, the date of his company's first major battle. I found the military symbol showing the location of my dad's battalion, 5th Battalion, 7th Cavalry. Then I found another that showed the location of his company, Alpha Company, near an inlet-type lake near the South China Sea. All I knew from the books I had read was that his company had been sent to sweep the area eastward toward the sea and, at one point, was sent to rescue a downed helicopter pilot.

Emotions are funny things. I had read a few accounts of what happened that day, the personal story of the first Alpha Company trooper to fall and the young family he left behind. Compelling as it was, it didn't bring me to tears. But as I studied this obscure map with military symbols, knowing what happened there—realizing this was the very spot in the world where my dad first watched his dead fellow soldiers being flown away on helicopters—this is when I cried.

For months, I've struggled over how to describe places like the Bong Son and An Lao regions, Kon Tum and Binh Dinh Provinces, Highway 19, and the many mountain ranges, all places I've only read about. And yet those who were there will tell you that a rice paddy is a rice paddy. The valleys, the mountains, the rivers, the highways, they're all pretty much the same. The only thing that makes any of them special is what happened there. What they remember is their experience, the fear, the fleeting moments of joy and comfort, the bonds of brotherhood made, and the hardships of life in the infantry. Their mental scrapbooks hold a disparate collection of anecdotes, reminiscences, and legends. Like stealing the colonel's jeep and heading toward town, crying beside a stream while trying to wash the blood from a fallen friend's radio—or the haunting vision of a dead fellow soldier being carried to the chopper, his eyes suddenly opening as if he were still alive.

When I was a kid, our family would turn out the lights, make a bowl of popcorn, set up the movie screen, and click through photographs on our Kodak Carousel slide projector. Sometimes we would look at Dad's pictures from Vietnam. My favorite was of him wading through a sea of six-foot-tall elephant grass with his rifle, unshaven, cigarette dangling from his lips. And yet this photo was curiously absent from the collection he sent me when I started this. I think he was embarrassed to have a picture of himself smoking.

Clicking through the slides, he would mention their names, which ones got killed, which ones made it. I never thought much about those faces, who they were before being sent to war, who they were to my dad. I knew that he was drafted and sent there on a boat, it was really hot, he got shot at, had some friends who were killed, and got a rock lodged in his arm that never came out. He did his duty when called upon, and that was all I needed to know.

The rest of the story has since resided only in the fading memories of my dad and those he served with. But what a tragedy if that story were never told. My hope is for their loved ones to see this war through my dad's eyes and learn something more about what they did there and what they went through.

It is largely a story of drudgery, deprivation, and of walking through jungles and rice paddies waiting to get shot at. There is pain, death, and regret. It is also a story of courage, with countless Bronze Star and Silver Star citations attesting to the bravery of Alpha Company's troopers. Aside from these harrowing acts of valor, it is more the daily acts of courage I hope to convey. The courage to rise from the dirt each morning and continue the march, the courage to obey, the courage to simply show up.

The National Archives maintains a record of all servicemembers killed in the Vietnam War. Pulling together the names and dates of deaths of those in my dad's company provided a starting point for research. I also searched memorial websites such as the Vietnam Veterans Memorial Fund's Wall of Faces, where fellow soldiers, family members, and hometown friends have posted their personal memories of those lost in Vietnam. Some posted their email addresses, and

I attempted to contact each of them. Many shared their personal memories and backgrounds of the fallen. I'd like to thank each of them and have noted their contributions in the Acknowledgments section.

Three books were written by those who served in my dad's battalion during the same year. In 1994, Captain Bernard Grady (Ret) published *On The Tiger's Back*, recalling his time in both Bravo and Charlie Companies. Another was published in 2009, *1966 The Year of the Horse* by Robert Powers, an infantryman in Bravo Company. Both men fought in many of the same battles as my dad, and their accounts contributed much to this story. Both have since passed on. If I could, I would thank them for what they wrote.

Published in 2007 by Joe Sanchez of Alpha Company, *True Blue, A Tale of the Enemy Within* tells of his experience as a cop in New York City but also includes memories of Fort Carson and Vietnam and the friends he made there. He also helped us find many other veterans from their old company. Thank you, Joe, for all of that.

Published in 2023 by Mike Toyne, *Brown Mule 7, Life of a 5th Battalion, 7th Cavalry Combat Wireman in Vietnam 1966-1967* tells of his older brother Leon's experience with the battalion during the same time, much of it based on letters Leon sent home to his grandparents. Leon Toyne was a combat wireman in the battalion's headquarters company. In June 1967, he was severely injured when a rock hit his head due to explosives they were using to clear ground, requiring several operations and a metal plate in his head.

Much thanks is due to my mom Carol for helping with our research and for proofreading several drafts of this book. And to my wife Misty, who has shown great patience and understanding, encouraging me to finish this project since it began. I also want to thank my dad for all the letters and photographs he sent home from the war zone, as so much of this book was written in his own words over fifty years ago.

When I asked about the letters, I wasn't expecting much. He said that he'd started reading them once and quickly fell asleep. He gave me a cardboard box filled with letters still in their original envelopes, bound in rubber bands and in chronological order. There were over a hundred letters. His dispatches were sent from some of Vietnam's most remote valleys and outposts, often scribbled in haste before another mission—or by flashlight under a poncho in the rain. They would travel over eight thousand miles across the ocean to be placed in a mailbox that stood across from a farmhouse along a rural county road in Wisconsin. Reading each of his letters from beginning to end was the closest I will ever come to time travel.

One letter provided an answer I had been desperately searching for. It had to do with their mission on October 4th 1966, the date of his company's first killed in action, and their mission to rescue that downed pilot. I had corresponded with the daughter of the first Alpha Company soldier to be killed that day. We exchanged whatever information we had, but neither of us knew if they had succeeded in rescuing the pilot. My dad couldn't remember much about that day, but his letter told of how they had actually rescued both the pilot and his gunner. I was happy to share this with someone for whom it meant so much.

The letters illustrated how in the dark my dad and his fellow draftees were about their fate during their training at Fort Carson and how rumors were their main source of information. They also provided a window into who my dad was then. I had tried to keep in mind how young he was and how different he may have been from the man I'd always known. You see, my dad is considered a pillar of reliability, an honest and responsible man who never drinks too much and hasn't touched a cigarette since before I was born. He worked for over thirty years as a maintenance electrician at a local factory, and I can recall how each morning his lunch pail sat waiting for him on our kitchen counter, sandwich and apple inside.

As I read the first of his letters, it all hit me like a ton of bricks. He was just a kid. His concerns were that of a typical twenty-year-old—cars, girls, drinking, and having fun—in pursuit of which he wasn't afraid to break the rules. And he was jazzed to become what was known as a *skytrooper*, flying into battle with a historic cavalry regiment once led by General Custer. He drew a picture in one letter to show his little brother what their Australian bush hat looked like.

He may have been a bit embarrassed by the adolescent nature of his letters and some of the stunts he pulled. Then again, who wouldn't be embarrassed by a weekly recounting of all their thoughts and aspirations from when they were twenty years old? But these are the things that give the story life, that make it real. The letters paint a portrait of a young man, anxious to make his family proud and utterly unprepared for the reality of this new war. He wrote at length about that first pitched battle they had fought on October 4th, asking his family if they had heard about Operation Irving on the news. But as their search and destroy missions dragged on, he wrote less and less about the actual combat.

The letters also depict a mother desperately concerned for the welfare of her boy "Willie." Along with her letters, she would send my dad packages of food, packets of Kool-Aid, copies of the local newspaper, and at one point, a raincoat. She worried if he was eating enough, was he losing weight, was he cold, and was he receiving communion? Years later, she would confide in my mom that she had been haunted by the specter of a soldier in dress uniform standing at her doorstep, telegram in hand. Of course, she wasn't the only one. She would correspond with other mothers in the area whose sons were in Vietnam and often ask if Will knew where this guy was or where that guy was. And where exactly was he, because the firebases and remote outposts mentioned in his letters were not shown on the maps of Vietnam published in their local paper.

As a kid, I considered my dad rather worldly. He had traveled to exotic places and fought in a war. He was a scuba diver and had been an astronaut. As a construction worker walking on narrow beams high above the city, he'd helped build the tallest building in Minneapolis, the IDS Tower. An electrician by trade but also an amateur inventor and photographer, he knows about astronomy, is an expert chess player, and can play both the guitar and the accordion. A jack-of-all-trades, he works on his own cars, builds things, and creates all kinds of electric gadgets. When I was older, I realized he hadn't really been an astronaut, and the photos on our basement wall were actually of Neil Armstrong. Nonetheless, I still thought of him as a Renaissance man.

He is typically the first to offer help when someone is in need. I can recall him stopping to assist stranded motorists on the side of the road, once giving a ride to a woman with two kids walking along the highway in the winter. Now retired, he still spends many hours each week doing handyman work for friends and local churches. Although he may not have been as strait-laced and responsible as he is now, his letters home show how his basic decency and regard for human life have always been part of his character.

In March 2018, I took my mom and dad to the National Archives near Washington, D.C. We were searching for anything related to my dad's unit in Vietnam but had no idea what we would find. What we found were his battalion's daily staff journals and situation reports covering each day of his combat tour. Typed up by some sweating Army clerk in a command tent somewhere in the highlands of Vietnam, many featured coffee stains and an occasional smear of reddish-brown Vietnamese dirt.

We spent four days scanning thousands of papers and one day visiting The Wall and other memorials. I came home and began sifting through the reports. It was mind-numbing and tedious, but occasionally, a piece of information would appear to help bring this story together. I'd been reluctant to travel so far, not knowing what we would find. It turned out to be a trip very much worth taking.

It is now September 2023 as I finish making revisions to this book that was originally published in 2018. Since that time, many more men from my dad's infantry company have reached out to share their own memories, accounts, and photographs, as have many additional family members of those in Alpha Company who were killed in action. Their memories are now part of this book, and the Acknowledgments section is about two pages longer.

# 1
# THE LETTER

It was hard to stay awake, real hard. He could feel himself once again slipping into that half-awake, dreamlike state that always seemed to take over while on watch. The rain had stopped hours ago, but the jungle was still dripping, as was the poncho over his foxhole. They had been attacked at night before, and it seemed just a matter of time before it happened again. It was everyone's worst fear. With only weeks or days left for him in Indian country, he only hoped it would happen after he left. A cigarette helped him stay awake while Quinn slept a few feet away. As it dwindled, a slide projector of sorts in his mind scrolled through the most haunting images of the last year, including the faces of his dead friends. The image that kept reappearing, however, was from an earlier time when he would have been hard-pressed to find this place on a map—that of an unopened envelope sitting on the kitchen table. It had been delivered to a farmhouse in Tilden, Wisconsin.

Tilden is the tiny farm town where my dad was born. In October of 1965, Wilbur Bowe was still living on the farm and helping with chores when he could. He had recently started a job at Johnson Manufacturing, a machine shop in the neighboring town of Chippewa Falls, working on a lathe and making parts. It was hard work, but unlike the farm, you were done when the clock struck five. It was Friday, and it was quitting time. "See you Monday, chief," he said as he punched the clock.

"Stay out of trouble," his foreman Ronnie Club quipped. "And try to drive on the right side of the road."

In small towns, traffic tickets are published in the local paper, so everyone knows when you run afoul of the law. Earlier that summer, Will and his buddy Larry Geisler had been cruising Main Street in the nearby town of Bloomer in Will's '56 Ford Custom. A car full of girls drove by. Will found himself driving alongside the girls on the left side of the road while Larry tried to get their attention. The mildly amused girls drove off in the night as red and blue lights flashed in Will's rearview mirror. "You're a good kid Will, but I can't let this one go," said Bloomer's police officer as he wrote the ticket.

Will loved the weekend, and he loved his car, almost ten years old but in good shape. As usual, hitting the town with his pals was the plan for the night. *Hang On Sloopy* played on the radio. He cranked the volume and sped down County Road B between Chippewa Falls and Tilden. Then came some news about the conflict in Vietnam, and he turned the dial.

He walked through the door to find his mom cooking supper as usual, but he could sense something was wrong. His father was usually watching the evening news about this time. Now the television was turned off, and he sat silently, staring at an unopened envelope on the kitchen table.

"This is for you," he said grimly.

Will looked back at his mom as she busied herself in the kitchen. There were tears in her eyes. He sat down to open the envelope. It was from the President of the United States.

"GREETINGS: You are hereby ordered for induction into the Armed Forces of the United States..." it began. A local board composed of his neighbors had selected him to serve his country. He was to report to the post office in Chippewa Falls at 8:00 AM on October 26th. He was twenty years old.

Vietnam had been in the news as America's involvement was deepening. However, very few battles involving significant numbers of American ground troops had taken place yet. It was rarely referred to as an actual war. Rather it was a "conflict" that the Special Forces, Air Force, and Navy had been involved in since the beginning of the Kennedy Administration, mainly as "advisors" providing weapons, training, and air support to the Republic of Vietnam in their fight against the communists. The Gulf of Tonkin incident had made headlines in August of the previous year. President Lyndon Johnson could often be seen on their television, making the case for our continued involvement. Marines had landed in Da Nang in May 1965, while the Army's 1st Air Cavalry Division had established its base in Vietnam's Central Highlands in July. A build-up of troops had begun, regular Army and Marine divisions were now arriving in-country, and the draft had recently been expanded. Until now, Will's life had been unaffected by the whole affair. Across the ocean and over eight thousand miles from Tilden, this obscure place they talked about in newspapers called Viet Nam would soon turn his life upside down.

Still living on the farm with Will was his fourteen-year-old brother Mike and their older sister Diane. She had suffered brain damage from a severe fever at age five and would live on the farm for as long as their parents, Eddie and Millie, could care for her. Will's two older brothers, Melvin and Darrell, already had families of their own, and Mel had started his own farm just up the road.

Darrell had joined the Army in 1954 and had been an airborne instructor. When he completed basic training, the family traveled to Fort Knox to see him graduate. Driving through Chicago on their way back, Eddie took a wrong turn at a stop-and-go light and was pulled over for driving on the sidewalk. The cop figured he was a drunk driver and started with the citation. Realizing he was just a lost farmer in the big city, the cop ripped up the ticket and helped him find his way out of town.

Twice during the 1950s, Taiwan came under attack from communist China. During the first of these attacks in January 1955, known as the First Taiwan Strait Crisis, Darrell's unit was called up to go and defend Taiwan. With their bags packed and the engines of their C-130s running, the mission was put on hold. The engines were shut off, and Darrell and his unit slept on the tarmac beneath the planes while diplomats negotiated a peaceful resolution.

Darrell became a trucker after leaving the Army. He and Will had a joint venture of sorts, a stock car they named PT-109 after John F. Kennedy's PT boat. Darrell did most of the driving, although Will gave it a go during one race and finished dead last.

Will had little interest in farming despite his upbringing. This was hard for me to understand as a kid. I thought the farm was the greatest place in the world, with all kinds of equipment to climb on, cats and dogs everywhere, and very little adult supervision. My cousins and I would ride the Honda three-wheeler all over the countryside, often flipping it. We shocked each other with the cattle prod and made forts out of bales in the hay barn. I always found somewhere to hide when it was time to go home. But for my dad, the farm was just a place where you did a lot of work. The cows had to be milked every morning and night, seven days a week, so your work was never really done.

Will had just graduated in 1964. Athletic, funny, and good-looking, he was well-liked at McDonnell Catholic High School, where he'd played fullback for the Macks. Known as "Grip," coach Ray Gripentrog had led them to a winning season during Will's senior year after going winless the year before.

After graduation, Will had attended Allied Machinist School in Chicago, the farthest he'd ever been from home, and Eddie had sent him off with a bus ticket and a twenty-dollar bill. Upon arrival, he needed a place to stay but didn't have enough money for the first month's rent. He made a deal with an apartment owner to pay it with his first check from the job that his school set him up with at a local chocolate factory. One of his favorite places in Chicago was the Adler Planetarium, where he took up an interest in astronomy.

One day, his younger brother Mike and his friend Larry Geissler made the bus trip down from the farm to visit him in the big city. Millie had packed sack lunches for the boys. Upon seeing all the candy at the factory, they dumped out their lunch sacks and filled them with chocolate.

You should know a few things about my dad's hometown. Settled by German immigrants in the nineteenth century, Tilden is a small unincorporated village between Chippewa Falls, home of the famous Leinenkugel's brewery, and Bloomer, which happens to be the rope jumping capital of the world. It is mostly dairy farms and cornfields. It is precisely halfway between the Equator and the North Pole, a fact made known to all who pass by along Highway 53, thanks to a billboard constructed by Will's brother Mike and some friends. Along with Chippewa Falls and Bloomer, it is one of the few places in the world where the name Bowe is routinely pronounced correctly, *Bo-vee*. There is a Catholic church, a motel, and two bars. One of these bars also serves as a banquet hall. Giant letters that spell "FOOD" are plastered on the highway-facing side of it. This is where our family has gathered over the years to celebrate weddings, anniversaries, birthdays, and a welcome home party for Mike's son Neil when he returned from the war in Iraq with the Wisconsin National Guard in 2005.

For a time, Mike served as Tilden's mayor-constable. When Eddie learned about his son running for mayor, he decided to run against him. It wasn't that he really wanted the job, he just thought Mike should have to run against someone.

The 1960s were known for protests, and Wisconsin farm country had its own civil unrest. Will and about ten others actually went to jail during an NFO (National Farmers Organization) protest over meat contracts in 1964. Protests would later erupt over milk prices, but no blood was spilled—only milk.

Many in the area were either drafted or enlisted into the military in 1965. Will's friend Don Mc Ilquham joined the Army and became an artilleryman. His next-door neighbor Allen Simon was also drafted into the Army, along with his friend from Bloomer, Charlie Rubenzer, and Bill Leidel, his coworker at Johnson Manufacturing. His childhood friend Ricky Mitchell joined the Marines. Like thousands of others across the country, Will would soon become a soldier trained to fight in the jungles of a foreign land. His journey would include many firsts. His first train ride, first voyage at sea, first ride in an airplane, first time in a foreign country—and the first time he saw a girl in a miniskirt.

*Bowe farm*

*Eddie Bowe*

*Left–right: Darrell's son Scottie, Eddie, Millie, Diane, Will, Darrell's son Randy, and Mike Bowe*

# 2
# FORT CARSON

*The sergeants here have never taught basic training
before and are about as dumb as we are.*

Leaves littered the sidewalk as Will approached the post office in downtown Chippewa Falls. The morning was cool and brisk. It smelled of fall, the kind of smell that reminds you of football. Eddie had driven him there in their big old family Oldsmobile. It was always easy to spot. Instead of placing each new license tab over the last year's, Eddie would just stick the colorful tabs all over the license plate. Will had already sold his '56 Ford Custom to his friend Larry. Dozens of young men were already there. Some looked anxious, others looked excited, but most were just joking around as they waited to report for induction. While standing in the first of countless lines in his Army career, Will met a fellow named Rodney Henning from Eagle Point, another small town near Tilden.

They were loaded onto a bus bound for the Federal Building in Minneapolis, Minnesota. After much poking and prodding, those found physically fit proudly raised their right hand and swore to defend the United States against all enemies for the next two years of their Selective Service obligation. They stayed at the Andrews Hotel a few blocks away. The next morning, they boarded a train bound for Fort Leonard Wood, where they were in-processed and given uniforms, haircuts, shots, and a written test to determine the occupational specialty they were best suited for. They quickly learned what "hurry up and wait" meant as they were herded like cattle from one station to another.

### 31 October '65

Hi Folks,

*Well, here I am. We've been issued clothes and given tests and a physical. It's been a lot of fun 'cause we ain't done nothing yet. There are six guys here from Chippewa County I know quite well. Without them I'd feel alone. Some of our guys got drafted into the Navy. I would have went crazy if I was in the Navy. This is okay so far, I hope. Well, how's everything at home, do any combining yet? We've had good sunny weather here. Did Larry find the title for the car?*

*Wish I was through with this part. We get sixteen shots. Some are given to you without the needle, they're blown into you. Ain't much more I know. Just having a lot of fun. I hate getting up at four in the morning. Well, who wouldn't? Oh yeah, we also got a haircut. Eighty cents those S.O.B.s charged us.*

*Well, see you in eight weeks.*

*Willie*

After a week at Fort Leonard Wood, Will and several others were flown to Colorado for basic training. After landing at the airport in Denver, they were herded onto buses bound for Fort Carson. After rolling through its main gate, rows of drab-colored barracks came into view.

Then the bus stopped. A drill sergeant appeared at the front of the bus and told them they had exactly one minute to get all of their shit off his bus. By design, their first task was an impossible one. They struggled to escape the bus as fast as they could, olive-drab duffel bags in tow.

"Put your bags over there," the drill sergeant yelled, "then form up over here—move your ass, privates!"

More drill sergeants emerged from behind the barracks, quickly descending upon the hapless gaggle of troops, each of them barking random questions, declaring what was wrong with them, or just telling them to move their asses. In their new green fatigues, the privates stood at attention in a crooked half-baked formation. The drill sergeants walked up and down their lines, immediately fixating on those who looked unusually awkward and mocking those who seemed excessively gung-ho. "Looks like we got a regular John Wayne over here," remarked one.

After their brief get-to-know-you session, they were split up into platoons and informed that their sorry asses now belonged to Bravo Company, 1st Battalion, 11th Mechanized Infantry (1/11th Inf). Mechanized meant they would operate armored personnel carriers—track vehicles like tanks, without the big cannon on top.

### Friday, 5 November '65

Dear Folks,

*Bet you never thought I'd end up out here. Neither did I. Pike's Peak is right next to us, about fourteen thousand feet up and covered with snow. Ninety of us came from Fort Leonard Wood by plane. Man, what a ride that was. To look at the land below was really beautiful, especially when you didn't have to pay for it. Well, how's the weather? It's just perfect over here, bright and sunny. Our platoon sergeant is very nice. We were standing in formation, and we told him the sun was getting hot, so he let us stand in the shade. We could have easily gotten the other one who is tough, mean, and a Karate-Judo expert. We got a pretty mixed-up gang of fifty-four here. One from Guam, Canada, and five different states, a half-dozen Negros, and two Indians. The little guy from Guam is a real comic.*

*You know, ever since I've been in the Army, I've been asked why I pronounce my name with the sound of a V. Today I was asked, and the guy says, "You must be German." Said he took German in school. You pronounce W like a V. So now I know.*

*How's everyone at home? I hope you got my address right, 'cause I'm expecting a letter from EACH of you. Also, I took out a five-thousand-dollar life insurance for a dollar a month. Don't know what the catch is. I guess I better close now. My arm is still stiff from a shot I received yesterday. I got one in the ass last Monday. The needle was at least two inches long, and that ached for two days. We all went to the dentist yesterday, and some got five teeth pulled. Good thing I brushed my teeth.*

*So long for now,*

*Willie*

*Send your zip code also.*

At Fort Carson, Will lived in Army barracks, ate Army food, and earned his first Army paycheck—just over sixty dollars after taxes. In 1965, an Army Private earned $87.90 per month, plus three hots and a cot. If sent to a war zone, he'd get an additional $65.00 in combat pay that was "worth every penny," as Will's Army buddy Marvin Bierschbach would later joke.

The soldiers typically trained six days per week, with most evenings off. There was a movie theater and bowling alley on post. They could find beer at the PX, a military convenience store. Overlooking Fort Carson is Mount Cheyenne, where NORAD is located.

Most draftees expected to be sent to Vietnam. Still, no one would be officially informed until completion of their AIT (Advanced Individual Training), which would follow their basic training. Also left unknown was the job or MOS (Military Occupational Specialty) they would be trained for and what unit they would be assigned to, but there was no shortage of rumors.

### Sunday, 21 November '65

*Dear Folks,*

*Well, I am bushed. Had K.P. (kitchen patrol) all day. Twelve hours of cleaning and mopping up the mess hall. I went to a football game yesterday, Air Force Academy against Colorado University. Colorado Won 19 to 6. I'll have to razz Gordy about that.*

*Tomorrow I'll take my M-14 and march three miles to the rifle range. We'll be doing this for the next two weeks. This physical exercise isn't nothing yet compared to my football exercise. I don't have anything to worry about compared to the weather I had in Chicago last winter. Man, that was rough.*

*When does deer hunting start? Say Dad, you should go back to Colfax hunting. This place where the deer cross over the dirt road where Schwabs from Bloomer got their deer. That's the very first place I'd go.*

*Reason I called Larry was some "wool" he tried to pull over my eyes. Why, there was no worry for me. The old Army will see to it I'm taken care of every minute.*

*This Henning kid from Eagle Point, we figure on going airborne. I imagine you don't like the idea, but it ought to be a real treat to jump out of a plane, haha!*

*Say, about putting my name in the paper. I wish I had told you before, but I am completely against it. It makes people think I am lonesome. If they want to write to me, they can find out my address.*

*What do you mean Mike dropped two subjects? He better sit on his ass and study. I don't care how good he is at ball if he flunks out of school.*

*I'm sure glad Dad is getting his eyes tested. I was thinking about a pair of glasses for a Christmas present. I don't know if I'll be home for Christmas. Heck, I'll be home two weeks later anyway, maybe even hitchhike on this fourteen-day leave.*

*We are having turkey for Thanksgiving. What are you having?*

*So Long,*

*Willie*

When they weren't training, they were either getting yelled at by their drill sergeants, cleaning things, or standing in line. The new privates learned that whenever you got a break in the Army, you smoked. Even if you didn't smoke, you smoked, as it lessened your odds of being tasked with some undesirable miscellaneous job, known in the Army as a "detail."

They would also learn drill and ceremony—how to march in formation, right-face, left-face, and about-face. "And there it is," exclaimed one exasperated drill sergeant, "the one who's gonna get his buddies killed in Vietnam 'cause he don't know his left from his right!"

### *30 November '65*

Dear Folks,

*It's almost 2 AM. We all have fire watch about once a week for an hour. So Ricky Mitchell is going over to Viet Nam. Two sergeants that take care of us guys are going over also.*

*Oh, last week I had a good argument with our three sergeants and everyone in our barracks. They almost made a laughing stock out of me. I asked a question. If you held a rifle horizontal to the ground and a bullet at the height of the rifle in the other hand. You fire the rifle and drop the bullet at the same time. And the two bullets will hit the ground at the same time. Only one fellow knew for sure I was right 'cause he took up physics in high school. I got a few bucks I'll make* on this bet. Father Rascey asked that same question when I was in fourth grade, and he better be right.

Did anyone get a deer yet? I am getting a little shooting in myself, only it's at targets. I guess I am fairly good at it. There is a right way and a wrong way and an Army way of shooting a rifle. If you ever call this M-14 a gun, it's ten push-ups for you.

Say Mike, that's mighty good to sell forty candy bars. The most I sold was two, and I ate them myself. Man, those two you sent me, I was really starving for. I'll buy two more if you have any left.

All I can say for the Army is that it's still a bunch of horse shit. It's been pretty easy so far. The sergeants here have never taught basic training before and are about as dumb as we are.

*Willie*

## Willie

The 1/11th Mechanized Infantry had a mascot of sorts. Earlier that year, a female brown bear cub had wandered into Canon City, Colorado. She seemed orphaned, so someone brought her to the Pueblo Zoo. Having no need for an extra bear, zookeepers brought her to Fort Carson, where the 1/11th adopted her. The battalion's sergeant major couldn't tell if the cub was male or female and named her Brutus. Officially, Brutus T. Bear—the T stood for "the."

A *Stars & Stripes* article noted how Brutus, being good-natured for a bear, had once attained the rank of Specialist-Five (SP/5) but was later busted down for biting a general's finger. As one soldier explained, "There was a sign saying, 'Don't put your hand in the cage,' and he did. There was some discussion over whether she should be promoted or demoted because of the incident, but the general's view prevailed. We thought she should have gotten a medal."

Brutus liked beer, and at a year old and 125 pounds, she already had a reputation as a heavy drinker. The article continued, "Although her Form 20 lists her Military Occupational Specialty as Terrain Analyst, her primary function is to assist in making this unit the colorful, high-spirited, and well-known battalion it is. Her Form 2166 reflects such rating factors as 'Frequently fails to get along with others, both on and off the job' and 'Requires a lot of supervision in relation to what gets done,' but the members of this battalion have complete confidence in her ability to excel as a mascot."

## 5 December '65

Dear Folks,

*I should wait until tomorrow night to write. I have such a hangover. Been drinking all last night and this afternoon. We got paid a whole big $61 last week. You know, I got paid $13 too much—for half a minute, anyway. You see,* the lieutenant was counting the money, and the First Sergeant asked me how I got to say Bowe with the sound of a V. I wasn't watching him count the money while I was explaining my name, until I got outside the door and counted $74. About to take off running when the First Sergeant hollered, "Bowe, come here."

The Army has plans for us with tanks and heavy guns, that is if I don't become an airborne paratrooper. We'll qualify on the rifle range this week and go to the gas chamber for a taste of tear gas. Next weekend I'll have a pass to go off post and hit the town. Some guys around here really get wild. They start to scrap every time they have a few beers. The beer is weak, but the air is thin, and it makes a big difference.

How does Dad like his new glasses? How is Mike going to camp in the cold? I guess we might camp out next week too. So no one got shooting at deer except Dad. I am not coming home for Christmas, I am sure. I'll graduate from basic in January and come home for fourteen days.

That argument about the bullet is still going on. You know, which one drops first. Well, I guess I'll close for now.

Your Son,

Willie

## Sunday, 11 December '65

Hi Mike,

I'll tell you what we all did this week. Monday, we went through the tear gas chamber. While inside, we all took our gas mask off to give our name, rank, service number, date of birth, and where we live. Man, you might say I was crying for an hour afterward. Damn, that was awful. Then Tuesday, went to the rifle range, and I shot expert. Boy, am I ever good. You'll need me to shoot your deer next year. Did you get to shoot any deer? Thursday night, we went through the infiltration course. That's crawling ninety yards over logs and barbwire while the machine guns fire bullets forty-four inches over our heads. December 20th, we'll go on our little old camping trip, carrying fifty pounds of equipment. During our march, there will be planes shooting at us. If we don't get off the road in time, we'll be full of holes. Maybe if they give me a few bullets, I'll shoot them down.

So how's basketball coming along? Yeah, I'd like to see how you got it set up. Looks like the Packers are tied with Baltimore. I watched part of that game today. Hey, Ma says you still have some candy bars left, and I'll buy them if you haven't eaten them already! Where the hell did you sell forty candy bars? Take 'er easy now. Write sometime this week.

Your big brother Willie

From November 1965 to January 1966, Will and his fellow trainees completed their Basic Combat Training, training that each soldier went through regardless of the MOS they would later be assigned. They ran several miles each morning and learned basic combat, lifesaving, how to use their gas masks, and marksmanship. Will qualified as an Expert Rifle Marksman.

### Tuesday, 20 December '65

Dear Folks,

Well, I thought I'd write this week to answer your letter. I received your box today. The very first thing I did was open it. I was eating a popcorn ball in one hand and fudge in the other, and the letter I received at the same time as the box. Here I was eating away, and I read, "Do not open until Christmas." Oh well, I didn't open two of the boxes anyway.

I haven't had a chance to go to town yet. Had guard duty and K.P. the past two weekends. I'll be kept pretty busy during the holidays. Going to the zoo and a hockey game, and maybe learn how to drive a tank. After that, it's just tests and monkeying around until January 12th, when we graduate. Then I'll come home by the 13th for fourteen days and then on my way to airborne… I hope I can get into it. Henning is pretty happy today 'cause he didn't think he would make the fourteen-mile march. Now he's sure of going airborne with me.

So Larry got picked up for speeding. Surprised he got away with it for so long. Received some cookies the other day from my foreman Ronnie Club. Then I got Christmas cards from quite a few people. I wish I could send them one back, but I'll write them a letter instead. It makes it worthwhile to get up in the morning when someone is thinking of you. Yeah, I got Dad's and Mike's letters. They should write more often. Mike signed it "little Skeeter." They called me that in high school, also. Have you got the Christmas tree up? Yeah, we got one here too. Sure wish I could ride home in Santa's sled. That would be a Christmas present and a half.

Don't worry about me drinking too much. It's the very last thing I can afford to do, except for New Year's Eve, maybe.

Merry Christmas and Happy New Year,

Willie

While standing in line to be measured for their dress uniforms for graduation, Will met Robert Wagner, a tall, barrel-chested guy from Seattle. "If I were just a half-inch bigger, I'd have a forty-inch chest," Will said.

"And if I were a half-inch bigger, I'd have a forty-two-inch chest," Wagner replied.

## 4 January '66 – 22 months left

Dear Folks,

Sure was glad to receive your letter. I am sure of this now, I'll be home on the 13th of January. I am catching a plane to Minneapolis for thirty-two bucks. From there, Don Mc Ilquham's buddy will take me home. Just tell Diane to listen for a car about breakfast time on the 13th.

So a lot of guys are wondering where G.I. Bowe is. I bet they think I am either in the Navy or the Air Force. After this, I am still going airborne. I'll be getting fifty-five dollars more each month, and I could use it. I heard that Allen Simon got into the Army.

Sounds like everyone had a busy holiday. I almost forgot it was Christmas. I didn't even get close to a bar on New Year's Eve, so us guys went to a Jerry Lewis show instead. Can't wait 'til I get home. It will be a treat, but I tell you, I am by far happier in the Army, even though it means that I might end up in Viet Nam. I ate my best meal in the Army, and I ate my worst meal here, too. Yeah, we got our "sea ration."

Larry wrote and said he had blood poisoning from barbwire he used to pull a fox out of a hole. He said he almost went nuts 'cause he had to stay in the house for three days. Oh yeah, this Packer game I watched last Sunday was alright, and a week before when they took a close one from the Colts. I'll have to tell Larry about that one. I guess I'll shave and hit the hay. Lights go out now at nine o'clock, and I've been writing for an hour in the can. I think this will be my last letter 'til I come home.

So long for now. I'll be seeing you soon,

Willie

Will Bowe (left) and Rodney Henning (right) at Fort Carson

# 3
# ARMY LIFE

*We have a new platoon sergeant named Burtis. A good man and was a cotton picker in Alabama. I could tell right away he was a farmer.*

Posted on a large board outside the orderly room one morning at the end of basic training was an alphabetical list of every man in the company. Next to each name was his assigned MOS. From Piqua, Ohio, Thomas Monnier was surprised to find 68W, the MOS for medic, next to his. He took this as good news, thinking he'd end up serving in a hospital somewhere. Scanning the list, he found a handful of others assigned as medics, including Bill Garcia, Mike Walker, and Michael Handley. The group was sent to Fort Sam Houston for combat medic training. Monnier soon learned that he would be serving nowhere near a hospital and that combat medics serve out in the field as members of the infantry company.

Will scanned the list with his pal Rodney Henning from Chippewa Falls. Both were found exceptionally qualified to be infantrymen, otherwise known as grunts. Next to Henning's name was 11B for Infantryman, and next to Will's, 11C for Indirect Fire Infantryman, also known as a mortarman.

For every infantryman in Vietnam, there were six or seven soldiers in other branches, such as artillery, aviation, engineers, transportation, and supply. Many draftees had hopes of doing something besides pounding ground for the next two years. But one difference between enlisting into the Army and being drafted was that those who voluntarily enlisted could choose their MOS, while draftees could not. The infantry was not a popular choice among those who enlisted, leaving a gap in its ranks to be filled by draftees.

Since they had stayed at Fort Carson through the holidays, they were allowed to return home after basic training, and so Will and Henning traveled home together. When they returned to Fort Carson in February, Henning was transferred to the 1/11th's Delta Company and Will to Alpha Company, along with Robert Wagner, Dennis Sherry, Richard King, and Bruce Madison. Alpha Company was led by their commanding officer (CO), Captain (CPT) A.J. Wise. Then all the Indirect Fire Infantrymen in the battalion, including Will, were temporarily attached to Charlie Company for advanced training on the mortars. They would return to Alpha Company after their mortar training.

*10 February '66 – 89 weeks left*

*Dear Folks,*

*Don't have much to say, and what I do have isn't good. I was in Alpha Company, 1/11th by some mistake for three days, and made a nervous wreck of me. Now I'm in Charlie Company. Got the letter you sent, envelope all marked up. Looks like it was all over post. This was how I got moved. From B Company to A, to C, to A, to C, to C 1/61st, back to C 1/11th. So you can see how it got mixed up.*

*Thought I'd be getting into a good company. We can't even take a shit without letting the sergeant know where we're going. This is worse than basic. They're so damn scared we might take off. A guy I know went AWOL this morning. They're on your ass all day long, and you can't even go anyplace, and doing work that's so meaningless. Don't be surprised if I go over the hill.*

*Didn't do much this week. Still a bastard of a company. Figure on starting A.I.T. next week. We're getting this sergeant that was in the Marines for nine years and just came back from Viet Nam. Puts on like he's tough, but I doubt it.*

*You know, Rod Henning is just across the street from me. Don Mc Ilquham is up about four blocks, and we see each other once in a while.*

*Will*

Indirect Fire Infantrymen operated the mortar weapon system in teams of four or five. Will and the others were trained on the 81mm mortar. Like portable artillery, it lobbed exploding projectiles at the enemy. Unlike full-scale artillery, it could be carried along with the infantry company, controlled by its commander, and fired with or without a forward observer to spot and adjust the rounds. The enemy in Vietnam also used mortars.

The 81mm mortar system stood just over four feet high when assembled. Weighing approximately ten pounds each, the mortar rounds were oblong-shaped with tail fins. They were muzzle-loaded, meaning they were simply dropped into the barrel, or tube, as it was called. Gravity and a firing pin at the bottom did the rest, propelling the round back out of the tube and into the sky while making a loud metallic "shunk" sound.

Will and his team members learned the duties of each position. They broke the system down, set it back up, dug the mortar pit, and set the base plate and aiming stakes. They split up the system and carried it on their many long marches out to the training ranges.

### 17 February '66 – 88 weeks left

Dear Folks,

*They seem to have eased off their "gung-ho, here we go" deal. Actually, I haven't learned anything yet since I came back from leave. All I did was drive this armored personnel carrier for about half an hour yesterday. Then we had to qualify for our A.P.C. license, and I passed my driver's test. Big deal, everybody did! We had this one sergeant teaching us how to drive, and he has never been inside one before. "Yeah," he says, "I'll have to get my license tomorrow, too." Huh? Well, that's the way they are around here. We got National Guardsmen right* with us, and they've done less than we have. Next week, I guess we learn some weapons or small artillery. We have a new platoon sergeant named Burtis. A good man and was a cotton picker in Alabama. I could tell right away he was a farmer.

This guy Barrow that I bunk next to has four years of college, and can he ever draw. Usually, he whips out pictures of fancy cars. We have quite a few Puerto Ricans in our barracks, and they all talk Spanish to each other. This Sunday, I figure on getting the gang to go skiing up on Pike's Peak.

Say, I got me a sleeping bag. They're worth eighteen dollars, and I'm going to send it home when I get a chance. I didn't steal it or anything. You see, if you were missing any of your equipment, you could get it replaced. I asked the supply clerk if they had an extra sleeping bag, and he said sure. Let me know about all that happens in the N.F.O.

Will

During their advanced training with Charlie Company, Will made friends with Kurt Elmer and Thomas Ragimerski, and a few black soldiers, Arnott Graham, Carl Evans, John Bronson, and Willie Harris, as well as a couple Puerto Ricans, Robert Figueroa and Angel Reynosa, all of them from Harlem, the Bronx, or Queens. Evans and Bronson were both tall and lanky. They could often be heard singing with Figueroa and Reynosa in the barracks, harmonizing to songs like *Under the Boardwalk* and *My Girl*.

Arnott Graham was short and muscular. He had come to the United States from the island of Trinidad in 1962 and spoke with a Caribbean accent. Graham recalled how Kurt Elmer's parents had emigrated from Germany and how he was the only white person he knew from Harlem. Graham's father had died when he was only four years old. Raised by his mother, he grew up in extreme poverty on the island. He came to America by himself at the age of nineteen, moving into a small Harlem apartment with two of his aunts. But it seemed that his aunts just wanted a "slave boy," as he put it, to do chores around the apartment.

Graham was working for minimum wage at a factory when he received his draft notice—with a token for the train, so there'd be no excuse for not showing up. He blew it off at first, but the notices kept coming. Eventually, one of his buddies from the 'hood got drafted. He figured Army life couldn't be worse than living with his aunts, so he took the train to the induction center at 39 Whitehall Street in Manhattan, raised his right hand, and became a soldier.

"I served with many great guys, and your dad was one of the best soldiers... one of the best human beings I've ever known," was the first thing Graham said to me. "Everybody loved Bowe. If ever I met a color-blind person, it was your dad. I almost felt like I wasn't black around him."

Graham spoke of the other New York guys, Ragimerski, Reynosa, Figueroa, Evans, and Bronson, and how they all liked to party. "I would have fit in better if I was into getting high," he said, "but it wasn't really my thing." One of Graham's best friends was Robert O'Brien, a big six-foot-two Irishman from the Bronx.

Will's new bunkmate Martin Quinn was also from New York City. "He and I hit it off from day one," he reminisced in his New York accent. "I remember Will moving into the barracks for our advanced training, and that was it. We became bunkmates at Fort Carson. He was a farm boy, so I figured he knew everything about the outdoors. I thought he'd be a good pal to have where we were going. A real comedian, he was always cracking us up and never took anything too seriously." He also told of how the sergeants often made Will re-shave his face because he could never shave his coarse beard close enough for inspection.

"It would drive me crazy," Quinn said about Will's messiness and disorganization. Will had a stocky frame with muscles from a life of farm work and a few years of football, while Quinn was tall and skinny. They were sort of like *The Odd Couple*, with Will as the sloppy and carefree Oscar, and Quinn as the serious-minded Felix. They came from very different worlds but forged a lasting friendship. The one thing they had in common was their parochial school background, both having been educated by Catholic nuns and priests during their childhoods.

"Friday, October 15th 1965," Quinn recalled the day he received his own draft notice. "I'll never forget it… with a token for the train. I told my boss, 'As of five o'clock today, I am no longer employed here. I'm leaving for the service.'" As he left, his boss gave him a medallion—a Miraculous Medal, he called it—commemorating the Virgin Mary's Immaculate Conception. He would wear it on a chain around his neck for good luck.

Although most were from various boroughs of New York City, there were others in their advanced mortar training, such as Marvin Bierschbach from Minnesota, Al Patrillo from Pennsylvania, as well as John Fulford and Fred Brodosi, both from Florida.

Marvin Bierschbach was from a little town called El Rosa near Saint Cloud, Minnesota. Like Will, he was raised on a farm, was unmarried, had recently graduated high school, and was not in college—a perfect candidate for the draft in 1965. To avoid a career in the infantry, he tried enlisting in both the Navy and Air Force, but they were all filled up. He cried when he received his draft notice. Nonetheless, he showed up. He had completed his basic training at Fort Leonard Wood and was slotted as an artilleryman. But his orders were changed at the last minute, and he was sent to Fort Carson to train in the "God damn infantry," as he put it.

Al Patrillo was a country fellow with blondish hair. His childhood friend Tom Ivey lived just across the street in their hometown of Susquehanna, Pennsylvania. Two years his senior, Tom recalled how Al was like an older brother to him and how they would make all kinds of mischief around their small town. They started out riding their tricycles together, playing marbles, making clubhouses from cardboard boxes, and flying balsam airplanes with long wind-up rubber bands.

They considered Tom's younger sister a pest and always tried to get rid of her, once sticking a ball of prickly burdocks in her curly brown hair. Tom's mother cried as it was but a week before her First Communion, and she would have to get her hair cut short. Once, they pushed her so hard on their swing set that she went flying and broke her arm. As she was his sister and not Al's, Tom faced the brunt of the punishments for their misdeeds.

Tom and Al would roam the woods and stone quarries, finding baby crows and rabbits, and bringing them back to their parents, who would tell them to put the animals back where they'd found them. They played hardball with other kids on a makeshift neighborhood ball field, and Al was always chosen first when picking teams. They rode their bikes to the lake to swim, where they always got an "electrocuted hot dog" and a bottle of Ma's Soda. They fished for trout in the stream, and Al would bring his rifle to shoot woodchucks. Al took up taxidermy when he was a teenager. His first mount was a Flicker, a bird that looked like some sort of woodpecker. Al was meticulous, explaining to Tom each step in the process.

After Al graduated in 1963, they spent less and less time together as Tom still had two years of high school left. Al went to work and bought his first car, a '57 Ford Fairlane hardtop convertible. It was his pride and joy, and he worked hard to fix it up. After receiving his draft notice, Al sold his car to a friend.

### *21 February '66 – 87 weeks left*

*Dear Folks,*

*Well, my weekend is a flop. I had planned on going skiing but can't go on pass until one o'clock in the afternoon. I'll have a pretty good idea where I am going soon. Rumors say we might go to Germany. I hope so. I should be making E-2 pretty soon.*

*It's lonely in the barracks now. Just about everyone is gone. Man, am I glad that I bought me that radio. It's really worth it. A lot of guys want to buy it from me 'cause it's the nicest around. I had it on guard duty one night. I was guarding these warheads with floodlights and live ammunition. An officer came to check on me. Had I gotten caught with the radio, it would have meant a stiff fine. Ask if I was sweating while he was talking to me.*

*The National Guard are all leaving after A.I.T. This is one mistake I made. I should have joined the Guard or some reserve. Then again, I never wanted to take a back seat.*

*So Mike is a Tender Foot, haha. That sounds pretty cute. I'd like to step on those feet. Make him write a letter some time. I almost forgot, send me the rest of my clothes if you can. I'd like my sweater, the red shirt, the short-sleeved yellow shirt, and blue pants. Well, so long. I'm going to the show now, it's only thirty-five cents.*

*Will*

Back in Alpha Company, those not slotted as mortarman were completing their own advanced infantry training. Among them was another Puerto Rican from New York City, Joe Sanchez. Eighteen years old, small in stature but in search of adventure, he'd tried to join every service in the military—including the Regular Army—but had been rejected based on his physical. "If I'd been born a dog instead of a person," he wrote in *True Blue, A Tale of the Enemy Within*, "I might have been something like a runt Doberman trying to be a K-9."

He was told to go to his local board and request his draft be pushed forward, as the standards for the draft were different. Being deemed unworthy to enlist but good enough for the draft was actually quite common. Soon Sanchez received his own letter from the President, along with a token for the train that would take him to the induction center at 39 Whitehall Street. Upon completing the very same physical he'd failed before, he was finally accepted as a draftee. At the time, his swearing-in was the proudest moment of his life.

Both Sanchez and Graham had completed their in-processing at Fort Dix, where they'd met Alan Weisman, a Jewish guy from New York. Weisman was engaged, and Sanchez met his fiancée while stationed there. He thought she looked a lot like Barbara Streisand. His first Army buddy, Sanchez looked up to Weisman. He was a few years older, and Sanchez had been impressed by his confidence while flirting with the stewardesses on their flight to Fort Carson.

### 13 March '66 – 84 weeks left

*Dear Folks,*

*Sorry I haven't written. I wasn't feeling too well today. I played hero and gave a pint of blood and felt pretty weak in the stomach. I wanted the day off to see the pretty nurses at the hospital.*

*Rod Henning isn't going to Viet Nam. He is trying like hell to, though. Don Mc Ilquham might. So far, I am not. Sometimes I wish I were going very much. You never know. I might yet. I hope not. About half have orders to go in May. What is Kenny Mueller's address? I have to tell him what to expect. Nobody ever told me anything, and that pisses me off. You know that Larry might be drafted, don't you?*

*My clothes came in good shape. I want you to send my white shirt and two or three good ties, my good overalls, and some of my underwear.*

*So Mike really likes the sleeping bag. I slept in them twice and warm as hell. Mike wants that little scooter. Get it for him! It'll be a good hobby. How I wish I had one at that age. Keep him out of trouble, haha! Well, I'll sign off like him.*

*From a Handsome, Muscular, Mighty, Great, Fabulous,*

*Willie*

Alpha Company claimed young men from all over the country—most from places you've never heard of—including twenty-six from Kentucky. Nicknamed "Juggy," Guy McNay was from Erlanger. Martin Quinn remembered him as a nice, quiet guy who was into cars. Drafted into the Army at twenty, he'd survived a rough upbringing. His older sister Annette Sebastian had been granted custody of Guy and his two brothers for abuse by their father and stepmother. "Juggy was a brother to me," Annette's son Walter remarked. He recalled seeing some of the beatings that Guy and his brothers took before coming to live with them when they were teenagers, and he was in grade school.

Also from Kentucky were grade school friends Gene Cross and Donald Duncan. Another was Bill Purdy. At eighteen, he was finishing high school and had just gotten into the ironworkers union when he received his draft notice.

Purdy remembers thinking of his friend, twenty-six-year-old Donald Rankin, as one of the old guys in their outfit. A devout Christian, he was the nicest guy you could ever meet. Along with his five brothers and one sister, Rankin had grown up poor in a family of tenant farmers amid the tobacco fields of central Kentucky. The first in his family to attend college, he was among a small handful of draftees in the company who had done so. However, he struggled to pay his tuition loans and dropped out with only one semester to go. He was drafted shortly thereafter.

Jim Hirschuber was from the small town of Stoddard, near La Crosse, Wisconsin. Drafted at nineteen, he got his notice the day before his wedding. Sent to Alpha Company from another basic training unit at Fort Carson was a small guy, Bobby Hansen. He was from New Jersey and became friends with Jim Hirschuber, Guy McNay, and Alan Weisman. The comparatively tall Hirschuber described Hansen as "always the life of the party," and the two became pals.

Thomas Erickson came from a poor family on the east side of Saint Paul, Minnesota. He had just turned eighteen and graduated high school when he was drafted. His older brother Marv was drafted a month later. While Tommy was at Fort Carson, Marv trained at Fort Bliss, and they exchanged letters.

In *The Faces Behind the Names* by Don Ward, Marv told of a time in 1963 when he was nineteen and Tommy was sixteen. He had just gotten his driver's license and took Tommy on a road trip to visit relatives in California in his old '53 Ford. Unlike other Minnesota families, they had never gone to the "lake" or on a summer vacation. They couldn't afford a motel, so they drove straight through to their grandmother's house. Marv recalled how while sightseeing between Los Angeles and San Francisco, "We even went to the 'lake' where we met a couple of girls and had a great time. The trip turned out to be the highlight of our young lives. We relived that vacation many times over."

### 24 March '66 – 83 weeks left

Dear Folks,

Well, here I am for two weeks in the fields, and it feels a bit like home. This place used to be a big ranch. Beautiful mountains all around here. The first two nights we spent in tents. Was it ever miserable, cold and windy. Thought I'd never live through it. Now we are in insulated tents with heaters, and it's a lot nicer. We had guard today, and I was picked to be Colonel Orderly, and now I sit in this hut 'cause I was the only one who knew how to type. Guess that was one time it paid off. Guys are suspicious about that sleeping bag.

Henning finally got his way and is going to Viet Nam. Don Mc Ilquham might go. Sergeant was telling us guys tonight about when he was over there. He was with the Green Berets or Special Forces. He was talking to us two guys for a couple hours. It must have been something to go through, alright.

Yes, Larry owes me exactly a hundred bucks. Do you ever hear anything about him getting drafted? No doubt he's scared. If not for the farm work, this would be the best place in the world for him.

I received those pictures and really got a bang out of them. I tried calling you guys last Sunday about 5:30, but everyone was out visiting. Figure on getting back to base about April 4th, so I'll call then. Ask Mike what he wants, like helmets, bayonets, cowboy boots. But only if he writes a letter. And Dad, too.

Your son,

Will

Sergeants are noncommissioned officers or NCOs. While commissioned officers—lieutenants, captains, and colonels—make plans and set policy, NCOs put those plans into action. Responsible for their direct supervision, they are expected to know their soldiers well and always place their needs above their own. In 2010, I held the rank of Specialist (SPC) in the Minnesota Army National Guard. Not yet a sergeant, I was assigned as a team leader, a position typically held by one. I was fairly inexperienced when I joined Officer Candidate School, the Army's commissioning program, and I had recently washed out.

"Well, Bowe," said Staff Sergeant (SSG) Brian Toohey, "the officer corps didn't want you, but we're gonna make you an NCO." My new squad leader had served in the 173rd Airborne Brigade during the initial invasion of Iraq in 2003. Anyone assigned to his squad found him a competent leader who always put the needs of his soldiers before his own, but also one you never wanted to cross. Failure to follow his instructions brought swift repercussions.

SSG Toohey had assigned several tasks for me as a new team leader during our 2010 annual training in preparation for our unit's deployment. One was to record the serial numbers of all three of my assigned soldiers' weapons and take accountability twice per day. Another was to record each man's blood type and allergies in case of emergency. Last, I was to memorize the *Creed of the Noncommissioned Officer*. I accomplished all this in short order, staying up late in our barracks memorizing the creed, which includes the following passages.

*My two basic responsibilities will always be uppermost in my mind: Accomplishment of my mission and the welfare of my Soldiers. I will not use my position to attain profit, pleasure, or personal safety. I will communicate consistently with my soldiers and never leave them uninformed. I know my soldiers and will always place their needs before my own.*

I awoke the next morning with these words etched firmly in my short-term memory. SSG Toohey never asked me to recite them. Instead, he asked me what I knew about my soldiers. Basically, I knew their names and blood types. While memorizing the words of the creed, I had missed the point.

Although he was nearly ten years younger than me, I looked up to SSG Toohey like an older brother. And I'll never forget the last time I got smoked in my Army career. Getting "smoked" or "scuffed up" is when your NCO dishes out punishment by making you do push-ups or to simply stay in the starting push-up position known as the "front-leaning-rest" for an extended period—usually mixed in with any number of physical ordeals until he's satisfied that you've gotten the point.

During that same annual training, our detachment stayed in what we called the "pig barn" barracks on Camp Ripley. I don't think they were ever actually pig barns, but they were old World War II vintage wooden buildings that were only used when all the other barracks were filled up. Among the units of the 1st Brigade, ours was typically on the bottom of the totem pole, and we were considered the red-headed stepchildren of our battalion. Since the entire brigade was training at Camp Ripley that August, this is where we found ourselves.

SSG Toohey told me to bring a big dry-erase whiteboard to the field during our training one day. I had my guys load it into a two-and-a-half-ton truck we called the "war pig" on our way out. We were participating in an exercise engineered by some civilian contractors and Regular Army personnel called XCTC or "ecstasy" as our platoon sergeant SSG Scott Corbin called it. We were in a convoy of Humvees. Our mission was to clear a bunch of buildings in a pretend Iraqi village with the help of some actual Iraqis who were roleplaying as Iraqi police. I was to have a small team of these Iraqi policemen lead the way. Approaching the first building, the Iraqis refused to go in, so I just barreled ahead and kicked the door as hard as I could. There was no give to it whatsoever. I fell flat on my back, and the door blew up. Now a pretend casualty, I waited for the medevac chopper to come and get me.

When the mission was over, sweating in the August heat, we all gathered around to listen to one of the Regular Army instructors tell us what we did wrong. Apparently, I should have just grabbed one of the Iraqi policemen and shoved him through the door ahead of us. On our way back to evening chow, I had my guys throw the whiteboard back on the war pig.

That night, everyone was milling about the barracks and getting ready for the next day's training. SSG Toohey asked me where the whiteboard was. I told him we had put it on the truck and forgot to bring it back in after chow. This is when the long-remembered smoking commenced. We had a very nice talk about life as I performed push-ups and other exercises to the point of exhaustion. With me sweating profusely, our conversation continued after the smoking, and the topic turned to how I could be a better NCO. Toohey wanted to impart to me his style of leadership, the kind that would make my guys jump into action without hesitation. This would require a more heavy-handed approach.

Our platoon sergeant SSG Corbin joined in, saying how being a team leader is the toughest job in the Army, how you needed to ride the Joes—lower enlisted soldiers—hard during training but also attend to their needs, how their problems were now your problems. Like Toohey, Corbin was former Regular Army. He'd invaded Iraq with the 101st Airborne and had been an air assault instructor at Fort Benning. To the Joes in the platoon, he was like our dad, and Toohey was like our cool—but also mean—older brother. Then Toohey said, "Bowe, do you know how to dominate a room?"

Corbin interjected, "Yeah, like this." He grabbed a folding chair and whipped it across the room. "What the fuck!" he yelled as the chair slammed against the wall. The barracks fell silent, and everyone fixed their gaze on SSG Corbin like a bunch of deer caught in the headlights. "That's how you dominate a room, Bowe." Then everyone returned to what they were doing like nothing happened.

SSGs Corbin and Toohey were hard on their men at times but also cared for them. Like all the NCOs in our detachment, they never ate chow until each of their men had gotten theirs. It may seem a small thing, mostly symbolic, but it was really just a mindset. At times, some of our soldiers would be sent to train with other units, and those units rarely thought to accommodate them in terms of food or anything else. This mindset ensured that the needs of the Joes would not be forgotten by their leaders. At the end of annual training, Corbin rented out a couple of houses on post for all of us to have a party in. We all respected SSGs

Corbin and Toohey, knowing they would do anything for us. They were examples of what we wanted to be as future NCOs.

Among Alpha Company's NCOs were SSGs Donald Burtis and Bobby Hayslip. From Georgia, SSG Hayslip was half-American Indian. SSG Burtis had grown up on a farm in Alabama and was the nicest of all their NCOs. He was big and tall and wasn't always yelling at them like the others.

SSG Kenneth Gregory was a veteran NCO who had served in the Korean War. "Are you guys having fun?" he asked Bobby Hansen at the rifle range. "Yeah, you'll see how fun it is when those targets are shooting back at you."

Another of Hansen's NCOs was SSG Elvin Wideman from Saint Louis, Missouri. When asked why Elvin had joined the military, his younger brother Ron offered, "Probably to get three meals a day," recalling how they had grown up in extreme poverty. Elvin was born the second of seven children, and Ron the youngest. They all attended Holy Family Catholic grade school, but only Ron went on to high school. The others all went straight to work. "Elvin was basically like a father to me," Ron reflected. "Partly because he was so much older, but also because our father was an alcoholic and had divorced our mother when I was just an infant."

Ron remembers his older brother Elvin as generous and kind but also saying to him, "Don't ask mom for anything because we don't have anything." Elvin had joined the Marine Corps in 1955 and served in Korea, then got out in 1960. Soon after, he was married and had a child. But within a year, he realized civilian life wasn't for him and re-enlisted, this time into the Army. He earned his high school diploma while in the Army and was a drill instructor at Fort Leonard Wood before moving to Fort Carson. When Ron was a kid, Elvin would drive him around Fort Leonard Wood to look at Army trucks and equipment. He once said to him, "Boy, I'll kick your ass if you ever join the Army." SSG Elvin Wideman and his wife Joanne had one more child before he left for Vietnam, giving them a son and a daughter.

Just like Will, Joe Sanchez had grown tired of being ordered around and of all the menial tasks that new soldiers typically do, like cleaning, polishing floors, and kitchen patrol (KP), all while getting yelled at by their NCOs. He remembers returning to their barracks after a long day of training to find all their stuff thrown out on the lawn because someone had forgotten to lock his footlocker. The soldier who had left his footlocker unlocked was made to carry it for the rest of the day.

In charge of Sanchez was Sergeant (SGT) Bill Chapman. Noting his poor attitude, SGT Chapman invited Sanchez to "vent his feelings," as it were, "off the record." Thinking he was free to speak his mind, Sanchez doubled down on the offer, swearing his sergeant a blue streak a mile long. Before marching out to the range the next morning, Chapman gave Sanchez a forty-pound rock to put in his rucksack, so he could "work off some steam."

Sanchez carried the rock along with the rest of his gear for several miles to the range and then back to the barracks that night. His buddy Alan Weisman joked, "P.T. Barnum must have been talking about you when he said there was a sucker born every minute."

Regarding his friend Arnott Graham, Sanchez remarked, "Graham was a swell guy, but he had a big problem with authority."

"My Army career was turbulent," Graham admitted. "I was sort of the black sheep of the company. If I felt I was being picked on, I rebelled. I received two or three Article 15 disciplinary actions for fights and scuffles at Fort Carson."

While he often bumped heads with his NCOs, Graham got on well with Alpha Company's commander, CPT A.J. Wise. He had been with Alpha Company for basic training and had no issues. But when he was attached to Charlie Company with the other mortarmen for advanced training, that's when the problems started.

"Charlie Company wanted to discharge me for failure to adjust," Graham said. "I'm sitting there with the Inspector General, Charlie Company's commander, and the chaplain. Then Captain Wise comes in and tells them how he thinks I'm a good soldier and wants to keep me in Alpha Company. My life would have turned out very different had he not stuck up for me that day."

### 17 April '66 – 79 weeks left

*Dear Folks,*

*About time I write again. Next Saturday we finish A.I.T. I can't go airborne. Short of men, so they say. But I am not going to give up. We'll get paid fifty-five dollars more if we train airborne.*

*I don't like to tell you this any sooner than I have to, but I think it best to say I am going over to Viet Nam by the end of the next three months. So I'll be home for a few weeks this summer. Many guys have orders to go in May. They showed picture slides of the country. Heck, I am looking forward to going over—for a day, that is. I am really surprised to see that all of the guys are anxious to go. Our Charlie Company captain has four Purple Hearts and was wounded three different times. He has pictures of the prisoners he has captured and killed. Our first sergeant was over there and got wounded also. He says he made over a thousand bucks a month on extra pay and bounties, so I'll make a few coins while over there. It isn't as bad as it sounds. Viet Cong are only five-foot-two to five-foot-four, haha! No, I do look forward to going. And I won't have two years of meetings when I get out, like in the reserves.*

*Camp Red Devil was miserable. Back here, I can relax with a can of beer, a bag of salty peanuts, swing music and a mild cigar. Tonight the colored guys are wild. Drunk as hell, and six or seven of them shaking dice, each with a fist full of bills. About the only thing you can live for here is the nightlife, otherwise you'd go bugs. I am still glad I am in the Army. Eighteen months and I am FREE GONE. Man, I am just holding my breath for that day, like waiting for Christmas when I was a little kid. High school was the same way. I'll make it one day at a time, and life will be so wonderful again. Sigh.*

*My buddy Charlie's having his girl come out here to get married. I got a hunch he'll want me to be his witness. He's a real swell guy. I think it's a good idea for him to be married. Maybe not. Two ways of looking at it in the Army. I guess I'll hit the hay. They shut the lights off, and now I'm sitting in the can.*

*Will*

Some soldiers had transistor radios to help kill the boredom of their downtime in the barracks. Will had one of his own and prized it dearly. Most of the music it played was of a familiar rock and roll sound he had grown up with. The Beatles were his favorite. His buddy Al Patrillo liked country music. Folk rock singers Bob Dylan and Simon & Garfunkel had recently become popular. Yet some of the sounds emanating from Will's radio were becoming very strange. New bands with odd names—Jefferson Airplane, The Grateful Dead, and Strawberry Alarm Clock—and cryptic lyrics that often sounded like nonsense. They were playing a new kind of rock known as psychedelic. Even the well-established Beatles had begun adapting to psychedelic rock's popularity. Society was changing. The America they would eventually return home to after their time in Vietnam would be remarkably different than the one they left in 1966.

A favorite pastime of SSG Bobby Hayslip and others, they often played dice or cards while in the barracks. Marvin Bierschbach recalled how they would gamble until one was completely broke, and the other had all the money. Then, in a basic form of loan sharking, the one with all the money would lend to the other at a rate of two to one—borrowing ten dollars to owe twenty—so he could keep gambling or buy smokes.

As soon as they were issued weekend passes, the men hit the bars in town. A bus took them there and back. A city slicker of sorts, Martin Quinn thought of Colorado Springs as a hick town in those days. "The bars downtown were all up and down the sidewalk," he recalled. "Carl Evans and John Bronson—these tall black guys we were friends with—always went to this one bar and had their girls lined up for Friday and Saturday night." A favorite bar of the officers was an Irish pub called The Golden Bee. Many found themselves at the tattoo parlor after a night of drinking.

Mixing Fort Carson's soldiers with booze and Colorado Springs townsfolk was a recipe for fistfights, often resulting in spaghetti western-style bar room brawls. "You a tough guy?" one thick-necked local breathed into Will's face. And his breath, to borrow a phrase from *Pancho and Lefty*, was hard as kerosene. A shoving match started, and Will got kicked out before any punches flew. Returning to post on the bus, an MP (Military Policeman) at the main gate demanded to see everyone's passes. Will had not been issued one that day, and he wasn't the only one. The MP ordered those without passes to wait outside while he checked the passes of those who had them. As three others awaited their fate outside the bus, Will slipped into the darkness, sneaking back across post to his barracks.

On another day off without a pass, Will and a buddy decided to climb the nearby Mount Cheyenne. This time, they returned to post through a large culvert to avoid the MPs at the main gate.

Joe Sanchez and Thomas Ragimerski also found themselves in a scuffle with some local boys while leaving the bar one night. Outnumbered, they were chased all the way back to the bus terminal.

There was a USO hall at Fort Carson where young women were bussed in from surrounding towns to attend dances with the servicemen. Sanchez was there one Saturday night. One of his buddies picked out the prettiest girl in the hall, betting that he was too chicken to dance with her. Sanchez was younger than most of his Army buddies and inexperienced with women, so he marshaled his courage. Her name was Teresa. She was twenty and lived in Denver. Not only did Sanchez get her to dance, he also got her number.

Sanchez called Teresa the next weekend. She wanted him to visit her in Denver, an hour away from Fort Carson. He didn't have a car, but one of his buddies did and agreed to drive. Robert Figueroa, Carl Evans, and Willie Harris decided to come along. They went out dancing with Teresa and her girlfriends.

As it was getting late, Sanchez's buddy who had driven them wanted to call it a night. The rest wanted to stay out, so Teresa said she would drive them back in the morning. After a long night of carousing, Evans, Figueroa, and Sanchez were checking into a hotel. Willie Harris came in the lobby saying, "Hey man, your girl's taking off."

Sanchez ran out to find Teresa waiting for him in her car with the engine running. "Let's go for a ride," she said. It was his first time with a woman.

### 21 April '66 – 79 weeks left

*Dear Folks,*

*I'll be home in July. Now all this is based on fairly reliable rumors. If I go airborne, it will all be changed again. We'll graduate this Saturday. Even heard rumors about going to Georgia for "airmobile" training, whatever that is.*

*All the National Guard taking A.I.T. with us have their noses in the air 'cause they're on their way home soon. They'll be cooled down when they're alerted this summer or later. They were all in the Korean War, they'll be in this one too.*

*Yesterday, I seen my first mouse here. I chased it and knelt on a cactus. Oh, it's painful. And I missed the mouse. Wanted to stick it down someone's neck.*

*If you have an empty box lying around, throw in some cookies and stick it in the mailbox. Just make an extra-large batch next time.*

*Your son,*

*Will*

Despite mixed feelings about Vietnam, Will thought, "If I'm stuck in the Army, I may as well be where the action is." He and Rodney Henning tried all they could to join the airborne corps. Combat medic Tom Monnier also tried, thinking that the war would be over by the time he finished airborne school. Still, no one was allowed out of the company. And so, it never really mattered what any of them wanted to do. Whether they wanted to be where the action was, or where it wasn't, or just in any service that wasn't the Army, or any branch that wasn't the infantry, or whether they wanted to jump out of airplanes—it mattered not to the Army. Their fate as ground pounders had been predetermined.

Most of the Army's main fighting units were already in-country, and the men anticipated being split up and sent to Vietnam as individual replacements. Royce Barrow had already received orders assigning him to the 4th Infantry Division in Vietnam. Fred Brodosi had been slotted as a door gunner for some other unit. Unknown to them was the fact that they were all desperately needed to fill out a brand-new battalion to be formed from those already assigned to the 1/11th Mechanized Infantry.

*Martin Quinn at Fort Carson*

*Cheyenne Mountain*

*Left–right: Molski, Elmer, Willie Harris, O'Brien, Figueroa, Sanchez
photo from Joe Sanchez*

*Angel Reynosa — CPT A.J. Wise*

*Marvin Bierschbach — Royce Barrow*

# 4
# AIRMOBILE

*They say it is a pretty comfortable war, so they say. You go out and fight a little, come back, take a shower, go to the P.X. and have a few beers.*

After their mortar training, Will, Quinn, Graham, Bierschbach, Patrillo, Reynosa, Figueroa, Evans, Bronson, Fulford, Ragimerski, Brodosi, Willie Harris, and all who had been attached to Charlie Company were brought back to CPT Wise's Alpha Company and assigned to 4th Platoon. Having completed their own advanced training at Fort Sam Houston, Tom Monnier and the other medics also returned to Alpha Company. Bill Garcia from California was assigned to 1st Platoon, Mike Walker to 2nd Platoon, Michael Handley, a tall farm boy from central Illinois, was sent to 3rd Platoon, and Tom Monnier to 4th Platoon.

It was the last week in April. The men stood in formation outside their barracks, awaiting a big announcement that would change everything. Their company, and in fact, their entire battalion, would stay together and go to Vietnam as an intact unit. Those who had already received transfer orders to other units, such as Royce Barrow and Fred Brodosi, would have those orders canceled. Upon deployment, the battalion would be released from the command of the stateside 5th Mechanized Infantry Division to join the 1st Cavalry Division in Vietnam.

Since their arrival in July of 1965, the 1st Cavalry had built airfields and firebases throughout the Central Highlands. The division's area of responsibility—the land it owned—was known as II Corps. Sandwiched between I Corps to the north and III Corps to the south, it was the vast middle section of South Vietnam. With few exceptions, policy was that no man would have to serve in-country for more than a year. The initial group of division soldiers had been in Vietnam for almost a year and would soon be rotating back to the states. Will and his friends represented the second wave of division men who would continue their mission.

The 1st Cavalry Division had three brigades. Each commanded three fighting battalions, except for 3rd Brigade, which had only two. Another battalion was needed. And so, the 1st Battalion, 11th Mechanized Infantry was officially renamed the 5th Battalion, 7th Cavalry Regiment—5/7th Cav for short—and now belonged to the 1st Cavalry Division's 3rd Brigade. Within this brigade, the 5/7th Cavalry would join the 1st and 2nd Battalions of the 7th Cavalry Regiment—the 1/7th Cav and 2/7th Cav—already in Vietnam.

It should be explained how the regiments associated with each of these battalions—the 7th Cavalry, the 8th Cavalry, and so on—were in name only. They had been kept part of each battalion's name for purposes of heraldry and esprit de corps, military jargon for flair. The modern Army was now organized by brigades rather than regiments. Many old cavalry and infantry regiments had existed since the Civil War or earlier. Brigades, however, had not been around that long, and they lacked the rich historical lineage of all these old regiments. And so it was that the names were kept, including that of the famous 7th Cavalry.

Formed exactly one hundred years prior, the 7th Cavalry had earned its fearless reputation during the Indian wars of the Dakota territories under the command of Lieutenant Colonel (LTC) George Custer. The 7th Cavalry saw action in the Philippine-American War at the turn of the century, in the Pacific during World War II, and in the Korean War. As portrayed by Errol Flynn in the 1941 film *They Died With Their Boots On*, Custer chose the popular Irish drinking song *Garryowen* as the regiment's official marching tune. "Garryowen" eventually became the phrase with which fellow 7th Cavalrymen greeted each other. The essence of cavalry esprit de corps, the song was played at every event where their band was present, and its rousing melody would become lodged in the memories of generations of 7th Cavalry soldiers.

### 24 April '66 – 78 weeks left

Hi Hot Dog,

Say there, kid. When are you going to drop me a few lines? How's school holding out, and when do those races begin? I think I'll see the races next Sunday in Colorado Springs. I should be home to see my car run this summer. Man, I miss the smell of burnt oil and the gunning of the engine.

You know this Alpha Company, 1/11th will be changed to Alpha Company, 5/7th. This is General Custer's cavalry unit. Going to wear an Australian bush hat and jump boots. Oh, it's going to be sharp. It'll be tough training. They're building a Vietnamese village outside of the Fort. That ought to be a laugh.

Henning and I got stoned last night, had to carry him back. I had K.P. with a big hangover today. This Ongsiner girl that chums with Carol Bresina, is her first name Sue? Henning and I have a five-dollar bet on it. I might get myself a tattoo next week. A beautiful eagle with mountains in the background. Think I should? I always wanted one. I asked Darrell if he wished he could take his tattoo off, and he said he did, so I hesitate. Oh well, write sometime.

Will

This (abridged) article appeared in Fort Carson's paper, *The Mountaineer*.

### Custer's Famous 7th Cavalry Returns To Life In New 5th Battalion

The new 5th Battalion, 7th Cavalry, first commanded by George Custer a hundred years ago, boasts a heritage of four Distinguished Unit Citations, two Korean Presidential Unit Citations, a Philippine Presidential Unit Citation, and the Chryssoun Aristion Andries, Greece's Gold Medal for Bravery. The 7th Cavalry was at the Battle of Little Bighorn in Montana June 25th 1876, when Custer's 264 cavalrymen faced over six thousand Sioux, Cheyenne, and Apache Indians. The result was history, and fourteen were awarded the Medal of Honor. The 5th Battalion, 7th Cavalry comes to life again at Fort Carson, not far from where it was first given the mission of guarding the western frontier in the days of Indian warfare.

The 7th Cavalry Regiment was formed July 28th 1866 at Fort Riley, Kansas. Its regimental crest, a horse-shoe shape with an arm and saber of the type used in the Indian campaigns. The blue and gold colors reflect the old cavalry. Across the top is "Garryowen." The regimental name Garryowen, Gaelic for Owen's Garden, comes from the 5th Royal Irish Lancers who frequented Garryowen near Limerick, Ireland. A tavern took the now-famous name, and there the traditional song was born. Later, across the seas, General Custer approved the name and song so popular among the tough Irish immigrants and Civil War veterans in the 7th Cavalry.

They faced such famous Indian chiefs as Crazy Horse, Sitting Bull, and Joseph of the Sioux. Indian campaigns were against Comanches and Nez Perce in Montana and Dakota, at Little Big Horn and Pine Ridge. Troops C, E, F, I, and L were annihilated at Little Bighorn, where Custer made his famous last stand. Later, they were in pursuit of Pancho Villa on the Mexican border. The regimental colors were flown in the Philippines as far back as 1878. During World War II, the 7th Cavalry won a Distinguished Unit Citation in Luzon and the Philippine Presidential Unit Citation. The 1st Cavalry Division made the initial entry into Japan, and the 7th Cavalry had the honor of escorting General MacArthur into Tokyo. Twenty-eight days after Korean fighting started, the 7th Cavalry Regiment was at Pohang-Dong for the first of nine campaigns.

The 5/7th Cav was still short of men, so many were transferred into the battalion from other units between April and May of 1966. One was Gerald Anderson, a towering fellow with glasses from Illinois. "I had trained on the large 4.2-inch track-mounted mortar," he recalled. "When I transferred to the 5/7th, they saw that I was a mortarman, so I was assigned to the mortar platoon—but they were using the smaller, portable 81mm mortars that I'd never seen before. I had a lot of learning to do before we left for Vietnam. I felt very welcomed by the guys in the platoon. I think we all felt the same. We knew we were going to Nam and wanted to get to know and trust each other quickly."

### 28 April '66 – 77 weeks left

*Well, I am in my Cowboy unit now. Getting our camouflage clothes next week. The only battalion on post to wear these. A new weapon's been issued to us, the*

M-16. It's like a twenty-two, but if you ever got shot in the foot, it could kill you. It's very wicked. Looks like a toy, very light and weird-looking. Two shots could cut a man in two. I got a few pictures of it to send you. If you're worried about me going airborne, no need. They're not letting anyone go. We're all going airmobile now. Going to train in helicopters. Just travel in them, not flying them. Don't know if we will get extra money for airmobile.

We start training Monday with a fifteen-mile march. We've been doing a lot of exercise this week, and I am stiff. Ought to make P.F.C. next month. These sergeants that have their bellies hanging over their belts. Oh, are they hurting. They have to work out with us also. Forty to fifty years old, and they're out running. They're pretty funny, and we tease the hell out of them. Even the cooks work out with us. Also, the big "bird" colonel. In Basic Unit Training, it will be intensified. Two hours of physical training each day. "We will be TRAINED Soldiers," says the captain.

Ricky Mitchell got into a few close battles. Sounds exciting. He can handle himself okay. This may seem funny to you, but I am glad I am in, as much as I hate this. If I hadn't been drafted, I am quite sure I would have enlisted.

I am in a platoon now with a bunch of hoods from New York City. They're some "cool cats." We're right next to the P.X., which is handy. My buddy isn't getting married until he gets home on leave. We figure on being in the fields quite often now. There's a firebase in Viet Nam called Little Big Horn, and our General's middle name is Custer. Ahem.

Adios,

Will

On April 30th, First Lieutenant (1LT) James Harmon's 2nd Platoon would assist with a firepower demonstration. A lot of brass—Army slang for important people—would be there, including the 5th Mechanized Infantry Division commander. "Everything was choreographed," Bill Purdy recalled. One of the many things set to explode was a Claymore mine, a small landmine that sprays bb-like pellets in one direction. During the demonstration, one 2nd Platoon soldier was napping on the ground, his feet propped up on a log. When the Claymore detonated, a pellet shot back in the wrong direction and went through one of his size-thirteen boots. Their platoon leader was not happy. The stray pellet wasn't their fault, but now 1LT Harmon had to explain to CPT Wise how his soldier managed to get hit on the bottom of his foot. Wise would have to explain it to their battalion commander, LTC Trevor Swett, who would then have to explain the incident to General Autrey Maroun.

On May 2nd, the battalion commenced Basic Unit Training. In this final phase, the men would learn combat insertion and extraction by helicopter, known in the industry as air assault. Today air assault is considered a special skill with its own schoolhouse at Fort Benning. Only soldiers of exceptional physical fitness are sent there, and those who graduate are given wings to wear on their uniform. In 1966, air assault wasn't considered a special skill but rather a basic job requirement for every fighting man in the 1st Cavalry Division. It was part of the new airmobile concept. Rather than marching long distances over contentious terrain, it envisioned airmobile infantrymen—skytroopers—flying into battle on steel horses.

With the advent of mechanized warfare in the First World War, the cavalry had traded in its horses for tanks. In preparation for the looming war in Indochina, they had swapped those tanks for helicopters. In 1965, the 1st Cavalry Division was officially designated the 1st Cavalry Division Airmobile. A catchier name, it was more commonly referred to as the 1st Air Cavalry Division.

The airmobile concept faced its first test in November 1965 when the 5/7th's sister battalions of the 3rd Brigade—the 1/7th Cav under the command of LTC Hal Moore, along with the 2/7th Cav and others—confronted a much larger communist force in the Ia Drang Valley of Vietnam's Central Highlands. The battle was depicted in the film *We Were Soldiers* based on Moore's book *We Were Soldiers Once... and Young*. Surrounded by the enemy, it promised to be a repeat of another 7th Cavalry commander's last stand, when Custer and his cavalrymen were butchered to the last man at Little Bighorn. And it would have been if not for the massive amounts of air bombardment, napalm, and artillery brought down on the enemy. The Ia Drang was the first major battle between regular American ground forces and their North Vietnamese Army (NVA) counterparts. The running five-day battle claimed over two hundred American lives and over a thousand NVA, and both sides claimed victory.

It wasn't just the infantry that was transformed by the airmobile concept. Assigned to the 1st Air Cavalry were artillery, engineer, transportation, medical, intelligence, military police, and signal units, all designated airmobile. With over four hundred aircraft, the 1st Cav's aviation battalions could quickly move them like chess pieces about the battlefield. The UH-1 Iroquois, or Huey, was the airmobile workhorse. Along with the larger twin-propeller CH-47 Chinook, it became the modern soldier's lifeline in the field. In airmobile training, the men learned how to board the Huey and how to jump off. They learned about centrifugal force and how not to fall out. They learned how to rappel by rope from a hovering Chinook. Loaded with over fifty pounds of gear, bodies sweating, and hearts pounding, they leapt to the ground and sprinted outward in all directions to secure the landing zone. Some would not become entirely comfortable with flying during their training. Once in-country, they would find that getting shot at helped to quickly overcome any lingering fear of heights. They would also find that, despite all the airmobile hype, they would travel mostly on foot.

### 3 May '66 – 76 weeks left

Dear Folks,

We have started helicopter training now. I just took a shower, had a beer, and am sitting on my bunk with a big blister on my foot. I don't know why we march so much if we're airmobile. I guess we have to practice running from the enemy, ha! We are in good shape, though. Can run three miles and walk eight with a forty-pound pack and still go bowling that night. Friday we're going to the pool to see if we can swim. If I pretend not to know, I might get time off during the workday to learn. I hope.

Seen two guys parachute from a plane today. Ah, that was cool. By the way, give Darrell fifteen dollars for the watch. Told him he'd have to give it to me if I ever made it through airborne.

We had a weapons firepower demonstration Saturday. Shooting at junk trucks and tanks. Man, the metal flew. Quite a show.

Heard some rumors today, like after Basic Unit Training, we might do some jungle training, either in Georgia, Panama, or Hawaii. Sounds alright.

Adios,

Cowboy Will

In basic training, the men had all qualified on the old M-14 rifle, which had a wooden stock. The new M-16 was smaller and lighter, made of steel and plastic, and seemed futuristic. Both featured a fully automatic setting—sometimes called "rock-n-roll"—firing continuously with the trigger held down. This made the rifle less accurate, however, and their clips only held twenty rounds. For accuracy and to conserve ammunition, most rarely used the full-automatic setting.

With their newly issued M-16s, they would again qualify at the rifle range. Each soldier would fire iterations, groups of targets in various positions. Alpha Company's Chester Millay from Kentucky was preparing to start his next iteration in the squatting position. He forgot that his rifle was still set on full-automatic. He was surprised and lost his balance when his rifle started firing on rock-n-roll, and he fell backward on his ass. "Luckily, the drill sergeant was further down the line and didn't see my stupidity," he said, "but the guys on my left and right had a good laugh."

### 22 May '66 – 72 weeks left

Dear Folks,

Guess it's my turn to write again. We were only out in the fields for five days. Now we're going out this Monday for another five days. It was awful weather out there. The last day had about two inches of snow and cold. It's a laugh.

*Those guys from the city are scared stiff of snakes. Got issued my bulletproof vest yesterday. Looks like something for the North Pole but can stop a bullet.*

*We had an inspection of rifles today. I didn't know our battalion commander had come for "inspection arms." Lt. Colonel Swett stands in front of me. I give him a big smile, and he keeps staring. "Don't you know how to come to inspection arms?"*

*"No sir," I said. Asked me a bunch of questions. The platoon leader's face turned red. It wasn't my fault. Anyway, it was pretty funny.*

*Captain Wise told us when we're leaving for V.C. land today. I wouldn't worry about it if I were you. My parents didn't raise no fool, even though you sometimes think so, ha! One of our sergeants has been there already. Rode shotgun (door gunner) on a helicopter. By the way, we're going by boat. I'll be feeding the fish every time I get seasick. Takes about four weeks to get there. Brother.*

*Everyone knows this battalion is lean and mean. They step aside when they see our distinguished camouflage neckpiece. Yeah man, tough, ha! Well, we do a lot of exercises and running. My gosh, that write-up of Allen Simon, ha! Is he a hero? Everyone has that type of training. Man!*

*Say, I might get a chance to jump. This friend I know made some jumps before, and he goes to Denver and rents a plane. I helped pack his chute last Sunday. Know not for sure if I can jump. If I do, I know I'll shit my pants, yeah!*

*Seen this show, "Sound of Music." It's been in this theater for twenty weeks straight now. Told Larry about wearing long underwear so we get used to the hot weather. I guess he believed me, ha!*

*Dad, I want you to watch this racing car of mine. Just make sure they're taking care of it and don't let it sit idle. Mike is darn lucky to be in the Boy Scouts. Man, I wish I could have been. Might say I am now, except a little bigger.*

*Your son,*

*Will*

Over in the 5/7th's Bravo Company was First Sergeant (1SG) Dayton Hare, a veteran of both World War II and the Korean War. Significantly older and more experienced than the other officers and NCOs in the company, he was small and wiry, grizzled by decades in the Army, and smoked cigars—a textbook First Sergeant. By now, he could have retired and avoided a final combat tour.

CPT Bernard Grady was Bravo Company's Executive Officer. In *On the Tiger's Back*, he recalls how 1SG Hare's stated reason for staying with the battalion was to earn his Combat Infantryman's Badge or CIB. 1SG Hare had seen his share of combat, but he had served as an MP in World War II and as an artilleryman in Korea. The CIB is only awarded to infantrymen serving in combat.

The stripes on a soldier's rank insignia signify where he stands in the hierarchy. Medals such as the Bronze Star with V device signify valor, while Silver Stars and Distinguished Service Crosses signify uncommon valor, gallantry, and extraordinary heroism. The unit patch worn on his left shoulder represents his division. That same patch, if worn on the right shoulder, says that he has served in a combat zone. The Combat Infantryman's Badge—a silver pin depicting a rifle adorned by a wreath and worn above his rack of medals and ribbons—means that he's been in actual combat. Many would gladly trade a few stripes of their rank insignia for the distinction of wearing the CIB. Now the head NCO of an infantry company, this was 1SG Hare's last chance to earn his. This was the reason he gave for staying with the company. But Grady suspected that he simply could not let his men—most only half his age and having never seen combat—go to war without him.

Known to the men as "Top," former Marine John Potter was Alpha Company's First Sergeant. He'd served in Korea, as had their commander, CPT A.J. Wise. 1SG Potter's face held scars from previous battles. At five-nine, he was physically imposing and built like a soldier, while CPT Wise was long and tall.

Among the few in the battalion who'd already been to Vietnam was the 5/7th Cav's Intelligence Officer, CPT Walt Swain. He'd survived two tours in the early sixties, in the swashbuckling days of remote Special Forces outposts, fighting alongside native highland tribesmen known as the Montagnards. Tall, square-jawed, blond and blue-eyed, Grady wrote of Swain's good looks, "If you needed to cast a green beret officer for Hollywood, Walt was your man." Swain loved adventure and danger but also had a fatalistic streak. Before departing, he told his wife he didn't expect to come home alive.

### 5 June '66 – 71 weeks left

Dear Folks,

*Our Lt. Colonel Swett is over in Viet Nam now, making reservations for us. He shouldn't have too much trouble, ha! Hope the scenery is pretty and the fishing and hunting good.*

*Henning's sister wants to pick us up when our leave comes. Better have the haying done. I doubt if I am physically fit for such heavy work. Be glad to see those green fields again. Only thing green in this state is the work clothes we wear. I bumped up my G.I. insurance, making it ten thousand now. Costs only two bucks a month.*

*Will*

SSG Sam Daily was a squad leader in Alpha Company's 1st Platoon. From Stringtown, Oklahoma, he was a career NCO. He was also the father of two girls and had just learned another child was on the way. As they prepared for Vietnam, SSG Daily was informed that he did not have to go. He had just spent over two years in Germany and would be kept stateside for at least a year before being sent overseas again. Four young soldiers from his platoon came to his home to ask him if it was true—that he really wasn't going to Vietnam with them. They were scared and pleaded for him to go with them. As an NCO responsible for the welfare of his soldiers, he felt compelled to see them through what he had prepared them for. He volunteered the next day.

SSG Robert Matulac was a veteran NCO who had enlisted in 1953 but had not yet served in Vietnam. He'd spent nine years in Germany, one in Korea, and the rest at various bases in the states. He was Asian-American, his mother of Japanese descent, his father from the Philippines. His father had joined the U.S. Navy and served as a cook aboard its ships. Despite being a cook, he told of a time when he was given a rifle and sent to fight the Germans in the Argonne Forest in the First World War.

As the communications NCO, Matulac was part of Alpha Company's command group, which included the commander, First Sergeant, medics, radio operators, supply staff, clerks, and drivers. He was the right-hand man for both CPT A.J. Wise and 1SG John Potter. Matulac was friends with SSG Sam Daily, who invited him to his house for lunch one day at Fort Carson. Daily was very proud of his wife and wanted him to know she was a great cook. He was also a bit superstitious. Driving back to the battalion area, Daily took an unexpected right turn. "Where are we going?" Matulac asked.

"Oh, nowhere," Daily replied, explaining that a black cat had just crossed the street. What Matulac remembers most about SSG Daily is how much his men respected him.

Another friend of Matulac's was Kazimierz Slomiany from Wallington, New Jersey. He had emigrated from Poland in 1960 and served as his family's translator. Drafted in 1965, he hoped to apply for citizenship after fulfilling his obligation to the Army. While at Fort Carson, Slomiany often went skiing along with Matulac, Earl Huber, and Tom Gruenburg.

From Oregon, Marty Scull, known as "Scully," was also friends with Slomiany. Scully's best friend was A.G. Hensley from Tennessee. Assigned to 1LT James Harmon's 2nd Platoon, they'd been together since basic training. He recalled how Hensley chain-smoked cigarettes and how he could just lean against a tree and fall asleep in less than a minute. Hensley rented a car one weekend, and they drove out to Pueblo in a gleaming blue Corvette. Hensley liked to drive fast. "Why a Corvette?" Scully asked. Hensley said it was like the one he had back home, and he missed driving it since they wouldn't let him bring it on post.

### 13 June '66 – 71 weeks left

Hi Mike,

*So school is out now, and I suppose you're spending your weekends camping. They don't sell fireworks in Colorado, so I can't get you any. Maybe I can sneak home a bomb. Maybe!*

*Working late all week. Wednesday, up at 3 AM and to bed at midnight. Also, we'll be riding in helicopters. No more bivouac camping, whoopee! Just fourteen working days left. We jumped off a thirty-five-foot tower with a rope tied around us. Our platoon sergeant Burtis got on top and wouldn't come down. No lie, he was up there for an hour, shaking like a leaf, haha! We were all nervous, alright. We're getting a lot of classes, and the guys go crazy for the movies we have about Viet Nam. Lt. Colonel Swett has taken some movie pictures of the exact place where we're going. Be seeing them pretty soon. Guess we'll be stars someday, ha! They say it is a pretty comfortable war, so they say. You go out and fight a little, come back, take a shower, go to the P.X. and have a few beers. By the way, I am pissed off 'cause they cut the free beer ration from six cases to three. Well, I guess you can't have everything.*

*Will*

    Before going to Vietnam, certain positions had to be filled and additional duties assigned. Each platoon in Alpha Company needed a radio operator, and their commander required two. This additional duty was assigned to certain infantrymen within the company. Royce Barrow explained how he wound up as a radio operator for CPT A.J. Wise and how it had nothing to do with his radio abilities. One of their sergeants came into their barracks, asking for volunteers to help with some projects. Barrow knew better than to ever volunteer for anything in the Army. No one else volunteered, and then the sergeant mentioned that he was looking for someone who could draw or at least had some "artistic ability." Barrow was an avid drawer and had many artists in his family. Reluctantly, he agreed to meet with their commander in the company orderly room. CPT Wise soon had him drawing up training aids, maps, targets, and other things they would use in their training over the coming months.

    CPT Wise liked Barrow and chose him as one of his radio operators, along with Donald Rankin, Bill Purdy's friend from Kentucky who'd been drafted shortly after dropping out of college. Barrow was from North Carolina and had also attended college. He had dropped out for a while to pay off expenses and save for one last year of tuition. Just like Rankin, he received his draft notice shortly thereafter. Barrow and Rankin were trained by communications sergeant SSG Robert Matulac along with the other radio operators in the company. Matulac's radio operator was Kenneth Rathyen. Among the platoon radio operators were Dave Fedell, Alan Weisman, Phil Jones, and Fred Brodosi. Rathyen had worked at a camera shop before he was drafted. Barrow planned to take many pictures while in Vietnam, so Rathyen helped him pick out a small 35mm camera that fit in his shirt pocket.

### 26 June '66 – 70 weeks left

Dear Folks,

Would you believe it if I said I was busy? Man, talk about losing sleep. But just one more week of training, and we can hang it up. Wish I was in basic. It was three times easier then. I like them choppers, though. Give quite a ride, fishtailing around. Ride in them just about every day.

Look on the map for the city of An Khe, Viet Nam. It's where we will be stationed. Central Highlands, right in the middle of the action, ha! Hope you're not losing sleep over this. Isn't that bad. I am not worried, and no one else is either. I heard the Charlie Company guys have got raffle tickets on which sergeants are going to get bumped off first. That seems a bit grim.

Got eight months in this damn Army today, and still no stripe. Most of us don't have one. Henning in Delta Company has had one for two months already. I am telling our C.O. to shove it. We're the best company in the battalion and still not treated right.

When are you sending the food? You know better than to ask a silly question like, do I want some cookies and doughnuts—of course I do! I'll send you some C-Rations, and I bet you'll never eat them cold. Have to get to a movie now.

So Long,

Will

Now that things were getting real, many started thinking harder about their fate. Some went AWOL (away without leave). Joe Sanchez's friend Alan Weisman struggled with the thought of going to Vietnam. He was known to speak his mind and once got into a shoving match with one of the guys over his feelings about the war. He considered becoming a conscientious objector and even spoke with a rabbi about it. The rabbi didn't give Weisman the kind of counsel he was looking for, explaining how their homeland was forged in war and how Jews have always answered the call to duty. Weisman confided to SSG Robert Matulac that he was afraid. "Well, you have to go," Matulac joked, trying to lighten the mood. "You're the only Jew in our company."

"I guess I have to go then."

The battalion commander took it upon himself to personally speak with Weisman. What he said is not known, but LTC Swett's words persuaded him to stay and do his duty.

Joe Sanchez had also developed misgivings. He regretted volunteering and was seriously considering going AWOL himself. He confided all this to Teresa, the girl from Denver that he'd been dating. She knew how much damage such a decision could do to his future. Whatever she said gave him the courage to carry on and changed the course of his life forever.

Then for reasons unknown, Sanchez was transferred to the 2nd Battalion, 20th Aerial Rocket Artillery (2/20th ARA), a gunship aviation battalion of the 1st Air Cavalry, and sent to Vietnam in early July. Gunships were modified Hueys armed with various types of machine guns and rockets.

As Alpha Company neared the end of their airmobile training, rules were loosened, alcohol flowed freely, and passes were doled out like candy. "It was just before going overseas," said Martin Quinn of the shenanigans of one particular night. "Sergeant Burtis rented out a room at one of the bars downtown. I was drinking rum and cokes and screwdrivers, and everyone got plowed. I don't even remember coming home that night."

### 1 July '66 – 70 weeks left

*Dear Folks,*

*We finally finished training. Wow, does it ever feel good. A parade, packing, shots, and turning in our gear is about all there is left. Been a long hard time, and I'll be glad to get home. We're going to try to rent a car this Sunday and watch the races at Pike's Peak.*

*We had a platoon party the other night. Sergeant Burtis said before we left, "Don't fool with my German wife."*

*The other sergeant said, "If anyone gets too wild and drunk, I'll smooch him in the mouth and kick him out," ha!*

*We got to the bar, and Elmer says to me, "Watch, I can speak a little German." He did alright. Now he'll be on detail for the next two weeks. The sergeant that warned us not to get too wild had his girlfriend—instead of his wife—spend the night, and he spent the night in the cooler for drunken driving and speeding. Another sergeant got into an argument with some guy over a woman, and the woman pulled out a pistol and cooled them off. Can't wait until tomorrow morning to hear what they have to say, ha!*

*Ricky Mitchell had a close call? Just cross your fingers. He'll be home in January, the way I figure.*

*Yeah, I almost dropped my teeth when I received a letter from Darrell. Says the car is the fastest one down there. Can't wait to see it.*

*See you all soon,*

*Will*

At the end of airmobile training in July, Donald Rankin and twelve others were sent for special jungle training in Panama. He wrote this letter while on his connecting flight back to Fort Carson.

*Chicago Airport—Tuesday Night*

*Dear Mom and Daddy,*

*We're finally almost back to Colorado. The flights have been smooth and pleasant. Panama was very interesting. We learned a lot, but the temperature, mud, rain, and insects were almost intolerable at times. I got hit on the head with a rifle butt during the first day of training. We were jumping from a truck, and the guy behind me jumped too quickly. It was only a small cut, but they sent me to the hospital that day and later in the week. That cost me a hundred points, and I didn't make Jungle Expert. I needed 800 points and had 765. The people in Panama are so poor that it is almost unbelievable. The main part of town is about like Irishtown. They think of everything to get your money.*

*Our trip from Charleston to Panama was unbearable. We got off the ground once and had to turn around and come back because the landing gear wouldn't come up. They repaired that, and then we took off again. I went to sleep while they were loading, so I didn't know when we took off. The second time we got full speed on the runway, and bells started to ring. The engine right next to our window went out. They got us stopped, and we went back to the terminal and stayed about two hours. Everyone was afraid to get on the third time, but we made it with no problems.*

*We just left the ground in a United jet! It is smooth, and the sunset is beautiful. It is red, orange, yellow, and then turns purple. We are flying toward it so we can see it a long time. We left four guys in Chicago. We thought we had an hour, but we only had twenty minutes. Some of the guys' families were there, and they didn't get to the ramp on time. They have tickets so they won't have any problem.*

*You should see my moustache. I really got quite a beard in the jungle, so I left the moustache. I'm sure the company commander will make me shave it off.*

*We wear a green and yellow scarf around our necks instead of a tie. There is an airborne unit that has the same. We ran into them in Panama, and they were going to whip us and make us take them off. However, we had plenty of guys, some knives and bottles, so they calmed down. One guy punched one of our men. Our guy punched him back, and he ran. The airborne really think they're something.*

*How are you all feeling? Is school out? I guess the weather is pretty now. I've been a little homesick the last few days. What do you all really think about*

*Nancy and our age difference? Sometimes, I think that maybe I'd like to marry her, but her family is such a bunch of goofballs. I'd hate to ask her to wait. But it would be ridiculous to get married before going overseas.*

*This is about all. Write soon.*

*Love,*

*Donnie*

Informed by her handlers that she could not go to Vietnam with them, Specialist-Four (SP/4) Brutus T. Bear—the battalion's only female soldier—may have been disappointed. It was hard to tell, as her face always wore the same blank expression. Their mascot would stay at Fort Carson and eventually travel to Vietnam after she had grown.

Before going to war, the men were given a two-week pass to return home, make arrangements, write their wills, and say their goodbyes. Some took the chance to marry their girls back home. Among them was Will's squad leader, SSG Bobby Hayslip. Another was Charles Bradford from Newport, Kentucky. Assigned to SSG Sam Daily's squad in 1st Platoon, he was known to his friends as "Charlie Cool" and sometimes spoke with a stutter. The youngest of ten, he was known by his nieces and nephews as "Uncle Charlie." He was very protective and quick to warn others not to mess with them. Some recalled him saying that he may just come home in a box. "Aww unc'," replied one of his nephews, "you're too mean to not come home." In any case, he wanted to ensure that his young bride Peggy was taken care of.

A friend of Bradford's in 1st Platoon was Michael Stoflet from Elkhorn, Wisconsin. Known as "Herbie" to his high school friends, he was also a favorite uncle of sorts—barely older than his nephew Steve Hubbard, who was starting his sophomore year of high school when Mike left for Vietnam. Steve told of how Mike's siblings were all named alphabetically, making Mike the second-youngest of fourteen, and how Mike had gotten his driver's license a couple years earlier and was always driving him around in his car. "Such a fun-loving guy," said his niece, Sally. "He played five-hundred pop-up, kick the can, and went skiing and sledding with us. He was always a kid."

"Mike was tender-hearted," his older sister Donna recalled. "If he came across money, he would always buy our mom something with it. When he got his car, he would take our daughters to the store for candy. He was always helping people and had a soft spot for animals."

"He was still young, and he'd just gotten a new puppy," Donna's husband Jim said. "He was so happy about it. 'What's his name' I asked. 'Six Thirty,' he said. I asked why, and he said, 'Well, he's not too dark and not too light. He's somewhere in between, so I named him Six Thirty.'"

Donna recalled Mike's unusually clean habits for a teenage boy, how he polished his white sneakers every night, and how their mother complained about his extra laundry. He had just turned twenty when he was drafted. "I worried," said Donna. "He was such a kind person. He'd never fired a gun before. I was afraid that the Army and the war would change him. I was working as a bank teller in those days. It bothered me—I remember people withdrawing large sums of money for college tuition just to keep their sons out of Vietnam." Mike had a sweet tooth, and she would send cookies in boxes packed with popcorn to keep them from getting crushed. Mike would write back, saying how he and his friends just ate the popcorn along with the cookies. Married to Mike's older brother Forrest, his sister-in-law Priscilla also recalled how he loved popcorn, how he would make a bowl of it every night, and how she had sent him boxes full of popcorn for Christmas at Fort Carson.

Mike's teenage sister Nancy had started a journal or scrapbook of sorts. She called it *Diary of a Soldier* and used it to record everything Mike wrote about in his letters, starting with his arrival at Fort Leonard Wood in 1965. Amid handmade collages and patriotic decorations, Nancy's journal documents all of Mike's training, how much he won and lost gambling, when they could or couldn't get beer—and how he'd volunteered to decorate and pass out candy during a Christmas program for children of an orphanage near Fort Carson. Pasted to its pages are photos of Mike's many nieces and nephews, another of him and his girlfriend Sharon holding hands and kissing on a couch. It tells of how Mike broke his ankle playing soccer during a company picnic in April and how his orders for Vietnam might get canceled as a result, "but he hopes not." According to Mike, their picnic saw a lot of drinking, ending in fistfights, broken noses, and stitches.

Thomas Erickson returned to visit his family on the east side of Saint Paul. His older brother Marv—drafted three months after him—was still in training at Fort Bliss and spoke to him on the phone before Tommy left for Vietnam.

On the last day of his two-week pass, Al Patrillo caught up with his neighborhood friend Tom Ivey. It had been a long time since they last spoke. Much had changed, and they had lost touch a bit, but Al was still like an older brother to him. Al told him he was headed to Vietnam the next day but didn't seem nervous. They talked about the classes Tom was taking, all the training Al had been through, how he'd shot "expert" at the rifle range—and how Al was excited about this local girl he'd been seeing. They had just gone out on a date the night before, and he seemed pretty serious about her.

Will traveled back to Tilden again with Rodney Henning, both sporting a cavalry-style moustache this time. Now they were good pals. On their caps, they wore the arm-and-saber regimental crest of the 7th Cavalry, and on their shoulders, the bright yellow shield and dark horse head patch of the 1st Air Cavalry Division. Arnott Graham was on the same flight from Denver to Minneapolis with

Will and Henning, a connecting flight on his way to New York. SGT Bill Chapman had driven Graham ninety miles to Denver so he wouldn't have to take the bus, and Alan Weisman had lent him money to pay for his airfare. During their flight, Will tapped him on the shoulder. "Wanna see something?" he asked, wrestling a bag down from the overhead compartment. Then he opened it up, revealing a mortar round he was bringing home as a souvenir.

"What a nut," Graham joked. "Imagine bringing a bomb on a plane these days! To this day, I can still picture the smile on his face."

Graham traveled back from New York to Fort Carson with Robert Figueroa, Angel Reynosa, and Robert O'Brien. They met up with another one of their Army buddies during a layover in Indianapolis. He was from Indiana, and his dad was there to see him off. He introduced his buddies to his dad, who shook hands with each of them until he got to Graham. He reached out, but the man just lurched back, refusing to shake the hand of a black man—and after shaking those of two Puerto Ricans and an Irishman. "Here I am going to war with his son," Graham reflected, "and he couldn't even shake my hand."

"Forget that redneck," said Reynosa. "Don't mean nothin'." But Graham never would forget, and for many years he held a grudge against the entire state of Indiana.

When it was time to return to Fort Carson, Eddie drove Will and Rodney Henning back to the airport in Minneapolis in the family Oldsmobile. Millie and Will's cousin Alice rode along to see him off. After some hugs and kisses, Will slung his duffel bag over his shoulder and headed down the concourse with Henning. As she watched them melt into the crowd, Millie asked Alice if she thought Willie would make it back alive.

*Will Bowe and Rodney Henning at Minneapolis Airport*

*Albert Patrillo and Mom — Charles Bradford with bride, Peggy*

*Michael Stoflet at Fort Carson*

*Sam Daily and family — Robert Matulac*

*Rappel tower at Fort Carson, U.S. Army photograph*

A.G. Hensley

LTC Trevor Swett (left) and generals watching firepower demonstration,
U.S. Army photograph

# 5
# SEASICK
*...and that was the good part.*

President Lyndon Johnson had dramatically increased troop levels since the beginning of the year when approximately 185,000 personnel were stationed in Vietnam. By August 1966, that number had grown to almost 300,000 and would swell to over 385,000 by year-end. At the time, just over five thousand Americans had been killed throughout the previous years of involvement. When the first soldiers of the 1st Air Cavalry Division were sent to Vietnam the year prior, it signaled a dramatic expansion of the war. Until then, the conflict had been the domain of the Special Forces and advisors who could call upon American aircraft to assist the South Vietnamese, who were then only faced with fighting the local Viet Cong (VC) guerrillas. Between that time and 1966, several regular Army and Marine divisions had arrived from the United States while thousands of regular NVA soldiers had poured into the highlands from North Vietnam via the Ho Chi Minh Trail. It was the beginning of the big war. The newly formed 5th Battalion, 7th Cavalry represented a massive doubling down in American commitment to that war—a crossing of the Rubicon—in keeping with the late President John F. Kennedy's inaugural declaration.

*Let every nation know, whether it wishes us well or ill, that we shall pay any price, bear any burden, meet any hardship, support any friend, oppose any foe to assure the survival and the success of liberty.*

At this time, most men were being sent to Vietnam as individual replacements rather than with intact units. Going to war essentially alone, they would cross the ocean on a commercial jet flown by Pan Am, United, or Flying Tigers. Arriving in Vietnam, they would be taken to a "replacement battalion" to be sorted out and assigned to whatever units needed them. Then they would be flown out to join their units in the field, arriving as strangers in their new companies. This is how the experience of the original members of the 5/7th Cav differed and what made it special. Most had been drafted in 1965 and trained together at Fort Carson. Now they would all go to war together, with only their most senior leaders bringing combat experience with them. Despite this, each of the battalion's companies would slowly but steadily disintegrate over the next year, and most of its soldiers would return home alone.

Many of Alpha Company's platoon sergeants and squad leaders had been to war before. Among them were Sergeants First Class (SFC) James Bonner and Marvin Hall, and SSGs Harry Coit, Kenneth Gregory, James Evans, and Cleofas Madrid. Of these veterans, most had not been to Vietnam but rather Korea. CPT

A.J. Wise was prior-enlisted and had been a communications sergeant in the Korean War, often reminding SSG Robert Matulac of this fact.

On August 2nd 1966, the battalion left Fort Carson in a mile-long caravan of buses. In the fog-laden San Francisco Bay, the aging USNS Gaffey awaited their arrival. Twenty-three years prior, she had first ferried troops to Guadalcanal during World War II, then to the Philippines and Okinawa. Like many of the 5/7th Cav's senior NCOs and officers, she had also been to Korea.

From a distance, the ship was a cacophony of noise and activity. By forklift and other means, immense loads of equipment, supplies, and food were being fed from the pier and over the gangway into a large opening in her massive grey hull. The soldiers spent hours napping on their duffel bags and smoking on the pier, waiting to get a taste of Navy life. They were finally herded onto the vessel, one company at a time. Lugging duffel bags on their backs, they were marched in a sort of half-assed formation into the opening in the ship's hull as the band played *Garryowen* on the pier.

The approximately 180 soldiers of Alpha Company were led in a general state of confusion down dimly lit stairwells, through long corridors, and into a large room filled with rows of bunks stacked four high. The ship smelled dank, of sea salt and mildew. As soldiers claimed each of their individual bunks by throwing their bags on them, it soon became apparent that there was not enough for each of them. Their sergeants advised them to start buddying up. Known in the Navy as hot racking, they would have to share bunks and sleep in shifts.

As the sun descended on the horizon, the ship's giant engines roared to life, belching black clouds into the sky, sending tremors through its frame, and arousing a renewed bustling and anticipation upon its decks. Will and hundreds of others gathered along the railing to watch the city of San Francisco disappear into the mist. For many, this would be their last view of American soil.

Shortly thereafter, Will hurried back down into the ship to puke in the toilet, as he was among the first to be hit by seasickness. They sailed out under the Golden Gate Bridge, where many had gathered to throw flowers and wreaths down to them. Then into the Pacific, commencing eighteen days of steady up-and-down motion amid its waves.

They spent their first two days trying to find their sea legs. For nausea, one of the cooks advised those on KP to eat an entire stick of butter. It worked for some. Conditions on the ship were cramped and hot. To avoid overcrowding in their quarters below, no less than a third of the men were required to be on deck during daylight hours. Most got over their seasickness after a few days. Will tried some pills from the dispensary, which helped a bit.

Charged with keeping over two thousand soldiers out of trouble for eighteen days at sea, their leaders quickly tasked the men with duties. Kitchen duty, latrine duty, guard duty, and every kind of menial detail. To avoid all this, Bobby Hansen and his buddy Jim Hirschuber hid out in one of the ship's lifeboats. They found that the boats contained survival rations, and friends brought them food from the galley. No one seemed to care that they were unaccounted for.

Hirschuber explained how they actually ended up in the lifeboats. Their bunks were located just beneath a giant heat pipe. It was already hot in their bunk room, but the temperature under the pipe was over a hundred degrees, so Hirschuber and Hansen went out to sleep on the deck. About 3:00 AM, the crew started hosing down the deck, and they were almost washed overboard. They climbed up and took cover in a lifeboat, and after that, they just decided to stay there. A volleyball game was being played on deck the next afternoon, and a wayward ball bounced into their lifeboat. "I'll go get it," came the voice of 1LT James Harmon. Anticipating an awkward moment, Hirschuber threw the ball back out. They expected to be found at this point, but there was no investigation.

The rest of the men attended classes and briefings to prepare them for what they would face in-country. In the mornings, they performed weapons training and exercised on the deck. There were even some impromptu boxing matches.

Arnott Graham was on KP duty during the first week, peeling potatoes and mopping floors. The galley was especially sweltering, and tempers were short. He got into an argument with one of the cooks, and then SSG Harry Coit, one of their veteran NCOs from Mississippi, stepped in. "I don't even remember what the argument was about, just that Coit was manhandling me," Graham recalled, "and then I shoved him. They said I punched him, but I don't think I did." The incident marked the beginning of bad blood between Graham and Coit.

Charged with assaulting an NCO, a special court-martial would decide Graham's fate. With LTC Trevor Swett presiding, CPT Walt Swain was assigned as prosecutor. A young lieutenant was Graham's defense counsel. CPT A.J. Wise argued that he should stay with Alpha Company and that he could oversee his discipline as his commander. Wise conceded that Graham may have had a chip on his shoulder—but he was a good soldier, and the incident wasn't all his fault.

Over the objections of CPT Wise, Graham received six months confinement and hard labor at two-thirds pay. He was put in the brig for the rest of the voyage, a small cement cell with a cot in the ship's bow. He was only given bread and water, but Kurt Elmer and Will sometimes brought him sandwiches.

The following was sent by Donald Rankin from aboard the Gaffey.

*August 12th 1966*

*Dear Mom, Daddy and all,*

*We're nearing Okinawa, and I can't wait. The voyage wouldn't be too bad if we weren't so crowded. I got seasick the sixth day and then had intestinal flu two days later. The sea is certainly boring after a few days. We've seen sharks,* whales, and flying fish. The flying fish are unbelievable. There are two thousand guys on the ship. Everyone gets along pretty well, and we're all in good spirits. They gave us G.I. haircuts again. It feels pretty good, but my head sunburns a lot.

You wouldn't believe how crowded we sleep. We are in double bunks, and we sleep head to toe. It is really hard to sleep with some of these smelly feet. Most of the guys are from my section that I sleep close to, so I make them take a shower at least every other night. Taking a shower is difficult because the shower room is at the end of the ship, and it is very easy to get seasick up there. You have to hold on to the railing to stay seated on the commode. This is about all. I will write as soon as we arrive.

Love,

Donnie

Will also sent a letter home from aboard the ship.

### 13 August '66 – 63 weeks left

Dear Folks,

Haven't quite made it yet. Left San Francisco on the 2nd and haven't seen land since and won't until we hit Okinawa on the 15th. Just can't wait 'til we get there. Been seasick twice. I don't believe I could take Navy life. You know, this boat—not worthy enough to be called a ship—is only going about twenty miles per hour. Imagine going to Minneapolis from home in a car at that speed.

There are about two thousand troops on this ship, about six hundred from our battalion. The weather is about ninety degrees. Got a very close haircut—well, everybody did—and my little moustache shaved off. We all look like we just got into the Army.

So far, we've seen flying fish by the hundreds, a few small whales, and a few sharks. Seen the prison of Alcatraz and the Golden Gate Bridge. We have class for about two hours a day and exercise. The rest of the time, we lay around and play cards, some for pretty high stakes. I guess we'll be in Viet Nam by next Thursday. I'll be so happy just to get off this boat.

Remember this colored guy I introduced you to at the airport, Graham? He's in jail for hitting a sergeant. Only guy in the cooler on the ship. It's pretty serious.

You know, it'll be almost a month before I'll be able to hear from you, since I left home that is. I hope you got my clothes and sleeping bag, and save them hats, they fit me well. My pants got dirty 'cause I was following a creek as the M.P.s were chasing me 'cause I went to town without a pass. Anyway, they didn't catch me, ha!

*I better sign off. The mail room is closing sooner than I expected. It's 6:00 PM Sunday now, and you're probably getting ready for church. Anyway, so long.*

*Up & down & up & down,*

*Will*

Also sailing to Vietnam aboard the Gaffey was Second Lieutenant (2LT) Winston Groom, fresh from his training at Fort Bragg. He was with a small psychological operations detachment and was appointed "Rumor Control Officer." For kicks, he started a rumor of his own. He mentioned to a group of young soldiers that he'd heard they were being followed by a Russian submarine. He wanted to see how long it took for the rumor to get back to him. In 1978, he would write one of the very first Vietnam War novels, *Better Times Than These*. The first part of his novel takes place aboard the Gaffey and was inspired by the events of this same voyage. In 1986, he would write another novel, *Forrest Gump*.

The life vest fiasco is one of the many incidents and shenanigans aboard the Gaffey that appear in Groom's novel. Despite suspicions swirling around the two who hid in the lifeboat, the identity of who caused the fiasco remains a mystery.

Two weeks into their crossing, a signal came over the ship's distress frequency. A crewmember was sent to check the life vests. Each vest was equipped with an electronic device that sent out a signal when deployed into the water. As expected, one was missing. Out of sheer boredom, it had likely been thrown overboard as a joke. Now every ship within the missing life vest's two-hundred-mile beacon was required by maritime law to spend no less than four hours searching for it. As the ship circled back and searched for the life vest, the men were put on lockdown and forced to stay in their sweltering, overcrowded bunk rooms while officers at every level took account of their men. With every man accounted for, the question of who had caused the fiasco remained unanswered.

Interrogations persisted until the ship encountered a massive typhoon that night. Anyone who wasn't sick before soon would be. Over and over, the ship rose with the swells, then crashed into the troughs, sending shivers, creeks, and moans throughout its aging frame. Going on deck for fresh air was too dangerous, so they stayed in their steaming bunk rooms, passing the trash cans between them. Marvin Bierschbach recalled holding on for dear life while trying to use the toilet and how seawater sloshed over the ankles of anyone trying to use the latrine. That night, Jim Hirschuber and Bobby Hansen went through the ship's engine room. They weren't supposed to be there, but they were curious. They found a trap door that opened up top. They watched the enormous waves rising above the deck and thought they would probably sink. The ship's captain would later say it was the worst storm he'd ever encountered.

The storm eventually subsided, and they docked on the island of Okinawa the next morning. The men were given a box lunch and kicked off to make way for the ship's resupply. As it was a military base, many tried to find the PX to buy stuff or call home, but most just got hammered with the free beer available on the beach. Getting over two thousand drunk soldiers back onto the Gaffey that evening was a challenge, and the shore patrol spent much of the night policing up stray troopers along the beach. The heat was stifling, and it persisted after darkness fell. Many slept on the deck that night in Okinawa.

They sailed for another two days before reaching Vietnam. By all accounts, Will's first voyage at sea was a miserable journey for all. He would not set foot on an ocean liner again for another forty-five years. "How we survived all that, I don't know," Bierschbach joked, "...and that was the good part."

*USNS Gaffey, photo by Marvin Bierschbach*

*Sailing under Golden Gate Bridge, photo by Marvin Bierschbach*

*1SG Ramon Esquivel standing far left, 1SG Dayton Hare sitting second from left with cigar, LTC Trevor Swett standing middle back row, photo by Royce Vick*

# 6
# SORRY ABOUT THAT

*All these years I read about these people in geography class,
and here I am, seeing it for real.*

At 4:00 AM on August 20th 1966, the USNS Gaffey laid anchor at the Port of Qui Nhon. Those awake on deck could make out the dark silhouette of mountains in the distance. Within hours the sun was beating down on them, and the ship was again a beehive of noise, movement, clanking, and yelling. Just before disembarking, the men were issued their rifles and forty rounds of ammunition, and they complained about not getting more. The ship was too large to dock, so Landing Craft Utility boats (LCUs) would ferry them ashore. They looked just like the landing crafts they had all seen in movies and newsreels about the D-Day invasion of World War II. They threw down their duffel bags and climbed down cargo nets into the landing craft. Amid the mass confusion, Will realized his helmet was gone. The walls of the landing craft were high, and they couldn't see where they were going. Rifles ready, many prepared to assault the beach under fire as they approached the shoreline. After a few minutes of anticipation, the ramp of the landing craft slammed down onto the sand, and... surprise! There was the band again, playing their familiar theme song. This time they were flanked by a cadre of generals and other bigwigs, division and battalion flags on display, and a gaggle of reporters taking pictures. People were lying about the beach, looking up at them in confusion.

Bob Matulac spoke of the vivid imaginations of the young troopers that day and how many thought they would be storming the beach. One was Don Shipley in Charlie Company, the first to land ashore. He explained how it wasn't just their imaginations. Aboard the LCUs, as a joke, many of their veteran NCOs had actually told them that they would be attacking the beach. "A bunch of scared kids," Shipley remarked, looking at a photo of his company coming ashore.

As they spilled onto the shore, Bravo Company's SSG George Porod was yelling at Will for not having his helmet. Alpha Company's 1SG John Potter told Porod to mind his own troops, then turned to Will and said, "So Bowe, where the hell *is* your steel pot?" They were immediately herded onto two-and-a-half-ton trucks. We called these trucks war pigs, but they were called "deuce-and-a-halfs" in those days. Most were taken to a nearby airstrip, crammed onto a giant C-130 cargo plane, and flown to Camp Radcliff.

Will, Kurt Elmer, and a handful of others stayed behind to guard equipment until more trucks came to haul it off. After loading the equipment and sending it on its way, they were taken to the airfield for the night. They stayed up late drinking at a makeshift bar called a "clubhouse" run by soldiers at the airfield. Holding up a can of beer, Elmer joked, "Only three hundred and sixty-four days left!" The next morning, another convoy of deuce-and-a-halfs would bring them to base camp to join their battalion.

Perched in giant open-air truck beds, they rumbled through the streets of Qui Nhon—immediately accosted by the smell of sewage, diesel fuel, burning garbage, and whatever the townspeople were cooking. The streets were lined with vendors and pushcarts and filled with hundreds of people on bicycles and scooters, their main form of transportation aside from a handful of French-manufactured cars. With arms stretched to the sky, throngs of children ran alongside the truck, begging for candy and food. Many young girls could be seen carrying their baby siblings. Whenever their truck got backed up in traffic and stopped, the boys would shout, "G.I. numba one!" offering to sell them sodas, cigarettes, and girly magazines. Some threw C-Rations and candy bars down to the kids and watched the ensuing melee. Leaving the children behind in a cloud of dust, they barreled out of the city and into the countryside.

Known as the gateway to the Central Highlands, Highway 19 was the main east-west route from Qui Nhon to An Khe and beyond to Pleiku. Along its winding path, Will observed the rolling mountains and floodplains. A patchwork of rice paddies stretched through valleys toward dark tropical tree lines. Thatch-colored villas and huts could be seen along their banks. The dust from the lead trucks coated everyone in a fine film of red Vietnamese dirt that clung to their sweat. The sun was intense, and it was approaching a hundred degrees. A lone farmer and his water buffalo could be seen working the fields. Women wearing conical straw hats could be seen in groups, working in the paddies, and carrying things along the road. It looked peaceful. The forests, however, were foreboding and mysterious, their thick canopies blocking all sunlight and creating a dark abyss beneath them. Will imagined himself walking into that abyss.

The forests stretched west into the highlands where they were headed. After nine months of training, he was finally here in the enemy's backyard. Now riding exposed in the back of the truck, he thought about how "Charlie" could be out there right now, watching him. He pictured what he might look like in Charlie's crosshairs and wondered if there was a bullet out there with his name on it. After a while, his thoughts returned to home, the farm, and his family. "If they could only see me now," he thought.

Soon they were winding through the mountains. Every few miles, they would pass a checkpoint manned by soldiers who looked bored. After what seemed an eternity but was only forty miles or so, they rounded a corner, and someone spotted something bright and yellow atop a mountain towering in the distance. Eventually, they could make out the profile of a dark horse within a yellow shield, and it was clear what they were looking at—the giant shoulder patch of the 1st Air Cavalry plastered to the side of a mountain.

After a few more twists and turns through plunging mountain passes, they arrived at Camp Radcliff. Located in the heart of the Central Highlands near the town of An Khe, the base camp was typically referred to simply as "An Khe." To the west loomed Hon Cong Mountain, displaying its giant 1st Air Cavalry patch on its side, leaving no doubt as to who owned the surrounding real estate. On its peak sat a security outpost and communications center for the camp.

Scratched out of the wilderness by the initial wave of division soldiers to arrive in Vietnam the year before, An Khe was still primitive, and many permanent structures had yet to be built. This was the 1st Air Cavalry Division's operating base, and here the new arrivals would behold the spectacle of the division's monumental operation. Chinook helicopters sling-loaded howitzers and ammunition crates while sky cranes resembling giant mutant mosquitos hauled disabled Chinooks through the air. Surrounding the vast perimeter were dozens of communication and guard towers. A rumbling colossus of lead, rubber, petroleum, and steel, all manner of war implements were on display—earthmovers, tanks, artillery, supply trucks, fuel tankers, C-130 cargo planes, transport planes, and endless rows of helicopters.

In August of the previous year, the site that would become Camp Radcliff was chosen by Brigadier General John Wright after searching the highlands for a location that could accommodate the division's over four hundred aircraft. General Wright knew, however, that an airstrip made of dirt would create terrible dust storms with every take-off and landing. The underlying grass and brush would remain but would have to be cut very close to the ground. The general had not anticipated that his advance party would include less than two hundred men, mostly high-ranking officers and NCOs. He gathered them in and began, "Gentlemen, you will all be issued a machete or a grub hook. They both do exactly the same job. We are going to cut brush until we have a golf course here. You may as well hang your rank insignia on a tree because until this area is transformed, we will all avail ourselves to this manual task. When the golf course is completed, you may then put back your rank insignia." The airfield at Camp Radcliff was thereafter known as the "Golf Course."

The newly arrived battalion had been given a large plot of dirt for its operating area. On their first day, the men worked into the night, erecting large tents to serve as barracks and a mess hall. They dug trenches around each to prevent water from future rains from running through them. They dug large holes to act as improvised bunkers in case of mortar attack. Soon everyone was covered in the red dirt of An Khe. An afternoon rain started. All the old-timers—those who had been there awhile—stripped off their clothes and showered in the rain. The new guys ran into their tents to get their soap and towels, but when they came back out, the rain stopped. They had just gotten wet enough to work up a nice soap and dirt lather and had no way to rinse off.

Formation was held before evening chow. CPT A.J. Wise said some commander-type stuff, and then it was 1SG John Potter's turn. "Your ration for tonight is two beers, and two beers only," he began. "We'll be formed up back here at oh-five hundred tomorrow—every swingin' dick—and bring your shovels."

The men were relaxing in their tents when mortar rounds started falling on the camp. Most landed near the perimeter wire, but soon the rounds came closer to the road that ran through the battalion area. One landed next to the colonel's tent, then another even closer to the road where many had gathered. The men hit the dirt and took cover in their makeshift bunkers.

Most spent the night trying to sleep while the base's howitzers fired artillery rounds toward distant hills. A Minnesotan with fair skin, Marvin Bierschbach had spent the day working shirtless in the sun. With his back burned, he'd sleep on his stomach for the next few nights. They eventually got used to the constant pounding of artillery and the relentless heat.

"Two men from Alpha Company got drunk," Bob Matulac recalled of their first night in An Khe. "Bobby Hansen and Tom Gruenburg. Gruenburg decided they should go into town and get some women. Hansen tried to talk him out of it, but he insisted. They climbed into Colonel Swett's jeep and took off. MPs at the main gate tried to stop them, but Gruenburg gunned it, and they jumped out of the way. On to An Khe they went with MPs following them, sirens blaring. The two wayward troopers finally stopped, surrounded by MPs with guns drawn. Into the stockade, they went. Captain Wise got a call from the MP in charge and went to pick up the two drunks. They reported to First Sergeant Potter the next morning. I thought he was going to blow his top. He stormed in and chewed them both out, and they seemed to melt under his wrath. Royce Barrow, Donald Rankin, and I were in the same tent as Potter, behind a sheet that served as a door. We could barely keep from roaring with laughter. Captain Wise warned that if Colonel Swett ever found out, they would never get out of this place."

At exactly 6:00 AM, "Goooooood morning, Vietnam!" could be heard crackling through transistor radios tuned to the Armed Forces Vietnam Network (AFVN), the Saigon-based radio station run by the United States military. The sign-on that kicked off the *Dawn Busters* radio show each morning was first used in 1965 by Air Force disc jockey Adrian Cronauer, as portrayed by Robin Williams in *Good Morning Vietnam*. That same trademark sign-on was continued by all who followed as hosts of the show, including future *Wheel of Fortune* host Pat Sajak. AFVN played block-formatted music—each genre played during a specific time block—along with news, comedy, and sports.

At night, troops could hear *A Date With Chris* featuring Chris Noel, a blonde bombshell actress and model turned AFVN disc jockey. In the early sixties, she'd been in movies with Steve McQueen and Elvis Presley, and magazine ads for Kodak cameras and the Ford Mustang. Offering words of encouragement and the fantasy of female companionship, Noel was the Allies' alternative to Hanoi Hannah, the North Vietnamese disc jockey who played American rock and roll along with communist propaganda.

The following excerpts are from an August 21st letter from Donald Rankin.

*Dear Mom and Daddy,*

*We arrived at Qui Nhon yesterday. There was an Army band and villagers to greet us. The mountains are very pretty, but the villages are dirty and smelly. Our living quarters are a scream. We have tents with cots and mosquito nets. Last night, I didn't get out my blanket and almost froze. It really cools off here at night. Today, it is very hot, but the wind is blowing.*

*The mortar shells burst about a thousand feet away all night. The first few make you jump, and then you forget about them. Our company area is safe. We have barbwire barricades with landmines and machine guns out there too. Plus, a huge light about one mile up on a mountain that lights up the whole valley.*

*Everyone is in good spirits. We all have G.I. haircuts again. That and C-Rations for food are the biggest objections.*

*I will write as often as possible. Next week, we will probably start operations, so there will be some long periods without writing. The helicopters will drop us our letters, even in combat, but we won't always be able to send them out. Tell everyone hello and write soon.*

*Love,*

*Donnie*

## 24 August '66 – 51 weeks left

*Dear Folks,*

*Finally getting a chance to write. It's like we expected, a lot of work. Got off on the 20th. We expected to land on enemy territory, but as soon as we hit the shore, the band was playing. I lucked out and stayed back on detail the first day to guard equipment while everyone else flew to An Khe. I was at this airfield and hung a little jag on my first night here.*

*We received our first operation order, and we're heading out, maybe for a few weeks. This place—Camp Radcliff or An Khe—is pretty big and secure, about a forty-mile perimeter. They shoot artillery rounds all night, which is annoying. I think she'll be alright once we get settled. Get a tavern built after we get most of the work done. Had to eat C-Rations for two days. Now the hot meals aren't too bad. Some ants around here are a little poisonous or something. Got up one morning and was bitten twice on the foot. Darn things sting. We get one Armed Forces Radio station here. Reruns of baseball games and fairly good music.*

*You'll notice I addressed the top of my letter with only fifty-one weeks left 'cause when I get out of here, if I still have to finish out my time in the Army, it will be like civilian life back in the states again. What did you do with my bombs, throw them away? Doesn't matter to me. Before I forget, try and get Don Mc Ilquham's address. He was in the fields, so I didn't see him before I left Carson.*

*Well so long,*

*Will*

    After setting up their battalion area, the men began their 1st Air Cavalry "Division Training." In an August 26th letter, Donald Rankin remarked how they spent most of their time digging ditches and attending class—but also that the relationship between the NCOs and the rest of them had improved, and they weren't giving them such a hard time as they had before.

    In Bravo Company's tent, 1SG Dayton Hare smoked a cigar while looking through a Pacific Exchange catalog. The military's version of a Sears catalog, it offered many of the same products at a lower price and was tax-free. Hare's wife had always wanted a set of fine china, but it always seemed too expensive. Bernard Grady recalled the First Sergeant circling a picture of the Noritake chinaware set he had picked. After a few more paydays, he would have it sent to his wife as a surprise.

## 30 August '66

Dear Folks,

*Try to write a few lines before work starts. We haven't moved out on our mission yet, not until Friday. Guess it'll be for a few weeks guarding a highway. One of the guys you met at the airport, Figueroa—Puerto Rican guy—was one of the few who got to town last Sunday. Well, he shacked up with a woman, and now he has the Clap, haha! We're giving him a rough time about this now. And now Graham is in the stockade. Doubt if we'll see him again.*

*Received those snapshots yesterday. The guys got a kick out of them. Oh yes, happy anniversary and happy birthday to Mike. That's quite some birthday present he has. He'll need a license to drive it, won't he? Better save it for me. Yeah, send me the newspaper for a few months. Rod gave me his Bloomer Advance. I'll be looking for them doughnuts today. I'm going to sneak off with them so I won't have to share. I can taste them already.*

*Well, I better get ready for a little night patrol. Last night, 1st, 2nd, and 3rd Platoons went out, and it rained for about two hours straight. They were a sorry-looking bunch this morning.*

*Will*

Since being transferred to the 2/20th ARA in July, Joe Sanchez found that being an infantryman in an aviation unit was rather boring. His job was to ensure the rockets on the gunships were mission-ready. More often, however, he found himself working as a battalion cook. "I'd been trained to kill the enemy," he recalled, "but instead, I was cooking breakfast." Ordered to get up early for KP duty for the third morning in a row, he finally refused. "What are you going to do," he joked, "shave my head and send me to Vietnam?"

Picking up a copy of the *Stars & Stripes*, Sanchez noticed a front-page story of the 5/7th Cav arriving in Qui Nhon. He walked across base camp to the 5/7th's headquarters tent and asked to come back. He managed to get the ear of both LTC Swett and CPT Wise, and so it was that he returned to his old company. He walked back to the 2/20th to pack his gear and start the paperwork. The battalion clerk was typing up his transfer orders. "Going to the 5/7th, huh?" he remarked. "Better send your mother some flowers."

Still at An Khe during their first week, certain platoons were sent outside the perimeter of the base camp. In these "get to know you" patrols, they marched overland for miles, learned how to cross fast-moving rivers using ropes, and set up ambushes for any approaching enemy. Although they served as practice for future patrols in more remote and dangerous areas, these were not just training missions. In 1965, the communications center atop Hon Cong Mountain had been overrun by Viet Cong sappers, soldiers trained to infiltrate and sabotage base camps and firebases. The enemy was known to harass and probe the perimeter of An Khe, and as they had already found out, mortar attacks were frequent. If close enough, they would hear the "shunk" of their mortar rounds launching from their tubes several seconds before raining down and exploding.

Now back with Alpha Company, Sanchez was on one of these patrols with 1st Platoon. He was paired up with Rocco Valentino, also from New York. In the pouring rain, they crossed some rice paddies and went through a village. Valentino didn't have his poncho with him. "Extra weight," he said. So they shared Sanchez's after setting up their ambush for the night. Sanchez kept watch for three hours, then woke Valentino up for his turn. Before he could fall asleep, he heard Valentino snoring. Will and the others in 4th Platoon were sent out on their own patrol outside the wire at the end of August.

### 31 August '66 – 48 weeks left

*Dear Mike,*

*Well, I guess you might say I have arrived in Paradise Island, as you call it. Paradise for snakes, bugs, and mosquitoes. Bugs here come in three sizes: four, five, and six inches. The other day we climbed up and down a ladder on a two-engine helicopter that hovered at thirty feet with hundred-mile-per-hour wind.*

*You should have been with me last night. I never had such a miserable time since I had K.P. on the ship. We had this little patrol—just like on T.V.—crossing rice paddies and sewage drains, and it rained for about four hours. Then we set up an ambush and waited. Took turns sleeping in the rain, and it was cold. Went through a small village with houses made of mud and grass roofs. Seems funny—all these years I read about these people in geography class, and here I am, seeing it for real.*

*Hey Mack, how did you swing this cycle? You're not even old enough to drive it. Let me know the first time you're picked up, ha! Say, old buddy. How about doing me a big favor? Send me some Kool-Aid packages. This will kill the taste of the water. We get it from rubber barrels, and it tastes like rubber. Took my chance to write 'cause it's drizzling this afternoon.*

*Just came back from supper—got two beers and two pairs of jungle boots—and I'm hitting the sack as soon as I seal this letter.*

*Take it easy,*

*Will*

On September 1st, staff officer CPT Martin Frey briefed an inspection team on the deployability of the newly arrived battalion and started planning their first operation. In just a few days, the 5/7th Cav would take over Highway 19 security from the 1st Battalion, 8th Cavalry.

It was a balmy seventy-eight degrees, and a full moon shone over An Khe on the night of September 3rd. As the soldiers of the 5/7th Cav slept in their tents, eight platoons of the 1st Battalion, 12th Cavalry were on patrol and in ambush positions outside the camp's perimeter. At 9:50 PM, the first of over a hundred enemy mortar rounds started raining down on the Golf Course, destroying dozens of helicopters. Sirens sounded as base defenses went on high alert, and the response was launched. Two aerial rocket artillery (ARA) gunships took off in search of the enemy mortar team as searchlights from the guard towers scoured the area surrounding the perimeter. Artillery batteries shot illumination rounds while firing several high-explosive rounds on preplanned targets. Within five minutes, the mortar attack had ended, and the enemy was trying to escape.

At 10:13 PM, a platoon from Bravo Company, 1/12th Cav spotted the retreating Viet Cong mortar platoon. A firefight ensued, but the enemy slipped away. At 10:30 PM, the base camp's reaction force—Bravo Company, 2nd Battalion, 5th Cavalry—air assaulted into the area. At 11:00 PM, guard towers detected hostile small arms fire, responding with machine guns and calling in mortar rounds.

The attack had come from somewhere north of the Golf Course. The area was kept lit through the night with spotlights from guard towers, AC-47 Spooky gunships, and illumination rounds from the artillery. Four soldiers of the 15th

Transportation Corps, an aviation supply and maintenance battalion, had been killed. Seventy-six had been wounded, and seventy-seven aircraft had been damaged or destroyed.

As the sun rose, more infantry companies poured in to search the area. They only found four impressions left in the ground by 82mm mortar base plates and three unfired mortar rounds—just outside the wire along the northwest corner of the camp. Ammunition expended in response to the mortar attack included 2,810 high-explosive artillery rounds, 428 aerial artillery rockets, 144 high-explosive mortar rounds, as well as 9,600 7.62mm rounds fired, and two five-hundred-pound bombs dropped by the Spooky gunships.

Donald Rankin wrote home the next day, saying the mortar attack had kept them up until 2:00 AM. "This place is so pretty," he lamented, "it's a shame these people can't get settled and enjoy the beauty and natural resources."

"They sure don't play games around here," Mike Stoflet wrote to his sister Donna. "Every night, there's a battle right outside our camp."

The following (abridged) article appeared in the *Columbus Enquirer*.

### Moment of Truth is Near for 1st Cavalry's Newest Battalion

*The moment of truth is fast approaching for the 1st Air Cavalry Division's newest battalion—the moment when its men will face death in the jungle battlefield hell of Viet Nam.*

*Some are worried. Maybe pint-sized Pvt. First Class Timothy Payne is, but he doesn't show it. "Man, those V.C. can't kill me," he said. "I owe too much money. I'm paying alimony." Payne is from Galien, Michigan. He is a little guy and has his troubles because of it. Like this afternoon when he and his buddies stood in line to get jungle boots. "Man, they've just got to have a size four-and-a-half," he said. The quartermaster did, and he and his companions laced up shiny new boots. They took a few tentative steps, and the new leather and canvas boots were immediately caked in oozy mud. The thick, black mud is everywhere this time of year in the central highland home the new unit—the 5th Battalion, 7th Cavalry—is hacking out of the jungle.*

*So far, they have not faced the enemy. They arrived in Viet Nam on August 20th to bring the brigade up to strength. But they know that any day now, they will trudge out into the jungle hunting for communists to kill. They also know that some may not come back—like some of the guys they have replaced. "But they're more than willing," said Sgt. Maj. Robert Meyer, a giant of a man from Newport, Kentucky. "We're ready."*

*From New Boen, Texas, Pvt. First Class James Harmon is one of the battalion's riflemen. He wants to start using it. Maybe it's because, lately, he's mostly been using a shovel. It takes a lot of digging to set up a new base camp, and it's men* like Harmon who do the work. "When we get through with this digging, we'll be able to get out and get those Viet Cong," Harmon said. "I'm ready to go." Harmon said he wouldn't mind the communist booby traps too much, figuring the cactus back at Fort Carson "are worse than these punji stakes over here." His buddies laughed and said he might change his mind later. The punji stake used by the Viet Cong is a needle-sharp sliver of bamboo that can cut through a man's boot and inflict a dangerous wound. Often tipped with buffalo dung, they can cause a potentially fatal infection.

The men have had extensive physical training and believe they are in good fighting condition. Battalion commander Lt. Col. Ted Swett of Columbus, Georgia could not be prouder. "Even eighteen days on a ship has not taken the edge off," he said. "Could you believe eighty-five laps around the sundeck is three miles?" Besides the physical training aboard the ship, the men fired their M-16 rifles off the fantail and attended lectures to learn about the war they will soon be fighting, the enemy they are out to kill, and who is out to kill them.

"There are advantages of coming to war as a unit," Swett said. "One of them is knowing the men personally. There's one problem, though. Some are going to get hurt." As he said this, the commander's grin disappeared. Then it reappeared, and he added, "But we feel we are big enough to take it in stride." The colonel said he could not ask for better troops. Three-fourths of his officers hold the Expert Infantryman's Badge, and over half have had Ranger training. "Fort Carson gave me the cream of the crop. The result is more troops will stay alive."

Their base camp is only two miles from the once sleepy village of An Khe, now a G.I. honkytonk haven where soldiers can buy anything from cold beer to female companionship. But passes are rare, and only a few have been there. There is too much work to do putting the finishing touches on a modern military fighting machine and its home camp. For example, there's a 1st Sgt. Haskell Westmoreland of Beckley, West Virginia. He's busy night and day whipping Charlie Company into shape. "We're over here for just one thing," he said, "and that's to kill Viet Cong."

 On September 4th, an advance party was sent to coordinate the 5/7th Cav's takeover of the Highway 19 security mission. As the men readied their packs for the field, 1SG John Potter hauled in a sack of mail. The tent bristled with excitement, and everyone dropped what they were doing. As the men milled about, reading letters and opening packages, Will noticed his buddy Al Patrillo sitting on his cot, letter in hand, staring at the ground. "It's over," he sighed. "She found someone else." Patrillo had just received his proverbial "Dear John" letter. He took it hard.

 "Sorry about that," said Will.

The following (abridged) appeared in the 1st Air Cavalry Division's newspaper, the *Cavalair*.

## 'Mules' Replace Tracks, 5/7th Grasps Airmobility
*Story and Photos by PFC Harold Morris*

Twelve months after the first skytroopers arrived in Vietnam, a new unit joined the 1st Cav's airmobile striking force. On August 20th, the 5th Battalion, 7th Cavalry joined the 3rd Brigade at An Khe, four months after transitioning from mechanized to airmobile. They came from Colorado where—as the 1st Battalion, 11th Infantry—they had trained with track vehicles on Fort Carson's wide-open spaces.

On April 1st, they received their new designation and began training for Vietnam. Armored personnel carriers were turned in while jeeps and mechanical "mules" were drawn in return. M-14 rifles were exchanged for M-16s, winter clothing for mosquito netting and flak jackets. Then the training began—tower rappelling, firing the M-60 machine gun, 81mm mortar, 90mm recoilless rifles, and grenade throwing. Twelve per company were sent to Panama for jungle training.

On August 2nd, they boarded the USNS Gaffey to cross the Pacific. The men took classes, fired their M-16s, and rappelled down the cargo hold of the ship. On August 20th, they docked at Qui Nhon, and a plane trip to An Khe placed the 5/7th in the division that same day. Tents had to be put up, trenches dug, and mess facilities established.

Then the in-country training started. The men visited the firing range, a hot five-mile march from camp. They zeroed their weapons and threw hand grenades. The "Garryowen Troopers" fired a quick reaction course. Moving through the woods, they were "attacked" to see how quickly they could bring fire on the enemy. Those going out on the first night patrol were "nervous but not scared."

Classroom instruction included field hygiene, prevention of malaria, types of snakes in the republic, and treatment of bites. The Explosive Ordnance Demolition (EOD) team demonstrated the types of booby traps and mines used by the Viet Cong. "Leave no duds on the battlefield, or 'Charlie' might shoot it back at you." Instructors demonstrated the different sounds made by various weapons, including the cracking sound of the enemy's AK-47.

Also on the agenda was a display of helicopters used by the "First Team" and demonstrations by the Pathfinders. On the final day of training, the 228th Aviation Battalion demonstrated the capabilities of a Chinook, stressing the importance of continual radio contact when approaching the landing zone. Two

Chinooks hovered above, and each dropped two troop ladders. Skytroopers of the 5/7th then climbed up one ladder into the aircraft and down the other to the ground, putting their new knowledge to use.

MACV Commander Gen. William Westmoreland paid a visit to welcome the 5/7th and spoke on the background of the communist insurgency. When asked about his men, Sgt. Maj. Robert Meyer responded, "The morale is very high—they're eager and ready for action."

WELCOME— Gen. William C. Westmoreland, MACV Commander, welcomes the "Garry Owen" troopers to their new assignment.

LET'S GO— Ready for the real thing, "Garry Owen" troopers start out on their first patrol.

ACADEMICS — Men listen attentively to instructor discuss map reading. They also learned about snakebite and booby trops,

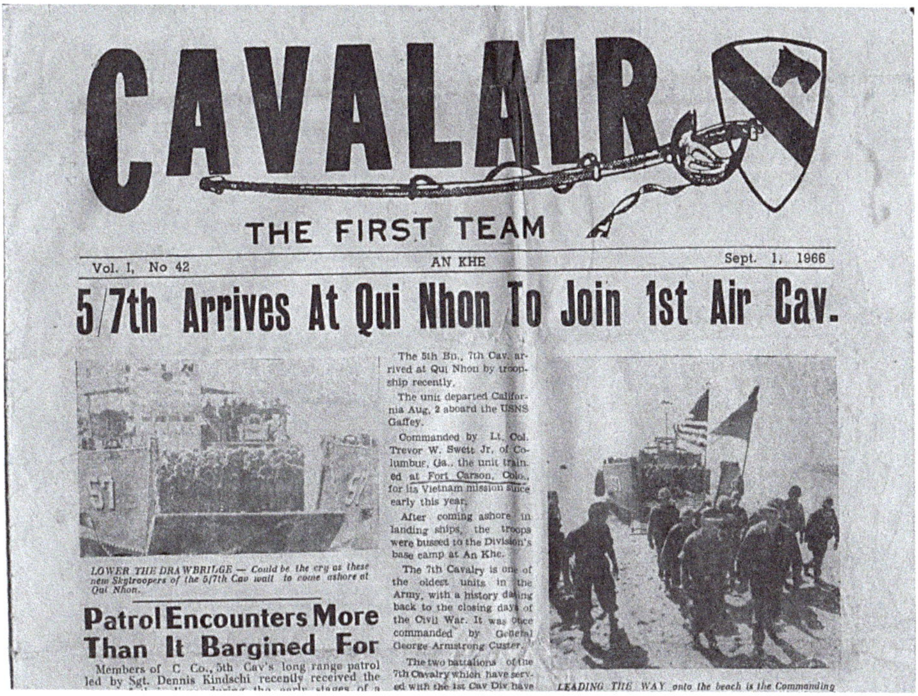

# CAVALAIR

THE FIRST TEAM

Vol. I, No 42 — AN KHE — Sept. 1, 1966

## 5/7th Arrives At Qui Nhon To Join 1st Air Cav.

*LOWER THE DRAWBRIDGE — Could be the cry as these new Skytroopers of the 5/7th Cav wait to come ashore at Qui Nhon.*

The 5th Bn., 7th Cav. arrived at Qui Nhon by troopship recently.

The unit departed California Aug. 2 aboard the USNS Gaffey.

Commanded by Lt. Col. Trevor W. Swett Jr. of Columbus, Ga., the unit trained at Fort Carson, Colo., for its Vietnam mission since early this year.

After coming ashore in landing ships, the troops were bussed to the Division's base camp at An Khe.

The 7th Cavalry is one of the oldest units in the Army, with a history dating back to the closing days of the Civil War. It was once commanded by General George Armstrong Custer.

The two battalions of the 7th Cavalry which have served with the 1st Cav Div have

*LEADING THE WAY onto the beach is the Commanding*

## Patrol Encounters More Than It Bargined For

Members of C Co., 5th Cav's long range patrol led by Sgt. Dennis Kindschi recently received the

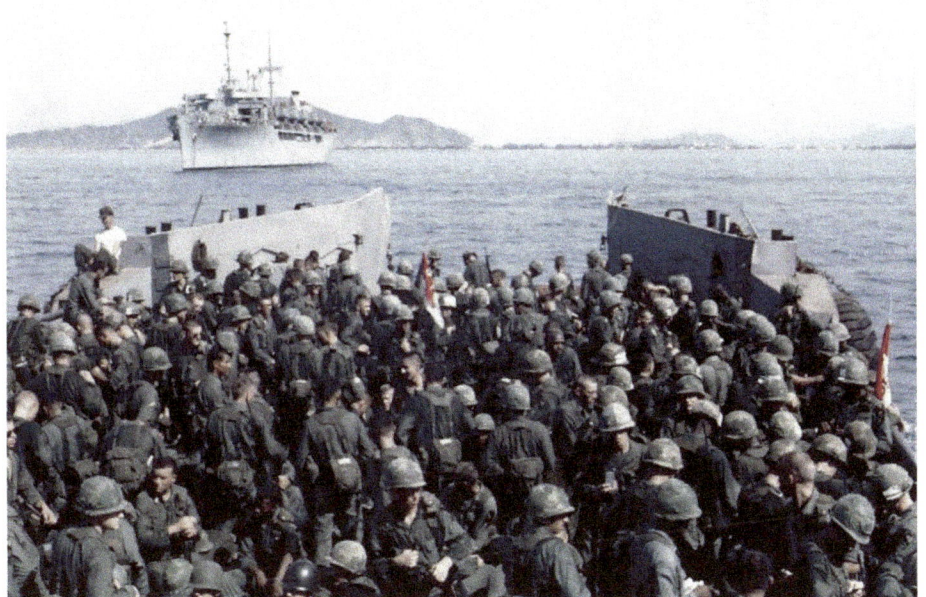

*5/7th Cav landing at Qui Nhon, photo by Royce Vick*

*Left–right: Quinn, Elmer, King, Anderson, Fulford, photo by Will Bowe*

*Aerial view of An Khe, source unknown*

*Hon Cong Mountain overlooking An Khe, source unknown*

# 7
# INTO THE JUNGLE
## (Operation Roadrunner)

*Yeah, I got—let me see—twenty-eight notches in my gun now.*

The opening scene of *We Were Soldiers* depicts the final defeat of the French during the French-Indochina War by the communist Viet Minh in 1954. The battle took place along Highway 19, then Route Colonial 19, about five miles west of the Mang Yang Pass. Winding through the highlands, the Mang Yang Pass is set between An Khe to the east and Pleiku to the west. Flanked by spectacular mountain rises on each side, it was the site of many enemy ambushes during both the French and American wars in Vietnam. That final battle was a slaughter, and over eight hundred French soldiers of Mobile Group 100 were hastily buried near Highway 19 in its aftermath (see Highway 19 map, page 334).

During the previous summer, the newly arrived battalion commander of the 1/7th Cav, LTC Hal Moore, had walked along this same battlefield. In his hand, he held a copy of *Street Without Joy: The French Debacle in Indochina* by Bernard Fall, which described that final battle in detail. Still visible from the highway were the white crosses marking the graves of those who died defending the French empire, only twelve miles from their new base camp at An Khe. He noted the adage, "He who controls the Central Highlands controls South Vietnam." He also knew that whoever controlled Highway 19 controlled the highlands. In fact, the North Vietnamese had once planned a major offensive in which they would use Highway 19 to split South Vietnam in two. The arrival of the 1st Air Cavalry in July 1965 delayed these plans for about ten years.

This (abridged) *Cavalair* article described a typical incident along Highway 19.

### Iceman Made Fatal Error When He Cheated Charlie

*Ice was a premium commodity when the Cav first arrived in An Khe. The ice arrived in an ancient truck from Pleiku. The iceman prospered on the inflated prices the Americans would pay for his product, but one day he made a fatal mistake. Accompanied by their Vietnamese counterparts, some military policemen checked on a stalled vehicle a few kilometers outside of town. They found the vintage iceman's truck. Inside was the iceman, bullet hole in head and very much dead. He had cheated, said a note in Vietnamese on the hood of the truck, and "grown rich on the dirty money of the Americans." But the real crime—according to the note—he'd cheated the Viet Cong tax collectors who controlled the road. So there was no ice in An Khe that day, nor the next, nor for quite some time.*

*5 September '66 – 47 weeks left*

Dear Folks,

*Don't have time to write 'cause we're leaving this morning. If I don't write for a while, don't worry. I'll write when I get a chance. No big thing.*

*So long,*

*Will*

In the early morning of September 5th 1966, the men of the 5/7th Cav departed An Khe, once again in a convoy of deuce-and-a-halfs. Dubbed Operation Roadrunner, their first mission was to secure this long winding road known as Highway 19 from An Khe to Pleiku. This included the Mang Yang Pass, where a deadly ambush had occurred just two years prior on allied Army of the Republic of Vietnam (ARVN) forces. Pleiku and An Khe were major bases, and many military convoys were made each day between them. There was also local civilian and merchant traffic along the route. The 5/7th Cav was now responsible for keeping the traffic safe and the Viet Cong at bay.

Each platoon guarded a checkpoint along the highway during the operation. As one squad of eight to ten soldiers manned their platoon's assigned checkpoint—and a hilltop base overlooking that checkpoint—the other three patrolled the surrounding jungle, also known as the boonies, the bush, or Indian country. Reaching 4th Platoon's checkpoint, the men jumped out. Leaving one squad behind, the rest headed into the jungle to search for the enemy.

The sun was beating on them hard as sweat stung their eyes, and the shade seemed inviting but ominous. Once again, Will stared into the abyss of the jungle as it swallowed one squad after another. Hearts pounding, he and his team would soon follow. "Move it, boys," grunted SSG Hayslip from behind. "Whatcha tryin' do, live forever?" Stepping into the forest, they found a dark, damp, pungent-smelling world, teeming with insect and animal life that made strange and exotic sounds, with monkeys screaming, the mating calls of geckos, and all manner of bird noises. The air was like a sauna, and with each breath, they felt their lungs fill with hot moisture. Droplets of water coated the foliage and quickly soaked their fatigues. Beams of sunlight filtered through the canopy, and within those beams, they could see the moist particles of jungle debris floating in the air. It was creepy, dark, and unwholesome. And so began the endless daily routine of hacking through forests, sloshing through rivers and rice paddies, and trudging over mountains in search of Charlie. Finding nothing, they returned to their hilltop base just before nightfall.

Alpha Company had three rifle platoons, 1st, 2nd, and 3rd Platoons, and one mortar platoon, 4th Platoon. Each platoon was led by a platoon leader, a 1st or 2nd Lieutenant, and a platoon sergeant, a Sergeant First Class or Staff Sergeant.

SSG Donald Burtis was the platoon sergeant in charge of Will's mortar platoon, and 1LT Sam Cathcart was their platoon leader. Each platoon had four squads, and each squad had two teams. Alpha Company's head NCO, 1SG John Potter, was responsible for running the company as directed by their commander, CPT A.J. Wise, who bore ultimate responsibility for the actions of his soldiers and their welfare.

On Will's mortar crew was their team leader, SGT John Fulford from Florida, Marvin Bierschbach from Minnesota, and John Bronson, the tall black guy from the Bronx. Their squad leader was SSG Bobby Hayslip from Georgia. Hayslip's other team was led by SGT Gerald Anderson from Illinois, with Al Patrillo from Pennsylvania, and Kurt Elmer and Martin Quinn from New York.

The men were on edge during their first night in the jungle. One of Bravo Company's platoons spent a great deal of ammunition on what they believed was a tiger "or something" approaching their perimeter, as noted in the battalion's situation report. In Alpha Company's 3rd Platoon, Bobby Hansen shared a foxhole with Donald Smith from Milwaukee. "Smithy would have been better suited for a typewriter than life in the infantry," he recalled. Hansen told of watching a black panther stalking by their perimeter one night and how a Vietnamese armadillo, or pangolin, gave them a great deal of trouble. Many flares were spent lighting up the area around the armadillo as it made a noise similar to soldiers shuffling along the ground.

Will's worst fear was to be attacked at night, but the darkness offered relief from the heat. Except for animal sounds and the distant thumping of artillery, it was mostly peaceful. Staring into the darkness, this is probably where you feel about as far away from home as you can possibly get.

According to the battalion's first two situation reports, Charlie was anxious to welcome the new skytroopers to the war zone.

*September 5th*

*10:25 PM—Alpha Company reports enemy probe of perimeter. Object believed to be a man set off two illuminating devices, was engaged with small arms fire and set off one more device.*

*September 6th*

*1:52 AM—Delta Company reports incoming light weapons fire.*

*7:45 AM—Morning sweep of Highway 19 complete, reported Green.*

*12:25 PM—Two unidentified persons seen heading west from Checkpoint 3, two hundred meters from highway. Soldiers of Alpha Company attempted to apprehend, but they avoided apprehension.*

1:50 PM—Jeep turned over on highway near Checkpoint 7. Medevac called for two individuals, lifted out at 2:10. SP/4 Gary Jefferis reported DOA. Injuries of PFC James McDonugh not confirmed at this time.

4:50 PM—Convoy received sniper fire departing Checkpoint 12. Bravo Company sent squad into area to search and seize with negative contact.

9:55 PM—Alpha Company 4th Platoon reports incoming M-79 grenade.

September 7th

8:05 AM—Bravo Company reports sniper fire. Do not know if VC or bandit. Patrol discovered punji stakes at coordinates BR 262-475.

11:00 AM—Bravo Company patrol found fresh tracks heading from northeast, one 80mm dud, and one 105mm high-explosive dud.

1:50 PM—Bravo Company reports thirty-five old emplacements with overhead cover found at 239-475.

On September 7th, Bravo Company was sent into the Mang Yang Pass, and one man was wounded while placing a Claymore mine. Later that night, Will's 4th Platoon took sniper fire twice, at 10:20 and 10:26 PM. They responded by firing their mortars and calling artillery strikes. At 2:30 PM the next day, a half-ton truck carrying MPs fell under machine gun fire from both sides, and one MP was wounded. The highway was closed for an hour while artillery and ARA gunships pummeled both sides of the road. Afterward, Bravo Company searched the area but could not find the enemy. Late that night, a Bravo Company soldier became the first in the battalion to take an enemy bullet, shot in the leg by a sniper.

## 8 September '66 – 47 weeks left

Dear Folks,

Here I am in a pup tent, and it's pouring out. It's drizzled just about every day now. Having a hard time getting my clothes to dry. Have to wash them in a creek below our hill. The last bunch of guys were here for about a month, so they had everything pretty well set up. Half of us stay up at night to guard. That's the night shift. The first night here, everyone was trigger-happy. We'd stare into the dark and would swear that this tree or that bush moved. We'd shoot a flare up and shoot a few rounds. Boy, everyone was a nervous wreck that night. Man, what a life.

Finally received your doughnuts today. Well, they were a bit moldy. We hadn't gotten any chow yet and were starving. So we ate them, mold and all. One guy said, "If we die of food poisoning, we'll die together." We're supposed to get two hot meals a day, but it hasn't been the case. Glad I brought some candy along. Say, I'd like you to do me a big favor. Send me a pair of overboots and a good *raincoat. Then I'll really be in business. I got a raincoat, but it's so awkward. Send it as soon as possible, and I'll be walking like a king. I best get some sleep now. I'll be waiting, hurry!*

*Will*

Will and his platoon headed into the jungle for another patrol. In most areas, the soldiers in each team formed a wedge—or V shape—spreading out to prevent a single grenade or mine from killing more than one. When patrolling through dense forests, however, they moved in a single file, following closely to avoid getting lost. Because they were moving on their own and not with the company, they left their mortar pieces back at their encampment.

They came to a clearing, crossed a rice paddy, and entered a tiny hamlet. A handful of women and children watched silently as the men searched their four or five small huts. "VC?" 1LT Cathcart asked the oldest-looking woman.

"No VC," she replied, shaking her head.

He motioned to the surrounding hills, "VC out there?"

The woman shrugged.

Later that afternoon, they trudged along a hillside of burned-out trees defoliated by Agent Orange. Each team of four followed the team in front of it. 1LT Cathcart and radio operator Fred Brodosi walked behind the first squad of two teams, while SSG Burtis moved with a laborious gait in front of the last squad. Somewhere in the middle, SGT Fulford led his team in a wedge formation, with Bierschbach following to the left and Bronson to the right, and Will following Bronson. Just in front of Fulford walked their squad leader, SSG Hayslip. "Listen, troops," he'd say in his southern drawl, "don't congregate—else there'll just be a puff of smoke circling 'round where you use to was."

A minute later, Hayslip was telling the stragglers to catch up. Just then, they heard the zipping of bullets flying by their heads and the snapping of branches and leaves, followed by the cracking of AK-47 fire. There was some yelling, and everyone hit the ground. Will tried to take cover behind a skinny dead tree. Lying in the rotting wet undergrowth, he scrambled to ready his rifle. For the first time, he fired it in anger—blindly into the forest in three-round bursts. As the men got online with each other and machine gunners emplaced their weapons, the attack was answered with an explosion of lead in the enemy's general direction. A blueish haze enveloped the platoon, and the forest's pungent odor was quickly overwhelmed by that of burnt gunpowder. Cathcart and Burtis both yelled, "Cease fire!" Then it was over. No one had caught a glimpse of the enemy.

It's been said that all war is hell, but contact's a bitch. This was considered "light" contact. Now they knew what the war looked like, what it felt like and smelled like. It wasn't exactly how they'd imagined it—just mass confusion and noise. They checked themselves for bullet holes and moved out while 1LT Cathcart radioed the company to report the contact.

"It ain't much of a war," remarked Burtis, "but it's the only one we've got."

Will looked at the skinny dead tree he'd used for cover and contemplated its uselessness. Fortunately, their superior firepower had provided all the cover necessary to survive that half-hearted attack.

No one said a word as they continued their march. Twenty minutes later, Burtis called for a break, and still, no one spoke. Bronson looked down at Will, and without a word, Will bummed him a smoke. His long black hands trembled as he flicked his Zippo. "Big tall black dude walking around in the jungle," he said under his breath, exhaling his first puff. "Those gooks are gonna shoot me first."

"Y'all scared of gettin' zapped now?" quipped Hayslip. "Don't be scared fellas. Anyhow, there ain't nothin' you can do when your number's up."

"Hell Bobby, I think I just shit my pants back there!" said Burtis—and the tension was broken, and Bronson laughed a deep laugh, and then everyone laughed, and they were back to smoking and joking.

A hard rain fell along with the darkness, and they took shelter in a tiny, abandoned cement building. With an ankle-deep stream of mud running through it, they sat on their helmets and tried to sleep while leaning against the wall.

3rd Platoon medic Michael Handley recalled one of their own patrols near Highway 19. Following a blood trail, 1LT William Nelson led them down a narrow path through the jungle. After some time—in great anticipation—they rounded a corner to find two old ladies chopping weeds and chewing on betel nuts, a common practice of old Vietnamese women. The betel nuts turned their teeth black, and apparently, the juice they spit out looked a lot like blood.

Bill Purdy of 2nd Platoon was on a night patrol with his squad during this time. A tall sergeant they called "Stretch" was leading them. In the darkness, Stretch fell ass-over-teakettle into a deep watery ravine. He wasn't hurt but had dropped his M-16 in the fall and couldn't find it. They climbed down and felt around for the rifle in the muddy water. Purdy recalled the voice of CPT Wise over the radio, "Don't even think about coming back without that weapon."

While the platoon sergeants were largely combat experienced and well-respected by their men, the lieutenants were a mixed bag. Land navigation skills were crucial as platoons often moved independently in this "small-unit" war. Some young lieutenants could barely read a map, however. The Infantry Officer's motto is "Follow me!" but Bob Matulac recalled how one of their platoon leaders was more apt to shout, "Move up, move up!" from the rear of the formation, unaware of what his men in front faced. In stark contrast was the leader of 2nd Platoon, 1LT James Harmon. A West Point graduate, smart and tough, he was respected by all. "He was head and shoulders above the others," said Purdy. "But he wasn't a 'spit shine' officer, and Captain Wise would occasionally remind him to shave. Rather than barking orders, he simply told us what needed to be done, and we always felt compelled to oblige."

### 12 September '66 – 46 weeks left

*Dear Folks,*

*Still raining out. Haven't seen the sun since we got here. Only problem is trying to dry our clothes. Getting three hot meals a day now. Sometimes it's real good, sometimes it ain't. We went on a patrol through these hills and seen how some of these people live. The houses are about three feet above the rice paddies and made of grass. You know, no matter how hard I have it, I'll always be thankful I was born in the U.S. We live like kings back home.*

*Last Tuesday, a guy got killed and two injured below our hill when their jeep turned over on a curb. Our medic had to give them first aid. His first big case.*

*Found a fishing pole in front of my bunker. Tried a little fishing down by the creek. Fishing poles here are thirty feet long. We use them for stakes and poles. Figueroa and I tent together and guard the west side of this hill.*

*How long did Leonard and Ken stay? I tell you, those two can join the Navy if they like. I had my fill when I was on the ship for eighteen days. I'd rather have my feet on this firm muddy ground. How did Ken's car look, pretty sharp? You know, if I bought a car over here, there'd be no tax on it. Do you know how much I could save on a new GTO? Here is some money that we get—not Viet Nam money, but military money we can only spend for some reason. We call it Monopoly money. Feels like five hundred bucks in my pocket.*

*Will*

Donald Rankin also wrote home on September 12th.

*Dear Mom and Daddy,*

*Received eight letters today. Boy, do I feel better. Today, one of our jeeps was fired upon. They stopped the jeep but don't know any particulars. Yes, that was our base camp that was attacked. They're still firing on it, but they usually don't do much damage.*

*We're doing pretty good. I'm used to being dirty and wet now. I had a narrow escape of my own today. We built a bunker of sandbags and logs. My tent was down, so I decided to sleep in it. The driest night's sleep I've had for a while. But I got up this morning, walked out, and it collapsed. It covered my helmet, weapon, duffel bag, and everything. It shook me up to think I might have been under there, but it broke my heart because it was such an awful job building it.*

*The natives have been unfriendly the past few days. That is a good sign that VC are in the area. We haven't seen any bad action yet. Today, one position received sniper fire, but he was soon run off. They think the VC are holding off until the monsoon gets worse.*

*I really feel a little homesick tonight. The day has been good, but sometimes the loneliness gets to me. Whalen and Earlywine are at my immediate position now. It is good to have someone from home, but we aren't real close. I guess because of our ages. But I'd probably be lost without them.*

*I'm feeling better about everything each day. My arthritis is bad on cold rainy days, and I have a bad cough at night. Doc gave me some antibiotic pills for the cough. I think it's from talking all day on the radio.*

*I'm learning my job pretty well. I've slowed down on being so gung-ho. There is little chance of me making E-5, so I'm just enjoying myself.*

*The commander got up yesterday morning in rare form. He grumbled and growled, stormed, and had a regular tantrum. I just stuck my head out of the tent and laughed. He doesn't have it any harder than we do.*

*Yesterday, I took a bath in the creek. It was cold but felt great after being dirty for fourteen days.*

*Also, send me that Cumberland College catalog sometime. I want to start working on this now. The Army pays a hundred dollars a month, and I might get out three months early to go to school. This is about all. Tell everyone hello.*

*Love,*

*Donnie*

On September 15th at 1:58 PM, Charlie Company's 2nd Platoon air assaulted onto an area known as Landing Zone (LZ) Quick. Aside from a punji stake wound, their patrol was without incident. But during their extraction, the helicopter crashed, killing one and injuring four others. They stayed at the crash site through the night and until the chopper could be recovered by a sky crane the following afternoon. Bravo Company suffered two wounded when soldiers guarding a bridge along the highway were hit by enemy grenades at 8:50 PM on September 17th.

That same day, Alpha Company received word that they would soon embark on their own company-size mission, dubbed Operation Golden Bee, in honor of their favorite bar in Colorado Springs. In a briefing attended by SSG Robert Matulac and the company's platoon leaders and sergeants, CPT A.J. Wise advised that they would be preparing for their first air assault.

Matulac awoke to a fierce burning sensation on his right foot the next morning. He went to see medic Bill Garcia. Removing his boot revealed two red bite marks. He thought it was a snake bite, but Garcia said it was from some sort of millipede. Matulac packed his gear and started down a trail toward the highway. His ankle started to feel numb, and soon he was tumbling down a hill. Having rolled his ankle, he was flown to Pleiku. With his foot in a cast, he reported back to CPT Wise the next morning but could not go on the company's first air assault mission.

### 18 September '66 – 45 weeks left

Dear Folks,

*Thank you for those cookies. Man, you couldn't have timed it any better. I had just gotten back from patrol that morning and was starving. They were in good shape, and the Kool-Aid really covers up the pill we put in our canteen for the water we get from the creek. The newspaper is good to read. Everyone else wants to read it too. At least I can read what's happening in Viet Nam, ha! Did you get my little Cavalair newspaper? The chow is getting better, the sun's shining, and it's beginning to look real good.*

*I got a letter from Allen Simon yesterday. He is with the 25th Infantry Division in a platoon of 4.2 mortars, which are bigger than ours. They're guarding Highway 19, same as us, but about ten miles west of here, near Pleiku. Sure would like to see the old boy. Are those boots and raincoat on the way yet? What did you guys do with those shells I brought home?*

*Will*

At 3:00 PM on September 20th, Alpha Company's platoons displaced from their positions, replaced by Bravo and Charlie Companies. In preparation for Operation Golden Bee, they moved to the battalion's forward command post—Eagle's Nest—overlooking the Mang Yang Pass. In the Army, "forward" means in the field where the action is, as opposed to "in the rear with the gear." A few hours later, the operation was postponed.

### 21 September '66 – 45 weeks left

Dear Folks,

*I bummed these papers and envelope off Rodney Henning. The last few days on our hill, we had a little excitement. Some V.C. or innocent hunter set off a trip flare, and we shot into that area with everything we had. It was at supper time. The guy who delivered the chow was in the creek taking a bath, and he jumped back in the jeep with no clothes to man the machine gun, ha! I was shooting my gun and eating a tough steak sandwich at the same time.*

*We moved from our last position to the top of this hill that Henning is on. We were supposed to go on a big mission, but now it's canceled. Hard to say where we're going. Rod's going on a little patrol today. My old squad leader joined the* long-range patrol, and now he's in charge of Rod. The most sure-footed sergeant I know, and Rod is damn lucky to have him. Wish I still had him. That guy who got killed in the jeep accident below our hill was a good friend of Rod and a good man. I knew him a little, also. Sure is a bad way to go.

We've been getting our Lifeline packs pretty regular now. Razor blades, candy, soap, toothpaste, cigarettes, but no beer. The beer is supposed to be free, but I heard they've been selling it on us—to locals back at camp—so we buy it off the Boom Boom wagon that goes by on our road.

To get back to my last letter, we guys were discussing what to do with my shells back home. The M-79 for a gear shift, 50 Cal for a radio knob, mortar round as a hood ornament, and I could put James Bond out of style. Then our platoon leader came up, and they mentioned about my shells. "Damn Bowe," Cathcart says, "did you really sneak all them home?" They all got a little chuckle out of it.

I received those boots and raincoat the other day. I could hardly wait for them to get here. Now if it would only rain. Cathcart was bitching 'cause he had to carry the box and newspaper up the hill for me. I got them all willed out in case I get bumped off. Now I have to worry about being knocked off by my own friends. The packages are expensive to send, so take it out of the money I send home. You may say it's alright, but not with me 'cause you have expenses and I don't. Also, next month chip in twenty bucks to the church for me. Not that the church needs it, but the Good Lord might give me some luck. I hope.

Old Pro,

Will

## 21 September '66 – 45 weeks left

Hi Fuzzy Face,

Mike, I'll be square with you. I haven't told anyone what's really going on here, or I'd have them all worried. I know I can trust you. Like the last hill we were on, it wasn't too bad. Most of us survived. I always told you I dug ditches, but I didn't say what for, did I? Burying V.C.s. I remember the time John got killed. His arm torn off. We thought we sent it home with him. But it was the wrong one, it was Andy's arm. Guess we all make mistakes. Like this last mission we were going on, they named it Suicide Mission. Thank God we didn't have to go. They were ready to give us the last sacrament. Yeah, I got—let me see—twenty-eight notches in my gun now. I suppose my days are numbered. When you gotta go, you gotta go. Now wait a minute. You're not believing all this shit, are you? Seriously, the biggest enemy here is the rain and the ants. Like that one time that trip flare went off, and we put a lot of bombs and lead into that area. I doubt we got anybody, but we killed a lot of ants.

*Did you shave before you went to school today? Yeah, or old Coach Grip will make you dry-shave in front of the class. Does he still tell stories of how good I was in football—the touchdowns, the tackles, the interceptions? Of course, this was only during practice. In the real games, I always let the other guys play hero. My weak point was being too modest. Like Darrell says, "I could have been a star, but they already had lights."*

*Bet you couldn't wait to get back to school. I know I couldn't, so I could get out of filling the silo. What do you have for subjects? I know, phy-ed, girls, skipping classes, and general science. Remember how good I was at it. All of them A's. I always believed in doing good at my studies, or not doing them at all.*

*I got them pictures you all sent. What color is that cycle of yours, and how does she run? Wish they would have been in color. And how are the races coming? I see Jerry Bresina is doing good in football, co-captain and all. Heard Green Bay won two games. Wish we could have brought our radios with us. What's the hit song back home? I almost forgot—say thanks to Ma and Dad for sending the clothes. It was just as I wanted.*

*Your hero,*

*Will*

Donald Rankin also wrote home on September 21st.

*Dear Mom and Daddy,*

*Everything is still going fine. We moved again yesterday. We are now on top of a mountain in the Mang Yang Pass. It is so beautiful. I wish that I had a camera to take some pictures. There were three thousand Frenchmen killed on this mountain in 1954. How the Vietnamese ever did it, I can't see. Everything is going well. We've only had three casualties from the enemy. They were minor. We had two guys killed in accidents. One in a jeep and one in a helicopter. This is about all. Tell everyone hello and write.*

*Love,*

*Donnie*

On September 22nd, after securing the battalion command post for two days, Alpha Company was notified that Operation Golden Bee was on again, now set for September 24th.

*The Saga of Western Man* was made for ABC Television at the start of the big military build-up in 1965. Unlike other Vietnam films, its perspective is not jaundiced by hindsight. Against the backdrop of an armada of helicopters flying over the mountains, the narrator observes of the highlands, "...it belongs to no one. Not to the Viet Cong who roam it, not to the South Vietnamese. It is no man's land. In Vietnam today, you will hold only the ground you stand upon."

The film follows an infantry company of the 1st Air Cavalry Division led by CPT Theodore Danielson, from their air assault atop a hill to their burning of enemy encampments, their wounded being flown away after a firefight, and their own Highway 19 mission. The narrator concludes, "Alpha Company, 1st Battalion, 8th Cavalry marches off again. One company and one company commander, in an army composed of companies... and they all are pretty much alike."

*Outpost along Highway 19, photo by Robert Matulac*

*Mang Yang Pass, photo by Harald Hendrichsen, 604th Transportation Co.*

*1LT William Nelson, photo by Robert Matulac*

*John Bronson carrying base plate, photo by Marvin Bierschbach*

# 8
# AIR ASSAULT
## (Operation Golden Bee)
*To the Viet Cong, they are known as the horse soldiers.*

While the 5/7th Cav secured Highway 19, other battalions of the 1st Air Cavalry Division launched Operation Thayer on September 13th 1966. In the Army's largest air assault operation to date, 120 Huey and Chinook helicopters airlifted five battalions—over two thousand combat troops—into positions surrounding the Kim Son Valley. Known as the Crow's Foot, the Kim Son comprises several river valleys converging in the shape of a crow's foot. From fourteen mountaintop landing zones, the skytroopers descended into the valleys, searching and clearing their respective hillsides, forming a steadily tightening noose around the enemy while allied ARVN battalions took up blocking positions to prevent his escape.

Thayer was the first operation of the Binh Dinh Province Pacification Campaign, designed to destroy the Viet Cong and NVA infrastructure throughout Binh Dinh Province. Part of the campaign was to prevent the enemy from confiscating the rice harvests from local farmers. As this was their main food source, it successfully encouraged abandonment and surrender among their ranks.

Within ten days, Operation Thayer had dislodged the communists from the Kim Son Valley. Now separated from their supply bases, the enemy fled eastward with the 1st Air Cavalry's 1st Brigade in relentless pursuit. On September 23rd, the NVA launched a nighttime attack on an ARVN command post. The attack failed, and they continued eastward into the coastal plains. Fleeing on foot, they could not outpace the skytroopers who pursued them through the air. Within days, two NVA battalions were trapped in an area of the Phu My plains between the Phu Cat Mountains to their south and the Nui Mieu Mountains to their north. To their east lay the South China Sea, and to their west—the Americans.

The 5/7th Cav would not join this large, multi-brigade, multi-national operation until the beginning of October. As Operation Thayer grinded on in the coastal plains, Alpha Company would kick off its own operation in the highlands—Operation Golden Bee, initially planned as a three-day mission.

### 23 September '66 – 44 weeks left

*Best get this letter written before dark. All I want to say is I'm going on a three-day mission, so I won't be writing. Well, I don't write that often anyway.*

*This is one of his buddies finishing his letter, as he is going to get our chow for tomorrow. When I get out of the service, I plan to visit you people.*

*PFC Quinn*

Donald Rankin also wrote home before their mission.

*Dear Mom and Daddy,*

*A very slow, cool, pretty day. It is the easiest day that we've had since our arrival. They were fattening us for a kill. Tomorrow, we are going on a full company operation. They haven't given us any details. So if you don't hear from me for a while, don't worry.*

*Is there enough money for you to make it on? If not, I think that I could arrange for the bank to give you part of my monthly payments. If I survive, I will get those others paid. If I don't, it won't matter because the insurance will cover it. This is about it. Write when you can.*

*Love,*

*Donnie*

At 8:51 AM on September 24th, the first choppers begin lifting Alpha Company's men from the pickup zone (PZ) at Eagle's Nest. The first wave will fly out in Chinooks and the rest will follow in Hueys. Amid the whine of their engines and the thumping of their blades, they run through a storm of reddish-brown dust and debris toward their flying war horses. The troop-laden choppers vibrate and strain upward. The soldiers can now view their battlefield from the sky as they skirt jungle treetops at over a hundred miles per hour toward LZ Brenda. Picturesque rolling hills, plains and meadows, winding brown rivers, triple-canopy massifs, mountains and valleys. Aside from the view, the open-doored choppers provide temporary relief from the heat.

Meanwhile, eight miles north of An Khe—on a remote enemy-occupied hillside partially covered with trees—all is quiet, save for the rustling of the elephant grass in the hot breeze. At once, the ground explodes, sending black geysers of dirt into the sky and shattering trees all about the hillside. The earth shakes as the concussion radiates for miles through the valley. The initial volleys of high-explosive artillery rounds are immediately followed by those of white phosphorous—sending up dramatic bright white burning plumes and setting everything around them ablaze. Next, exploding canisters of tear gas fall from Chinooks flying above, engulfing the hillside in a choking white haze.

An armada of helicopters emerges over a distant ridgeline. Departing from the formation, gunships on each side now drop headlong into the valley like angry hornets, spraying a hail of lead and rockets into the area around the landing zone. Those who had given away their position by taking shots at them are now hunted relentlessly by the attack helicopters. Each is laden with over a thousand pounds of hate—7.62mm machine gun rounds for killing men and aerial rockets for dug-in bunkers. Spewing bullets at over six thousand rounds per minute, the gunships carry Gatling gun-style armaments known as miniguns. Laced with red tracer rounds, each minigun's torrent of lead takes on the appearance of a red snake. As the gunships circle, the troop ships move into a stepped formation and descend toward the landing zone while door gunners on each chopper strafe the surrounding tree lines with their M-60s.

Descending into the noxious haze, the skytroopers can be seen to be wearing gas masks. The most eager are leaning out and standing on the skids, clinging to the chopper with one arm and clutching a rifle with the other. One has a pack of smokes strapped to his helmet, another a bottle of bug dope. Even from a distance and through the grime on their fatigues, the large patches on their shoulders can be recognized. To the Viet Cong, they are known as the horse soldiers.

The men had been told that an enemy force was holed up on this hill. Such an assault precluded any attempt at stealth. As expected, the enemy had quit the hill during the artillery barrage. Alpha Company's first air assault was not without incident, however. Yelling over the noise and thumping, each chopper's crew chief had advised the men to jump out the right side, closest to the hill. Perhaps because he had been trying to don his gas mask over his glasses at the time, a young and eager lieutenant in 1st Platoon didn't get the message. As the rest of the men jumped out the right side, he took a flying leap out the left shouting "Garryowen!" and taking his radio operator with him. They fell about twenty feet, and the lieutenant broke his ankles. They all learned how deceiving the tall elephant grass could be, making you think you were closer to the ground than you actually were.

The artillery had left a wicked mess of a landing zone, with brush fires and jagged remnants of splintered trees scattered about the hillside. Through the tear gas haze and past intermittent fires, the troops sprinted out in all directions to form a secure perimeter, just as they'd been trained. Their training had not prepared them for assaulting onto such a ragged landing zone, however, and four others were injured while jumping out of the choppers. The last wave dropped onto LZ Brenda at 10:46 AM.

At 11:06 AM, Alpha Company started along "Route Red" to commence their search and destroy mission. As they set out, many noticed razor-like cuts on their arms that had been inflicted while running through the elephant grass. Assisted by a scout dog platoon attached to the company, they would pursue the Viet Cong through dense jungle for the next five days, encountering many small villages or hamlets, enemy camps, and river crossings.

The following photos are from a *Cavalair* article on Alpha Company's first air assault mission by SP/4 Jerry Condon.

Member of Company A directs landing of helicopters before assault.

Troopers Assault onto gas prepped LZ Brenda.

Capt. A.J. Wise directs movement of his company before fire touched off during operation.

*Choppers waiting to load and en route to LZ, photos by Will Bowe*

# 9
# LIFE OF A SKYTROOPER

The following was inspired by Minnesota veteran and author Tim O'Brien's *The Things They Carried*. His novel tells the story of an infantry platoon in Vietnam through the many things each man carried. In this chapter, I've attempted the same based on the experiences of my dad and his fellow soldiers of Alpha Company and the 5/7th Cavalry.

When the company marched, two rifle platoons led the way, followed by the command group and mortars in 4th Platoon, with one rifle platoon taking up the rear. This allowed CPT A.J. Wise to direct mortar fire in support of the rifle platoons when they encountered the enemy.

Each man carried his standard-issue M-16 unless he carried a grenade launcher or machine gun. On his load-bearing vest, he carried at least two plastic canteens of water, no less than three twenty-round clips of M-16 ammunition, at least two fragmentary grenades, at least one smoke grenade, and perhaps, one or two white phosphorous grenades.

Inside his helmet or "steel pot," he carried letters from home and, if he had a girlfriend, photographs. Mike Stoflet carried cash in his helmet, faded out from the constant dampness, some of which he mailed home to his mom. He told her not to bake cookies as she was then recovering from open heart surgery but to send him some store-bought ones instead. "Mother sent me those pictures," he wrote to his sister Donna. "I only hope I can find a place to keep them out here. I have them in my helmet now, the only place they'll stay dry."

Strapped to his helmet, he often carried a small plastic bottle of bug juice or a pack of cigarettes. Martin Quinn carried Marlboros when he could get them, Al Patrillo carried Pall Malls, and Will smoked Camel non-filters.

On his back, he carried his rucksack, to which was attached a shovel or "entrenching tool" and a flashlight equipped with a special red lens for use at night. The rucksack held a raincoat poncho that could also be used for shelter or as a stretcher for carrying the dead and wounded. In his rucksack, he also carried a light blanket called a poncho liner, a mosquito net, a rifle cleaning kit, and a few personal hygiene items. In a waterproof bag inside his ruck, he carried extra socks and footpowder to prevent jungle rot. Although issued a six-pound "bulletproof" flak jacket and a small inflatable sleeping mat, he would likely deem both unworthy of the extra weight—and no extra fatigues, as helicopters would bring these as needed.

In one of his fatigue pockets, he carried the *Code of Conduct*, issued by President Dwight Eisenhower and printed on a wallet-size card that read in part:

*If I am captured, I will continue to resist by all means available. I will make every effort to escape and aid others to escape. I will accept neither parole nor special favors from the enemy.*

*If I become a prisoner of war, I will keep faith with my fellow prisoners. I will give no information or take part in any action which might be harmful to my comrades. If I am senior, I will take command. If not, I will obey the lawful orders of those appointed over me and will back them up in every way.*

*When questioned, I am bound to give only my name, rank, service number, and date of birth. I will evade answering further questions to the utmost of my ability. I will make no oral or written statements disloyal to my country and its allies or harmful to their cause.*

They carried cans of food called C-Rations. Cases were flown in on resupply helicopters called log ships, along with ammunition and supplies. The log ships' downdraft kicked up dust and debris as they landed—covering the men in dirt, blowing away their papers, and making a mess of their encampment—yet they were always happy to see them.

Some log ships were Hueys, and some were Chinooks. Any helicopter was an ideal target for enemy mortars and rocket-propelled grenades, so the men would rush to the chopper and form a human conveyor belt, unloading the supplies as fast as they could.

Martin Quinn would head straight for the C-Rations, hoping to find his favorite meal, Spaghetti and Meatballs—a bonus if it contained his favorite dessert, the Pecan Roll. Highly prized by all, the Pound Cake would be saved in the bottom of one's rucksack for special occasions, best served with Fruit Cocktail or Peaches in Heavy Syrup. One wildly unpopular item was the Ham and Lima Beans, often called Ham and something quite profane. Also scorned was the peanut butter, which was usually rock hard with all the oil separated. C-Ration Cheese Spread and Tabasco sauce helped make certain meat items palatable. Each meal box contained a Meat Unit can, a Bread Unit can, a Dessert Unit can, and an accessory pack that included salt, pepper, instant coffee, gum, toilet paper, and four commercial-grade cigarettes. They never knew what brand they would get but could often make trades for their favorite. The free smokes served as currency for the few who didn't smoke.

They carried heat tabs, but a more effective way to heat their C-Rations was to use a small amount of C-4, a plastic explosive for clearing landing zones. The putty-like material burned fiercely when lit but would not explode without using a detonator or "blasting cap."

Most ate their rations straight from the can, but some attempted gourmet meals. In fact, several C-Ration cookbooks were published in this effort. Quinn recalled crawling from their ponchos at first light to find Will cooking some sort of concoction in their helmets and asked, "What the hell are you doing with our steel pots?"

"I'm making breakfast," Will replied. "What does it look like?"

To open his C-Rations, each man carried a P-38 can opener or "John Wayne," usually on the necklace used to carry his dog tags, the small metal plates that bore his name, service number, blood type, and religion. On that same necklace, Quinn also carried the Miraculous Medal of the Virgin Mary that his boss had given him before he left.

When they were lucky, the log ships also carried hot meals. They came in box-shaped insulated "mermite" containers and would be ladled onto paper plates. Sometimes they brought Lifeline packs containing personal hygiene kits, candy, chewing gum, and cigarettes. Quinn always hoped for the one with Chuckles candies. The log ships represented their only connection to "The World" as they brought bags of mail and current issues of the *Stars & Stripes*. For whatever reason, they rarely had fresh uniforms.

Sometimes the log ships carried a chaplain accompanied by an assistant. The chaplain's assistant carried a Gospel, chalice, the body and blood of Christ, and all things necessary for a proper field service—as well as an M-16 rifle, as he was also tasked with protecting the chaplain, who traveled unarmed.

Military chaplains are unique from their civilian counterparts in that they minister to soldiers of all different faiths, regardless of their own. Many soldiers find Jesus during basic training, mostly to avoid their sergeants and work detail on Sundays. In the fields of Vietnam, service wasn't necessarily held on Sunday but rather whenever the chaplain could make it there. The services were held at their encampment or outpost, typically improvising an altar with boxes of C-Rations or ammunition. Each chaplain served the spiritual needs of an entire battalion scattered over three thousand square miles. The services were short on ceremony but meaningful to those who attended.

One chaplain of the 1st Air Cavalry, CPT Henry Hilliard, conducted over five hundred services in the field. He earned his Air Medal—awarded for performing twenty-five air assaults—several times over and two Bronze Stars for Valor. He was also awarded the Soldier's Medal for rescuing a wounded pilot from the flames of his burning helicopter.

Firebase Mary had a small roofless chapel built by the artillerymen who manned the outpost. Named in honor of the patron saint of the artillery, Saint Barbara's Chapel was surrounded by a small picket fence. A row of little wooden benches served as pews, and on its altar of stained ammo boxes was placed a brass cross carved from a 105mm canister.

The 5/7th Cav's chaplain was a Catholic priest, Major (MAJ) Thomas Widdel. Both a soldier and a priest, he was built like an NFL linebacker, but his manner was more that of a priest. In his mid-forties, he wore glasses and a receding hairline. He wore the same jungle boots and uniform as those he ministered to, with a clerical stole draped over his broad shoulders. He carried their confessions, prayers, and petitions, and offered them up to the Lord. Known to the men simply as "Doc," 4th Platoon medic Tom Monnier was also Catholic. He recalled giving his confessions to Father Tom and how his altar was made of water cans.

When not holding services in the field, Father Tom stayed at his tent at LZ English, a major outpost near Bong Son with an airfield and field hospital. This is where most of the dead and wounded of the 5/7th Cav were flown into from the field. He requested to be notified of any incoming casualties. In his memoir, Bernard Grady notes the many contradictions and ironies of a chaplain in the Vietnam bush. He also recalls the many trips he made to the medical tents with Father Tom during the later months of their tour when he served as the Battalion Adjutant. Often waiting as the medevac chopper or "dustoff" landed, Father Tom would be there to comfort the wounded, most of whom were only half his age.

Last in the row of medical tents at LZ English was the Graves Registration unit, also known as the morgue. Parked outside the Graves Registration tent was a refrigerated truck used for storing the bodies of the dead until they began their journey home. This tent is where the dead were first brought and where Father Tom sometimes found himself. Graves Registration could usually identify the dead by their dog tags. Still, military regulation required two individuals to positively identify each body. Although identifying the dead of his flock was not his official duty, it became a rather routine one.

In his rucksack, Al Patrillo carried a camouflage fedora that he wore whenever not wearing his steel pot. SSG Robert Matulac carried a journal. After checking on his men and digging in for the night, he would pull it out of his rucksack and record the day's events along with his personal thoughts. In a small plastic bag in one of his fatigue pockets, Royce Barrow carried the 35mm camera that fellow radio operator Kenneth Rathyen had helped him pick out before leaving Fort Carson.

They carried pens and notebooks for writing letters, small Bibles and Rosary beads, jackknives, Zippos, sunscreen, packs of presweetened Kool-Aid, candy, snuff, checker sets and decks of cards, hometown newspapers and Playboy magazines, an assortment of trinkets, and watches with illuminated dials for guard duty at night.

A few also carried a stash of pot, which could easily be obtained from sources at base camp or locals in the towns. Joe Sanchez didn't carry any himself but decided to join in one night and wrote about it in his book.

*We were in this Godforsaken place, and the guys had nowhere to go. They amused themselves by getting high. The more sensible ones stuck to marijuana—hell, it grew anywhere in that climate. I think some guys were doing worse stuff. I stayed away from all of it—until one night when I was up on this spooky, lonely hill with two other guys, one Mexican-American and one Irish-American, who were passing a joint. They gave me a hit. A lot of people say your first hit doesn't do anything. Me, I reacted. I went smack into the Twilight Zone.*

*First, the stars got real bright. They started shooting. Then, I could see my teeth shooting out of my mouth, too. Not really, but to me it seemed perfectly real. I felt like I had gone into another dimension, and I thought everybody I saw was in it, too...*

Eventually, Sanchez realized someone had taken his M-16, and a lieutenant was bringing him to the commander. CPT A.J. Wise read him the charges. Sanchez responded by flipping him off. They put him in the lieutenant's tent to sleep it off. The next morning, CPT Wise gathered everyone who'd been up on that hill and ordered Sanchez to point out the guys who gave him the pot. With the guilty parties standing before him, Sanchez claimed he couldn't recognize them. After all, it had been dark out. Despite talk of legal action, nothing ever came of it.

Most carried a machete for hacking brush, vines, and bamboo—also for snakes, tarantulas, scorpions, and millipedes. Over thirty species of venomous snakes inhabited the region, including bamboo vipers and the fabled two-step snake, named for the number of steps its victim would take before dying.

Bobby Hansen was sitting around bullshitting with the guys when he felt something moving underneath him. He stood up to find he'd been sitting on a snake, and everyone just ran off without their rifles.

Marty Scull was on guard one night and trying hard to stay awake. Sitting in his foxhole along the company perimeter, he could barely see anything. Hearing a faint rustling sound, he saw a dark figure out of the corner of his eye. His heart jumped into his throat as he realized something had moved into the foxhole with him—a seven-foot snake. In a panic, Scully grabbed his machete and hacked its head off. It took a while to calm down. Staying awake was no longer a problem for the rest of his guard shift that night.

SGT J.C. Jackson had the misfortune of having a cobra spit venom in his eyes. Rendered totally blind, he was flown to a field hospital. When the wounded were flown out of the field, medics would gather their gear and store their weapons in a locked cage near the field hospital. Eventually, SGT Jackson recovered his sight. Before returning to the field, he was brought to this cage to retrieve his weapon. Among the stacks of countless M-16s, he could not find his own, so he simply grabbed one that looked functional. When it was discovered that he no longer had his issued weapon, he was made to pay for it out of his Army paycheck. He may have been the only soldier in the company to get spat in the eye by a cobra, but he was not the only one to suffer the injustice of having to pay for a lost weapon after being medevaced.

Each radio operator carried the PRC-25, a twenty-three-pound radiotelephone more commonly called the "Prick Twenty-Five." With its three-foot antenna bouncing above the radio operator's head, it was like wearing a sign that said, "Shoot me!" They carried extra batteries and an additional extra-long antenna for improved range while encamped.

As assistants to the commander and platoon leaders, radio operators had to be calm under fire, and it helped if they could read a map. They soon became a hub for both official information and the rumor mill. A bond of sorts was formed among them, especially between Donald Rankin and Royce Barrow. They were always together since being chosen by CPT Wise as his own radio operators at Fort Carson and got on as best friends. Rankin handled communications between Alpha Company and the platoons on what was called the company net. Barrow communicated with the battalion command post on the battalion net. Kenneth Rathyen manned the radio for SSG Robert Matulac. Dave Fedell was the radio operator for 1st Platoon. Alan Weisman was the radio operator for 2nd Platoon leader, 1LT James Harmon. In 3rd Platoon, Phil Jones was 1LT William Nelson's radio operator. Fred Brodosi manned the radio for the mortars in 1LT Sam Cathcart's 4th Platoon. Tasked with the additional duty of directing mortar fire, Brodosi carried a plotting board and a book that indicated which size charge to use at specific distances.

Machine gunners Bill Purdy, Bobby Hansen, and Robert Wagner carried the twenty-three-pound M-60 machine gun while assistant gunners Ed Raciborski, Brian Ravese, and Guy McNay carried extra barrels and metal ammo boxes and extra chains of ammunition draped about their shoulders.

Grenadiers Rocco Valentino, Al Patrillo, John Kruetzkamp, and A.G. Hensley carried the M-79 grenade launcher. Resembling a sawed-off shotgun, it was sometimes called a "thumper" for the sound it made. To prevent friendly fire incidents, its grenades would only detonate after traveling thirty meters, a problem for close-in fighting, and so grenadiers also carried a .45mm pistol. Each squad had one grenadier, who typically followed just behind the point man, who was the first in line when marching through the jungles and rice fields. In 2nd Platoon, Marty Scull often walked point, followed by his squad's grenadier, A.G. Hensley, his best friend from Fort Carson. Another grenadier in 2nd Platoon was John Kruetzkamp, one of Bill Purdy's friends from Kentucky.

Kruetzkamp liked carrying the .45mm, mostly to have it with him at night. The only problem, whenever they found an underground tunnel, he was called upon to go in and search it. These countless tunnels enabled the enemy to simply melt into the earth when pursued by the Americans. They had already been used by the Viet Minh during the French-Indochina War. As the NVA and Viet Cong moved mainly at night, this underground network was their refuge by day. Many contained command centers, mess halls, and medical facilities. Their openings were well-hidden beneath the brush, usually covered by a trap door, and often booby-trapped.

Most of these tunnels turned out to be empty, but not always. Those who did not surrender or escape would die by flamethrowers or white phosphorus grenades. Bob Matulac noted how regular grenades were ineffective in tunnels, as their blast did not go around corners. He advised the men to use white phosphorus whenever possible, as it would continue to burn while depleting the tunnel of oxygen. Finally, the bodies would be removed, counted, and stacked. This unpleasant task of entering the tunnels with a flashlight and pistol, then dragging out the charred enemy bodies, was usually given to the platoon's lowest ranking or newest members.

Kruetzkamp was crawling into one of these tunnels with his pack still on. He was in deep when someone dropped a grenade into an opening at the other end, sending a wave of agitated fruit bats his way. In a panic, he struggled to turn himself around and get out, but the entrenching tool attached to his pack was caught on some rocks. The bats were all over him in the pitch blackness, and he felt like he couldn't breathe. It took him a while to calm down after shimmying his way out. Later, Kruetzkamp gave his pistol to one of the new guys, and he seemed pleased to have it. Days later, they came upon another tunnel, and Kruetzkamp was called up to go in. "Here you go," the new guy said, trying to give him back the pistol.

"Why do you think I gave it to you?" replied Kruetzkamp.

Combat medics Tom Monnier, Mike Walker, Bill Garcia, and Michael Handley each carried Novocain, Darvon, syringes, scissors, bandages, compresses, gauze, and tourniquets. They carried ointments, salves, zinc oxide, and antiseptics for treating the various funguses and infections carried by their fellow soldiers, as well as pills to prevent malaria. They distributed a small white pill to the men each day to prevent a virulent strain known as falciparum. For the more common form of malaria, they doled out another pill every Monday. Large and orange, this is how the men knew which day of the week it was. Malaria's symptoms included fever, uncontrollable shivering, convulsions, jaundice—and in severe cases, damaged vision, kidney failure, and brain dysfunction. Some avoided ingesting the pills, hoping to contract the disease and to be sent to a hospital where it was comfortable and dry. To prevent dysentery, they distributed water purification tablets. The men dropped these into their canteens to treat the water derived from streams, resulting in a swill called "iodine Kool-Aid."

One good thing about being in the mortar platoon was that it was usually not out front while moving through the jungle and not the first to get shot at or to hit a booby trap. The downside was the heavy equipment the mortarman carried. In addition to the standard infantryman's load, each carried part of their team's mortar system. One man carried the tube, another carried the bipod, another the ammunition—each round weighing about ten pounds—and another carried the most awkward component, the base plate. Each component weighed over thirty pounds.

There were many ways one could die in Vietnam, and enemy fire was just one of them. The ground they walked was riddled with booby traps made from grenades, artillery and mortar rounds, or anything else that could explode—hidden beneath the earth and activated by unseen tripwires. They were psychologically devastating because, just like the enemy, they were also invisible. Not the deadliest, but perhaps the most feared, was the Bouncing Betty. Activated by three tiny prongs that were easily concealed in vegetation, the relatively small mine had two charges. The first popped the mine up about three to four feet, waist-high—or more to the point, ball sack-high—before the second charge exploded, sending shrapnel into the victim's midsection. Many areas were also riddled with punji stakes, which were also usually invisible until it was too late.

Platoon leaders—lieutenants who were tasked with knowing where they were going—carried maps, compasses, and binoculars, as did the forward observers, whose task it was to call for artillery fire.

Others carried Claymore mines and flares to place around their encampment at night. Gerald Anderson carried letters from a girl back home and blocks of C-4 to clear landing zones while others carried the blasting caps. He also carried a .45mm pistol and extra ammo clips for his M-16 as he was always afraid of running out of ammunition.

They carried massive amounts of explosives and firepower, and the battalion recorded many "death by misadventure" incidents—Claymores exploding prematurely, pistols and grenade launchers discharging into feet, flares discharging into hands, and ammunition dumps catching fire.

The M-72 light anti-tank weapon or "LAW" was a rocket launcher that functioned as a mini bazooka. They were designed to blow up tanks, but in Vietnam, they were used for destroying dug-in bunkers. Bill Purdy told of a soldier who was firing the LAW but hadn't properly aligned something in the mechanism. It misfired. He lay wounded, and they all thought he was dead. This soldier had a buddy, and they had agreed that one would get the other's stuff if he got bumped off. His buddy was going through his pockets when the wounded soldier yelled, "Hey man, I'm not dead yet!"

John Kruetzkamp recalled a lieutenant shooting off a flare beneath a tree, sending branches down on his head. He'd also gripped the mechanism too high and burned his hand. He laughed, noting how the lieutenant was awarded a Purple Heart.

Along with this foot-borne arsenal of weaponry and supplies, they carried the dirt and the mud, the leeches and other tropical parasites, and the persistent stench of the rice paddies and jungle decay. Some carried a sense of patriotic duty, some their faith in God, others just a sense of resignation. In the pit of their stomachs, they carried a deep homesickness. On their shoulders, many would also carry the weight of regret—for what they did or didn't do, or for something they lacked the courage to do.

CPT A.J. Wise carried experience from his time in Korea, responsibility for the mission, and his inflatable sleeping mat. Accountable for the actions of his men as well as their very lives, he carried what was perhaps the heaviest weight of all.

*Marching through rice fields and following stream, photos by Will Bowe*

*River crossing, John Bronson in foreground*

*Gerald Anderson (left) and Kurt Elmer (right), photos by Will Bowe*

*Viet Cong fighter pulled from tunnel*

*Father Tom Widdel and assistant, photos by Marvin Bierschbach*

*Marvin Bierschbach*

*John Bronson (left) and Carl Evans (right), photos by Will Bowe*

# 10
# SEARCH AND DESTROY

*Wish you could have seen us. We sure were bad-looking—beard, mud, and torn clothes—but I am in good shape.*

On the first day of Operation Golden Bee—after setting out following their air assault on LZ Brenda—Bill Purdy became one of the first to suffer the pain of a punji stake wound, along with one of their scout dogs. The stake went straight through Purdy's hand and broke off while hacking through jungle brush. Despite the many injuries, the company kept marching all day and into the evening.

Just before 7:00 PM, CPT A.J. Wise brought the company to a halt on some tree-covered high ground where they would bivouac for the night. He briefed the command group, platoon leaders, and platoon sergeants on the next day's mission. The platoon sergeants were to then brief their squad leaders, and they, in turn, were to brief their own men. SSG Robert Matulac would ask the lower enlisted men what they knew about the next day's operation and usually only received blank looks in response.

When dark came, the men would form a cigar-shaped perimeter, along which each team of two or three would dig a foxhole, each serving as a make-shift guard post. Vegetation often blocked the view, so "fields of fire" were hacked out in front of each position. Machine gunners and assistants dug emplacements for their M-60s, and a trench was dug in the middle to serve as a latrine.

Several Claymore mines were placed out beyond their perimeter. The Claymore is an anti-personnel mine, shaped like a large, thick, curved plate, the convex side imprinted with the words: FRONT TOWARD ENEMY. It was placed wherever the enemy would likely approach and stuck into the ground using built-in stakes. Detonation wire was strung back to the operator's guard position. When activated by its remote detonator or "clacker," the mine would explode, spraying metal balls in a shotgun-like pattern. Set out further were trip flares. When the enemy, or sometimes an animal, stepped on its wire, a bright burning flare would shoot straight up into the air, emitting a loud hissing sound and illuminating the surrounding area.

Finally, small teams were sent farther out in ambush positions—listening posts or stakeouts—to detect any approaching enemy before they could attack the sleeping company.

The poncho each soldier carried was simply a large plastic sheet with a hole and hood in the middle that could be used as a raincoat. When buttoned together with two other ponchos and using some sticks, they formed a small tent-like shelter known as a hooch. While two of his buddies slept, one man kept watch. They would take turns through the night, earning two hours of sleep for each hour on guard.

Martin Quinn hated the chore of digging in at night. "Will was good at digging foxholes, though," he remarked. "Getting through the rocks and roots was hard, especially after humping the hills all day. I'd set up the tent while Will dug a little trench to keep the rain from flowing in." He laughed, recalling how Will was more likely to use his helmet for cooking. "When it was on, it was all cattywampus, John Wayne-style, with the chin straps dangling. I'd say, 'Will, you might want to strap that thing down. Charlie's out there, and your head is a big target.' And he'd just say, 'Aw, why bother.' He was a character and took everything lightly, and I was a nervous wreck most of the time. But all his joking around did so much to lift the spirits of everyone in the platoon."

They moved out again at daybreak. At 7:55 AM, the scout dogs picked up the enemy's trail, leading them to an area where at least ten Viet Cong had slept the night before. At this time, a request was sent from the company, through battalion, to the 3rd Brigade command. The request was granted, extending the operation for an additional two days. They moved out again the next morning toward a suspected Viet Cong encampment. The next two days brought more of the same, taking only light contact from the elusive enemy.

The following excerpts are from the October 8th issue of the *Cavalair*.

## 5/7th Succeeds in Combat Test—Search Led By Angry Lieutenant
*By SP/4 Jerry Condon*

*Alpha Company of the 1st Air Cav's 5th Battalion, 7th Cavalry destroyed major elements of an expansive Viet Cong supply network north of An Khe in a five-day sweep mission tagged Operation Golden Bee. The operation, which ended September 28th, was the first combat test of any of the battalion's companies since its arrival in Vietnam on August 20th. Until now, the unit has been responsible for Highway 19 security between An Khe and Pleiku.*

*The sweating skytroopers kicked off Golden Bee on September 24th with a five-wave air assault onto LZ Brenda, thirteen kilometers north of Camp Radcliff. Artillery splattered the knotted jungle minutes before ships began carting the heavily equipped "Garryowens" into the landing zone.*

*Throughout the operation, communications and troop movement were hampered by densely foliated hills strewn with punji stakes and narrow paths the company had to hack through the jungle. "It's difficult to control a tactical formation in vegetation this thick," remarked company commander A.J. Wise. While enemy contact was light, the company destroyed fifty-three work and sleeping huts, dozens of bunkers, concealed crop fields, stockpiles of harvested crops, and thousands of newly made punji stakes. Automatic weapon* ammunition, rice caches, meat animals, and crude punji stake factories were also uncovered. An estimated twenty guerrillas were pushed out of the supply channel as Alpha Company humped through fifteen kilometers of jungle and broken trails near the banks of the Song Ba River.

German Shepherds of the 25th Infantry Scout Dog Platoon attached to Alpha Company were used to track fleeing enemy soldiers and to seek out trails and paths. "We'll shoot anything that moves," radioed the angered leader of the scout dog platoon, 1st Lt. Teddy Hampton. "Tell everyone to lay down and be quiet." Moments earlier, four Viet Cong had escaped him and his sergeant following a close-range firefight. The two were seeking the source of previous enemy sniper fire as elements of Alpha Company checked out scattered huts and bunkers further to the rear.

1st Lt. Hampton and Sgt. Manuel Ybanez began their tedious search on a hidden path while their four dog teams awaited further instructions at the jungle entrance. Four pajama-clad soldiers had popped out of an adjoining trail just ten meters ahead of the tiny recon patrol. "It was the first time 'Charlie' had walked right into us," Hampton said. "Two had automatic weapons, probably AK-47s, and the other two had carbines." Hampton and Ybanez hit the ground and opened up with their M-16s as enemy bullets bounced in the trees around them. One Viet Cong clutched his chest and sank to the ground but was carried away by the others as they escaped into the jungle. Capt. Wise brought two squads into the area, blanketing the jungle with M-79 and machine gun fire. Then Wise sent a ten-man search party after the guerrillas, but the two dog handlers soon spotted drag marks and blood on a path the foursome had used as an escape route.

Bundles of bamboo still moist from cutting were found on secret trails, indicating that "Charlie" had fled just moments before. Artillery fired from the Cavalry base camp potted portions of jungle in the path of the oncoming infantrymen. "It's not a heavy troop concentration area," pointed out 1st Lt. James Ulrich, a forward observer attached to the unit from the 1st Battalion, 21st Artillery, "but they must have thought the best place to store supplies was right under our noses."

Battalion Intelligence Officer Capt. Walt Swain stated, "Original reports indicated that the area had a drug collection point. But nothing we have found as of yet can substantiate this."

Hampton and his sergeant hurriedly grouped three dog handlers and a radio operator around them, then set out with a rusty brown and black German Shepherd named Prince in the lead. Prince—handled by Pvt. First Class Darrel Melton—had been wounded earlier by one of the tens of thousands of punji stakes scattered throughout the area. As the scout patrol followed a blood trail left by the retreating guerrillas, Prince alerted his followers to enemy booby traps and led the patrol through a maze of paths. The rear man of the Viet Cong foursome haphazardly planted punjis behind them as they raced through the torrid jungle. More than an hour later, the patrol surrounded three sleeping huts and a bunker complex where the four had stopped "to pick up food, packs, and a new supply of punji stakes," according to Hampton. The village contained cotton supplies, corn rations, batteries, musical instruments, and miscellaneous trinkets. "They're headed toward an aid station across the river," the lieutenant remarked. But night closed in, and the weary platoon leader decided to wait until morning to continue the chase.

An instructor at one of my NCO courses explained what search and destroy meant. "Basically, it's walking around looking for a fight." It was audacious if nothing else. There was a method to the whole thing—but to the Joes, it often felt like they were just wandering around and waiting to get shot at. The lower enlisted often had little idea where they were, where they were going, or when they would get there, only that they were on their way.

On a typical search and destroy mission, CPT A.J. Wise would receive orders from the battalion—when to commence movement, where to search, what to look for, and the location of their final objective. He would be advised by Battalion Intelligence Officer CPT Walt Swain of suspected enemy locations. 1LT James Ulrich, his forward observer, advised him of what assets were available to assist them should they encounter heavy resistance. The gunships were often called upon as they offered a lot of accurate firepower. Huey gunships were eventually deemed too slow and too easy to shoot down with the enemy's rocket-propelled grenades and would be replaced by the AH-1 Cobra in 1967. With no passenger or cargo space, it was designed specifically as an attack chopper. Made apparent by its alien appearance, the Cobra had but one purpose in life—killing.

Artillery batteries held hilltop firebases throughout the region and could also be called upon, either by CPT Wise or his forward observers. Attached to Alpha Company from the 1st Battalion, 21st Field Artillery, 1LT Ulrich's forward observer team included his recon sergeant and radio operator Danny Garrity.

They were searching for Charlie but found that he was more likely to find them, often taking a few shots and slipping away completely unseen. Charlie was usually outgunned and rarely challenged them in force. Following the company like a phantom, his objective was not to overrun the Americans but rather to demoralize them. The men learned, however, that with artillery and gunships, you didn't have to see Charlie to kill Charlie. Although they seldom saw the enemy alive, they found plenty of their dead and counted them all.

River crossings represented an opportunity for the enemy to attack but also their only chance to bathe and wash their clothes. When they felt it was safe or were simply desperate enough, they would strip off their clothes and wade into the river, bars of soap in hand, while others pulled security.

On September 28th, the men of Alpha Company used ropes to cross a large river called the Song Ba as they reached their final objective of Operation Golden Bee, arriving at PZ Linda at 2:30 PM. Someone threw a smoke grenade to signal the incoming choppers. A pop and a hissing sound, billows of purple spreading along the ground, then twisting into the sky. They smelled like sulfur, not a pleasant scent but one that would become welcome, often associated with the end of a long mission. By 4:10 PM, the final lift was bringing the last of Alpha Company back to An Khe, ending their first air assault operation.

Meanwhile, the rest of the battalion prepared for their own return to base camp. That morning, a coordinating party from the 2nd Battalion, 12th Cavalry arrived at the Eagle's Nest to plan their own takeover of the Highway 19 mission scheduled for the next day. That evening, the 1st Air Cavalry Division Commander, Major General John Norton, arrived to be briefed on the battalion's experiences and recommendations. With Operations Road Runner and Golden Bee complete, the 5/7th Cav prepared to join the 3rd Brigade and others in a much larger and more dangerous operation that would be a continuation of Thayer.

## 29 September '66 – 43 weeks left

*Well, we finally made it back from our mission yesterday. We had a few broken bones and punji stake wounds. Then after we came back to An Khe, we heard what we did on the radio. What a blow-up. First music I heard since the 5th of this month. We are going to Bong Son tomorrow, a long ways from here, so not much of a rest.*

*This last mission, we ran into about four V.C.s, killed one, or wounded him bad. Burned down a bunch of houses. Wish you could have seen us. We sure were bad-looking—beard, mud, and torn clothes—but I am in good shape. I don't know how often I'll be able to write, so don't worry. What I'd like is to send some V.C. souvenirs home.*

*We wrote to a girl in our newspaper, Berg from Spring Street. She announced her engagement, and about twenty of us guys signed our letter to her. Everybody reads my paper. I forgot to mention that you only need a five-cent stamp on the letters, and it still goes Air Mail. Now you can send five for the price of two.*

*I got your candy and long johns and paper. This letter may be a little mixed up, but I am in a hurry and mixed up, too. I'll write the next chance I get.*

*Will*

It was the end of September 1966. Alpha Company's men had survived each of their jungle patrols along Highway 19 and their first air assault. Several had been wounded, but still no fatalities for the company—and they had shot up a few Viet Cong and taken some prisoners. As a battalion, the 5/7th Cav had suffered many more wounded and two fatalities, resulting from Delta Company's overturned jeep and Charlie Company's helicopter crash.

To their east, the 5/7th Cav's sister battalions of the 3rd Brigade, the 1/7th and 2/7th Cavs, were closing in on the enemy regiments that had been pursued from the Kim Son Valley into the soggy coastal plains of Phu My during Operation Thayer. The operation ended on October 1st 1966, with over two hundred of the enemy killed, at a cost of thirty-five American lives. In terms of body count, it was a success. Operation Thayer had prepared the battlefield. The next phase of the Binh Dinh Pacification Campaign would exploit it.

*Will Bowe in elephant grass*

*Will Bowe carrying base plate, followed by Angel Reynosa,
crossing the Song Ba on September 28th 1966, photo by Fred Brodosi*

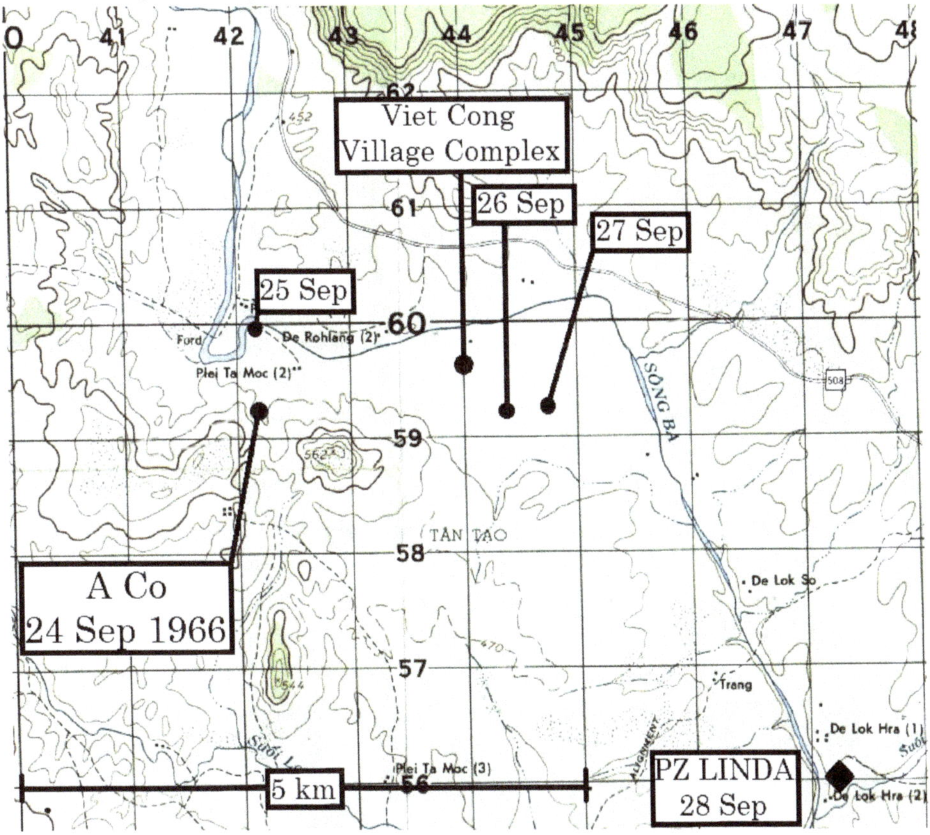

*Operation Golden Bee, 24–28 September 1966*

# 11
# THE FIRST TO FALL
## (Operation Irving)

*We guys make up all kinds of silly stories like that. Sorry if I had you worried.*

After spending but a day back at base camp, the 5/7th Cav moved out for its next operation at 9:00 AM on September 30th 1966. Again in a convoy of trucks, they headed east from An Khe along Highway 19, winding their way back out of the highlands and down into the coastal plains. This was the same route Will and others had taken to An Khe after landing in Qui Nhon, only now they were headed in the opposite direction. Will thought back to that time in August when he'd imagined how Charlie could be out there watching him. It seemed so long ago but had only been five weeks. They passed a burned-out armored personnel carrier on the side of the road, just like the ones they'd trained on back at Fort Carson. It looked to be the victim of a rocket-propelled grenade or something. They turned left and headed north along Highway 1.

Running between six and twelve miles inland from the South China Sea's coastline, Highway 1 stretched north through the Phu My plains, then further through the Bong Son and beyond (see Battle Maps, pages 330–334). Dominated by vast flooded rice paddies, the terrain differed remarkably from Operation Golden Bee's dense highland jungle. Known as the breadbasket of Vietnam, the regions of Bong Son and Phu My are among Vietnam's most fertile.

Highway 1 was the main north-south route through South Vietnam, the deadliest stretch of which had been dubbed La Rue Sans Joie—The Street Without Joy—by French troops during their own war, inspiring the title of Bernard Fall's book. Camp Hammond was an old French outpost just west of Highway 1, near the town of Phu My. Thirty miles north along Highway 1 near the town of Bong Son was LZ English. Though smaller than the highland base camps of Pleiku or An Khe, English and Hammond were major outposts with airstrips that could accommodate large cargo and transport planes.

The battalion forward command post headed for Camp Hammond while each of its companies headed for PZ Bradley, just off Highway 1. From here, the companies airlifted to separate LZs along a north-south axis about two miles west of the highway, north of Camp Hammond. Charlie Company was flown to the northernmost LZ Suzie, Bravo to LZ Hooker, and Delta to LZ Thomas. Alpha Company was flown to the southernmost LZ Ike, its final lift arriving at 3:25 PM.

With lifts completed, each company patrolled its own area for the rest of the day. When dark came, they sent out ambush teams, and this was all repeated the next day. They made no enemy contact, however, as the NVA were waiting for them on the other side of Highway 1.

Meanwhile, key leaders attended briefings at Camp Hammond on a massive operation that would feature the 5/7th Cav's first battalion-size air assault. A reconnaissance platoon was attached to Alpha Company, while pathfinder and engineer teams were attached to others.

Commencing the next day, Operation Irving would be a continuation of Thayer, intended to finish the communist forces that had fled into the coastal plains from the Kim Son Valley, scattered and desperate but relatively intact. Battalions of the 1st Air Cav's 1st Brigade would attack NVA positions from the northeast, along the coast of the South China Sea. At the same time, battalions of the 3rd Brigade, including the 5/7th Cav, would push toward the coast from the southwest. It was deemed a new operation as the 1st Air Cavalry Division would now be joined by legions of ARVN and Republic of Korea (ROK) troops. With three ARVN and five ROK battalions joining the two American brigades, this joint operation would involve over seven thousand combat troops. Just like Thayer, Operation Irving kicked off with five battalions of skytroopers air assaulting into battle positions in the early morning hours of October 2nd 1966.

At 6:45 AM, Bravo Company lifted off from its position, descending at 7:11 AM onto LZ Opal, atop a hill just northwest of the Song Ca and Siem Giang rivers, in the middle of the Phu My plain. Phu My was a vast swampy lowland area bordered by the highlands far to the west, the Nui Mieu Mountains immediately to the north, the Phu Cat Mountains to the south, and to the east—a large inlet lake of the South China Sea—Vinh Nuoc Ngot. The enemy was known to be somewhere around this inlet.

Alpha Company lifted off at 8:16 AM, assaulting onto a hill dubbed LZ Topaz at 8:31 AM. Between the two rivers, Alpha Company's LZ was just less than a mile southwest of Bravo's.

At 9:23 AM, both Charlie and Delta Companies assaulted onto LZ Bloodstone, another mile southwest of Alpha Company, securing what would serve as the 5/7th Cav's command post. Early that afternoon, battalion command arrived by Chinook to set up shop. From their tents here on the banks of the Siem Giang, LTC Trevor Swett and his staff would direct each of the companies during the operation.

To their northeast, on the opposite side of what would soon become a vast battlefield, battalions of the 1st Brigade took up positions near the coast, surrounding enemy regiments that occupied the village of Hoa Hoi, just north of the Vinh Nuoc Ngot inlet. The 1st Brigade attacked immediately. A few hours into the fighting, leaflets were dropped on the village, warning civilians to evacuate and occupiers to surrender. The assault was paused at one point to allow about two hundred villagers to escape.

As the battle raged around Hoa Hoi, those units massed to the southwest—including the 5/7th Cav—ran patrols in their own areas to catch enemy fighters fleeing from the 1st Brigade. Only two enemy fighters were killed by the 5/7th, but over fifty were taken prisoner. Again, each company sent out ambushes and waited through the night.

Early the next morning, battalions of the 1st Brigade reattacked Hoa Hoi ferociously while the 5/7th and 1/7th Cavs continued their own area patrols. Alpha Company patrolled in a loop pattern. Again they made enemy contact, killing a handful of fleeing enemy fighters and taking more prisoners. They returned to LZ Topaz before dusk and sent out ambush teams as the sun set on the battlefield.

Of the approximately three hundred enemy soldiers that had occupied the village of Hoa Hoi, over two hundred were killed, and over thirty were taken prisoner by the 1st Brigade.

### 3 October '66 – 42 weeks left

*Dear Folks,*

*You wouldn't believe what we did this morning. We watched combat from the top of a big hill called Topaz. Must have been at least two thousand men and twelve armored vehicles blowing the hell out of these villages below us. Just like watching a movie. Some joker yelled, "Popcorn and peanuts, get 'em while they're hot!" You might have heard of this operation named Irving. Might take a week or more to finish. This other unit cut off a battalion of N.V.A. last night, and something like 160 got killed with the help of the Navy. No one in this company has been hurt so far in this operation. Even we killed a few V.C. and captured a bunch of them. Man, there are more choppers around here than birds. Sure am glad I'm in the mortars. You see a little action, and yet you're fairly safe. Tomorrow, we'll make a drive eight miles to the sea, and about a million villages to clear out. So that's the story so far.*

*I received one of your packages, and a mouse chewed a hole in it. That didn't make a darn bit of difference.*

*Combat Will*

Donald Rankin also wrote home on October 3rd.

*Dear Mom and Daddy,*

*We're now a part of Operation Thayer. We're on top of another mountain. The sea is on one side, with rice paddies and palms on the other three sides. Today I had to carry a baby up this horrid mountain. Yesterday, we captured forty-one VCs, killed two, and wounded two. In these two days, we've found medicine, documents, and everything. The 12th Cavalry killed 169 VCs where we're going. We're still doing okay. No deaths and few casualties from the enemy.*

*Received a lot of mail tonight. That makes the day better. You, Suzie, Nancy, Bob Schweitzer, and a guy from college. I wish I had sent my money home. I'll probably get it wet and ruin everything in my billfold. Tell everyone hello. Save one of those pictures to send to Nancy. This is about all. Will write when I can.*

*Love,*

*Donnie*

Alpha Company received its final briefing on the morning of October 4th. Their mission was to finish what 1st Brigade had started. Both the 5/7th and 1/7th Cavs would push northeastward toward the sea, in the direction of the previous day's fighting between 1st Brigade and the NVA, searching villages and taking prisoners.

Before heading out, Tom Gruenburg and Earl Huber would always find SSG Robert Matulac. As a lucky insult, Matulac would say, "Go get yourself shot," or "Go catch a grenade." It seemed to work as neither had been wounded yet.

Alpha Company's men trudged down the hill from LZ Topaz into the soggy Phu My plain. 3rd Platoon led the way, followed closely by 1st Platoon. In 3rd Platoon, Robert Wagner and Guy McNay took turns carrying their machine gun. In 4th Platoon, SGT John Fulford led his team, Marvin Bierschbach, John Bronson, and Will, as they lugged their mortar pieces. Following in 2nd Platoon, Marty Scull set out on point for his squad, followed by his buddy A.G. Hensley with his M-79 grenade launcher.

Leading 1st Platoon was 1LT Barry Gallagher, who had recently replaced the lieutenant who had broken his ankles during their first air assault in September. He'd volunteered for the draft shortly after finishing college with the guarantee of Officer Candidate School and married his high school girlfriend during basic training. After his commissioning and airborne training, he'd volunteered for service in Vietnam so that he could choose which division he would be assigned to. At Fort Benning's jump school, he'd watched 1st Air Cavalry soldiers going through airmobile training with their helicopters and had decided this was the division he wanted to join.

Intelligence reported a regiment-size force was occupying the small fishing village of An My, just south of the now-destroyed village of Hoa Hoi. Set along the northwest corner of the Vinh Nuoc Ngot inlet, this village was their final objective. As the forward company for the battalion, Alpha was to lead the attack on the village after covering several miles on foot.

The terrain here was at sea level and dominated by rice paddies and mangroves—trees and shrubs with twisting exposed roots that grow in salty tidal backwaters. They marched through a wide flooded valley dotted with small villages, staying between the two rivers that ran in the same direction as their advance. At times the water was nearly waist-high, even higher for Bobby Hansen.

To Alpha Company's left, Bravo Company and ROK soldiers marched in the same direction on the other side of the Song Ca River. On their right, their attached recon platoon and ARVN forces moved with them along the other side of the Siem Giang.

They came upon many small hamlets along their march. Searching through one, Hansen's buddy Smithy stabbed a stack of hay bunched up around a pole with his machete. He didn't realize a pole was inside. With its handle slippery with sweat, his machete got caught on the pole, causing him to lose his grip, inflicting a large gash on his hand. Their medic bandaged him up and sent him to the rear.

Eventually, the village of An My came into view along with the South China Sea. The river on Alpha Company's right, the Siem Giang, could be seen winding through the middle of the village before emptying into the inlet lake. Just then, Hansen overheard the traffic from Alan Weisman's radio. Amid crackling static, he could hear yelling and gunfire—and the radio operator on the other end saying Bravo Company had two wounded in action. Above them flew an H-13 scout ship—a small, bubble-shaped observation helicopter with just a machine gun for weaponry, seating only a pilot and gunner. The scout ship would direct the attack of the gunships and draw fire from enemy positions so they could be targeted. Hansen and Weisman watched as it flew on toward the village and disappeared over the trees.

Farther off to Hansen's left moved another soldier, followed by a CBS reporter, through the mangroves. As they got closer to the village, the lead platoons came under vicious machine gun fire from fortified bunkers outside the village. At the same time, enemy fighters erupted from spider holes shooting bursts of AK-47 fire and disappearing back into the ground. Hansen watched the soldier to his left take three rounds that nearly flipped him over. He could see the reporter lying beside him in the water beneath the mangrove branches and wondered if he'd also been wounded.

Troopers of the lead platoons were scattered about, and many were getting shot. Everyone was taking cover, lying in the water behind the rice paddy dikes. They struggled to return fire as their rifles were jamming. What had been an organized formation quickly dissolved into chaos. The platoons and squads were all mixed up with each other, and their sergeants struggled to keep control of their men. The enemy they had faced in Operation Golden Bee had been more intent on fleeing than fighting. On this day, the enemy was forced to surrender or fight.

Hansen saw two enemy soldiers approaching about a hundred yards in front. He shot only two rounds before his own weapon blew up. Some grenadiers attempted to take out the bunkers with their thumpers, but many M-79s were also rendered useless as they had recently been submerged while taking cover.

The only weapons that seemed to be working were their machine guns. The thick muck was sucking them down, and Hansen became completely stuck. Two others struggled to pull him out.

At 2:30 PM, the H-13 scout ship was shot down by enemy machine guns. In addition to taking the village, Alpha Company was now faced with a rescue mission. CPT A.J. Wise radioed 1st and 3rd Platoons, directing them to extract the pilot and his gunner wherever they were, alive or dead. The chopper was in the area but out of sight, and they would have to search for it while fighting continued. All they knew was that it went down somewhere southeast of the village. After some searching, the helicopter's gunner came rushing to them through some brush. He was exhausted and scared. His pilot had hurt his back in the crash and couldn't move. The gunner led 1st Platoon, followed by 3rd Platoon, toward the downed chopper that lay smoking in the water amid the mangroves with its injured pilot. But to reach the chopper, they needed to cross the Siem Giang, then a wide-open area of deeply flooded saltwater paddies—or salt dikes, as they were called—that looked something like cranberry bogs. The recon platoon secured their river crossing as they waded through the Siem Giang and started across the salt dikes.

Halfway across the dikes, they fell under machine gun fire from enemy bunkers near the village. SSG Sam Daily, who had volunteered to go to war at the pleading of his men, found his squad in danger. He attempted to lead them in a flanking movement but was pinned down by gunfire from one of the bunkers. SSG Daily, Charles Bradford, and a third unknown soldier were off to Bobby Hansen's left. Everyone yelled at them to get down as they directly assaulted the bunker, allowing the rest of the squad to move to safety. Hansen watched as the first round hit Daily and knocked him back off his feet. Bradford continued while firing his M-60, followed by the third soldier. They had nearly reached the bunker when they were both struck down.

3rd Platoon medic Michael Handley recalled helping to save Jessie Lane, one of the many wounded that day. He also tried to save Daily as he lay in the swamp, but he was too far gone, as was Bradford. Back at Fort Carson, Will had briefly known Bradford as "Charlie," who'd married his young bride just before departing for Vietnam.

"He saved my life that day at the cost of his own," recalled Barry Gallagher. "We were moving along the dikes when the VC popped up out of holes and started shooting at us. Charlie was right behind me and saw a VC about to shoot me. He knocked me out of the way and took a bullet that was meant for me. I killed the VC. Charlie died in my arms with his friends touching him. Not a day goes by when I don't thank him for my life."

Twenty-one years old from Newport, Kentucky, Private First Class (PFC) Charles Bradford would be awarded the Silver Star.

The third soldier who'd joined the assault was wounded but would survive. Sometime later, he would write to Daily's wife. Over time, the letter was lost, but she recalled some of the words. "Your husband died a hero," it began. "I am telling you how it happened. We were in a rice paddy when we were attacked. Sergeant Daily ordered us to go for cover. He said, 'Get back, get back, that's an order!' Two of us disobeyed and stayed with him. We were all shot, and I was playing dead in the water. Two North Vietnamese soldiers came and kicked us to make sure we were dead. One wanted to shoot us all in the head, but the other convinced him to leave." Sam Daily would be awarded the Bronze Star for Valor.

*Staff Sergeant Sam Daily distinguished himself by heroism in action on 4 October 1966 while serving as a squad leader during the extraction of a downed helicopter pilot from hostile territory in the Republic of Vietnam.*

*As his company came under intense enemy fire from several fortified bunkers and dikes, Sergeant Daily led his squad in an aggressive flanking action, but heavy enemy fire pinned the squad down before it could reach the objective. Exposing himself directly to enemy fire, Sergeant Daily executed a one-man assault on the bunker, which had effectively halted the forward progress of his squad. He was successful in suppressing the enemy fire sufficiently to enable his squad to resume its advance but was mortally wounded while doing so.*

*Sergeant Daily's determination, devotion to duty, and concern for the welfare of his men are in keeping with the highest traditions of the military service, and reflect great credit upon himself, his unit, and the United States Army.*

As the battle continued, 1LT Gallagher found himself pinned down behind the dikes near 2nd Platoon leader 1LT James Harmon. They looked at each other and said, "John Wayne." Then they rose up, yelling at their men to follow them into the fire. Their men had little combat experience, and the two leaders feared they would be left to run through the flooded expanse alone. Instead, their men immediately emerged from the water, fought like hell, and overran the enemy.

"It was my first time in real combat," said 4th Platoon medic Tom Monnier. "I was shocked, thinking, 'This is for real.' It was hard to get it through my mind that people were actually trying to kill each other. I didn't know what was going on or that we were looking for a downed helicopter. Then I saw it lying in the water up ahead. I saw Lieutenant Harmon and his medic, Mike Walker, making their way toward the chopper. Later, I was treating a guy who'd been shot up badly. He told me to take off his wedding ring and send it to his wife. I didn't take his ring off, though, just told him he was going to make it."

Fred Brodosi, who knew Monnier simply as "Doc," was helping him with that same wounded soldier when they heard the report of their first killed in action come over his radio. "The first time I was ever scared for my life," he recalled.

As his own weapon was useless, Bobby Hansen had picked up Daily's rifle to carry on the rescue mission. After nearly three hellish hours of fighting, searching, and more fighting, they finally reached the downed chopper at 5:20 PM. Hansen's fellow 3rd Platoon soldier, Dennis Sherry, had found a small reed boat and used it to ferry the injured pilot out of the knee-deep water of the mangroves. Then they put him on a field stretcher and carried him back to the rear.

Smithy was already in the rear and waiting to be medevaced. Radio operators Royce Barrow and Donald Rankin were there with SSG Robert Matulac and others in the command group. They had radioed for a dustoff but were still taking fire from fighters scattered among distant spider holes. They were told to lay down a suppressive fire and let loose with everything they had while Matulac guided in the chopper. The reeds of the rice paddy were blown flat into the rippling water as it hovered while teams of men carried the injured pilot and a few of the wounded to the dustoff. Smithy climbed aboard, and they were off.

Meanwhile, 1LT Gallagher and a few of his men were using another reed boat to bring back one of their own wounded along with the body of Charles Bradford. But as the sun was setting on the flooded battlefield, they became lost and separated from the rest of the company, having only a .45mm pistol, two M-16s, and a nonfunctional radio between them. Eventually, they were missed, and a few soldiers came to lead them out.

As Alpha Company's mortars were set and firing on the village, Bravo Company was picked up and airlifted to the other side as a blocking force. Robert Powers was a soldier in Bravo's mortar platoon—one of the battalion's first replacements who had just arrived in Vietnam a few days earlier. In *1966 The Year of the Horse*, he describes a chaotic scene as their Hueys descend on the other side of the village. Door gunners strafe the tree line while he and others jump six feet down into the swamp. They become instantly stuck in the thick bottom layer of muck, exposed and unable to move. Engulfed in a blue gunpowder haze, bullets whistle by as they struggle to move their legs.

Bravo Company advanced toward a tree line, regrouped, and ran through to a clearing to establish their fighting positions. Powers and his mortar platoon started lobbing shells while the rifle platoons unleashed their machine guns.

SSG Cleofas Madrid—one of Alpha Company's Korean War veterans—took out many of the occupied spider holes during their attack and would be awarded the Silver Star for his actions.

Trapped and desperate, many enemy soldiers tried to escape by crossing the Vinh Nouc Ngot inlet, some swimming, others in little fishing boats. Their attempts were unsuccessful. The enemy was engaged with massive force until cease-fire was ordered. A Navy battleship could now be seen positioned in the South China Sea. Within minutes, it began shelling enemy positions within the village of An My and continued for about an hour. It was dusk when another medevac arrived to fly out more of Alpha Company's wounded—Jessie Lane, Jerry Brown, Danny Rogers, Rolland Slocum, and Marvin Hall—along with the bodies of Sam Daily and Charles Bradford.

Infrequent gunfire and artillery bombardment continued as darkness fell. Illumination rounds were lobbed by the battleship throughout the night to light up the village and prevent the enemy's escape. Illumination rounds are artillery shells that burst high in the sky and continue to burn brightly, lighting up several square miles of terrain as they slowly descend by parachute, each emitting a piercing hissing sound along with a smoke trail that spirals above. As they rock back and forth beneath their parachutes, so do the shadows of everything on the ground. The thumping of helicopters could be heard constantly through the night. Guided by flashlight and radio, medevac choppers landed, then quickly disappeared into the darkness with more of the dead and wounded.

Gene Cross from Kentucky was walking along the dikes of a rice paddy that night when he was shot in the head. The sniper's bullet went through his helmet but only grazed his scalp, leaving a scar that remains to this day. All he remembered was seeing a flash of light, then waking up in the muck as their medic revived him. Apparently, he'd kept all his letters from home in his helmet. His letters were mostly ruined but were thought to have saved his life. Robert Wagner had taken a bullet through his ear that also ripped through his chinstrap.

"It was so dark that we had to hold onto each other's packs as we walked," remarked Fred Brodosi of their endless slog through the rice paddies and salt dikes that night. Following Brodosi was medic Tom Monnier, wet, exhausted, covered in other people's blood, and lugging an enemy machine gun. They had no idea where they were or where they were going, each man just following the one in front of him. Monnier was small, and the machine gun was big. He fell behind and started losing sight of Brodosi. Fearing he would be lost in Indian country, he threw the machine gun into the muck and sloshed through the swamp as fast as he could to catch up.

Alpha Company suffered one more fatality on October 4th. Bobby Hansen's buddy Smithy, wounded by his own machete, was en route from Camp Hammond to An Khe for treatment along with soldiers of other units. While flying through a dense fog near An Khe, their transport plane crashed into the side of Hon Cong Mountain. There were no survivors. PFC Donald Smith, Jr. was twenty years old from Milwaukee, Wisconsin.

A hard rain fell the next morning as Alpha and Bravo Companies moved into the village. They expected resistance but encountered none, finding only a smoldering apocalyptic scene. As the battleship sailed away, they searched the destroyed village. Several dead NVA fighters were found in dugouts and trenches, their bloody bodies crumpled and in awkward positions. The survivors had escaped with the weapons of the dead. Unlike the Viet Cong, who typically wore black pajamas, many of these NVA regulars wore khaki uniforms and pith helmets. At 8:20 AM on October 5th, after clearing the village and destroying the enemy's rice caches, Alpha Company was airlifted to Camp Hammond to recover. They were replaced by Charlie Company, who would be left to count and stack the bodies.

The men got showers and fresh clothing at Camp Hammond. They stripped off the grime-laden fatigues they had worn since leaving An Khe in August, piled them on the ground, and set them ablaze. As it would turn out, they would have to make these new fatigues last even longer. After recovering at Camp Hammond for the afternoon, Alpha Company was flown to LZ Opal.

## 6 October '66 – 42 weeks left

*We finally got started with our drive to search out these villages. October 4th, I guess it was. It was going along fine, seeing how these people live. We took a bunch of prisoners. It was late in the afternoon when the N.V.A. shot down a chopper. Our company went out to rescue the two pilots. It took about two hours to get there and when we did we got attacked. A Sergeant and a PFC I knew quite well got killed as the company got closer to the chopper. Six or seven got wounded. It's something I never want to live through again. We rescued the pilots. One thing I am glad we got is those choppers with rockets and machine guns, and also the medical ships. They really saved the day. We didn't fool around to see how many V.C. we killed. Yesterday we showered and shaved and got clean clothes. Now we are back as a reserve.*

*I received your long letter yesterday. I put it in my helmet and had the helmet upside down, and now it's soaking wet. To answer your letter, I am not starving. I doubt if I lost any weight, or very little. It rains an awful lot where we are now, and it gets darn cold at night. No, it isn't true what I wrote to Mike. I said in the letter that I was just kidding. We guys make up all kinds of silly stories like that. Sorry if I had you worried.*

*I got to talk to Rod about two weeks ago. Yes, he might get to train in the Green Beret camp for six weeks. This is because he is on long-range patrol, and I am not. No, I didn't see Allen Simon. I guess I was about ten miles from where he was, and he might have seen me if he drove past that little place where we were along the road. Larry Geissler said Allen saw me too. He might have.*

*Looks like the hog prices are very good. Is that the highest it's been all year? I am eating the package of popcorn and marshmallows. The marshmallows got a little sticky this morning 'cause I left them in the sun. You won't have to bother with these packages every week 'cause Lifeline packs come pretty often now with the free candy bars.*

*Will*

*Sam Daily — Charles Bradford — Donald Smith*

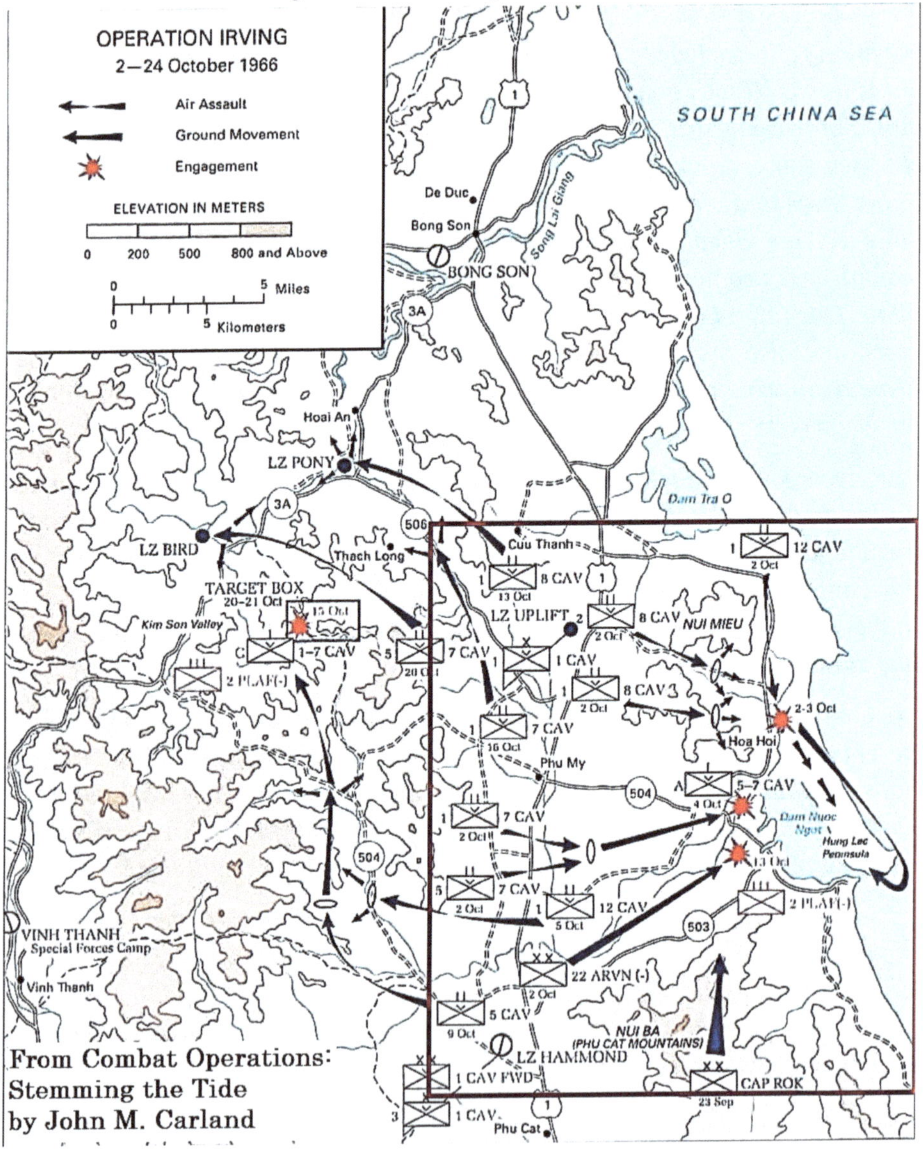

From *Combat Operations: Stemming the Tide* by John M. Carland

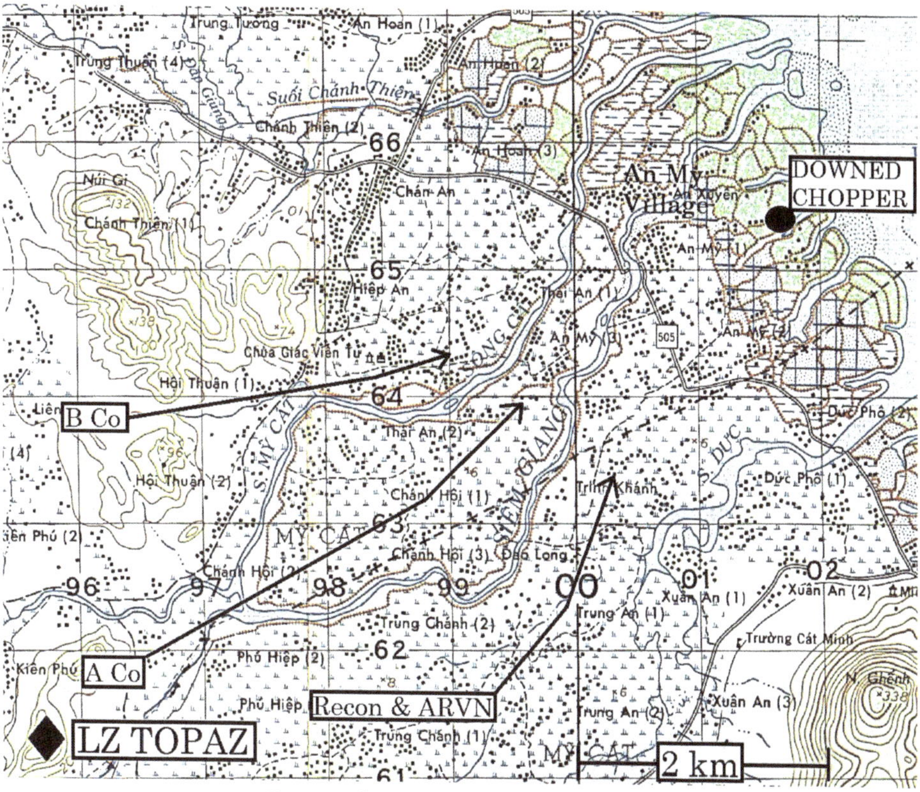

*Route of march, October 4th 1966*

*Donald Rankin carrying child, photo from Tony Rankin*

*Bell H-13 scout ship, source unknown*

*Sam Daily leading soldiers on October 4th 1966*

*Barry Gallagher — Larry Abegglen and Michael Handley*

*James Harmon and 2nd Platoon with prisoners, photos by Robert Matulac*

*A.J. Wise with villagers*

*Medic aiding wounded villagers after battle, photos by Robert Matulac*

# 12
# DELIVER US FROM EVIL
*Now we don't have to make up war stories like we did before.*

Most who have been to war will tell you that the worst part was not the fighting but rather the living conditions. I used to wonder why soldiers in Vietnam carried cigarettes strapped to their helmets. I know now that it was the only place on them that wasn't always wet. Waking each morning soaked from the morning moisture, they marched for hours through dew-covered foliage. The jungle's dampness would start to evaporate in the late morning heat, only to be replaced by their own sweat. They wore the same fatigues for weeks or months on end. Soaked with sweat and bug dope, they felt like greasy rags, and the men found that wearing no underwear was preferable to wet underwear.

The endless daily marching over rough terrain took its toll on their feet, made worse by the constant wetness. Dry socks were worth their weight in gold but hard to come by, and their feet deteriorated each week in the field. To varying degrees, they all suffered from trench foot, as it was called in the First World War—jungle rot, as it was called in Vietnam. Many also suffered fungal infections that itched and burned.

The rice paddies and streams were rife with giant leeches, which were not painful—but the wounds they left were as they began to fester. Their razor-like teeth could not be felt but caused profuse bleeding. After crossing a river, SSG Robert Matulac looked back and saw blood soaking Al Patrillo's trousers. "What happened, are you wounded?" Matulac asked. Patrillo looked down to find a host of leeches in his pants. Despite their size, they could flatten themselves to where they could penetrate even the most tightly-laced jungle boots.

Some rice paddies held unusually high levels of both human and water buffalo waste. 1LT Barry Gallagher's platoon had taken fire, and he was lying prone in one of these paddies that served as a communal toilet. By day's end, his body was covered with giant red bumps, and it felt like his skin was on fire. He was flown to the aid station at LZ English for treatment, where Army doctors—who had never seen a case quite like this—gathered around and took photos. He was told that the rash was from some kind of parasite that thrives in the toilet water paddies.

If they weren't walking through leech-infested rice paddies, they were walking through elephant grass, with its sharp blades inflicting cuts along their arms and hands, or through thorny jungle vines that did the same. Like those left by the leeches, these relatively minor wounds simply refused to heal in the perpetual moisture, causing pain and oozing puss as they became infected. Sooner or later, they would all feel the wrath of Vietnam's fire ants. Unlike the leech's, its bite was felt immediately. If disturbed, a colony would attack en masse, leaving welts that also itched and oozed for weeks. Martin Quinn suffered many such infections on his hands and arms. "Doc would pour antiseptic on them," he recalled, "and it stung like hell."

The most time I've ever spent wearing the same uniform is about a week or so, and I was miserable. The farthest I've ever had to march with my rucksack is twenty miles, with dry boots, on a flat road, and in comfortable weather. After the first ten miles, my legs became stiff, and my stride shortened. It took a couple days to recover. Now I imagine that same trek, carrying an M-16 and mortar tube, in hundred-degree heat, with wet socks, through swamps, and over hills, knowing I would do it all again the next day. On training missions, the longest I ever went without sleep was about forty-eight hours. One of the first things you learn about sleep deprivation is that you can start dreaming while standing and with your eyes open. Considering these physical ordeals, the parasites, the infections and diseases, the lack of sanitation, the weight they carried, and the fear that followed them, one can scarcely grasp the misery of an infantryman in Vietnam.

Following the battle of October 4th, the 5/7th Cav continued search and destroy missions in the Phu My plain. On the night of October 5th, Alpha Company set up blocking positions near LZ Opal to catch enemy fighters fleeing from Bravo and Charlie Companies' search and clear missions. Alpha Company's men moved out on their own patrol the next day. Meanwhile, Bravo Company took fire from another village near An My. Several secondary explosions were heard the next morning as the village of thirty huts was burned to the ground. A squad from Charlie Company was reported lost at 2:30 PM on October 7th. By 3:55 PM, they had been found and were flown to their company's command post.

Alpha Company moved out again on October 8th, crossing many rice paddies and learning how they were great places to get shot at. Earthen dikes rising less than a foot above the water crisscrossed each of them. While the dikes provided easy passage, it was safer to remain low and slosh through the gray-colored muck, which was thick and sticky and often had a rotten stench.

While crossing one of these paddies in water just above his knees, Will's platoon started taking fire from a nearby tree line. As rounds whizzed by their heads, everyone crouched in the muck and returned fire, hunkering down behind the dikes—except for an unusually tall soldier. "Tall Lee Roy" towered above the others. Everyone yelled, "Lee Roy, get down!" but he just stood there on the dike, looking around. Will could see the enemy's green tracers streaking by him on each side. Tall Lee Roy mysteriously survived without a scratch.

Before nightfall, they marched up another hill called LZ Ruby, where they would encamp. That night, Charlie Company soldiers killed two Viet Cong passing through their ambush positions on nearby LZ Topaz.

In the early morning fog of October 9th, Alpha Company moved back down into the valley to search a village known as Vinh Nhon near the banks of the Song Ca. They returned at dusk to LZ Ruby with a prisoner found hiding in one of the huts. Will was told to guard him. Bound and blindfolded, he sat Indian-style on the ground. He didn't look like much, scrawny and maybe seventeen years old at most. Whether he was Viet Cong or not, he was of military age. Unless politically connected, young men in South Vietnam were not allowed to sit out the war.

Assisted by their Vietnamese interpreter, one of their officers came to interrogate the prisoner. Removing the blindfold, he lit a cigarette and offered it to the man. Looking straight ahead and avoiding eye contact, the prisoner declined. The interpreter started jabbering rapid-fire questions in Vietnamese while pointing to various spots on a map. The prisoner gave short answers and refused to look at the map. The interpreter grew agitated and seemed ready to assault the man, but the officer calmed him down. Soon a chopper arrived with some military intelligence people to pick up the prisoner.

Sometimes they would find members of traveling musical propaganda troupes among the captured. Their battalion's Intelligence Officer, CPT Walt Swain, wanted to know the purpose of their costumes, instruments, and props. His interpreter explained, "Bob Hope show... for VC."

They often encountered enemy soldiers seeking to surrender before a fight even started. Their malnourished bodies would emerge from the bushes, often waving a white cloth and making motions toward their mouths, signaling their hunger. "Chieu Hoi!" they called out, referring to the Army's "Open Arms" program that gave amnesty to those who turned themselves in. They were cared for and fed, then used for intelligence. Some became Kit Carson Scouts, serving alongside American troops as guides and interpreters.

The Chieu Hoi program was promoted by psychological operations units, such as that of 2LT Winston Groom. From airplanes, they dropped thousands of leaflets over enemy areas, encouraging their soldiers to surrender with the promise of good food and humane treatment. In a memoir for *Smithsonian Air & Space Magazine*, Groom wrote, "I dimly remember one of the infantry platoon leaders telling me over drinks in the tent that passed for an officers' club that the North Vietnamese soldiers were using our leaflets as toilet paper—his men had stumbled on an area in the jungle littered with the evidence. This led to us discussing a plot to embed the leaflets with itching powder or some other unpleasantness, but nothing came of it." A 1967 1st Cavalry Division report contemplated cigarettes to promote surrender among the enemy.

*Psywar Cigarettes. The effort to make VC and NVA read Chieu Hoi Messages could reach a new dimension in effectiveness if persuaded to read leaflets. While the enemy may destroy leaflets, he would certainly be reluctant to destroy cigarettes with psywar messages on them.*

As the intelligence folks flew off with the prisoner, Will spotted a lone man in black pajamas, a Viet Cong or innocent farmer, walking along the dikes of a rice paddy far across the valley. He motioned to Patrillo, who came over and offered Will one of his Pall Malls. Whatever the man was, he wasn't supposed to be there, according to the Korean soldiers patrolling the valley. Water and mud splashed up all around him as they opened fire. He dashed for cover as distant shots echoed through the valley. They watched the man sprint along the tops of the dikes, falling once into the muck, then stumbling and running again toward the trees at the edge of the rice paddy. No one knows if the running man survived.

### 10 October '66 – 41 weeks left

*Dear Folks,*

*You know that big fight we had? This guy got shot in the helmet, and the bullet came out the side and just scratched his head a little. He told me he was shaking like a leaf after that. We had a few heroes too. One dragging his buddy back to safety after being hit. Another bringing back a machine gun under heavy fire. Now we don't have to make up war stories like we did before.*

*Just sitting on this big hill and searching the villages below us. Then we move to another hill and another one. Down in these flat lands is where most of the people live. Coconut trees all around, sugar cane, peanuts, onions, and a few other crops they raise besides those darn rice paddies.*

*Caught a guy yesterday. Our interpreter claims he is a draft dodger from the South Vietnamese Army. Just like some of us back home.*

*This little book is what the village chief gave me. He is up on the hill with us. He brought his bike along with him. This is their main transportation. They have cement houses in some villages, usually the church or chief's house. I guess these were made by the French people that were here. Well, I guess I'll go dry my clothes while the sun is still out. Every morning we wake up soaking wet.*

*Rice Paddy Daddy,*

*Will*

In the early morning of October 11th, Alpha Company again descended from LZ Ruby to search more villages. They searched for weapons, stockpiles of rice, and any men of military age, who were usually conspicuously absent. Entering was dangerous, as they could be occupied by enemy soldiers. Consisting of crude wooden houses with grass roofs and dirt floors, they were inhabited mainly by women, children, and old men who looked like Confucius. The villagers had few possessions and subsisted on whatever the land provided. Most worked harvesting rice.

It was humid, and the sun was beating hard as they approached their first village of the day, which had also recently been searched by ROK forces. Marvin Bierschbach heard some muttering ahead and noticed the men stopping to look at something on the ground as they entered the tiny hamlet. At first, he couldn't tell what it was but figured it was something dead by the many flies swarming about. As he and John Bronson drew closer, they perceived the head of a Viet Cong. He'd been buried up to his neck by the Koreans and left to die, a practice the Viet Cong themselves often inflicted on their enemies. "Well," said Bierschbach, "there it is."

"Yep," replied Bronson, staring down. "There it most definitely is."

Assisted by their interpreter, 1LT Cathcart and SSG Burtis were talking to a small elderly man. With gray whisps of hair on his chin, he seemed to be the village chief. He was shrugging his shoulders and motioning toward the hills. There were pigs in pens, dogs and chickens roaming about, and children staring at them from the entrances of huts. Amid the animal sounds and Vietnamese chatter, Tom Monnier heard someone yell, "Hey Doc, come up here!" Al Patrillo and Fred Brodosi were waiting for him at the entrance to one of the huts. Painful screams emanated as he approached. Inside was a young woman in labor, on a hammock, with two other women at her side.

In combat medic training, Monnier had learned basic stuff, how to give shots and IVs, how to put a band-aid on a bullet hole, but nothing for this situation. He stepped back out and yelled, "Hey, does anyone know how to deliver a baby?" The men responded with blank looks. He felt helpless but figured these women had been giving birth out here for hundreds of years and probably knew more about it than he did. He gave the woman some Darvon for the pain.

"Hey Doc," Patrillo yelled through the door, "we gotta di di mau!"

Monnier hoped for the best as they set out for the next village.

They trudged on, searching one after another, and if weapons were found, they would set the village ablaze. Amid the smoke and crackling sounds of their burning huts, they would relocate the people as humanely as possible—a sad task, but villages used by the enemy to store weapons and food were considered legitimate military targets. Many criticized this policy, as it alienated otherwise neutral or even friendly inhabitants. But the men of Alpha Company didn't get to make policy. This is what they were ordered to do in service to their country. And so, the soldiers had little more than pity and C-Ration candy to offer the villagers who were caught in an impossible position. Using terrorism, assassination, and rape as weapons, the Viet Cong and NVA would confiscate their rice and force the men into service. Resisting them meant death. If found to be helping them, however, the Americans would destroy their homes.

The villagers often greeted the men with smiles and even food. Other times, they remained expressionless and impassive, and that was always a bad sign.

Their true loyalties could not be known, nor could they be distinguished in any meaningful way from the enemy. And yet, they were to be treated with a certain level of respect. Sent to Vietnam by some guy they didn't know to kill some other guy they didn't know, and admonished not to kill anyone that didn't deserve killing, the humanity of these impossibly young soldiers would be tested. By all accounts, Alpha Company's men treated the villagers with as much compassion as they could. Donald Rankin wrote to his old college roommate, Blair Richards, in whose wedding he'd been best man. He told of the heartache he felt for the poor people of rural Vietnam and how he wished he could help them. Mike Stoflet also felt for the villagers they encountered, once writing to his older sister Donna about how he and a few others had visited an orphanage near An Khe and given the children candy.

Alpha Company returned to LZ Ruby at the end of the day. Everyone had grown accustomed to the leeches and knew how to remove them quickly and painlessly, either with a squirt of bug dope or by burning them with their lighter. While setting up for the night, Martin Quinn noticed something in his pants. He wasn't surprised to find a leech but was disturbed to find it stuck to the right side of his ball sack. Because it was so deeply embedded, neither bug dope nor fire could remove it. He walked over to their medic. "I've got a problem Doc," Quinn said, dropping his drawers. The look on Doc's face offered little reassurance. By now, the leech was fully engorged, writhing about, and weighing heavily on his scrotum. After much discussion with the other medics, it was decided that the leech would be cut out. Doc began sterilizing his tools, first with alcohol and then with his Zippo lighter for good measure. Before getting cut, Quinn needed a shot of Novocain. He stared nervously at the needle as Doc tapped the air bubbles out of the syringe, then closed his eyes and braced himself. Fortunately, the anticipation turned out to be worse than the procedure.

While pulling guard duty that night, Will's platoon sergeant came to him with an unusual question. SSG Donald Burtis stood before him with PFC Bruce Madison, asking if he could teach them how to pray. As darkness fell upon them, the three skytroopers joined hands and bowed their heads as Will led them in the same prayer Jesus taught his disciples.

### 12 October '66 – 41 weeks left

*Dear Folks,*

*Did you ever hear of our Operation Thayer? There have been about three thousand killed in this operation so far. Life here seems so cheap. But the village people are always happy to see us. Some of these people are Catholic. In this hut, they had a picture of Christ and Mary. Thing is, they both had slanted eyes. Went to Mass yesterday, the fourth time since I was back on leave. I go every time I get a chance—well, everybody goes now.*

*My platoon sergeant is Catholic and told me before Mass started that he never was to church in twenty years. He mentioned about confession, and I encouraged him to go, and he did—received communion also. Last night, I pulled guard with him and Madison and had to teach him some prayers. He wears a rosary around his neck now. I think everyone says his night prayers out here.*

*Just waiting as a reaction force today. A bit tired from sitting up bullshitting last night. This one cat from college knows about flying saucers, hypnotism, and reincarnation. Man, he made it sound so real, and he's really smart too. I don't know, but it seems to me that it mustn't be true. I'd like to check into this when I get home.*

*It's been almost a year since I've been in the Army. Doesn't seem like it. Seems more like a hundred years since I was back in Fort Leonard Wood. Boy, what changes I went through since high school days. I read in the last newspaper you sent that Melvin got picked up for a traffic fine. Ha!*

*Will*

*Our Father, who art in Heaven, hallowed be thy name. Thy kingdom come, thy will be done, on Earth as it is in Heaven. Give us this day, our daily bread, and forgive us our trespasses, as we forgive those who trespass against us. Lead us not into temptation, but deliver us from evil.*

 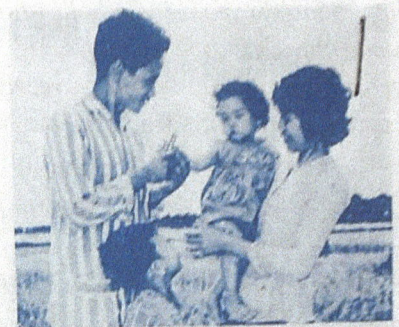

*Chieu Hoi leaflet from the National Archives:*
*Do you want to die and be buried in an unmarked grave—or come back to your family and enjoy the government's protection?*

*Marvin Bierschbach*

*Soldiers being picked up in rice paddy, photo by Will Bowe*

*River crossing in Bong Son, photo by Robert Matulac*

*Tom Monnier (Doc) — Viet Cong prisoners*

*Fred Brodosi — Robert Matulac and A.J. Wise*
*Photos by Tom Monnier*

# 13
# WAR WITHOUT FRONTS

After a few more days of searching and destroying in the Phu My plain, Alpha Company was flown to an artillery firebase known as LZ Garnet on October 15th. They would pull guard duty here for the next two days. At 5:10PM, a PFC Lee was reported missing. Three small patrols and an H-13 scout helicopter searched for him through the night.

Relatively safe compared to the areas they patrolled, firebases represented a rare opportunity to rest. The men still pulled guard duty and slept in shifts in the dirt, there were typically no buildings, showers, or even outhouses, but at least they weren't slogging through the bush all day. Some firebases, such as LZ English and Camp Hammond, were more developed. These had larger perimeters and guard towers, were accessible by road, and may have featured a field hospital, chow tent, and perhaps a beer tent or clubhouse. But most were like LZ Garnet, small affairs with no such luxuries, located on hills and mountaintops accessible only by foot or helicopter. Dug-in artillery positions were surrounded by sandbags and bunkers constructed by the artillerymen. Around their perimeters were more bunkers used by the infantrymen who kept guard.

During the battalion's operations, one company was often designated as a reserve or "reaction force" and kept on call at a nearby firebase while the rest went on missions. Whenever a company in the field encountered the enemy, the reserve would be flown in to assist. Being on reserve allowed you to rest while the others humped the hills. When called into action, however, you could count on being dropped into combat. When flying the company out in waves, the flight crews would sometimes inspect the chopper for damage between lifts. To the troops, this meant that they would soon be jumping into a landing zone under fire—a hot LZ.

Their time at LZ Garnet gave the men a chance to write letters. They simply wrote "FREE" in the corner of the envelope, and it would be delivered free of charge. Will mostly wrote to his mom, Millie. Marvin Bierschbach wrote to his girlfriend, Jane. Joe Sanchez wrote to Teresa, the girl he'd lost his virginity to in Colorado. Bobby Hansen also had a girl to write to. Jim Hirschuber wrote to his wife, Charlene. Fred Brodosi wrote home on the back of C-Ration boxes, and his little sister would use his C-Ration letters for a middle school report. SSG Robert Matulac didn't have a girlfriend but was pen pals with a girl in San Francisco. Tom Erickson wrote to his older brother Marv, who had also been drafted in 1965. Before long, however, Sanchez would receive his own Dear John letter from

Teresa, saying she had met someone else, as would his buddy Alan Weisman, from his fiancée.

Mike Stoflet wrote to his girlfriend Sharon and sisters Donna and Nancy. He'd been near Sam Daily and Charles Bradford when they were killed and wrote of how scared he was. "You probably heard on the news about that big battle we had on October 4th," he wrote to Donna. "We lost two men from my platoon. You really start thinking when your buddy next to you gets shot down like some kind of animal. By the way, I'm not telling any of this to Mother, so please watch what you say to her." While Nancy kept recording Mike's Army experience in her *Diary of a Soldier*, Donna couldn't help but think of how her little brother—such a kind-hearted person—just didn't belong there. She kept sending cookies.

During their time on the various firebases, the men read the *Stars & Stripes* and the funny papers, told dirty jokes, played cards, and smoked. They talked about cars, women, sports, and who was their favorite girl on *Gilligan's Island*.

Bobby Hansen and Alan Weisman discussed the cars each would buy when they returned to The World. Hansen would get himself a '68 Plymouth with a Hemi engine. Weisman planned to buy a '67 Jet with a 428.

Tom Monnier was friends with the other medics, Michael Handley and Mike Walker, radio operators Kenneth Rathyen and Donald Rankin, and fellow 4th Platoon soldiers Fred Brodosi and Paul Lussier. SSG Elvin Wideman was an experienced soldier and former Marine in 3rd Platoon who often helped out the younger guys. "You could just tell he was a leader," Monnier said. One night, Wideman showed him how to heat coffee in a paper cup by burning a small chunk of C-4 and how the flame would heat up the coffee without burning the cup.

Will became good friends with Al Patrillo. His mother often sent packages of treats to be shared. Patrillo also received coffee tins filled with homemade cookies from his childhood friend Tom Ivey's mom. Still, Tom was never very good about sending letters to Al as he was often busy with college homework.

They were sitting on sandbags, eating C-Rations, and talking about what they would do when this was all over. Patrillo told Will how he planned to move to Wisconsin to start a taxidermy business with him. Will could never tell if he was joking or not. It started drizzling rain. Martin Quinn muttered something and went off for his poncho. "At least it's a warm rain," Will grinned.

"Man, don't you ever bitch about nothin'?" asked John Bronson, eating Spaghetti and Meatballs out of a can. "I only wish I could be so happy-go-lucky."

The Army has a way of bringing people together. As a soldier, you'll often find yourself in close quarters and forming bonds with those you would have never known in civilian life. As Communications NCO, SSG Robert Matulac's position was at the company level, so he got to know almost all of the men in the company, at least a bit. For a time, I was the full-time Admin NCO of my own unit. Working at the company level, I quickly learned which soldiers had personal problems and marital issues, which ones had drug and alcohol problems, and which ones had problems with the law. Whenever a soldier got in trouble, I was among the first to find out.

Aside from bringing together people from disparate backgrounds, the Army is also where those who don't fit into most social circles often find the most acceptance and appreciation. I think of a young soldier named Joseph Parker-Widga. He was barely out of high school when he showed up at our annual training in 2010. He was quiet and seemed a bit scared of his sergeants. He spoke with a sort of Elmer Fud-like impediment. Our platoon sergeant, SSG Corbin, had an aversion to long names, and so he called him "P-Dubs."

Years later, after another annual training at Camp Ripley, P-Dubs and I were back at the armory, our last stop on our way home. He was the only one there, aside from myself. He couldn't see out of one eye as it had become infected with something from the field. He wore what were often referred to as "birth control glasses," the very non-fashionable eyewear issued to soldiers by the Army. He was the only soldier I knew to actually wear these after basic training. They weren't pretty, but they were sturdy and practical. I didn't think he should drive, so I offered him a ride home. "No thanks, sawgent," he said, "my brotho's picking me up."

P-Dubs was different, and he found friendship and appreciation among the young men in our detachment, perhaps more than he ever found outside the Army. He was good with the radio and all the digital equipment that we used as forward observers. Most of all, he was a good friend to his buddies in his platoon, known as someone who would never refuse a helping hand.

I was the only one in the office when my friend and boss, SFC Adam Petersen, called to inform me that P-Dubs had killed himself. We had all known P-Dubs for over six years.

He had been on temporary orders through the summer, helping out SSG Adam Walton in the supply room. Only a month before, those of us on the full-time staff had gone on an outing to a Twins baseball game in Minneapolis, and we brought P-Dubs along. While watching the game, we talked for hours at a bar in the stadium overlooking the field. He seemed happy and not as shy as he used to be. I can picture him sitting there smiling as if it were yesterday. He'd struggled with the physical fitness test and had been stuck at the rank of Specialist for the last four years. But he was passing it now, and we talked about putting in his promotion packet for Sergeant. I tried to convince him to come to the topless bar with us after the game. He wasn't interested, saying he needed to get up for work the next morning. Even before asking, I knew this would be his response. He went home early that night while the rest of us got drunk.

His death was well-planned. He'd organized his belongings, tied up loose ends, and left letters for those he worked with about where to find things. To SSG

Walton, he left his rifle. He didn't want to put anybody out, as if simply making arrangements for an extended trip.

I was alone in the office again a week later. I was about to leave when I got a call from the military chaplain who was to conduct SPC Parker-Widga's funeral the next day. He didn't have much to go on for his eulogy. I told him I would gather some information and send it to him. I looked through his personnel records and found a recommendation for the Army Achievement Medal that P-Dubs had been awarded following his deployment in 2011. That was helpful, but I also thought his family should know what he meant to us. I didn't intend to write his eulogy, but that's just how it worked out. It's sad to say it, but it would have been a rather small gathering if not for all the fellow soldiers who showed up for his funeral on that cool October morning at Fort Snelling. I would never have known someone like P-Dubs if not for the Army. Having known him is one thing that makes me glad I joined.

Will described his own company as a mixed-up bunch. Growing up in rural Wisconsin, he'd never really known people of other races or who spoke with northeastern accents. Now he was part of an infantry company cobbled together with blacks, whites, Italians, Puerto Ricans, and others. They had come from farms, cities, trailer parks, suburbs, and ghettos, from all corners of the great republic. The one thing most of them shared in common was their modest economic background, some coming from extreme poverty. Few were there by choice, but they all depended upon each other now for survival.

After a long night lost in Indian country, the wayward PFC Lee found his way back through the jungle, returning at 6:55 AM on October 16th.

Later that day, giant sky cranes descended on LZ Garnet to carry off the artillery where Alpha Company's 4th Platoon had been pulling security. The artillerymen departed in their own choppers. Quitting the firebase and ending their brief reprieve, 4th Platoon flew back to LZ New Diamond to rejoin the company.

### *17 October '66 – 40 weeks left*

*Dear Folks,*

*No, I am not in the hospital if that's what you're thinking. It is just an envelope and paper the Red Cross gave us. Good news, I believe this operation is almost over. Rumors are going around saying we might go in tomorrow. We in the mortars were guarding an artillery unit for two days. Man, what I wouldn't give to be in the artillery. Good food and lots of it. Sit on top of a hill and take it easy. Now we're back with the company.*

*Our C.O. doesn't seem to give a damn about us in the mortars 'cause we have it easier than the rifle platoons. That's why we always get cheated out of our sup-*

plies. I think he's getting too big-headed since that big rescue mission our company made. I read in the newspaper you sent about our company rescuing those helicopter pilots.

This battalion calls our operation Irving. The Koreans call it Tiger. Also, we had the South Vietnamese Army out here and a couple of other battalions, and they called this whole operation Thayer. Some of the guys read in their letters from home that we were on the Chet Huntley Program, making the news.

It hasn't rained now for almost a week. It quit just like that. Otherwise, we were wet twenty-six hours a day. Now everyone is getting a real fine tan.

I saw Rodney Henning a few days ago. They were teed off because they had to go back out when we took over their position guarding the artillery. Rod says they're all going to quit the Long Rang Patrol 'cause they aren't getting the privileges they were promised.

I got your package of fudge and doughnuts. I just munched away for an hour or so last night while on guard. If you're going to send tomatoes, send them in a coffee can. The shoe boxes get pretty squashed. In the next package, send a stick of summer sausage and a big chunk of cheese. The cheese the N.F.O. sent us, you know who got it? The generals and colonels, we'll never see it.

Hey, I might be going on a five-day vacation on the 28th to Hong Kong. This is called R&R, rest and recuperation. If my name turns up, my buddy Quinn said he'd lend me a large sum of money. He and Figueroa claim they're going to visit our farm after the service. Two big city slickers from New York that have never seen a farm before. My buddy Brodosi got his pictures back, and the one he took of me crossing the river, and I am sending it to you. I think this picture was taken on September 28th.

I'm sending a little package for Mike. Well, I best not say. Hey Mike, if you don't have anything to do after school, ask the librarian for Project Blue Book. Also, The Shafer Mysteries and books by Charles Fort. These all tell of flying saucer sightings. Let me know what you find out. I got your letter Mike, but you can't put a back address as just the town. It doesn't make any difference, as long as the zip code is on it.

I guess the Orioles sure did a job on the Dodgers, huh? I read about them in the Army newspaper. Heard about Willie Davis making them errors. And Larry is all for the Baltimore team. Did the Yankees really finish in last place?

You know, when we got nothing else to talk about, we talk about our plans for when we get out of the service. This is my plan. First, I'll take a forty-eight-hour bath. Then I'll buy a set of fine clothes and jump in my '67 Thunderbird that I ordered from Viet Nam tax-free and drive home from California. Then I'll raid *the refrigerator for three weeks if Ma hasn't kicked me out by then, ha! Then instead of working at Johnson's, I'll work in Minneapolis or Milwaukee for more money and overtime to pay for the car. Then I'll use this G.I. Bill that pays over a hundred dollars a month for thirty-six months of school. Maybe night school to be a construction welder. Farming is too much for me to manage. And then, I'll take up astronomy for a hobby and build an eight-inch lens telescope.*

*I heard a rumor that in June '67, the battalion will start rotating back to the states, starting with the lowest ranking first. When the 1st of June comes near, I'll try like hell to get busted to E-1.*

*Chow time now. Sounds like a big bargaining center. Trade two cans of this for a can of that. I can get some good trades. You'd be surprised what I would trade for a fruit cake. Well, I must eat now. Man, is it ever hot out.*

*Will*

One of the most dangerous parts of taking out an ambush team was returning to the patrol base in the dark. Known as a passage of lines, the team leader would inform those guarding the perimeter that they were leaving and when they would return. Guard duty ran in shifts, however, and the message wasn't always passed on to the next guy. At 8:18 PM on October 18th, two Bravo Company soldiers were shot by their own men while returning from ambush positions. It was dark and raining, and their dustoff was delayed. Under poor flying conditions, they were finally medevaced at 9:44 PM. One would die before reaching the field hospital.

At 4:10 PM on October 19th, Alpha Company was flown west, air assaulting onto LZ Buckner, high in the Central Highlands. This is where other battalions of the 1st Air Cavalry had commenced Operation Thayer back in September. The terrain was steep, rugged, and thickly vegetated. Just like Phu My, however, it was still very wet, with rice paddies and flooded streams running through the fog-laden valleys below. The rest of the battalion flew into the same area the next day, with the battalion command post setting up shop at LZ Duz.

This new area in the highlands represented the most frightening terrain. Here the jungle's thickness reduced the infantry company to fighting on par with the enemy. Their mortars were often rendered useless amid the tangled vines. Attack helicopters could rarely be used with both enemy and friendly hidden beneath the jungle canopy. Calling for artillery would be difficult for 1LT James Ulrich and his team of forward observers, trying to keep track of their location and determine the enemy's grid coordinates when they could only see but a few feet in any direction. Reinforcements could be called upon should they run into a larger enemy force. But with no place for the choppers to land, this would be severely complicated. While searching intently for the enemy, no one actually wanted to find him here. In the depths of the jungle, the company was on its own.

The area was riddled with landmines, booby traps, and punji stakes. For medevacs, they would use a hoist to sling-load casualties through the trees. Rather than moving in wedge formation, now each platoon marched in a line. The terrain was punishing, and they never walked on flat ground. Thorny "wait-a-minute vines" constantly latched onto their rucksacks, weapons, and equipment, frustrating their already slow movement. The hacking became impossible, with virtually no room to swing the machetes, their handles slippery with sweat. When dark came, they found themselves digging in on a steep mountainside. Fred Brodosi set his rifle between two trees to keep himself from rolling down the slope. The next day brought more of the same.

Black clouds darkened the sky on the third day, October 21st. The rains that had briefly subsided now returned in torrential fashion. Alpha Company was now on the west side of the southernmost claw of the Crow's Foot that formed the Kim Son Valley, and through it ran a river called the Soui L`on. It was a narrow valley, only a quarter-mile wide in some areas. On the other side loomed a dark jungle-covered hill where enemy encampments were suspected. Over a thousand feet above the valley floor, its peak disappeared into the low-hanging clouds. Brigade had ordered the 5/7th to search and clear that hill. The plan was to attack from all directions at dawn the next day, with Bravo Company advancing from the opposite side of the hill, Charlie Company from the south, and a company from the 1/7th Cav from the north, each leaving one platoon back as a blocking force.

## 21 October '66 – 40 weeks left

Dear Folks,

*Now I am teed off 'cause the chopper came and blew away the letter I was writing. We didn't go in like I figured, and it started to rain again. Son of a gun. We went up in the mountains. Still a lot of leeches around here. I don't know if Rod got his raincoat or not. Wish I had mine, but it's too much to carry when we're moving. Food is picking up. Haven't been hungry for a long time.*

Wet Will

It was still raining at 6:00 AM the next morning when the companies moved out to surround and search the hill. Moving in from the west, Alpha Company needed to cross the Soui L`on, which had now developed into a raging torrent. It suddenly widened and engulfed the entire valley, flooding their encampment. It became very deep and proved impossible to cross. The company from the 1/7th encountered the same while moving in from the north. An airlift was contemplated to get them across the river, but the relentless downpour prevented this.

Alpha Company and the company from the 1/7th Cav spent the night in blocking positions along the flooded rivers as showers continued.

The rain finally eased, and at 9:31 AM the next morning, Alpha Company was airlifted across the river. The jungle was wet and dark. Its ground was exceedingly steep, muddy, and littered with soggy deadfall and jagged rocks. Their progress was agonizingly slow. Reaching the top, they found an abandoned enemy camp. Bunkers made of logs and mud surrounded a handful of crude bamboo huts. All that had been left were stockpiles of rice. This was typically airlifted out and distributed to local villagers. But no landing zone was available, so the rice was burned along with the encampment. Then the men dug in to spend the night atop the hill.

That night, Donald Rankin wrote to his younger brother Wayne.

*Dear Wayne, Martha, and children,*

*Received your letter with those cute pictures several days ago. However, it has rained for three solid days and nights. Yesterday, the river overflowed, and we were in knee-deep water before we knew what happened. We are in very jungley territory between Phu My and Bong Son. We haven't seen too many Viet Cong, but the mosquitoes, rain, ants, and leeches are enough. The leeches are four and five inches long sometimes. They are really hard to keep off.*

*I guess Jr. is glad to be home. With luck, I'll be home by this time next year. That really seems far away now. I received the card and letter from Wayne about a month ago. I thought that I had answered, but we move around here so much that it's hard to remember anything. Tell everyone hello. I'll write more later.*

*Love,*

*Donnie*

The next morning, Alpha Company moved east through the jungle and down the opposite side of the hill. They encamped on the banks of the Nuoc Lang River in a valley that formed yet another claw of the Crow's Foot. This valley was even narrower than before, only about six hundred feet across. Here they would have little standoff from the enemy approaching from the jungle.

Rankin wrote as they prepared for another airlift set for the following day.

*Dear Mom and Daddy,*

*Received your letter this afternoon. A nice easy day. Very hot but tolerable. I got about nine letters. Everybody, Sarah Jane Bell, Gene's sister, Mrs. Gibson, you, Suzie in California, Suzie Crockett, some woman in Arizona I don't even know, and several others.*

*Tomorrow we're going into a "hot" landing zone, so it'll probably be a few days before I write. I don't even know the area. This is all. Will write more later. Tell everyone hello.*

*Love,*

*Donnie*

    Their next air assault would mark the beginning of another major operation for the 1st Air Cavalry Division. Despite hopeful rumors of returning to base camp at the conclusion of Operation Irving, Alpha Company and the rest of the 5/7th Cav would stay in the field as the division rolled into its next operation, through November and into December.

    Operation Irving concluded at midnight on October 24th 1966, a resounding success as over two thousand enemy soldiers had been killed and over a thousand had been taken prisoner. Over fifty Americans had died to make it happen.

    As it had been said, "In Vietnam today, you will hold only the ground you stand upon." In this war that the French had called guerre sans fronts—war without fronts—progress could not be measured in territory. The enemy's territory was not the objective as it had been in previous wars. Rather, the enemy himself was the objective, and success was measured in terms of body count. By this measure, the 1st Air Cavalry Division was winning. Despite their many wounded, as night fell on October 24th, the men of Alpha Company had suffered only four fatalities. This was just the beginning—the deadliest month was yet to come.

*View of Central Highlands from helicopter, photo by Will Bowe*

# 14
# LIFE AND DEATH IN THE JUNGLE
## (Operation Thayer II)
*That's how much they loved their men.*

Every soldier in Vietnam was entitled to five days of official rest and relaxation, known as R&R, during their year-long tour. Available destinations included Hawaii, Tokyo, Taipei, Singapore, Kuala Lumpur, Bangkok, Manila, and Hong Kong, still a British colony at the time. Hawaii was popular among married officers and senior enlisted men, as they could arrange to meet their wives there. Royce Barrow was going to Hong Kong near the end of October but didn't have any money as he had nearly all his paycheck deposited into a savings account. And so, his friend Donald Rankin lent him sixty bucks.

As Operation Irving was terminated, Operation Thayer II commenced on October 25th 1966, bringing more of the same search and destroy missions in the plains and highlands of Binh Dinh Province. November brought the monsoons, daily downpours that fell in sheets, wind-driven storms, increased humidity, and an opaque early morning fog that blanketed the lowlands.

Alpha Company airlifted from the banks of the Nuoc Lang. Flying three miles west, they air assaulted onto LZ Falcon atop another large hill just west of the Soui L`on. With Bravo and Charlie set in blocking positions in the valley below, they marched northeast along a jungle-covered ridge, ending their patrol that night on the banks of a rice paddy in another part of the Crow's Foot.

On October 26th, the battalion was flown to a new area about three miles southwest of the Crow's foot. Suitable landing zones were scarce, so small teams of combat engineers equipped with explosives and chainsaws were attached to each company. Chinook choppers lifted the battalion headquarters and Delta Company to LZ Pluto, followed by Bravo Company air assaulting onto LZ Venus, Alpha onto LZ Mars, and Charlie onto LZ Mercury. Most of the LZs were at high elevations. Alpha Company would remain at LZ Mars for the night, a cleared-out area that sat along a saddle leading up to the area's highest mountain. Winding through an expansive valley to their southwest, the large Song Con River could be seen turning from amber to violet in the waning twilight.

In the night, Martin Quinn shook Will awake for his turn at guard. He took off his watch with illuminated dials and gave it to Will. In the distance, little more than the skyline of mountains across the valley could be discerned, and the foreground before them was nothing but black shapes. Sitting in their foxhole, Will studied those shapes, waiting for one to move. The vast void was filled with insect and animal noises as the moist air carried the faintest sounds for miles. The distant thumping of artillery echoed through the valley.

Filling his mind were images of home—Dad filling the silo with a cigarette dangling from his lips, Mom working in the kitchen, Mike riding his bike, and their old collie Chester chasing along the yellowish sandstone driveway that ran through the farm. He tried to concentrate on the dark shapes and think of more immediate concerns. He needed his own illuminated-dial watch. He wondered when they'd get to rest at another firebase. He wished his feet were dry.

He thought about how it was October now, and how it would feel like football weather back home, and how it would smell—the leaves, the grass, the popcorn and hot cocoa from the concessions stand—and how there really were no seasons in Vietnam, just rainy and dry seasons that went from wet to hot. And the images from the past continued. His old Ford Custom and his friend Larry Geissler, the night they were all dressed up with their prom dates. Coach Grip leading them onto the field on a beautifully cool Friday night beneath the stadium lights—a vision of midwestern Americana, with the marching band, and the rocket's red glare, and cheerleaders doing flips and cartwheels, and fans holding up signs that said, "Go Macks!" and waving banners and flags, American flags and Vietnamese flags. Looking for Eddie and Millie, he saw Vietnamese children in the stands shouting, "G.I. numba one!" and SSG Burtis walking the sidelines with a clipboard.

And then it was the last game of the '63 season, where they were losing to Prairie Du Chien in a drizzling mist. He stood there, helmet in hand, as the players and referees walked off, abandoning the football that lay near the fifty-yard line of the muddy field. The announcer was reading off the names of local boys who'd been killed in Vietnam, and a hard rain fell. Fans with umbrellas shuffled down the bleachers. He looked up into the rain and watched the clock on the scoreboard wind down to zero. And then he was staring at the black shapes in the wilderness, and he was in Vietnam, and it was raining.

He pulled out one of two remaining Camel non-filters. He lit it beneath the ledge of their foxhole, careful to keep its glowing end out of sight. SSG Bobby Hayslip whispered, "You awake?" Will looked back and nodded. "Any smokes left?" They spoke quietly in the darkness for a while, then Hayslip continued checking on his men.

Alpha Company set out for LZ Venus the next morning. Venus sat atop a mountain that towered fifteen hundred feet above the valley. The troopers spent the morning hacking through two miles of densely forested ridges. Then they crossed a small stream to begin their steep ascent. They climbed doggedly. Weighed down by their equipment, 4th Platoon's men struggled to keep up, dropping base plates and mortar tubes while negotiating the rocky terrain. Carrying the base plate, Will followed close behind Quinn, often grabbing onto his belt to keep from falling behind. "I know that base plate's heavy," Quinn finally said, "but I can't carry both of us!" Burdened by extra chains of M-60 ammo, Bobby Hansen walked point, chopping through vines and bamboo as they scaled the ragged slope.

A lieutenant of one of the rifle platoons grew impatient and accosted the men of 4th Platoon as they approached the tree-covered summit. From here, dozens of five-hundred-pound bomb craters could be seen about the mountain and in the valley below. They descended a short distance toward LZ Venus, a cleared-out area on the other side of the summit. It was mid-afternoon as the battalion command chopper approached with LTC Trevor Swett and his staff officers, followed by a log ship with three replacement soldiers.

SSG Robert Matulac walked through the trees toward the LZ as the choppers touched down. He saw SSG Donald Burtis clutching a newspaper, smoking and joking with one of the engineers. A few feet away, Will and Quinn argued over who would dig their foxhole. Bobby Hansen had just finished digging his own and headed toward the LZ, hoping to get some mail. Matulac had a bad feeling. He was about to warn the men that the area was not yet secured. As he approached, Burtis and the engineer were hit by a sudden burst of sniper fire. Will and Quinn dropped their shovels and ran for cover behind some large trees. Matulac dove into one of the bomb craters, followed by LTC Swett and his staff officer, MAJ Victor Bullock. Matulac saw the log ship's door gunner jumping around to avoid enemy bullets while maneuvering his M-60. Then Rocco Valentino came running, jumping into the same crater and landing right on top of LTC Swett. Hansen had left his weapon behind while heading toward the chopper and was lying defenseless on the ground as bullets flew by.

CPT A.J. Wise was on the radio, calling in gunships and a dustoff. Matulac and Donald Rankin returned fire while leapfrogging each other up the hill. MAJ Bullock sprang out of their crater and rushed to help medic Bill Garcia care for the wounded engineer.

Will and Quinn fired their rifles into the jungle-covered high ground from where the sniper fire came. Will could hear Burtis yelling for help but couldn't see him. For a moment, he hesitated, unsure of where Burtis was or how to get to him amid the flying lead. Then 1SG Potter stepped out through the cloud of gunsmoke like John Wayne and dragged Burtis back to the cover of the trees. Burtis had taken two bullets in his stomach. His fatigues were soaked in blood, and his hands were shaking.

They continued firing blindly into the jungle until the gunships arrived to pummel the surrounding area. With the help of some others, Will and Quinn hefted Burtis on a poncho and carried him to the LZ. Burtis was a big man, and it took all their strength. Medic Tom Monnier scrambled to hook up an IV as they waited for the dustoff.

The three new soldiers hadn't even landed in the field before getting shot at and were reluctant to get out of the chopper. Matulac climbed up and shoved them out. "Fresh meat," grunted Bronson. "Welcome to the jungle." In their clean fatigues and shiny boots, they stood in stark contrast to the ragged veterans.

The dustoff arrived, and they loaded up Burtis and the wounded engineer. The chopper dipped its nose and began its ascent, blowing a storm of dirt in the faces of the squinting troopers. Will and Quinn watched as it disappeared into the sky, wondering if Burtis would survive. Will thought back to their time at Fort Carson, how he was scared of heights and had refused to go down that rappel tower, and how just two weeks ago, he'd taught him those prayers while keeping watch on LZ Ruby. More than his platoon sergeant, Burtis was a friend. That moment of hesitation during the firefight now filled him with regret, wishing he'd been the one to drag him to safety. Their squad leader, SSG Bobby Hayslip, would take over as platoon sergeant for 4th Platoon.

After the wounded lifted off, the men were ordered to march back out to find the snipers. Dejected and exhausted, they trudged back into the jungle—but the enemy was long gone. They returned to LZ Venus at dusk.

They continued down the opposite side of the mountain the next morning. After covering a mile or so, they stopped on a hill near the Song Con. Here they cut out another landing zone with the help of the engineers, dubbing it LZ Sun.

One of the new guys who'd arrived on the command chopper was Malcolm Brouhard from Wheatfield, Indiana. He'd just completed his training when he married his young bride on October 15th, ten days before shipping out to Vietnam. He was nineteen, and she was eighteen. On the Wall of Faces, his younger brother Dick recalled the following.

*Malcolm loved to play basketball and was good at it. I remember when we had moved to another house that sat on the edge of two school districts. The coaches from both schools came to our house and asked my parents to send Malcolm to their school, basically fighting to get him on their basketball team.*

*One night, he and a friend were driving in the country and came upon a duck in the middle of the road, and they stole the duck. The farmer saw them and started chasing them down the road without any headlights on and a loaded rifle. Somehow the police got involved. They let my brother and friend go but arrested the farmer for driving without headlights and carrying a deadly weapon.*

*Then there was the day he left for Vietnam. I was a junior in high school. I knew he was leaving about the time I was getting out of school and thought I would miss the train. I took off running toward the station, hoping to see him before he left. The train was pulling away when I got there, and Malcolm was at an outside window. I waved goodbye, and he was pointing at his wedding ring, reminding me that he had someone very special to come home to.*

### 28 October '66 – 38 weeks left

*Dear Folks,*

*I hope you guys got my last letter, October 21st. You see, we were camped along this river and had a flash flood. Some of the guys got their letters back. I didn't, so I don't know if it got through or not. I had sent those pictures back, so let me know if you got them. I lost the first page of that letter when a chopper flew over the tent. Oh well.*

*The sad part of this letter is my platoon sergeant got shot yesterday. It came from some snipers. But he is in good shape. We've been humping the hills lately, and it's been really rough going. You want to know why we get wet almost every day? It's because we are always moving, and there's no time to build a decent shelter. Yes, I do have my raincoat, but not with me. It will come in handy once we get into base camp. I believe in December for a few months. Only seen Rodney Henning twice since September 5th. Did you ever read in the paper about the 1st Cav Division or Operation Irving? Well, that's us. It is us in the 5th of the 7th Cav along with the 1st of the 7th, the 1st and 2nd of the 8th, and the 1st and 2nd of the 12th, combined with the Koreans and Vietnamese Army—and it's also called Operation Thayer. It's hard to explain.*

*Did you get the picture of me crossing the river? I got those pictures of Mike, Darrell, and Diane. I see you still have those letters hanging up, and Mike is trying on my shirts, ha! Yes, he can wear my clothes, except for those hats. I see Darrell needs a shave, and the lawn needs cutting. You guys better shape up. I really like them pictures, wish I could keep them. I missed R&R this month. I have a chance for Bangkok on November 12th or Tokyo on the 24th. If I do, I sure will call home—you better believe it. I'd best close, starting to pour rain.*

*Jungle Will*

The 5/7th Cav had been searching for the enemy in the Kim Son and Song Con Valleys for nine days, finding only rice caches and punji stakes while taking light contact from snipers. On October 29th, they encountered two mines, wounding nine of the battalion's men. That same day, Alpha Company turned eastward, covering three miles into the mountains. They continued their search in the Song Con area for another day until Alpha Company was airlifted to Camp Hammond. While the others pulled security, 1LT Barry Gallagher's 1st Platoon was designated quick reaction force for the 3rd Brigade.

On October 31st, Mr. and Mrs. Leroy Stoflet received a letter from their youngest son, Michael. "They say we'll be able to go back to base camp by the holidays," he wrote, "but I don't think I'll make it that long."

Not much was happening the next day, November 1st. Mike Stoflet was writing another letter to his mom. His platoon leader, 1LT Gallagher, was told that he could send in some men to see Nancy Sinatra's USO show. He sent five of them up to a pickup point from where they would be flown to An Khe.

Minutes later, at 1:30 PM, 1LT Gallagher's radio crackled with an urgent call from CPT Wise. Two helicopters of the 1st Squadron, 9th Cavalry had been shot down. During their rescue attempt, one of their scout platoons had run into an entire battalion of Viet Cong and was pinned down just outside a village near Bong Son. As the quick reaction force, Gallagher's platoon would be flown in to assist. The five who thought they were going to see Nancy Sinatra sing *These Boots Are Made for Walkin'* were quickly rerouted. They linked up with the rest of 1st Platoon as they air assaulted under heavy fire into a large rice paddy.

Just beyond lay the village where the Viet Cong were holed up. After crossing the paddy and starting through waist-high grass, machine gun fire erupted from dug-in bunkers near the village. Rocco Valentino barreled back between Gallagher and radio operator Ray Malinowski, busting the cord that ran between the handset and radio. Malinowski had an extra cord and managed to fix it while lying in the high grass, but they remained pinned down.

Gallagher had noticed some hedgerows at the edge of the village. They could be used for cover if they could just make it there. Through the thick grass, he yelled the order to his men, and they pushed on, low crawling through the grass. Mike Stoflet was out in front and pushing on toward the bunkers. Amid deafening gunfire, Gallagher heard someone shout "Medic!" and watched SP/4 Bill Garcia rise from the ground. He had only advanced a few steps before he was shot in the head. Gallagher crawled to Garcia in the muddy grass. He was unconscious, but his reflexes were still working.

He called for a dustoff but was denied as the area was too hot. Then he felt an intense surge of wind at his back. "I turned as a helicopter suddenly landed behind us," Gallagher recalled. "Two men jumped out under heavy fire and grabbed Garcia, put him on the chopper, and took off. The two men were LTC Trevor Swett and MAJ Robert Jennings. That's how much they loved their men."

At 4:17 PM, the 5/7th's Bravo Company was dropped onto a nearby hilltop called LZ Suzan to join the assault. A downpour commenced as they advanced across the wide rice paddy toward the village. Night fell as the battle continued. After nine hours of intense fighting, the troopers managed to overrun the enemy, though most had escaped into the mountains. They had killed over forty Viet Cong, all of whom had been left behind by the retreating enemy battalion, a sign that they had been beaten badly.

Three soldiers of the 1/9th Cav had been killed in action, as had seven of the 5/7th's Bravo Company. Among the dead was Bravo Company's beloved First Sergeant, Dayton Hare. Several Viet Cong fighters had been concealed in spider holes dug beneath the hedgerow approaching the village. They had waited until 1SG Hare and a handful of others were upon them when they opened fire. Forty-four years old and a veteran of two previous wars, he lay dead outside a village named Quang Ngheim. He would be awarded the Silver Star and Purple Heart. He had also finally earned his Combat Infantryman's Badge. Shortly thereafter, some friends pitched in to send his wife that Noritake Chinaware set he had picked out for her.

During his tour, 1LT Barry Gallagher had four different medics in his platoon but considered SP/4 Bill Garcia the best. "He constantly checked the conditions of the entire platoon," he recalled, "how their feet were as the constant wet would cause rot and took care of punji stake wounds. He died because he cared so much for his fellow troopers." Despite the efforts of LTC Swett and MAJ Jennings, Garcia died before reaching the field hospital at LZ English. From Pacoima, California, he was twenty years old.

Steve Hubbard's favorite uncle, twenty-one-year-old Mike Stoflet, who Garcia had died trying to save, also lay among the dead in the pouring rain. "I told him not to go in," his sergeant told a war correspondent afterward. "He should have thrown a grenade in, but he just said, 'No sweat, I'm going in.' He went through the door, and a machine gun shot him down." He would be awarded the nation's second-highest military honor, the Distinguished Service Cross.

*The President of the United States of America takes pride in presenting the Distinguished Service Cross (Posthumously) to Private First Class Michael Howard Stoflet, United States Army, for extraordinary heroism in connection with military operations involving conflict with an armed hostile force in the Republic of Vietnam, while serving with Company A, 5th Battalion, 7th Cavalry, 1st Cavalry Division.*

*Private First Class Stoflet distinguished himself by exceptionally valorous actions on 1 November 1966, while his unit was being airlifted to reinforce a besieged American unit. As his platoon proceeded north from the landing zone to assist the friendly unit, it came under intense automatic weapons fire from several fortified Viet Cong bunkers. Private First Class Stoflet's squad continued to advance until it was pinned down approximately seventy-five meters short of the hostile positions. Realizing the perilous position his comrades were in, he dauntlessly began a one-man assault on the insurgent emplacement. Despite the murderous volume of fire directed at him, Private First Class Stoflet succeeded in safely reaching the bunker and immediately found an opening through which he could get inside. His first attempt to secure the position was nearly fatal, as a burst of automatic weapons fire sent him reeling backward with a slight head wound. Momentarily stunned, Private First Class Stoflet again disregarded his safety to vault back into the small opening. In this courageous effort to overcome the enemy, he was mortally wounded.*

*His unimpeachable valor in the face of overwhelming odds enabled the platoon to overrun the Viet Cong position and accomplish its mission. Private First Class Stoflet's extraordinary heroism and devotion to duty, at the cost of his life, were in keeping with the highest traditions of the military service and reflect great credit upon himself, his unit, and the United States Army.*

High school friend Karen Gramenz recalled how Mike's was the first military funeral she had been to and how it still haunts her. Classmate Steven Schinke wrote on the Wall of Faces, "Mike was smart, fun, full of life. He was quick to laugh and even quicker to elicit laughter from others. I can only presume that Mike's award was in recognition of the selflessness and derring-do that he so often displayed in school being made manifest in Vietnam with his squad. Even today, we miss him."

The day before his body was returned, Mrs. Stoflet received that final letter Mike had written on November 1st. His older sister Donna recalled how she could see the scar from the initial round that had grazed his scalp. Months later, she would come home to find on her doorstep the last box of cookies she'd sent him—returned to sender and marked "Deceased." Her daughter Terry, who Mike used to drive to the candy store, wrote a poem about his final days, trying to explain—in the words of a sixth-grader—why he did what he did. His younger sister Nancy made one final entry in her *Diary of a Soldier* journal, "November 1st 1966—Was killed in Viet Nam."

Alpha Company's 1st Platoon and Bravo Company searched the village as the dead were evacuated in the dark, and rain continued through the night. The next day, Bravo Company returned to LZ Susan to recover while Charlie Company was flown in to continue the search with 1LT Gallagher's 1st Platoon.

### 2 November '66 – 38 weeks left

*Dear Folks,*

*We finally got a little rest. We're pulling guard at a French security camp called Hammond. Very little worry, and can see for miles around. Don't know for how long. Might leave again 'cause of some fighting going on. If we stay here, I've got a stack of letters to catch up on. So tell Darrell, Mel, Mike, Ronnie, Larry, Doris, Pat, Connie, and Steve that I'll write them all a letter when I get a chance.*

*I tell you, those summer sausages and cheese you sent sure came at the wrong time. When we got here, I ate so much I couldn't move. Then Sergeant Hayslip came with two packages for me. The next day, I took out my dirty old rusty machete and sliced off a couple chunks of meat. It's been a long time since I had a taste of spiced meat and cheese. Still have a few packages of Kool-Aid left.*

*I guess you misunderstood me. Astronomy is not an animal. It is the study of the universe. Remember the time I wanted to learn how to stuff animals, taxidermy? Well, this guy from Pennsylvania took it up, and he made it sound really interesting. This is what Dad and Mike could do for a little hobby. Just get the address out of Sport & Field. For only ten bucks, they'll show you how to mount all kinds of animals. I'm going to try it when I get home. If you want me to buy you Chinaware or a souvenir, let me know. May God take care of you all.*

*Will*

While the others rested at Camp Hammond, Alpha Company's 1st Platoon and Charlie Company continued their search for the enemy, with Bravo Company rejoining them on November 3rd. They ended their mission just after noon on November 4th, searching and clearing a village on the banks of Dam Tra-O, another inlet-type lake near the South China Sea. The 5/7th Cav regrouped at Camp Hammond that night.

The following are excerpts from a letter Donald Rankin wrote on November 5th.

*Dear Mom and Daddy,*

*We're still at the Forward Support Area. It is really great! It gives us time to relax and catch up on letter writing. Yesterday, I got a package from Martha Barnes Lee and Dr. and Mrs. Simpas in Paris. Also, Carolyn sent me a fruit cake from North Carolina. Everyone has really enjoyed it all. I have too much, so about all the company gets a share. I feel kind of guilty. The expense for mailing the stuff is outrageous. Should anyone mention a box, tell them not to spend money on soap. The Army sends us an accessory pack, and soap is the only item that there is enough of.*

*Things have been quiet except for 1st Platoon. They were committed the other day and had two killed and two wounded. It really ticked us off. They should commit us as a company. They sent them to help a battalion that isn't too swift anyway. I'm sure 1st Platoon was being typical aggressive Alpha Company and had no backup support. That platoon has suffered all the killed in action and twelve of our wounded. I was part of that platoon until I was made radio operator. Bravo Company also had heavy losses in that battle. I'd hate to know who they were. Those two real close buddies from Michigan are in that company. We were always together until we became Alpha Company, 5/7th.*

*An NBC news cameraman went with us on a short escapade yesterday. Look closely at the news, and you might see some of us. I don't think I'm in any of them. This is about it. I'll close because I have about fifteen letters to answer.*

*Love,*

*Donnie*

Later that afternoon, Alpha Company was replaced by Bravo and sent out on another mission. The men were told to load up into the back of some deuce-and-a-halfs. At 2:15 PM, they left Camp Hammond, moving north along Highway 1. Turning right onto Highway 504 at the town of Phu My, they headed east toward the coastal plains and steaming rice paddies where they had fought their first major battle. Six miles in along the muddy highway, the convoy stopped at a small bridge spanning the Song Ca, and the troopers jumped out. Less than a quarter-mile away was the Song Ca's twin river, the Siem Giang. On its banks, they could see the ruins of An My, where they had fought on October 4th.

Over the next two days, Alpha Company's men would cover over thirteen miles on foot, making their way around the Vinh Nuoc Ngot inlet. On November 6th, they headed north, crossing another river that emptied into the inlet. Then they marched into the jungles of the Nui Mieu Mountain range. They climbed nearly a thousand feet to the range's southernmost peak, then returned in the same direction, taking a surrendering Viet Cong prisoner during their descent.

Quitting the jungle, they marched out into the sunlight toward the narrow Hung Lac peninsula that separated the inlet from the South China Sea. Moving south along the sandy peninsula, they bivouacked among the dunes and set out ambushes for the night. There was beauty here along the sea, white sand beaches and palm trees. Sampans and other small fishing boats could be seen floating atop the turquoise water. For once, it wasn't raining, and the scenery was a welcome change.

They moved inland at daybreak, traversing around the southern banks of the inlet. They crossed a river and came upon a village where they took five more surrendering Viet Cong. Then they crossed another river and returned to where they had started the day before. They set out their ambushes and spent one last night in the Phu My plain.

The next morning, they set off smoke grenades to mark their position, and Chinooks arrived to lift them off. By 7:45 AM, they were at LZ English, and by 8:37 AM, Hueys were dropping Alpha Company's men onto LZ Catalina, atop a mountain on the north edge of the Cay Giep range where the Bong Son River— known to the Vietnamese as the Song Lai Giang—empties into the sea. They searched for remnants of NVA regiments fought by Charlie Company in their recon mission the night before. It had been a fierce battle, with gunships, artillery, and naval gunfire brought to bear on the enemy. They found nothing. The battalion regrouped at Camp Hammond the next day.

Alpha and Charlie Companies set out again on the morning of November 10th. Again in a convoy of deuce-and-a-halfs, they headed north on Highway 1. When they hit Highway 504, they linked up with a mounted reconnaissance platoon from Delta Company driving armored personnel carriers. They would provide security escort as Alpha and Charlie Companies searched and cleared the many villages along the highway. At 8:14 AM, they came upon a small bridge that had been burned by the Viet Cong. Engineers were dispatched to rebuild it. They continued searching and clearing the next day, finding five more bridges that had been destroyed. They returned to Camp Hammond on the 12th.

Soldiers were always needed to replace the dead, wounded, and those who'd fallen ill. In mid-November, Donald Duncan arrived on a log ship resupplying Alpha Company in the field. From Kentucky, he was the grade school friend of Gene Cross, the soldier who'd survived being shot in the helmet on October 4th. Unlike the replacements who had just arrived in Vietnam, Duncan had come with the original group in August and had been working in the 5/7th's supply shop at An Khe. He'd gotten into a disagreement with his sergeant and had volunteered to come out to the field. Will thought he must be nuts. Leaving the company was Robert Henry, whose brother had just arrived in Vietnam. The Army didn't want to have both serving in a combat zone at the same time, so Henry was sent to Korea.

### 13 November '66 – 35 weeks left

*Dear Folks,*

*Guess it's been a while since I wrote. Wrote to Mel and Darrell. I'll have to write to Darrell again 'cause I wasn't in a good state of mind.*

*We've been moving a lot, and now we're back at Camp Hammond. This morning, this Vietnamese interpreter was teaching me Judo. Man, he weighs about thirty pounds less than me, and he threw me all over the place. I can handle myself against anyone in my platoon, but this cat's too good. Been having a lot of fun with these Soul Brothers (colored people). They're out of sight. Singing and telling jokes, make you die laughing. I get more sleep when we're humping through rice paddies or jungles. Here we're either playing poker, rolling dice, singing, or getting canned up. And then, in the next day or so, we'll go chase V.C.*

*Last week they pulled a dirty trick on us. Told us we had to attack this hill with eighty V.C.s on it. Man, we were scared. And all there was on the hill was N.B.C. taking movies of us. Talk about pissed off. I'd like to... can't say. But the next guy with a camera will be a guy without a camera.*

*This letter got a little wet from the shower we just had, and this dang tent ain't too good either. Man, it's getting hotter than hell out now. I don't care how hard it rains or how many hills and rice paddies we go through, as long as we don't have to fight. When the weather is bad or we're tired and miserable, I always say it could be worse. In fact, the guys here don't understand me. One cat said if I slept in a rice paddy it would be okay, as long as the water wasn't flowing, ha! As long as I don't go through another October 4th, I'll be happy.*

*I remember the first time we searched a village. We were sharp, on our toes, and scared. Now we stumble into a village, flop down in their yard, and make ourselves at home. Only people left are the kids, women, and old men. Kids here are like the kids back home. Give one a piece of candy, and you got the whole village holding their hands out. The old men give us coconut juice. When these people get old, they look like they're a hundred when they might only be fifty years old.*

*We got a guy here, Henry, leaving for Korea. Lucked out. Man, I sure hate to see him go. Heard Graham is coming back from the stockade soon. He'll be back in again, ha! Figueroa bought a twenty-dollar watch from a Vietnamese. Very nice watch, but doesn't work, ha! Just shook hands with Henry. That old fart got my razor too. Says he'll send it back. Yeah, I bet he will.*

*No, Rodney doesn't read the Chippewa paper. Not mine anyway, 'cause I very seldom see him. But I guess his mother sends him the Bloomer paper. I don't know why Rod is discussed. The only company that hasn't fought yet. I guess that's why he always wants to see some action. He should be in Alpha Company. We've seen the most action so far.*

*About forty shopping days left until Christmas, huh? If you guys send me a watch, I'd be real happy. The one I had in Colorado went haywire. If you do, send one with illumination dials. It comes in handy for guard duty at night. Heck, they're singing Christmas carols already. Wish they wouldn't. Makes me homesick. If I get on R&R, I'll send you all presents.*

*Will*

Donald Rankin also wrote home on the 13th.

*Dear Mom and Daddy,*

*Just returned from four days of tramping around the China Sea area. We've been there so many times that it's getting like home. The people recognize us and try to give us food. We captured four VC men and two women. One patrol killed a VC and got his weapon. That area is east of Phu My. It is supposed to be pacified now. The 9th Division is going to move in and occupy the area. Then, we'll move on to some other VC stronghold. Today, we'll go to church services and get our equipment ready to go to Bong Son for four days. We will be a blocking force there. That is usually a very easy job.*

*We're beginning to get a lot of new guys in the company. They are beginning to take seven or eight at a time from the 5/7th battalion and put them in others. This is because we're all due to leave Viet Nam the same time. Should we all stay together, they would have to replace a complete battalion next August. Everyone is really angry that we're getting split up.*

*Several of the guys made E-5 yesterday. Sometimes, I think about being a fire team leader or squad leader and realize that I'd be responsible for the lives of about nine men. However, someone has to do it. So, if the opportunity comes, I might take it. Captain Wise told me last week that if I could get into Warrant Officer school, he would release me. I'd sure like to be a helicopter pilot, but three more years is a long time. Eight to ten months of that would probably be spent over here.*

*Did I send you Nancy's address? Send her a picture for me. It is a real pretty morning. There are a lot of low-flying clouds, and the sun is half-shining. It is good that the clouds are here. The temperature must be a hundred degrees already. This is about all. Tell everyone hello and write soon.*

*Love,*

*Donnie*

On November 14th, Alpha Company air assaulted into the Bong Son plain near Dam Tra-O Lake. They searched and destroyed for three days while a civic action team provided medical services to a nearby village just east of Highway 1. They returned to Camp Hammond on the 16th.

While waiting as a reserve force at Camp Hammond on the 17th, the company was alerted at 3:25 PM. Once again, the 1/9th Cav had made contact. An hour later, they were headed into the highlands, descending onto a mountaintop between the Kim Son Valley and another called Valley 506. In pouring rain, they moved south through the mountains, eventually linking up with a platoon of the 1/9th. Following a creek bed, they kept moving until late in the night and bivouacked in the jungle. They marched northwest the next morning. Again they came up empty-handed and slept in the jungle.

*Michael Stoflet — Dayton Hare — Bill Garcia*

*Michael Stoflet funeral, photo courtesy of Sally Stoflet*

*Father Tom Widdel and Tom Monnier*

# 15
# VALLEY 506

*Just one of those mental pictures that stick in your mind.*

"Everyone remembers that day," remarked Bobby Hansen in his New Jersey accent, speaking of November 19th 1966. He recalled how his squad leader, SSG Elvin Wideman, had received a Dear John letter from his wife just a few days earlier and how his own girl had stopped sending letters weeks ago. LTC Trevor Swett had flown out early that morning to meet with CPT A.J. Wise. He'd also brought an important communique for Alan Weisman. Swett commanded hundreds of soldiers yet remembered Weisman from Fort Carson and how—despite his grave doubts—he'd persuaded him to do his duty. The message informed Weisman that his aunt had passed away and left him over a million dollars. "The only millionaire sleeping in the bush tonight," Weisman joked.

LTC Swett's command chopper took off, and the men continued fruitless searching in the mountains. At 10:07 AM, they were lifted three miles southeast. In an effort to surprise the enemy, the landing zone was not prepped with artillery and bombing in the typical fashion. They assaulted onto a sea of elephant grass in an open area atop a giant hill mass. The sides of the hill were dark and densely forested. 1st and 4th Platoons moved down with the command group toward the rice paddies in the 506 Valley and continued plodding around the base of the hill. Meanwhile, 2nd and 3rd Platoons split up, each hacking through the jungle on opposite sides of the hill.

After four hours of searching, 2nd Platoon radioed, saying they had found human shit on the ground. They kept moving. At once, they found themselves face-to-face with dozens of Viet Cong fighters peering out from well-established bunkers. For what seemed like several seconds but was only a half-second or so, they just stared at each other. It was strange how the enemy had not been expecting them. The jungle surrounding the bunker complex was thick and had likely blocked the sound of their choppers landing.

Gunfire erupted, and they all dove for cover. From behind a fallen tree trunk, 1LT James Harmon yelled, "Keep your heads down!" Lying next to him was his radio operator, Alan Weisman. During a lull in the gunfire, Weisman looked up briefly, attempting to locate the enemy positions as he radioed CPT Wise. He was shot in the head and died there next to Harmon.

2nd Platoon held its ground for the next hour. At 2:30 PM, 3rd Platoon was picked up by choppers and dropped into a position from which they could reach them. They had to climb uphill through broken trails and thick jungle, cross a large ravine, then move around a large knoll to reach 2nd Platoon. Led by 1LT

William Nelson, among those in 3rd Platoon were Bobby Hansen, Jim Hirschuber, Earl Huber, Bill Boyce, John Fitzpatrick, squad leader SSG Elvin Wideman, radio operator Phil Jones, machine gunners Robert Wagner and Guy McNay—and a new guy, Eddie Woodruff, a replacement who had joined the company in October.

The 5/7th Cav would later be recommended for a Presidential Unit Citation. In that recommendation were narratives of their many battles. According to this narrative, "Link up with the platoon in contact by the air assaulted platoon was not possible because of the dense vegetation, darkness, and a large ravine separating the elements." Hansen said the actual reason for their failure to link up with 2nd Platoon was that they were sent up the wrong trail.

Moving around the knoll, they spotted footprints. A few feet in front of Hansen, Huber was on point when he said, "Hey, there's some bunk—," and before he could say "bunkers," the whole forest in front of them exploded. They had been sent around the wrong side of the knoll, right in front of the enemy bunkers, which were now only fifteen feet away. Huber was the first to go down, shot in the leg. The pistol grip of Boyce's rifle was splintered by a bullet that also ripped through his leg. Hirschuber was standing behind a small nub in the ground that held a large tree, and there he took cover. Just to his right, Fitzpatrick was shot in the chest.

SSG Wideman called up his machine gunners. As they rushed forward, McNay was shot in the shoulder, and Wagner fell into a hidden pit filled with punji stakes, and one went through his leg. Hansen found himself pinned down in a fold in the ground next to a tree. As fragments of bark and branches rained down on his back, he watched the tall grass before him being mowed short by the enemy's machine guns. Others in the platoon got online with those in front, and he was able to move back a bit. Huber was badly wounded but smiling as Hansen bandaged his leg. "The war's over for you, pal," Hansen joked. "You'll be boozing it up with the nurses in no time. Hey—why don't you shoot me in the leg, and I'll go with you!"

On Hansen's right, SSG Wideman and radio operator Jones came online. "Come on with me, Jones," Wideman said, and they crawled through the brush toward the bunkers. Jones was hit by four bullets, one through his helmet, one through his pack—another cut through the wire of his radio, and another shot off the antenna.

Wideman continued on a one-man assault, throwing grenades and killing many enemy fighters in their bunkers. Eventually, he was hit by machine gun fire. Crawling back through dense thickets, he'd almost made it to his men when he was hit again, and he ceased to move. Their platoon leader yelled at them to move up, not realizing most of the lead soldiers were already wounded. Wideman was lying about four feet in front of Hansen and Jones and exposed to the enemy bunkers. They were about to make an attempt to drag him back, but the new guy had already moved up in front of them. "It should have been me to go up there with Jones," Hansen remarked about Eddie Woodruff, "but he was already up there. He just stood up and got shot."

Hansen and Jones managed to pull Woodruff by his ankles back down into the brush, but they couldn't reach Wideman. Woodruff had a sucking chest wound and needed to be medevaced. Hansen and Jones wanted to carry him down the hill. They vowed to return, but 1LT Nelson ordered them to stay and fight. As they held their positions through the night, only those who could make it down on their own could be medevaced.

Bravo Company had been flown into a blocking position in the 506 Valley. Charlie Company had also been alerted and was standing by at Camp Hammond, but rain and darkness prevented their take-off.

4th Platoon had dug in at the bottom of the hill when the fighting started, between the tree line and the rice paddy, in a semi-open area where they could fire their mortars. Full artillery could not be used as friendly and enemy were too close to each other. Will and his mortar team, John Bronson, Marvin Bierschbach, and John Fulford, lobbed high-explosive shells at enemy positions nonstop through the night. Others did the same, while some fired continuous illumination rounds to expose any escaping Viet Cong. Fred Brodosi recalled the resupply choppers landing in the paddy, filled to capacity with mortar rounds. Bierschbach remembers this as one of their longest sleepless nights in Vietnam.

The night sky filled with fiercely burning illumination rounds as Huber limped down the hill. "I got a million-dollar wound," he said to SSG Robert Matulac while waiting for the dustoff.

"You forgot to get your lucky insult," Matulac joked.

Matulac recalled this as his scariest night in Vietnam. The casualty collection point was near the edge of the rice paddy, and his job was to call in the medevac. Using flashlights and ground flares to guide in the choppers, he felt like an easy target.

The men advanced on the bunkers at daybreak, only to find the enemy's dead and weapons left behind. The new guy had died during the night. "We could've saved him," Hansen said regretfully. From Napa, California, PFC Edward Woodruff was twenty-four years old. Their squad leader, SSG Elvin Wideman, who Woodruff had died trying to save, was also dead.

Mangled enemy bodies littered the blood-soaked ground. Blood trails could be seen leading from the bunkers into the jungle. Staggered about the hillside, the bunkers were elaborate affairs, fortified by large logs and packed down with dark, reddish-colored mud. Most emptied into tunnels where they found more weapons and bodies lying in pools of semi-coagulated blood. The weapons were gathered, the bodies stacked and counted.

The battle-weary men of 2nd and 3rd Platoons descended like ghosts through the morning fog. They walked along a trail to where the company was gathering near the banks of the rice paddy. Matulac walked in the opposite direction, intending to find his friend Alan Weisman. He saw that many were badly wounded. Then came radio operator Phil Jones with a hole in the front of his helmet. As Jones walked past, he noticed another hole in the back. "Are you hurt?" Matulac asked.

"Nope," Jones replied.

Hirschuber recalled Curtis Zechman's neck bleeding and how he was completely unaware that he'd been shot. The bullet had lodged beneath his skin and was still stuck in his neck. He didn't believe it until he felt the bullet for himself.

Matulac and a few others carried Weisman down the hill. Dead bodies are heavy, and their muscles were weak. They bumped his head on the chopper door while lifting him in. "Sorry, Alan," Matulac said, forgetting he wasn't really there.

My dad remembers watching the dead being carried down the hill that foggy morning. As rigor mortis had set in, the arm of one was sticking straight up as they carried his body to the chopper. Just one of those mental pictures that stick in your mind.

Among the dead were PFC John Fitzpatrick from Franklin, Wisconsin, and SP/4 Coley White from Wiley Ford, West Virginia. With five killed in action, this was the most fatalities Alpha Company had taken in a single day.

Leaving behind his wife Joanne, their son Joseph, their daughter Sharyl Ann—and his younger brother Ron, who thought of him more as a father—SSG Elvin Wideman would be awarded the Distinguished Service Cross.

*The President of the United States takes pride in presenting the Distinguished Service Cross (Posthumously) to Elvin Joseph Wideman, Staff Sergeant, U.S. Army, for extraordinary heroism in connection with military operations involving conflict with an armed hostile force in the Republic of Vietnam, while serving with Company A, 5th Battalion, 7th Cavalry, 1st Cavalry Division (Airmobile).*

*Staff Sergeant Wideman distinguished himself by exceptionally valorous actions on 19 November 1966 while serving as a squad leader with elements of the 7th Cavalry on a search and destroy mission near Bong Son. When the lead element became heavily engaged with a Viet Cong force, his platoon moved forward to provide fire support. As the unit maneuvered into position, it was suddenly pinned down by intense automatic weapons fire from several fortified bunkers to their immediate front. Pinpointing the insurgent positions, Sergeant Wideman directed three of his men to cover him as he dauntlessly crawled forward alone. When he arrived at a point near one bunker, he threw a grenade into it and destroyed the emplacement. With complete disregard for his safety,*

*Sergeant Wideman then ran through the fierce hostile barrage to another emplacement, where he killed all the Viet Cong with his rifle. Unmindful of the inherent dangers, Sergeant Wideman courageously advanced toward another bunker a few meters away. As he raised up to toss a grenade, he was mortally wounded by machine gun fire. With the last effort of his strength, he flung the grenade into the emplacement, killing all the insurgents inside.*

*His conspicuous gallantry saved many of his comrades from death or injury and contributed immeasurably to the defeat of the Viet Cong force. Staff Sergeant Wideman's extraordinary heroism and devotion to duty, at the cost of his life, were in keeping with the highest traditions of the military service and reflect great credit upon himself, his unit, and the United States Army.*

Over thirty Viet Cong had been killed, and an enemy camp destroyed. The men formed human conveyor belts to remove all that was left in the enemy bunkers. They hauled out weapons, ammunition, fifteen pounds of clothing, an inch-thick stack of documents, and one of those funny-looking grenades with a handle called a ChiCom.

Relieving them in place, Charlie Company helicoptered in at 10:00 AM. Those same choppers flew Alpha Company back to Camp Hammond to recover. Bravo and Charlie continued searching for what was left of the enemy. Over the next two days, they found many more dead Viet Cong fighters in the surrounding jungle, along with abandoned weapons and equipment—frag grenades, AK-47 rifles, machetes, mines, anti-tank grenades, rocket launchers, Bangalore torpedoes, more documents, over a thousand 7.62mm rounds, and over a ton of rice.

Donald Rankin wrote home the next day, November 21st.

*Dear Mom and Daddy,*

*Yesterday, we returned to the forward support area after a very gruesome week. Most of it was spent cutting through the jungle hunting Viet Cong. Sunday, our 2nd Platoon went on a patrol and walked right into the middle of a Viet Cong camp. Our 3rd Platoon was flown in to help them, and they ran into an even larger group. They fought for about three hours. It got dark, and both platoons had to stay in the jungle all night. We fired mortars around our two platoons all night to keep anyone from getting to them. Yesterday morning, the rest of Alpha Company, along with another platoon from another company, went up to bring out the dead and wounded. We had five killed and eight or ten wounded. It was sure a sad morning yesterday, but we are lucky that all of those two platoons weren't killed. There was at least a company of Viet Cong hidden in the thick trees and vines with bunkers that our mortars would hardly shake. Jones had a close call. A bullet went through his helmet, shot his radio antenna off, and cut the handset off. He didn't even have a bump on his head.*

*Yesterday afternoon, they brought us back in. We're all doing pretty good. My feet are kind of rotten. We get ringworm and impetigo all over us if we don't put zinc oxide on every little scratch. My left ankle is swollen, but the soreness has gone. I guess it is from the rough walking and jumping from the helicopters!*

*The other day, we jumped from the helicopter and ran for cover. I tried to jump what I thought was a small puddle. I tripped and went in up to my neck. We all got a big laugh out of it. That afternoon and night, we walked for six hours along a creek through thick jungle, rain all the way, to get to a platoon that had encountered the Viet Cong earlier that day. We didn't encounter any action but were we beat.*

*I'm still receiving a lot of mail and packages. There are about ten or twelve letters in my helmet that I haven't had a chance to answer. Suzie sent me a box yesterday. I'm about sick from eating so much. We stuff ourselves after having nothing but C-Rations for six or seven days.*

*I'm still considering being a helicopter pilot. What do you all think? I would probably be back in the states by January. Go to Alabama for nine months and then be reassigned. Also, I'd probably have to come back here for twelve months. That wouldn't be too bad. The VC don't like to shoot at helicopters because they carry some really potent machine guns and rockets. Should I do that, I would get E-5 pay and clothing allowance—and if I didn't get my commission, I'd still be E-5 and get a good job. My commander talked about it last night. At first, he wouldn't say much, but twice in the last three weeks he has suggested that I try it.*

*Yesterday, I got a new uniform. I had worn the other one for two and a half months. It was getting a little frayed. The weather has been unbearably cool and rainy. Some nights, we almost shook our teeth out. This is all for now. Maybe I'll have time to write more after this week.*

*Love,*

*Donnie*

  A few days later, a log ship arrived with supplies and two more soldiers from the rear-echelon. Like Donald Duncan, who had arrived the week before, they'd also been working in the battalion supply shop at An Khe. Unlike Duncan, they had not come to the field by choice. One was a thin black fellow named Robert Cain. The other was Russell Ferrebee. Nicknamed "Porky," he was a chubby, disheveled soldier whose helmet was usually crooked and who was always getting yelled at by his sergeants. Both were nice kids, Bob Matulac recalled. It is not remembered what they had done, only that they had pissed someone off at base camp and had been sent to the field.

Bill Boyce—the one who had gotten his rifle shot up with fragments stuck in his leg—could not find his weapon after recovering from his wounds. Just like SGT J.C. Jackson, he would receive a bill from the Army. He opted to make payments on his debt, sending the Army exactly one dollar each month.

Due to the incident with SSG Harry Coit aboard the Gaffey, Arnott Graham had been in Long Binh Jail since arriving in-country. A military stockade near Saigon designed to hold approximately four hundred prisoners, the facilities at Long Binh were makeshift, and conditions notoriously harsh. Soldiers were sent there for everything from drug possession and going AWOL to rape and murder. A tall fence topped with concertina wire and guard towers surrounded the perimeter. Most prisoners were kept in tents with wooden floors.

Racial tensions were simmering throughout the Army just as they were back home. The squalid conditions of the stockade only aggravated matters. On September 5th 1966, those tensions boiled over. Graham recalled how it all started when a couple of bad dudes attacked two guards. One was about six-foot-four, and the other was also a big guy. They were both troublemakers, and one was in for attempted murder. The attack sparked a riot that continued until the following day. Graham wanted no part of the riot and just wanted to survive.

The next morning, the compound was filled with tear gas to subdue the prisoners. Graham hid in one of the sandbag bunkers built to protect against mortar attacks. He held a wet towel to his face as the gas burned his skin and eyes. He thought he would suffocate and was nearly unconscious when the gas finally lifted. Many had been seriously hurt at the outset of the riot, and some guards had been nearly beaten to death. Many more were injured when a company of MPs stormed in to take charge following the gas attack.

Now in the last week of November, Graham was about halfway through his six-month sentence. He was reading a copy of *Stars & Stripes* when he learned of Alpha Company's battle on November 19th and how Alan Weisman had been killed. He sat there contemplating his friend's death when a voice came over the intercom, "Prisoner Graham, report to the front gate for release." Although he'd only served half his sentence, they desperately needed replacements, and he was being sent to the field. He would continue at two-thirds pay for the full six months, however. Soon he was on a resupply chopper headed for Alpha Company in the jungle.

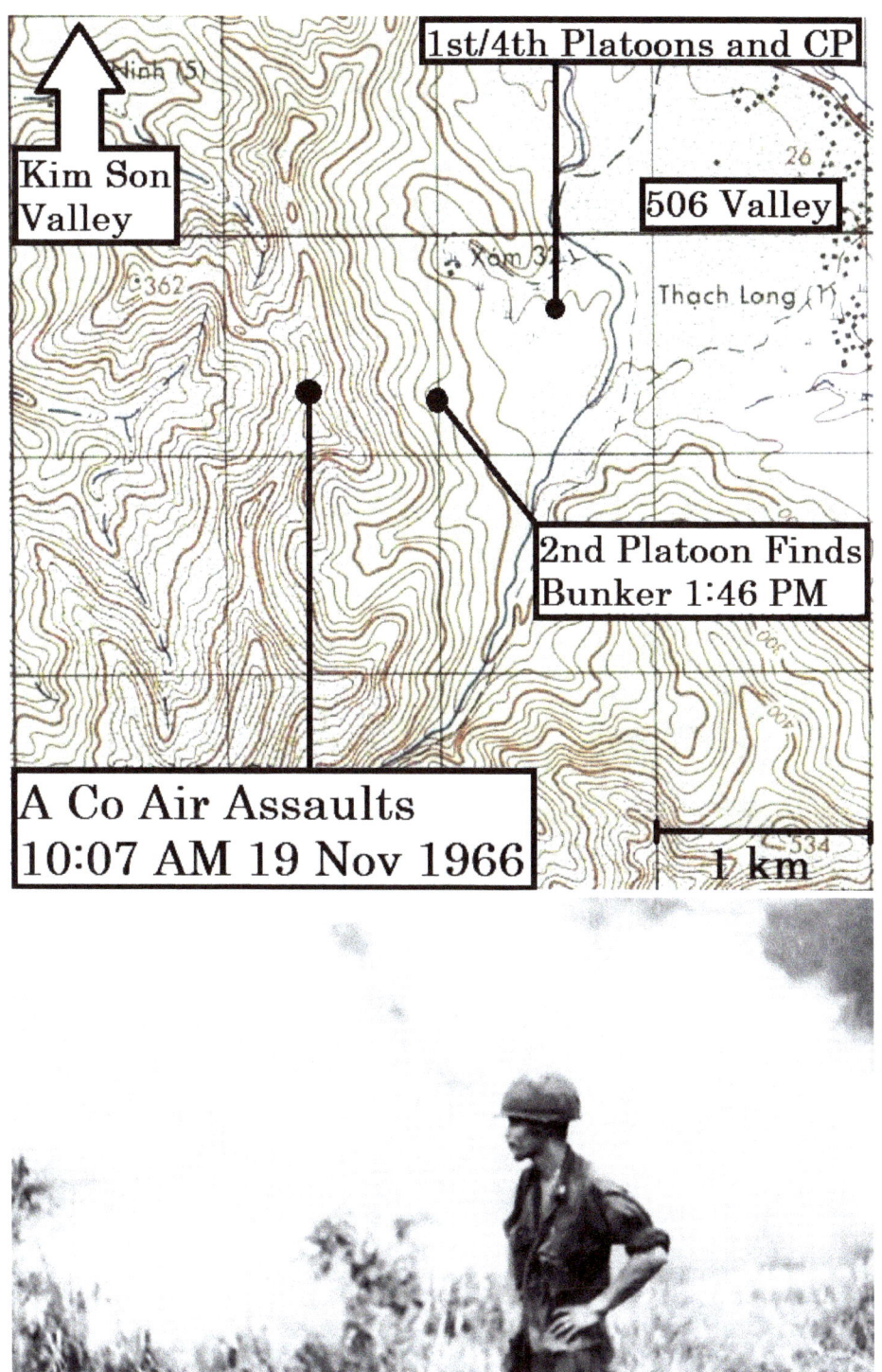

*Robert Matulac marking position for choppers*

*Edward Woodruff — Coley White*

*Elvin Wideman — John Fitzpatrick*

*Bill Boyce, photo by Robert Matulac*

*Martin Quinn with captured enemy weapon, photo by Will Bowe*

# 16
# THANKSGIVING

*Today the heavens cried for him.*

The following (abridged) excerpts are from a Viet Minh officer's diary quoted in Bernard Fall's *Street Without Joy*.

*...but the planes dived upon us without firing their guns. All of a sudden, Hell opens in front of my eyes. Hell comes in the form of large egg-shaped containers dropping from the first plane, followed by other eggs from the second and third planes. Immense sheets of flame extending over hundreds of meters strike terror in the ranks of my soldiers. This is napalm, the fire which falls from the skies.*

*Another plane swoops down behind us and again drops a napalm bomb. The bomb falls closely behind us, and I feel its fiery breath touching my whole body. The men are now fleeing in all directions, and I cannot hold them back. There is no way of holding out under the torrent of fire, which flows out in all directions and burns everything in its passage. On all sides, flames surround us now... His eyes were wide with terror. "What is this, the atomic bomb?" No, it is napalm.*

It was Thanksgiving Day. The morning of November 24th 1966 started like any other as Alpha Company's men rose from beneath their ponchos. Five days had passed since their battle on the 19th. They did what soldiers in the field typically do in the morning, relieving themselves, checking for leeches, and smoking a cigarette or two. The few who took them off at night checked their boots for snakes or other wildlife. Those who practiced field hygiene brushed their teeth or even shaved. Some made instant coffee in their metal canteen cups.

Amid the clanking and grumbling of a waking infantry company, Donald Rankin penned another letter to Blair Richards, his old college roommate. He wrote of how he planned to return to Vietnam after this was all over to help the poor people of the villages recover from the war. Addressed and in its envelope, he stuck the letter in his pocket, intending to send it on the next log ship.

Well into their third month in the field and in nearly constant rain, their feet were in rough shape, and many were falling ill. They had been promised new fatigues and an extended recovery at An Khe. But for now, Operation Thayer II marched on. The plan was for Alpha Company to act as a blocking force for Charlie Company's sweep through a village. Then they would fly to Camp Hammond for Thanksgiving dinner.

The day before, Alpha Company had been dropped into the mountains between the Kim Son and An Lao Valleys. Perhaps the most beautiful in the Central

Highlands, the valley of An Lao also had a reputation as the deadliest. Dominated by steep, towering mountains covered with dense triple-canopy jungle on both sides, the expansive river valley was dotted with villages. At its southernmost reaches, the valley curled sharply to the west, then back to the north, creating a fishhook shape. Following the previous day's air assault, Alpha Company had marched north, approaching the edge of that fishhook. They had encamped on a small hill overlooking a vast rice paddy about a half-mile wide.

On the other side of that rice paddy, a large village of about twenty small huts known as Van Hoi was occupied by an NVA battalion. The rice paddy wrapped around the south and west sides of the village. A small river ran through the village. To its north rose lightly wooded foothills that intermittently cradled terraced rice paddies and eventually led up to a large forested mountain called Nui Dat Set. It was monsoon season, and the rice paddies were all deeply flooded.

Joe Sanchez had been sent to LZ English for some medical treatment and was to return to the field that morning. He was waiting to board a Chinook headed out to resupply Alpha Company, but the crew chief told him there was no room and he would have to wait until tomorrow.

It was still early morning when Alpha Company's men started down the hill and across the expansive rice paddy toward Van Hoi. As they approached, slow-moving fighter planes flew above, strafing suspected enemy positions surrounding the village with their guns. One of the pilots gave SSG Robert Matulac a thumbs-up as he flew by. He felt his radio operator Kenneth Rathyen was following too closely. "Spread it out," he said. Just then, large casings from another plane's machine guns landed on Rathyen's helmet, causing him to go cross-eyed.

Alpha Company would move around to the north side of the village and serve as a blocking force for Charlie Company as they swept through the village from the south. Charlie Company's landing zone would be just south of the village—in the middle of the same wide-open paddy Alpha Company was now crossing—and so Alpha Company's 3rd Platoon was left here to secure the LZ.

After crossing a ravine on its southern edge, the rest of Alpha Company—surprised they hadn't taken fire yet—skirted cautiously around the western edge of the palm tree-laden village. They did not enter but did encounter a small handful of out-lying huts in their path. They searched the huts, finding only the usual women, children, animals, and old men. They continued on, wading through more rice paddies, eventually reaching their blocking position at the base of a long-rising foothill about three hundred yards northwest of the village. They waited here for several minutes.

At 9:00 AM, the first wave of Charlie Company's platoons descended toward Alpha Company's 3rd Platoon in the rice paddy on the opposite side of the village. All hell broke loose as machine gun fire erupted from the village. 3rd Platoon's

Bobby Hansen was carrying an M-60 machine gun as he watched Charlie Company's troops jump into the water. He couldn't hear the gunfire beneath the thumping of the choppers but could tell by the expressions on their faces that they were getting shot at. The NVA had simply waited for the choppers to arrive before unleashing their guns on what they'd thought was a secure landing zone.

CPT Bernard Grady had recently taken command of Charlie Company. He told of how they came in under heavy fire from the village during their approach, how the choppers banked evasively to the right and ascended, and how he and his men were forced to jump out at a height approaching twenty feet. With only earthen dikes providing cover and a wide expanse to cross, Charlie Company sloshed toward the village with Alpha Company's 3rd Platoon.

The rest of Alpha Company started back toward the village from the opposite side. Machine gun fire broke out from its northwest corner, and everyone lay in the muck behind the dikes. Water shot up about fifty yards in front of Matulac. Then another round splashed about ten yards closer, then another even closer. Searching for the sniper, he recalled reading about the battle in the Ia Drang Valley the year prior and how many snipers were positioned in trees. He saw a row of trees just north of the village. From left to right, he began firing into each one. After putting a few rounds into the fourth tree, he saw a rifle drop. He shot a few more rounds and watched a body fall to the ground.

The battle intensified, and throngs of civilians could be seen running from the village. With many already lying wounded in the muddy water, Charlie Company's men struggled across the rice paddy as the village was pummeled by artillery and mortars.

Fighting continued with little movement for about twenty minutes until two bombers descended from distant clouds to their south. Troopers on both sides of the village set off smoke grenades to mark their positions, then hunkered down in the muck behind the dikes. Radio operator Royce Barrow could hear the rumbling of their jet engines growing louder. As they approached, he watched green tracer rounds shooting up at the bombers as canisters of napalm cartwheeled through the air. Erupting walls of flame shook the earth and sent ripples through the muddy water as spinning pieces of huts flew about the burning village, and the sky was on fire.

A third jet approached just as Charlie Company prepared to assault the village. Both of its bombs fell tragically short, directly on top of one of Charlie Company's platoons. Just outside the blast zone, CPT Grady felt an intense thermal wave flash across his skin as flames spread across the water, and he saw mud, helmets, and men sent flying in all directions. Amid the confusion, screaming, and the smell of napalm—like that of burnt rubber and gasoline—he waded through the paddy to find that one of his men, Private-Two (PV2) Eddie Lopez, had been killed instantly. Several others were severely burned. Through the handset of his radio, Barrow heard the voice of CPT Grady yelling over the battalion net, "Tell them to drop the bombs on the damn village, not us!"

Grady stayed on the radio, trying to call off that final jet. It banked for its final run at the village, then dropped its last bomb. It hit the curved base of a palm tree near the village and was lobbed back out into the paddy. Grady and his men watched the giant oblong canister wobble through the air above them for several seconds before bellyflopping in the water, splashing them with mud. Fortunately, this last one was a dud.

Heavy fighting subsided following the bombing. Alpha Company's 3rd Platoon was picked up by choppers and dropped into a position far to the northeast of the village to block any surviving fighters from escaping into the mountains. The rest of Alpha and Charlie Company cautiously advanced through the smoldering village. Marvin Bierschbach recalled finding the bodies of snipers around the surrounding trees and how some were hanging from those trees. Many more dead were found within the village. Little was left aside from burning huts, dead animals, and a few live ones scurrying about and making a terrible racket.

At LZ English, a chopper that was to bring Alpha Company's Thanksgiving dinner was quickly repurposed as supply clerks threw out food containers in exchange for crates of ammunition.

At 1:17 PM, Bravo Company was flown in from Camp Hammond to replace 3rd Platoon in their blocking position, and 3rd Platoon was flown back to rejoin Alpha Company. As they descended near Alpha Company's position, Matulac watched green tracers from a distant tree line rip through the choppers as the men jumped into the muck. The helicopters seemed to be magnets for enemy bullets, and again they were under fire. They were supposed to have jumped out on the side opposite of the enemy fire, but Bobby Hansen jumped out the wrong side with his assistant gunner, Brian Ravese. Matulac recalled the sight of Ravese, who wore thick glasses, trying to link up with Hansen after being separated during their landing. Sergeants were yelling at him to go one way and then the other. Mud and water exploded all around him as he splashed and struggled through the waist-high muck.

The choppers flew away, and there was a lull in the fighting. CPT Wise rose to his feet along with his radio operator, Donald Rankin. Over the company net, he advised the platoon leaders that they were moving back to their original blocking position at the base of the long-rising hill. As Rankin followed, Wise took only two steps before a sniper's bullet meant for him struck Rankin in the head. Death came instantly as he splashed into the water under the weight of his radio, his rifle and helmet, grenades and bandoliers of extra ammunition. Those nearest looked down to see Rankin lying face up in the water, eyes open as if looking up to the sky, blood spreading out around his head. CPT Wise was still holding the handset attached to the radio on his back.

They returned fire, and Matulac removed the radio from Rankin's back and strapped it to his own. With rifles slung over their shoulders, three men pulled Rankin's body from the muck while two others stretched a poncho. Quinn, Hansen, Will, and a few others started carrying his body back toward the hill, and a hard rain fell. Martin Quinn, who wanted to live, recalled how he was always afraid of getting shot, yet while carrying Rankin through the waist-high water for what seemed an eternity, he felt no fear, only numbness and exhaustion.

After crossing the wide rice paddy, they struggled up the long-rising hill, and a dustoff descended as they reached a flat area near the top. Several wounded men were loaded on in the pouring rain, and then Rankin, and my dad recalls how part of his skull was missing as they heaved him onto the chopper.

Beyond the hill lay another rice paddy, and beyond that, a dense jungle ascended into the mountains. 1LT Barry Gallagher's 1st Platoon passed through the command group to lead the way down the back of the hill and through the rice paddy. Fearing an ambush, he argued but was ordered to keep moving. He sent one squad to the right, across from a wooded area on the other side of the paddy, another to the left, then started through the middle with the rest of his men. About halfway across, machine guns erupted from the wooded area. Several men fell immediately, chaotic fighting resumed, and Gallagher radioed for gunships.

Matulac was taking cover next to one of their medics when 1SG John Potter walked by. "Top, they're still shooting out there!" he yelled.

"I know," replied Potter as he trudged into the paddy. He dragged back one of the wounded to Matulac and the medic, then went back out for another of their wounded, and then another.

As Alpha Company troops pulled their dead and wounded from the water, Charlie Company pursued the enemy through the jungle for about two miles, to another small village near Bravo Company's blocking position, where eight were taken prisoner. They had shed their uniforms and weapons but were determined to be NVA regulars. Under intense interrogation by ARVN interpreters, none would give up where they had stashed their weapons.

Five more Alpha Company men had just been killed. Will, Bierschbach, and a few others used their own ponchos to cover the bodies. One of them was Gene Cross's grade school friend, SP/4 Donald Duncan, the supply clerk who'd volunteered to come to the field just a week before. Also among the dead—SP/4s Robert Cain from Sumter, South Carolina, and Russell Ferrebee from West Union, West Virginia—the two who had been sent to the field for pissing someone off at base camp. It had been their first and only combat operation.

Also killed was nineteen-year-old PFC Malcolm Brouhard, the replacement soldier who'd just gotten married in October and had been with Alpha Company for less than a month—the one whose younger brother recalled pointing to his wedding ring from the train window as he left for the war.

Also nineteen years old was PFC Thomas Erickson from Saint Paul, Minnesota. In *The Faces Behind the Names*, Tommy's older brother Marv recalls, "Tom's last letter home was dated November 22nd 1966. My mother received the letter two days after she was informed of his death. I lost a brother, a friend, and a good part of my childhood memories on November 24th 1966, but my mother lost one of her children. My mother had been through a lot in her life, including a number of surgeries, divorce, and poverty, but nothing took the spirit out of her like the violent death of her son. She died less than five years later, and I know she thought about Tommy every day."

The rain had briefly stopped, and the five dead were still lying in the field. Matulac had called in another dustoff. Circling above, the pilot radioed, asking when their last contact was. "About an hour ago," Matulac advised. The pilot refused to come in, saying the LZ was too hot. Matulac was still carrying Rankin's radio. He'd tried to find someone to take it but couldn't. He walked off to a secluded area near a small stream. He knelt down to wash off the blood and brain matter from his friend's radio. Even after the deaths of his friends Sam Daily, Bill Garcia, and Alan Weisman, he'd managed to keep hold of his emotions. But as he started his task, something inside him broke open, and he just knelt in the stream and cried.

It was getting dark, and a Chinook was en route with their Thanksgiving dinner. Box-shaped mermite containers filled with turkey, gravy, mashed potatoes, cranberry sauce, and all the fixings were on board. The chopper took sniper fire as it approached, and the crew started hastily throwing down food containers as they hovered twelve feet from the ground. Robert Wagner tried to keep the containers from falling over as they dropped. Except for some spilled gravy, he succeeded. The sniper was suppressed, the chopper landed, and the rest of the food was unloaded. "I was in tears, unloading a box of vegetables," Barry Gallagher recalled. "The chopper blew back the ponchos covering my men. I'll never forget the look on the crew chief's face when he saw the bodies."

Matulac told the pilot of their five dead. He said they couldn't take them as they would have to decontaminate before hauling more food. Matulac was desperate and threatening the pilot. He finally agreed. Gerald Anderson recalled how scared he was, how he sometimes couldn't breathe, and how they unloaded turkey and then loaded dead bodies onto the same helicopter.

There was more than enough to go around, and it started raining again as they ate their Thanksgiving meal. Royce Barrow recalled how they hadn't eaten all day and were starving, and how he couldn't eat because his best friend was dead, and how he still owed him the sixty dollars he'd borrowed for R&R, and then he stopped abruptly—because he had to—because after fifty-some years, he still feels the same pain he felt on that day. "He was liked by everybody, not an enemy in the world," he said of Donald Rankin. "My best friend and good buddy."

CPT A.J. Wise had spent as much time with Rankin as anyone since bringing him on as his radio operator at Fort Carson, often sharing a tent or foxhole. Some noted how he was never quite the same after Rankin's death.

Joe Sanchez was still at LZ English. That afternoon, he had watched a medevac chopper land with the first of Alpha Company's casualties. Frantic activity started about the field hospital. Through the rain and mud, Sanchez and SP/5 Richard Cantale rode a mechanical mule, a small utility vehicle, toward the medical tent. They came upon a row of jungle boots in the mud outside the tent. Next to the boots were helmets filled with rainwater and blood.

The next day, Cantale wrote a letter home. It was featured in *Dear America: Letters Home From Vietnam*, edited by Bernard Edelman and published by W.W. Norton & Co. The book was later made into an HBO documentary.

*25 Nov 66*

*Hello dear folks:*

*It's going to be hard for me to write this, but maybe it will make me feel better.*

*Yesterday after our big dinner my company was hit out in the field while looking for VC. We got the word that one boy was killed and six wounded. So the doctor, medics and the captain I work for went over to the hospital to see the boys when they came in and see how they were.*

*The first sergeant came in the tent and told me to go over to the hospital and tell the captain that six more KIAs were coming in. When I got there, they asked if anyone from A Co was there. I just happened to be there, so they told me that they needed someone to identify a boy they just brought in from my company. He was very bad, they said. So I went into the tent. There on the table was the boy. His face was all cut up and blood all over it. His mouth was open, his eyes were both open. He was a mess. I couldn't really identify him.*

*So I went outside while they went through his stuff. They found his ID card and dog tags. I went in, and they told me his name—Rankin. I cried, "No, God it can't be." But sure enough, after looking at his bloody face again I could see it was him. It really hit me hard because he was one of the nicest guys around. He was one of my good friends. No other KIA or WIA hit me like that. I knew most of them, but his was the first body I ever saw and, being my friend, it was too much. After I left the place, I sat down and cried. I couldn't stop it. I don't think I ever cried so much in my life. I can still see his face now. I will never forget it.*

*Today the heavens cried for him. It started raining at noon today and has now finally just stopped after 10 hours of the hardest rain I have ever seen.*

*Love,*

*Richard*

Weeks later, upon returning home from Rankin's funeral, his old college roommate, Blair Richards, would receive a letter in a mud-stained envelope. Dated November 24th 1966, someone had found it in Rankin's pocket and put it in the mail. "The envelope was muddy," Blair noted on the Wall of Faces, "but the contents still ring out to me. He was concerned about the innocent people of Vietnam and was troubled that he couldn't do more for them."

A dark thunderhead loomed in the distance as night fell. Alpha and Charlie Companies remained in the field while Bravo Company airlifted to Camp Hammond with the prisoners. Robert Powers of Bravo Company recalled guarding one of the wounded NVA soldiers they had taken to Camp Hammond that night. Lying on the ground, he was visibly in pain. Powers covered him with his poncho and waited for some military intelligence officer to come and pick up the prisoner. His small act of compassion was acknowledged with a pained nod of the man's head. Their own Thanksgiving meal had just arrived. Powers struggled to eat as much of it as he could before the rain washed it all off his paper plate. By the time he'd finished, the prisoner was dead.

Meanwhile, Alpha Company's men prepared for a long night in the field. At once, the drizzling rain grew into a torrential downpour, filling their foxholes with water as they dug in near a tree line at the edge of the valley. As Will and others had given up their only form of shelter to cover the dead, they gathered whatever ponchos they had left. Under a makeshift tent of sorts, they huddled together as the downpour continued.

About 3:00 AM, a shot rang out, followed by a scream of pain. Bobby Hansen recalled how he thought they were once again under fire. Actually, one of their new replacements had just shot himself in the ankle. It wasn't an accident. His shattered foot was treated by their medics, but the monsoon was too intense for a dustoff to come in. Amid the pouring rain, his cries could be heard through the night. And so ended my dad's worst day in Vietnam.

### *27 November '66 – 32 weeks left*

Dear Folks,

*I am finally getting to write. I am just going to say I am in bad shape. Ain't been dry for almost a week and have very sore feet. Man, am I ever getting sick of this damn rain. I guess we're going back to base camp for a couple of months. You must know by now that I spent a night with Rod on one operation. Well, I am sending this letter now. Write more soon, I hope.*

*Will*

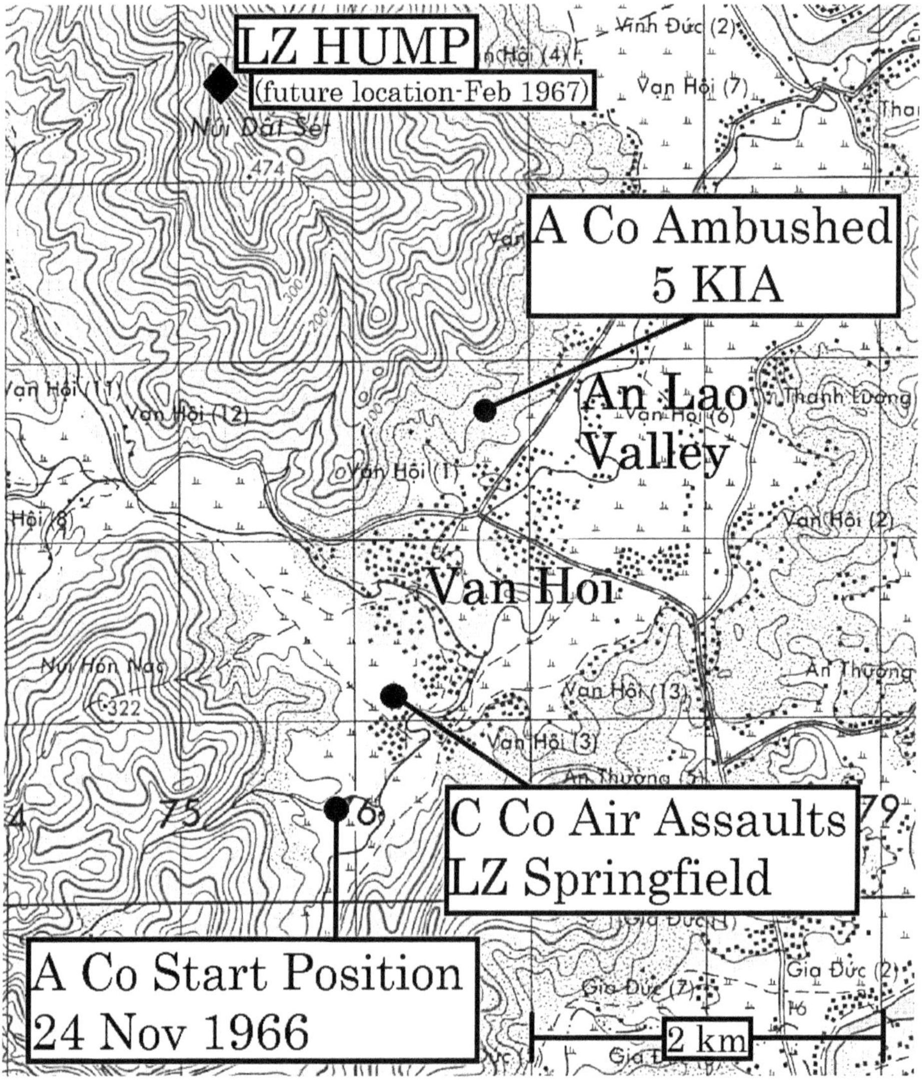

*Robert Cain — Russell Ferrebee*

*Donald Rankin — Malcolm Brouhard*

*Thomas Erickson — Eddie Lopez*

# 17
# THE BEST DAY

*How some people make a career out of the Army, I'll never know.*

The rain continued the day after Thanksgiving. The battalion had planned to bring both Alpha and Charlie Companies back in, but poor flying conditions prevented this. And so, Alpha Company marched a short distance up into the jungle-covered side of Nui Dat Set Mountain and spent another night in the area. The next morning, they moved back down into the valley. At 11:37 AM, they were airlifted to Camp Hammond, where they pulled security for the rest of the month.

On December 1st 1966, LTC Trevor Swett relinquished command of the 5/7th Cav to LTC Charles Canham. He had fallen ill and could no longer continue. Battalion commanders in Vietnam were not typically held in high regard by the lower ranks, and change of command ceremonies are among the most boring events in any young soldier's life. Yet LTC Swett was well-respected by all and genuinely cared about each of the hundreds of soldiers he led. He had been with them since their days at Fort Carson and was a father figure to many. He spoke of the honor of leading such a fine group of men and remembered, by name, each of those who had given their lives. "There was not a dry eye in the formation," said Barry Gallagher.

That same day, Bravo Company suffered six killed in action in a confrontation known as the Battle of Phu Huu II in the Kim Son Valley. One of the six, PFC Lewis Albanese, would be awarded the Medal of Honor.

### 3 December '66 – 32 weeks left

*Dear Folks,*

*Sorry for not writing as often as I should. We were pretty busy last month. Well, we're a few days from going back to An Khe. I feel pretty sick now. First time since I've been in Viet Nam. We've been here at Camp Hammond for almost a week. Rodney is the head of his company? Maybe his platoon but not his company. He is pretty sharp—I know, he can carry a radio. Yeah, I got a letter from Don Mc Ilquham the other day. He is going to be in the same place I am now, Camp Hammond.*

*Hey, guess what—the Bloomer high school Homemakers of America girls sent me a shoebox full of goodie bars. I'll have to write a thank you letter. What makes you think I can play that recording you sent? I think I can play it on this guy's tape recorder. Someone just told me I got a box from a church. Guess I'll go up to the command post tent and get it. It's supper time now, and I only ate* a can of fruit today. Wondering how we get beer? The Army sells us beer from the states, and the Vietnamese sell beer of their own.

So Mike got lost while hunting, ha! Well, he'll still have a chance to get one. I should be getting a letter from Larry telling me about his buck.

R&R is five days but takes about ten for travel and getting ready. I hope to go in January or February. All I'm looking forward to now is rest and the Bob Hope show.

Will

*7 December '66 – 31 weeks left*

Dear Folks,

And now we are very sure of going back to An Khe. A five percent chance of going. This makes the 999th rumor so far. Well, that's about all for now. Forgot to say that half the company is sick or something.

So long,

Will

At 10:45 AM on December 8th, the ragged battle-weary men of the battalion started back to An Khe in a convoy of trucks. As Operation Thayer II continued in the field, the 5/7th Cav officially took responsibility for Camp Radcliff's defense, known as Green Line duty, on December 10th.

Since leaving An Khe in September, engineers had built wooden barracks for the battalion. They had also constructed a mess facility. Named Hare Hall, a small three-foot-tall cement pedestal and plaque stood just outside its entrance in memory of Bravo Company's fallen First Sergeant, Dayton Hare, who was killed on November 1st along with twelve others, including Alpha Company's Michael Stoflet and medic Bill Garcia.

Although a drastic improvement from their life in the field, An Khe was not exactly Club Med. The men worked long hours in the heat, guarding posts and manning towers along the perimeter. The buildings and tents were infested with rats, and each month, the medical detachment at An Khe administered rabies shots to approximately ten soldiers that had been bitten by rats, monkeys, dogs, mongooses, banana cats, or other potentially rabid animals. Platoons were sent out on night patrols outside the perimeter—but at least they could return to base camp in the morning, where their standard of living seemed luxurious.

Observing the routines of those who worked on base, it became clear to many of the infantrymen that they had chosen the wrong profession. Soldiers in the artillery, armor, and other combat arms branches often refer to those in non-combat arms branches, such as supply or signal, as POGs—People Other than Grunts. Of course, infantrymen consider anyone not in the infantry to be POGs, combat arms or not. In Vietnam, they had a more colorful acronym. REMFs, for Rear-Echelon something or other.

For the first time in months, the men of the 5/7th would get showers, new fatigues, and three hot meals a day. There was a chapel that showed movies at night and a clubhouse where they could get beer. In their new wooden barracks, freshly showered and in their new fatigues, many rested on their bunks, allowing their bare feet to luxuriate in the air. Despite their ruck marches at Fort Carson, nothing could have prepared their feet for what they'd endured. Most were in bad shape, but some had it worse than others.

When Arnott Graham had gotten out of Long Binh Jail in November, rather than returning to 4th Platoon, he'd been assigned to 1LT Barry Gallagher's 1st Platoon and was friends with 1st Platoon soldiers Joe Sanchez and Leonard Pelullo. "Lenny was an Italian kid from Philadelphia," he reflected. "Great kid, everybody loved him. We were out in the field, and he had the worst case of trench foot I'd ever seen. I told him to go see the medical officer to get a profile. Hopefully, he'd get sent back to base camp to recover. But Captain Maize just chewed Lenny out and accused him of malingering."

Sanchez recalled Pelullo lying on his bunk. He was also letting his feet air out and heal, eating Christmas cookies from his family in Philadelphia and listening to a tape recording they had sent of themselves. "I'm not going to die here," he said.

"Of course not," replied Sanchez. "We'll both make it home together."

"I can see it in my mind as if it were yesterday," Martin Quinn said of a similar memory. "Will was sitting barefoot on his footlocker in those new wooden barracks we only saw maybe once or twice. He was writing a letter home, and I could tell he was depressed about something. Can't remember what. Maybe it was just the holidays. Unusual because he was usually the one cheering us up. 'Don't worry, man, it'll all work out,' I said."

Quinn recalled how Al Patrillo also had a tape recorder and how he and Will used it to make recordings to send to their own families. He also told of how there were certain tents at base camp and how he could smell the pot a mile away.

### 13 December '66 – 30 weeks left

Dear Mike,

*Now that we're back at An Khe, I'm getting my teeth checked. Sure is nice here. First night I slept without waking in three months. Last night was the first time I seen a T.V. since I left the states. First time I heard music in over two months. Man, was it nice to listen to the radio again. Turned the knob "click" and music. Wow, outa' sight! They've got a movie screen set up here, which I seen a couple nights ago. They had a beer tent selling burgers and hot dogs. It rained, and we got wet but enjoyed it. Won thirty bucks playing cards, which should break me* about even. General Norton is coming to visit us. Lately, we've been on perimeter guard. We have the dump grounds nearby, and it stinks.

Now that we've got it easy and not much to do, they've turned us into an engineer company. They've got us building roads, believe it or not. We're supposed to be getting a little rest. Yeah, we worked half the day, and the road wasn't even supposed to be there. How some people make a career out of the Army, I'll never know.

Yes, we were going on all kinds of operations before we came back to camp. Some real bad ones, too. Bravo Company went on one, got sixty V.C. and six of their own killed. Captured a hundred pieces of equipment and made a big haul. Altogether they've killed 154. Alpha Company's killed 83, Charlie Company about sixty, and Delta Company fifteen. Rod's platoon killed the fifteen. A guy I knew in Bravo Company got the highest medal award, Congressional Medal of Honor. Wounded three times, saves two of his buddies, kills eight V.C., runs out of ammo, charges this bunker with a .45 pistol, and gets killed. Well, now he's a hero. Wish he'd been more careful. Some of our guys didn't make it either. I doubt if you saw us in battle on November 24th. They might have mentioned it. Well, we should be taking it pretty cool for a while.

A bunch of our guys got transferred to the 1st of the 7th Cav. I wish now that I had been. The guys say it's great. Our mortar platoon has almost more chiefs than Indians—five leaders and six workers. The rest are sick or transferred. I'd hate to leave my friends, but I can't stand these big heads. Say, I'm going to try and be a door gunner on a helicopter. Chances are slim, but I'll try.

I hope we can get to town before Christmas. Our C.O. is so chicken to let us go. If so, I'll send some presents home. I bet we don't get to see the Bob Hope show. Something will come up, I know. I heard Phyllis Diller is coming with him. Man, that ought to be a real pair.

So, no deer this year, and you got yourself lost, ha! I had a good laugh when Ma said that. It won't be the first time, either. Basketball is in season now. How I wish I could handle the ball. I can just feel it at my fingertips and "swish" through the net it goes. So you have a team going this year? I know it ought to be great.

Will

    The men would soon get to visit the town of An Khe and were briefed on the off-base rules. Venereal disease was rampant, and each soldier was required to purchase a condom in order to receive a day pass. Taking a military bus into town, they found many shops and restaurants catering to American soldiers. The town was only a few blocks long in each direction but bustled with activity. Ever present in its streets were crowds of children, many offering to shine boots or selling sodas, some simply begging, while others tried to pimp their "sisters." There were many "G.I. bars" in town with Filipino bands playing American music. The red-light district was called Sin City, a series of small buildings with bars in front. It was cordoned off from the rest of the town, and an MP checked passes at the gate.

Some shops sold military "surplus" supplies and uniforms. While they rarely got new fatigues in the field, these shopkeepers had plenty. There were laundries where rear-echelon soldiers could get their uniforms cleaned and pressed. The shop owners would provide free beer as they waited for their laundry.

Many were seriously ill during this time. Despite the big orange pills they took every Monday, some had contracted malaria, including Guy McNay, who was still recovering from being shot in the shoulder on November 19th. A few days into their stay, Will fell ill with some kind of poisoning or dysentery. A cold sweat set in, and his face turned pale. His bowels churned, then loosened violently. To make it worse, SSG Bobby Hayslip was sending him on a night patrol—but his team leader, SGT John Fulford, insisted he stay back and recover. Will was forever thankful for this.

Green Line duty was the battalion's best chance to take care of dental and medical problems. 4th Platoon medic Tom Monnier had a hernia operation. Placed on light duty for a month, he went out on short trips with the doctors to do inoculations and routine medical procedures for local villagers. "It was my best duty in Vietnam," he recalled.

### 14 December '66 – 30 weeks left

Mike,

*The dentist hardly did any work on my teeth. They were in good shape, and I only brushed three or four times. Did you get my Christmas card? Don't believe that card. The only chapel we ever had was an open field with cases of C-Rations for an altar. We never came close to an actual church. Now I'm listening to this messed up radio station. They play rock and roll in the morning and then this horrible classic jazz in the evening. What can you expect when it's an Army station? Our sergeant swears my radio was on twenty-four hours a day at Fort Carson. You know, I listened to the Packers playing the Colts. What a game. Be sure and mention it to Larry—he sticks up for the Colts. Are the champions of the NFL and AFL playing each other in the "Super Bowl?" Should be some game, alright.*

*Hey, are you going to learn taxidermy? I know you're busy, but Dad's taking it easy this time of year. I got a letter from Mrs. Henning saying I should write to my folks more often. I know, that was just in November. It won't happen again. Ask Dad if Larry has paid everything on my car.*

*Wish I had a little drink here. Rod and I really hung one on last time. And I got sicker than a dog that night, whew. I guess I don't have any worries for now. A roof over my head, dry and warm, and plenty of candy. Everyone's healthy, and the cows are giving plenty of milk. So now I'll sack out, listen to some crummy music, or write another letter. Ma says you dig on art. Send me some of your work. Oh well, Fuzzy Face, ha! How do you like my electric razor?*

*Easy Sailing (so far),*

*Will*

One day at An Khe, Joe Sanchez was ordered to guard a young sergeant who had gone AWOL. "I'm not going back out there," he said to Sanchez. "I need to go home to my wife." He had left base camp and hitchhiked to the Saigon airport. He'd planned to buy a ticket and board a plane back to the states until he saw American MPs guarding the airfield. He turned to run but was caught by the MPs. Sanchez thought back to Fort Carson and how Teresa had talked him out of going AWOL himself. He just felt sorry for the guy.

In mid-December, Martin Quinn flew to Hong Kong on his five-day R&R. Meanwhile, on December 19th, their mortar platoon and a platoon from Delta Company were transported to a densely forested hilltop half a mile outside the base camp's perimeter called LZ John. As part of the battalion's new base defense plan, it was to become one of many fortified outposts encircling Camp Radcliff. Gerald Anderson recalled building the outpost.

*Some big-shot general saw this small hill and decided it would be a good outpost. Of course, the mortar platoon was assigned to build it. It was covered with trees and brush, so we had to cut out fields of fire to see any approaching enemy.*

*Then the powers that be said, "The more secure, the better." So now all the vegetation had to be removed, but it was impossible. We were saved when the engineers sent a dozer to knock everything down. It made a circle around the hill and a flat top for our weapons. We built sandbag bunkers and parapets for our mortars. We dug emplacements for M-60s, a .50 caliber machine gun, and a 60mm recoilless rifle. We had all the ammunition we wanted.*

*It was really good duty once we had it built. The ranking NCO was Bobby Hayslip. We did harassment and interdiction firing into the forest every night. We sent out small patrols into the forest every other day to see if we were being observed by the enemy. We took turns sleeping and lounging in the bunkers until the rats decided to move in. Bob Hope was doing his show at base camp, but we never got to see it. After the outpost was completed, some high-ranking officer wanted to watch us from a chopper while we demonstrated how much firepower we had. It was a great success.*

## 21 December '66 – 29 weeks left

*Dear Folks,*

*Been working hard on a hill just outside base camp, building bunkers and clearing land. Worked almost two days before they realized we needed a dozer.*

*I got a package from Larry with a coconut in it. As if we don't get enough of these in this country, ha!*

*I wonder if we'll have Christmas Day off. Seriously, the way things are going, it'll be the first day we've ever gotten off work in Viet Nam. We won't see the Bob Hope show for sure, and I counted on it so much. We were only given a few cards to send, so wish the Hennings a Merry Christmas for me. Hope you all have a fine Christmas and New Year.*

*Will*

After five days of work, LZ John provided very basic shelter with tarps and ponchos stretched over sandbag walls. It rained steadily on Christmas Eve as Patrillo, Evans, Bierschbach, Elmer, Bronson, Will, and Henning sat on ammo boxes, and mud flowed through their bunkers. The Drifters' doo-wop rendition of *White Christmas* played on Will's transistor radio as they enjoyed what remained of their beer, smokes, and treats from home. The AFVN disc jockey read a public service announcement, "Pet monkeys are amusing but also dangerous since they often carry rabies and tuberculosis. Army veterinary services provide the tests and inoculations required to ensure a healthy life for your pet. If you have a pet monkey or any kind of pet, please visit the Army veterinary detachment near you."

"That reminds me," Patrillo joked, handing Will a Pall Mall, "you're just about due for your shots! Enjoy these smokes—probably our last until we get back to base camp."

"Maybe we could go in to see the medics," Will suggested. "Elmer and I both have ringworm."

And so it was that Elmer and Will were allowed to take a jeep into base camp the next day. They saw a doctor and were given some ointment for their ringworm. Stepping out of the medical tent, they heard an emcee's voice emanating from distant loudspeakers. Unfortunately, they had been ordered to report immediately to company headquarters. Elmer looked at Will and said, "What are they going to do, shave our heads and send us to Vietnam?"

There on a large stage was Bob Hope, walking about with his golf club in hand. Elmer and Will pushed their way close enough to hear his jokes. Other celebrities were there, including Phyllis Diller, Anita Bryant, and Vic Damone. Later, the Korean Kittens, Joey Heatherton, and some other Playboy models showed up to remind the boys what they were fighting for.

"You were supposed to be back three hours ago!" fumed 1SG Potter when the two finally reported to the company shed. They were put on KP duty, cleaning pots and pans at the mess hall for the rest of the night—a small price to pay for an afternoon of laughter and pretty girls remembered as my dad's best day in Vietnam.

### 27 December '66 – 29 weeks left

Dear Folks,

No, I am not in the fields. Those are other units of the 1st Cavalry. We are just half a mile from base camp. We're building a well-fortified outpost. We have about thirty-five guys here. We built a bunker. Took three days to build and fell down three times. We killed a seven-foot-long boa constrictor. And by the way, our chapel is the ground we stand on 'cause we don't have one yet.

Rod and I spent Christmas Eve together, listening to Christmas carols on my radio. It was raining and mud ankle-deep, and we felt so lousy that night. I sometimes get so sick of this damn Army. But guess what? I had a wonderful time on Christmas Day. Me and Elmer were allowed to go into base camp for ringworm. The doc gave us both a forty-eight-hour profile.

Christmas dinner was out of this world. Oh yes, and we seen the Bob Hope show. Ended up on K.P. 'cause we sneaked off. Oh well, it was worth it. Man, did we have a blast. That Hope is really crazy. And Phyllis Diller, wow, she was out-of-sight, and the other sexy women, wow. Don't forget we'll be on T.V. January 18th, so don't miss it. I had a wonderful time, with a lot of luck and a bit of pull. And poor Rod is here helping our platoon build this outpost. Man, was he ever pissed 'cause me and Elmer got profiles, ha!

I was very happy to receive the wristwatch. It is so useful. I liked it very much. Also, your box of candy and the tape recording. I played it on this recorder I borrowed, and you guys sound so nervous, ha! But it was so wonderful to hear you all. I'm going to tape over it and send it back so you can hear me.

Let me know if you're getting all my letters. I know I wrote four to you in December and two to Mike. And Mike is getting a little swift. Better cool his heels a little. No doubt you're getting my letters late because of all this Christmas mail.

Will

Martin Quinn returned from his R&R just after Christmas. Now that most of the work had been done, he found a relaxed atmosphere at LZ John. It was boring but relatively safe. They passed the time playing cards, taking pictures, finding things to kill, and throwing around an old football. They usually didn't carry their air mattresses in the field—but they were staying put for a while—so

Quinn and Will brought theirs out to the outpost and set them on some empty ammunition crates to use as makeshift beds. Patrillo's R&R in Hong Kong was coming up in about a week, and Quinn lent him his camera.

Other platoons in Alpha Company pulled duty in the base camp's guard towers. SSG Robert Matulac manned the radio in the battalion Tactical Operations Center. "Alpha Company manned about five towers," he recalled. "One night, one of the towers asked if they could fire a few rounds toward the camp's interior. 'No!' I said. They radioed back, saying that a tiger was circling around the base of their tower and looking up at them. I attempted to get permission for them but was denied. So, I just told the tower to make sure they aimed straight down at the tiger. Meanwhile, Sergeant First Class Marvin Hall was in his tent, cleaning his rifle. It was in pieces when he was bumped by someone from outside his tent. Angry that he'd made him drop the parts of his M-16, he cussed and gave back a hard elbow jab. But instead of getting an apology, he got a large growl from a tiger! He scrambled to get his weapon together. But by the time he did, the tiger had disappeared into the brush."

Arnott Graham also found himself manning one of An Khe's perimeter towers. Two soldiers were required to be in the turret at all times. Several were assigned to this one tower and took turns. With two up top, Graham and the others were smoking and joking below. It was cold and rainy. They wanted to warm up, so they strung their ponchos between the support beams. They filled a large metal bucket with sand, poured on some gasoline, and set it on fire. This kept them warm for a while. When the flames dwindled, someone decided to pour on more gas. The fire wasn't entirely out when the additional gasoline was poured on, however. The five-gallon gas can blew up and started the whole tower on fire. As it burned, the two in the turret could only climb about halfway down and were forced to jump. Now severely burned, the fellow with the gas can was himself on fire. He rolled around in the mud until the flames were out. Also destroyed was an M-16 left in the tower and a Starlight Scope, an expensive night vision device. After surveying the destruction and cussing them all out, one of their sergeants remarked, "You're all gonna have to re-enlist to pay for this."

On December 27th, everyone's worst nightmare befell another company of the 1st Air Cavalry. Two batteries of artillerymen occupied a firebase in the Kim Son Valley known as LZ Bird. Infantrymen of Charlie Company, 1/12th Cav were providing security but were severely undermanned. They had just received many replacements, most of whom had not yet seen combat. Just under two hundred Americans occupied the firebase. In the darkness, about seven hundred NVA crept to within fifteen feet of their perimeter wire. At 1:00 AM, they stormed the firebase en masse. Communications were knocked out and hand-to-hand fighting ensued. Several howitzer positions were defended to their death while illumination rounds fired from LZ Pony bathed the combatants in an eerie light.

Shouting at their men to get down, 1LT John Piper and SSG Robert Underwood loaded and fired two 105mm Beehive rounds directly at the enemy troops engulfing the firebase. Designed to stop mass infantry attacks, the Beehive releases over eight thousand burning steel flechettes that fly like insects in all directions. In a *Soldier of Fortune* story by Al Hemmingway, radio operator SP/4 Clint Houston remarked, "It was so haunting. It screeched like a million bees. I saw a big hole in their ranks, and then I heard screaming. Those bodies were ripped to shreds. Then they fired again with the same results. The assault was stopped dead in its tracks."

With the assistance of ARA gunships, the enemy was beaten back after two hours of hellish combat. The rising sun revealed a grizzly scene as the bodies of nearly thirty Americans and over two hundred North Vietnamese lay strewn about the outpost. Sixty-seven Americans had been wounded. Charlie and Delta Companies of the 1/8th Cav were flown in to relieve the beleaguered defenders and pursue the fleeing enemy.

Following the battle, some units of the 5/7th Cav were also flown in from An Khe to join the pursuit. Bravo Company's Robert Powers recalled having his Christmas break cut short when he and others were sent in. Alpha Company's SSG Robert Matulac arrived at LZ Bird at dusk the evening after the attack. "It looked like a disaster area," he said. "The emplacements were still there, but no guns or equipment. Just paper, scraps of cloth, some empty boxes, some barbwire. Two of us went down to the lower emplacements and found flechettes scattered on the ground. There was an eerie atmosphere to imagine the battle that was fought there."

Milling about the abandoned outpost, Matulac noticed some papers with handwriting lying about. He bent down to pick one up and brushed off the dirt—a half-finished letter dated December 27th. Minutes later, they marched into the surrounding jungle to search for Charlie.

*Aftermath of LZ Bird, photo by Robert Matulac*

*Joey Heatherton at the Bob Hope show, source unknown*

*Sin City, photo by Will Bowe*

# 18
# THE OUTPOST

*No, I don't need a toothbrush. But tell the doc I have one, and thanks anyway.*

Although often used for heating coffee and C-Rations, C-4's main purpose was for blowing up trees. A remote detonator and blasting caps were used to make it explode. They would strap the block-like charges of C-4 to tree trunks with the blasting caps in place. Extra charges were used on a particularly large stump at LZ John, and the explosion sent a rock into Will's arm.

### 30 December '66 – 28 weeks left

Dear Folks,

Lucked out again. I got a small stone in my upper right arm. So this means about a two-week profile. You see, I just got back with my platoon yesterday and was helping Sergeant Hayslip blow this stump with C-4. We were using a large amount, and I said I was going to split to the other end of our position. He set it off before I got there, and a rock hit my arm. Didn't hurt too bad, but Doc said I better have it x-rayed. They found the rock. Then they operated but couldn't get it out. Have to wait for it to heal now. It was really neat. I worked two hours and bingo, back into camp. Rod didn't like to see me go in. "Out here two hours and going back in again," he says. "He's just faking, sergeant." I told him I had to get another fifth of whiskey. He told me you wrote him a letter, and he wanted me to tell you to tell his folks that he's still working his ass off at our position and hasn't had much time for writing.

There's something funny about this Army. In civilian life, you never want to get hurt. In the Army, you're always hoping to get hurt. I am in a building that looks like Louie Simon's shed, on a bunk with a soft mattress and clean sheets. Breakfast and dinner served in bed. This is what I like, wow. I hope I can get a pass to go to town later. Packers should be playing on the radio today. It's almost five o'clock by your most splendid watch.

This is a news clipping of the Bob Hope show. He said in his show that Dean Martin would be elected to distribute liquor licenses and Mickey Rooney would distribute marriage licenses. And in Saigon, the best things in life are not free but rather off limits, ha!

I know it won't rain now that I have a roof over my head. Don't forget to tell Mrs. Henning that our platoon is putting Rod to work building bunkers and chopping logs in six inches of mud, ha! Oh well, today marks the end of another year. The doc says I'll be here a few more days. So wish the Green Bay Packers well and not me. I like it here, despite the needles. So long, from a cool, clean, dry, and comfortable son named,

Will

Gerald Anderson recalled New Year's Eve back on the outpost. "We had our own little celebrations," he said. "Not much alcohol was available, but Staff Sergeant Bobby Hayslip managed to get a bottle of Scotch and some Tab for a mix. So Bobby and I had a little celebration sitting atop the hill to welcome in 1967. By the way, Scotch and Tab are a terrible mixture."

### *1 January '67 – 28 weeks left*

Dear Folks,

*Did we ever have a wild time last night, Kool-Aid and cookies. It's noon now, and this very minute, everyone back home is having a rip-roaring time. The doc said he'll sew me up tomorrow. I wrote Rod a letter about how nice it is here and that the work best be done when I get back. I can see him now, swearing a blue streak at me, ha! Got some Vietnamese kids here with New Year's noise makers. They're cute. Act like kids back home.*

*The Packers are playing today. I'll hear it on the radio tomorrow. I started a good paperback, "The Mob's Man." Tells about his start playing hooky and small robberies, then into a big syndicate. Seen a funny show last night about a guy on his first date that reminded me of Larry. Just reading, writing, and listening to the radio. The station here plays eight-year-old rock and roll as if it were on the top fifty. I know that music will always be part of my life. I'll have a tape player in my car and a stereo set someday. You know, I'd rather have music than a new car, tractor, or T.V. Makes you feel real good. Maybe because I hadn't heard it for so long. Full of needle holes,*

Will

Fred Brodosi hadn't been seen for some time. Will ran into him one night at the clubhouse while recuperating at base camp. Amid the smell of spilled beer and cigarettes, he told Will how he'd broken his ankle while descending a mountain. It happened sometime after the battle on November 19th, and he had spent Thanksgiving at a hospital in Qui Nhon. Then he was put on light duty and sent to An Khe to help the engineers build their new wooden barracks.

### *8 January '67 – 27 weeks left*

Dear Folks,

*No, I am not alive, just a ghost writing. Now the last time we had a battle where we got a little scared was Thanksgiving Day. Now we probably won't see any action until March. Like Rod and Delta Company, today they're going on a little*

patrol. Nothing more dangerous than you crossing the highway to get the mail. So don't get worried.

Ma was wondering if I kept all my letters. Well, how many will a steel helmet hold? Only a few. Been looking through these old pictures you sent long ago. They sure look nice. My nights must be restful 'cause I never dreamt so much about home before as I did the past week. Is it dry here, you asked. Are you kidding? I can't remember when it ever was dry. Behind our mess hall is worse than our pig pen. By the way, our mess hall is really beautiful. Tin roof, wooden walls, and cement floor. Say, if you can get a small Wisconsin flag, send it over. We'll hang it up in our mess hall.

Great news, getting out of Viet Nam in six days. Six more paydays, that is, ha! Three years ago today, I was in high school. Two years ago today, I left for Chicago. The 12th will be one year since I graduated basic training. And today, I sit with a sore arm in Viet Nam.

Got out of the hospital yesterday, but I've got another week on light duty. Tried to hit the town, but First Sergeant Potter says, "No pass if you're on profile." Okay with me, but the minute I am put on detail, I'm heading to town. Got a haircut today. Been over two months. I wonder how long they would have let me go. The surprise of the year, the mess hall is having coffee breaks now twice a day, ha! I almost dropped my teeth. I'm quite sure now that I am going to Hong Kong in February. Just had to talk to the right guy.

How are you feeling Ma, did you get an operation on your stomach? I hope it's okay. Yeah, I know we can eat meat on Friday. Besides, we're allowed to eat meat 'cause we're in the service. No, I don't need a toothbrush. But tell the doc I have one, and thanks anyway. What do you mean you can't send food? It ruined so much the ants and bugs all jumped in their boats and moved out.

Had a few beers with Fred Brodosi at the clubhouse last night. I talked with some guys with this artillery unit that got hit by the N.V.A. Heard a rumor that Allen Simon's 25th Infantry Division is going to Bong Son. Brodosi said our chaplain needs an assistant. Man, my worries would be over if I could get that job. I'll have to look into this. Never wanted to be one, but it's a different story now. Seen enough killing. Going to see about being a gunner on a chopper, too. It's a slim chance about getting out of the infantry, but what do I got to lose?

I asked Elmer about the many phrases in The Mob's Man, like "heist job—he has been burned—the numbers racket—and policy racket." You see, he lives in Harlem—the roughest section of New York—but is the finest guy I know from there.

I'll get a camera someday. Or say, if you want to buy me a 16mm pocket-size camera, that is what you can send me for my birthday. I should clean my radio.

*Been almost a year now that I've had it. Guard it with my life. No finer radio around. Guys here have great big radios and can only get one American station, ha! I listened to all these football games too. Read that the Super Bowl ain't going to be so great. Nobody's going to see it 'cause it's being played neither in Green Bay nor Kansas stadiums. Biggest game of the year, and nobody sees it. What a joke. Well, it's supper time. Mike better get to writing!*

*Will*

Between December and January, several soldiers from the 5/7th had been transferred to the 1/7th and 2/7th Cavs. Among them was Joe Sanchez. In *True Blue, A Tale of the Enemy Within*, he describes the events of his twentieth birthday in January 1967 while serving as a radio operator in the 2/7th.

*After dinner, I settled back and started a letter to my mother. I told her all the stuff that sons in a tight place make up to tell mothers they don't want to upset: how nice the weather there was, how quiet things were at camp, how safe I felt—anything that would make her think I wasn't really in harm's way. Just as I was writing this, I looked up and saw helicopters in the direction we had just been brought in from. They were firing ARA (aerial rocket artillery) rounds at the target below.*

*"Saddle up," we were told. There was enemy activity, and we'd have to go back out in the field. The lift choppers arrived. We were put aboard, four to six per chopper. They took us back to where we had been that afternoon and put us off near a village. We were to search out a suspected VC camp. The enemy was nowhere to be seen—and that's the worst kind. We heard him, though, and pretty soon we were likely to feel him.*

*Sporadic automatic fire broke out whenever a patrol got too near the enemy's position, but so far, nothing had really popped. Fred Booker, our forward observer and a British Army veteran, was on an embankment. Then some of us started down the embankment. Our platoon leader went ahead. I stepped aside to let him pass. Some of the group followed him, and I wound up picking up the rear.*

*That was when the grenade came at us and exploded. I remember calling out in Spanish, "Oh, my God, Mom, I've been shot in the head," and thinking I was going to die. I felt burning sensations in my arms, legs, groin. Then everything went from fast to slow-motion. I saw Booker tumble down the embankment to my right, and to me, he looked like a store mannequin floating in some Twilight Zone. Even the leaves blown off the trees seemed like they were hovering instead of falling. I was coughing from the battle smoke, and then it seemed like I couldn't move at all. I suppose my brain had shut down from the concussion—that's what they said later. All I know is I was aware of everything, but my body* wasn't moving or responding at all, and it was only when I heard the ringing in my ears I realized I was actually coming back to life.

In fact, I could move now. I managed to limp out of the crater I was in and I saw a trooper on the ground taking cover. Then someone came up to me, forced me to the ground, and called for a medic. As I was lying on my back being treated, I could see jets flying overhead and bombing the area near us. It turned out four of us had been seriously wounded by shrapnel, and that we had killed four Viet Cong in return, but I didn't know that yet. I don't remember much about being airlifted out except that the medevac pilot gave me a thumbs-up.

On January 11th, Will's buddy Rodney Henning was sent out with Delta Company to participate in Operation Washita II. Henning and his team set up an L-shaped ambush along a dirt road just outside the town of Bong Son. About dusk, a lone figure emerged on the road in the distance, approaching their position. The men quietly switched their selector knobs from safe to semi-automatic. They couldn't discern if they were seeing an enemy fighter, a civilian, or perhaps one of their own men. Team leader SSG Bealer Caudill ordered them to hold their fire. About fifty yards up the road, the figure suddenly vanished. Caudill asked for two volunteers to go investigate with him. Henning, Caudill, and Jimmie Dir cautiously stepped through the trees along the side of the road. As they approached the area where the figure had disappeared, they spotted a man crouching in the bushes, raising a rifle. At once, they fired their weapons. The man had fired but one errant round before he was killed. From his body, they collected his AK-47, gas mask, and documents.

### 14 January '67 – 27 Weeks Left

Dear Mike,

*Got myself an office job—C.Q. runner—stay up all night and don't do a darn thing. We got a typewriter in here, and I'm seeing if I can still type. Man, this is the life of Riley. Like the guys say, "I'm getting over like a fat rat and clean as an onion." Today is the first time I wore underwear in over three months. It took too long for our clothes to dry with underwear on, so we threw them away. All these cooks and office clerks have rain suits and buckle boots. Only place I get my shoes dirty is coming from the mess hall and into the clubhouse to have a few beers. The only bar in the division that doesn't have liquor. Oh well!*

*I found out about being a door gunner. Turns out you have to re-up to get that job. Guess I'll settle for being a ground pounder. I heard Rodney Henning got himself a shotgun off a dead V.C. I guess he can send it home if he likes. I hope I can get a V.C. rifle to send home.*

*Almost 1:30 AM. Sergeant Fulford is making coffee so we can stay awake. My faithful radio helps, but it's starting to go on the blink. Sergeant is all wrapped* up in a sleeping bag to keep warm. You know, we should go on a hike when deer hunting comes. Take our sleeping bags and camp out until we get one. When I get to town, I'll buy you all a little present. I'm sure I'll get there soon. Think of what I'll be doing a month from now on R&R.

Just heard that Queens, New York has a big fire going from the riots. Got a few buddies from there.

Win any basketball games? Next time tell me how school's going and send a picture of your modern art. Well, I can't think of anything else to type about. And be sure you type back, I mean write back, Fuzzy Face.

White Collar Worker,

CAPTAIN: WILL E. BOWE

On January 15th, the Green Bay Packers defeated the Kansas City Chiefs in the world's first Super Bowl, and Will returned to LZ John. Al Patrillo had just returned from his R&R. He told the guys about a girl he'd stayed with in Hong Kong, and they were checking out his photos when a helicopter landed on the outpost. They figured some colonel was coming to check on them and tried to look busy. Then a beautiful blonde in a miniskirt jumped out of the chopper. The only celebrity known to travel South Vietnam in an open-doored helicopter, AFVN disc jockey Chris Noel was there to visit.

During her time in-country, Noel survived mortar attacks, sniper fire, and helicopter crashes, and the North Vietnamese placed a ten-thousand-dollar bounty on her head. The following is an excerpt from her IMDb biography.

*A tour of a VA hospital in 1965 altered her destiny forever. Based on her minor pin-up celebrity, Chris impulsively auditioned for the Armed Forces Network and started hosting her own radio show for the G.I.s in Vietnam, frequently flying to that war-torn country and visiting remote areas considered too risky for Bob Hope's USO shows. She became the G.I.s' favorite sexy radio and show personality while putting her own life on the line. As it turned out, Vietnam veterans would become her prime mission and life's work long after the war.*

The guys gathered around to meet Chris as she posed for photos and signed pictures. Fifty years later, there's one thing my dad remembers most about this day. It was the first time he saw a girl in a miniskirt.

### 19 January '67 – 26 weeks left

*Dear Folks,*

*Well, back to the grind. My arm feels fine. Had K.P. the first day off profile. Now I am back to filling sandbags. My dear radio went haywire. Am I ever lonely without it.*

*Supposed to have been out in the fields again, but I guess we ain't going until later. We might get attached to another unit to guard an R&R center in Viet Nam—just a rumor. We're getting "bad news" Burtis back again. He was our old platoon sergeant that got shot three months ago. He came out the other day. Showed us his wound and the bullet that hit him. Got shot twice. Actually, he and I get along pretty good. He put me in for E-4 last October. But when he got shot and Hayslip took over, my name got wiped off the list. Bound to make it pretty soon.*

*About a dozen guys came by yesterday, all neatly dressed and clean. We asked how long they'd been here, and they said six days. What, six days? Man, did that make us feel good. They're six days, and we're six months. Oh boy.*

*I sent a few negatives to have developed for Quinn, so send them back as soon as you get the prints. These are color. These other guys want the negatives as soon as you send them back. This is the place we've been the last month. We had just got here and were still neat and clean. Our company commander, A.J. Wise, sitting on the sandbags with a rifle and a mean grin.*

*I got a letter from Joanne today, Alice Yohnk, the Hennings, and your letter with those downright good pictures. Hey, why do you write the names on the back of them pictures? Don't you think I know who they are, gee! I hear it is very cold, like thirty below. I don't think I want to be home now, ha! Guess you were a little worried around December 12th.*

*Received your birthday cake the other day. Lit the candles and sang happy birthday. They kept asking, when are you going to open "our" package? Sure glad we got "our" package today. We all liked the cake, and it was in fine shape. Frosting was a little off, but still okay. Yes, I got Mike's candy bars long ago. Yes, I still have the raincoat. I believe the rainy season should end soon. No, Ricky Mitchell isn't stretching it when he said it reached 135 degrees down by Saigon. It's about 110 in the sun today, and it's January.*

*You know, I could call home from base camp, and it wouldn't cost anything. But I'd have to be in base camp and would have to wait my turn. And when you talk, you'd have to say "over," and then I would talk, and then I'd say "over," and so on. I'll wait 'til I get to Hong Kong, but I hear it costs fifty dollars for three minutes. I'll just reverse the charges, ha! …I just heard that a call home would only be about nine bucks for three minutes. That's just how fast rumors change. People here are like old women, gossiping.*

*So Charlie Rubenzer is re-enlisting. Wow, what a nut. Re-enlisting is worse than being shot at. If I don't get out of the Army when I leave here, I could bring natural death on basic trainees. Man, what a time that would be. "It's five after 4:00 AM, and you're not off the sack yet? Didn't shave, huh? Buckle not shiny,* boots not polished?" I can see it now. In fact, I hope I don't get discharged from over here. Got to get even for what they done to me. Give them a ten-minute break, they expect five, and you only give them three. Inspecting rifles, "Dirty front sight, dirty rear sight. What are you trying to do, grow a garden?"

Mike done alright in the Klondike Race. He'd better write and tell me about it. That darn Dad must have folded this one letter 'cause I gave up trying to refold it. Ought to write more so he can get in practice. Well, ain't much else to say. I listened to the whole Packer game. Really whooped them.

Will

Martin Quinn at LZ John

*Left–right: Jim Marshall, Carl Evans, and Bower at LZ John*

*Kurt Elmer at LZ John, photos by Martin Quinn*

*I shook Hands with her WOW She had Mini shirt Also a movie star*

CAVALAIR

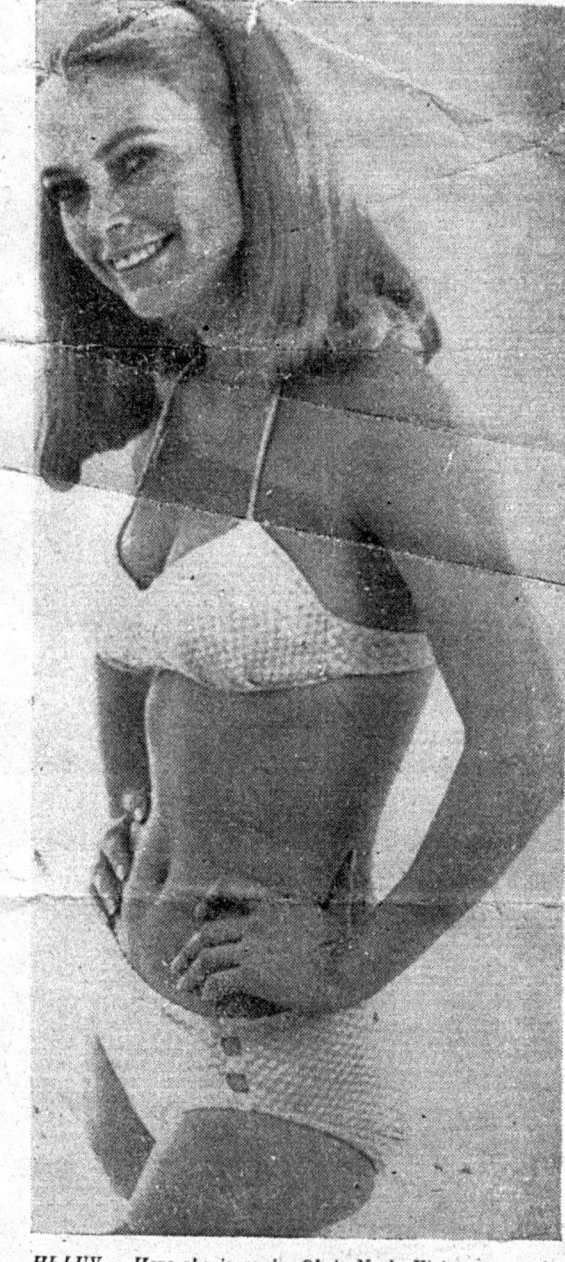

HI LUV — Here she is again. Chris Noel, Vietnam's vocal sweetheart over Armed Forces Radio. She visited the Cav Wednesday and Thursday, charming the troops at the Red Cross center and the 2nd Surgical Hospital. The lads of the 1/7th were the lucky ones. They had a real date with Chris for lunch. But even they should appreciate this different view.

# 19
# RETURN TO AN LAO

*I am hoping we can even the score.*

As January 1967 ended, the 5/7th Cav prepared to rejoin Operation Thayer II and the real war beyond the outskirts of An Khe. Alpha Company's roster had dramatically changed due to casualties, sickness, and transfers. Many replacements had arrived, and most had not seen combat. Led by SGT John Fulford, Will's mortar crew was still intact with Marvin Bierschbach and John Bronson. After three months in the hospital recovering from malaria and being shot in the shoulder on November 19th, Guy McNay returned to the company. Strings had been pulled by a high-ranking military family member to get him stationed outside Vietnam. Instead, he requested to return to Alpha Company.

### 1 February '67 – 24 weeks left

*Folks,*

*We're heading back to the fields. Don't know what they have in mind, but rumors have been good. Went rappelling out of a helicopter the other day. Jumping out as high as our big silo is back home. One guy nearly busted the rope. When I seen that messed up rope, it didn't give me much confidence. Here's a picture of our old platoon leader, Lieutenant Cathcart. He was transferred in January to a post office job. A nice guy but not too swift.*

*I got the newspaper you sent. Read that Larry got into a little wreck again, ha! Been getting "boo-coo" mail lately. That means a lot of mail. Got a birthday package from Mrs. Henning. Connie Geissler told me you got a little high at Ken Nelson's party, which you didn't mention. Ahem!*

*The camera you sent is here, but I have to go back to camp tomorrow to get it. And then, if Rod is back, we'll try to soak up some beer. Even if he isn't, I am still going to. I am dying for a dozen cans of beer. Can't wait to get that camera. Thank you a whole lot.*

*Will*

On February 4th, Alpha Company was flown in transport planes to LZ Two Bits. From here, Alpha and Delta Companies were to air assault onto the peak of Nui Dat Set Mountain. At an elevation of over fifteen hundred feet, it overlooked the An Lao Valley and the village where they had fought on Thanksgiving Day. It would become an established firebase dubbed LZ Hump—but for now, it was undeveloped and densely vegetated, with no place for choppers to land. And so, at 10:06 AM, one of Delta Company's platoons rappelled onto the mountaintop from Hueys hovering above the treetops. Among them was Will's buddy Rodney

Henning. Either his rope was too short, or the chopper was hovering too high, and he hurt his neck in the fall.

Alpha Company followed, climbing down rope ladders from Chinooks, something they had only trained for. "In rappelling, a man can reach the ground from sixty feet in about four seconds," CPT Theodore Danielson of the 1/8th Cav once quipped. "And if somebody's shooting at him, I guarantee he'll make it faster." The same could not be said of an air assault by rope ladder, however. One of the lifts reported hovering for seventeen minutes while unloading its troops. In the middle of Indian country—each with forty pounds of gear climbing down a rope ladder attached to a helicopter hovering at forty feet—it's hard not to imagine all the things that could go wrong. Everyone was anxious to get their feet on the ground, and the guy following Martin Quinn kept stepping on his hands.

The men spent the day cutting and clearing. A company of engineers was flown in, and a sky crane lowered a dozer. As the area was cleared, Chinooks lowered howitzers, ammunition crates, and artillerymen. Like giant flying hippos, more Chinooks descended from the sky, dropping their loads and flying off again. Meanwhile, those below commenced the herculean task of establishing a new firebase. The battalion command post descended at 11:30 AM. The command chopper crashed when one of its blades hit a tree, but no one was seriously injured. Will took many photos here, and Royce Barrow showed him how to best operate his new camera.

### *6 February '67 – 24 weeks left*

*Dear Folks,*

*So now we're on this high-ass hill. I've taken quite a few pictures. This camera is almost too nice to have out here in the boondocks. I keep it wrapped in plastic in my ammo pouch. I'll send the film home when I go on R&R. It's getting dark, and I'll have to close. Working hard clearing the hill.*

*Will*

*7 February '67—Morning now. Log ship hasn't come in yet. Elmer gave me this picture he took of me on our way to the Bob Hope show.*

At LZ Hump, one company would guard the firebase as the others patrolled the surrounding areas. Returning to their real job of searching and destroying in the jungle, the men descended the mountain. Since their arrival in August, when they were fresh off the boat and eager for action, they had learned how to survive on C-Rations, Kool-Aid, instant coffee, and cigarettes. They had learned the reality of this new war, how to put one foot in front of the other, and how to endure. They had learned about death, how it often struck randomly in this place, and how unlikely they were to find Charlie before he found them. The hardened troopers now stepped quietly through the depths of the deepest dark forest, eyes darting back and forth, scanning for tripwires and Bouncing Betties, ears strained to hear the faintest sound. This is how it started—but eventually, the hyper-alertness combined with the physical exertion and extreme heat became exhausting. They inevitably reverted to clumsily plodding through the jungle like mules, or as some would say, "like a clanging band of gypsies."

They descended further, into the An Lao Valley, returning to the village where they'd fought on Thanksgiving. While searching the remnants of Van Hoi, they took sniper fire, killed one Viet Cong fighter, and called for a medevac following a violent encounter with a water buffalo.

"The water buffalo didn't seem to like us," said Bill Purdy, recalling a close call of his own. While moving through a rice paddy, one became agitated and started charging toward him from a distance. Purdy couldn't outrun the buffalo in the muck. With a full clip in his M-16, he started firing. With his clip half empty, the beast was still charging as others in 2nd Platoon fired their rifles. The buffalo eventually collapsed only a few feet from where Purdy stood.

Each company patrolled through the valley and surrounding mountains for the next week. As they were likely mined, the men avoided the dusty clay-like trails now cracking in the heat of the dry season. Sniper fire was frequent, but no one encountered the enemy in force. Each day they found abandoned bunkers, tunnels, hastily dug graves, rice stockpiles, punji stake pits, and a variety of booby traps. Found in an abandoned bunker complex was a twenty-inch stack of papers. Among them was a photograph of a captured U.S. Navy pilot and a photocopy of his identification card.

The battalion's former Intelligence Officer, CPT Walt Swain, had recently taken command of Rodney Henning's Delta Company and quickly earned their respect. Henning's platoon was designated a Long-Range Reconnaissance Patrol, or LRRP. They were sent on missions that required stealth. This prohibited noisy air assaults and required them to move farther on foot, enduring longer periods without helicopter support. The idea was for the LRRP to find the enemy units, allowing regular elements to fix and finish those units.

Henning had recovered and returned to the field following his rappelling incident on LZ Hump. On February 7th, his platoon found a human skeleton amid several half-dug foxholes on a jungle-covered mountainside. Later, they found themselves lost in elephant grass while attempting to follow a creek bed. Dusk fell upon them as a battalion of Viet Cong approached. Henning turned off his radio. Still undetected, they crouched in the six-foot-high grass and waited for the enemy to pass. Instead, they hunkered down right next to them in the elephant grass. Amid the sounds of soldiers settling in and Vietnamese banter, the men sat silently with their backs to each other, clutching their rifles. It started raining. Concerned that light could reflect off their wet helmets, they covered them with camo netting. It was a long, wet, sleepless night. As the men held their breath, the enemy soldiers finally moved out just before daybreak.

While operating out of LZ Hump, the battalion counted eleven enemy killed, three wounded, and three taken prisoner. The week also saw nine of the battalion's men wounded by mines, punji stakes, and snipers. On February 9th, Alpha Company was lifted back to LZ Hump to guard the firebase.

### 10 February '67 – 23 weeks left

*Dear Folks,*

*Everything's going smoothly so far. Only rained once since we've been here. But man, has it been hot, and I got a real nice tan. We're back to building bunkers and filling sandbags. Every four to five days, a company comes in for about a day. Food has been quite good. Ice cream and chicken, and a beer or a Coke the past few nights. One thing the Army really surprised me with is no more steel pots, only soft caps. I almost dropped my teeth. Rod said he hurt his neck pretty bad and hit a punji stake a while back. Don't mention it to Mrs. Henning.*

*Yes, Joanne told me she is expecting in June. I'll be an uncle eight times. No, I wouldn't like my bedroom painted pink. My goodness, of all colors. But so long as it isn't Army green, doesn't matter to me.*

*Will*

After his friend's death, SSG Robert Matulac had written to Donald Rankin's mother, and they began corresponding. Dated February 11th, the following was found among the collection of letters sent home by Donald Rankin.

*Dear Mrs. Rankin,*

*I'm glad that my letter answered your questions. In reference to your query, Thanksgiving Day over here was the day before Thanksgiving back home.*

*I also want to thank you for the invitation to stop by and visit. If I am around that part of the country, I will be sure to stop by and pay my respects. I showed your letter to everyone in the section, and they were quite interested in the postcard and happy to hear from you. Donald always talked about his family and the country where he had lived, so I feel that I almost know all of his friends and family personally. If I can be of any more assistance to you, don't hesitate to write.*

*Sincerely,*

*Roberto Matulac*

*P.S. We are now operating in the same area where Donald was hit. I am hoping we can even the score.*

AP Photo by Catherine Leroy—Helicopters, supposed to be able to land on a dime, found they couldn't touch down on narrow hilltops in the central Vietnam coastlands, February 1967, but that didn't stop them from delivering right on the money. Engineers blasted drop areas clear, and the giant Chinook choppers dropped their soldiers of the 5th Battalion, 7th Cavalry regiment to participate in Operation Thayer II some 15 miles southwest of Bong Son, which is some 300 miles northeast of Saigon.

*Alpha Company descending on LZ Hump, photo by Bill Purdy*

*Soldiers at LZ Hump, photo by Will Bowe*

*Chinook at LZ Hump, photo by Royce Vick*

*Sling-loading howitzer and ammunition, photo by Will Bowe*

*Sky crane lowering dozer at LZ Hump*

*Left–right: Al Patrillo, Martin Quinn, and Fred Brodosi, photos by Will Bowe*

*Lining up for hot chow at LZ Hump, photo by Will Bowe*

*Left–right: Kurt Elmer, Paul Lussier, Will Bowe, and Al Patrillo*

*View from above the clouds at LZ Hump overlooking An Lao Valley*

*Al Patrillo, photos by Will Bowe*

# 20
# LZ Santana
## (Operation Pershing)

*Some action on my perimeter. May be an animal… checking it out now.*

With 1,757 enemy killed at the cost of 242 American lives, Operation Thayer II had been the 1st Air Cavalry Division's longest sustained operation since its arrival in Vietnam. Quitting LZ Hump and ending the historic operation, the 5/7th Cav would be airlifted in waves to the Operation Pershing area on February 11th. Dark clouds were gathering as Alpha Company, following the others, lifted off at 5:05 PM. As they touched down on the rocky LZ Santana, the skies turned angry. The downpour was such that the battalion command post could not make the final lift following Alpha Company as planned. No cutting or clearing was necessary this time as LZ Santana sat atop a sparsely vegetated rocky hill five miles west of the sea.

In the pouring rain, the companies immediately marched east down the hill into the northern Bong Son as the mountains filled with thunder. The terrain was similar to Phu My but more densely populated, with villages everywhere. Operation Pershing would not officially commence until 12:00 AM on the 13th, as a truce was being held through the 12th in observance of Tet, the Vietnamese New Year. Despite the supposed truce, there was plenty of hostile activity. The men spent the next two days searching and clearing villages as scout ships flew above, drawing small arms fire. Each company took contact and a handful of prisoners.

Alpha Company returned to the base of the long-rising rocky hill leading up to LZ Santana at dusk on February 12th. Instead of staying together as a company, each platoon staked out its own perimeter—some in rice paddies at the base of the hill, others in nearby sweet potato fields. It was part of their new battalion commander's strategy. Aside from hit-and-run sniping and mortar attacks, the Viet Cong would only attack in force when they outnumbered an American unit. The purpose was for one of the platoons to bait such an attack, then quickly envelope the enemy with the rest of the company.

Another new tactic was to send out five-man reconnaissance teams, ahead during patrols and in ambush positions at night. Each recon team's call sign was a different number "Custer," and there were nine teams within the battalion.

"One of our recon teams with Staff Sergeant Harry Coit and Jim Hirschuber spotted a large group of NVA approaching their position," Bob Matulac recalled. "They hid in some elephant grass, hoping the enemy would pass. However, the NVA surrounded them and settled down. They called in the enemy position, and I asked how close they were to the NVA. 'If you want to talk to one of them,' Coit's voice whispered through the radio, 'I could give the handset to the closest guy.' Hirschuber had to keep a button pressed down on the radio to keep it silent. He swears he could hear his own heartbeat while waiting for the enemy to pass."

The rice paddies at the base of LZ Santana were terraced, forming a series of steps leading up to the rocky hillside. The water was only ankle-deep as it was the dry season. This is where 4th Platoon set up their position on the night of the 12th. Amid hushed cursing and grumbling, Will and the others settled in to sleep atop the paddy's soggy earthen dikes.

The command group established a separate perimeter with 1st Platoon farther up the hill among the mounds of sweet potatoes. Kenneth Rathyen had replaced Donald Rankin as radio operator for the company net. Royce Barrow still manned the battalion net. They dug a foxhole next to a clump of trees in the center of the perimeter. Here they monitored the radios, replacing the regular antennas with extra-long ones for better range at night. CPT A.J. Wise checked on his men, then went to sleep.

In a crude graveyard atop a ten-foot embankment overlooking a small creek, Arnott Graham set up with one of 1st Platoon's ambush teams. The graves here were just mounds of dirt with no markers. Graham was told that Charlie Company would sweep through, trying to push the enemy into their ambush. Down below the embankment, where tangled twisting tree roots approached the creek, he set up a trip flare and a Claymore mine. He ran the wires and clacker for the Claymore back up to the embankment. Graham was paired with a new soldier in the company, and they took turns sleeping and watching from their position.

Graham's friend Lenny Pelullo shared a foxhole with a young black soldier named Donnie Ward. Graham recalled how Ward was always sharing baked goods sent by his mother. Pelullo and Ward had dug in about fifty yards from Graham's position, just beyond the command group.

The moon was about half-full as Barrow and Rathyen took turns sleeping and monitoring the radios. At 11:23 PM, Rathyen reported shots fired in the distance. 3rd Platoon radioed back that they had just shot and killed an escaping prisoner. Charlie Company radioed that they were approaching the area. Rathyen informed 1LT Barry Gallagher, and he informed Graham. He watched Charlie Company's men quietly slosh through the creek bed. Convinced there was no enemy in the area, Graham hunkered down in a more comfortable spot between a grave mound and hedgerow, about thirty feet away from his clacker.

The following transmissions between the companies, recon teams, and the battalion's forward Tactical Operations Center (TOC) were recorded in the battalion's daily staff journal on February 13th.

*3:00 AM—Custer 6 to TOC: Ten minutes ago, rifle shots started down the valley from my location, three to four shots fired four different times. Believed to be the echoes of artillery rounds firing over the valley.*

Graham's trip flare shot up a few minutes later, hissing and illuminating the creek bed below. He scrambled back to his position on the embankment, grabbed the clacker, and looked down. Whatever it was had vanished. If it had been the enemy, he'd missed his chance. 1LT Gallagher crept up in the dark to see what happened. "Detonator jammed, sir," Graham whispered.

Barrow awoke to monitor the radios. At 4:00 AM, he reported the company's status as green, meaning all clear. He lit a cigarette, cupping it with his hand to avoid detection. He heard branches cracking outside their perimeter, and another trip flare shot up. He sent the following transmission.

*4:14 AM—Alpha Company to TOC: Some action on my perimeter. May be an animal... checking it out now.*

Just as he lifted his thumb to end the transmission, a grenade exploded in the foxhole of Pelullo and Ward. Then more grenades exploded about the perimeter, and Barrow saw brilliant streams of green tracer rounds coming from several positions. "We're taking fire!" he shouted, hitting CPT Wise on the boot. Some of the men guarding the perimeter threw grenades instead of firing their rifles to avoid revealing their positions. Amid the gunfire, 1SG John Potter jumped to his feet. "Top, get down!" yelled Barrow.

Then 1SG Potter was shot in the knee. "That son of a bitch shot me in the leg," he complained as a stream of sparks mysteriously rained down on Barrow.

Sharing a foxhole with CPT Wise was his forward observer, 1LT Ulrich. He sat up and scrambled to get his boots on. "I've been hit, sir," he said. Wise asked him where. "In the neck," he sputtered. These would be his last words, and he died in the arms of his radio operator, Danny Garrity.

Graham was pinned down between two grave mounds. Two Viet Cong fighters were so close that he could hear their banter. "I could have reached out and touched them," he said.

The fighting ended after about ten minutes. Among the dead were 1LT James Ulrich from Brecksville, Ohio and SP/4 Carl Mueller from Covington, Kentucky. Killed immediately in their foxhole were PFCs Leonard Pelullo from Philadelphia, Pennsylvania and Donnie Ward from Pollocksville, North Carolina.

*4:26 AM—Alpha Company to TOC: Activity has stopped. Probing throughout perimeter from the east at 1st Platoon and company command post location. Getting illumination.*

Danny Garrity called in the illumination rounds, revealing an eerie scene of grim-faced men tending to the wounded as their shadows swayed back and forth. In the darkness and with enemy still in the area, it was too dangerous for the medevac to come in. The men stayed at one hundred percent alert—which is to say that no one slept—for the rest of the night.

Graham contemplated his trip flare that had gone off about an hour before the attack. By missing his chance to blow the Claymore, he may have allowed the enemy to get in position, or so he thought. He'll never know if it was the Viet Cong or just another animal that tripped his flare. Still, he'd blame himself for the deaths of his friends Lenny Pelullo and Donnie Ward. Some said Rocco Valentino had been sleeping while on watch that night. True or not, he was blamed. Considering how sleep-deprived everyone was, he was probably not the only one.

The *Philadelphia Daily News* ran this article about Leonard Pelullo.

### **Memory Honored in a Pizza Parlor**

*"Lenny" Pelullo carried an old-fashioned silver certificate dollar bill in his wallet for years, recalled Vincent Tacconelli, a neighbor who runs a pizza parlor a few doors from the Pelullo's. When he received orders for Vietnam, Tacconelli warned him about carrying the currency. "Such a nice guy. We wanted to kid him a bit," Tacconelli said. "We told Lenny if he was captured with the silver certificate, the Viet Cong would think it was a map and try him as a spy." Before leaving, Pelullo turned it over to him for safekeeping. Hearing of Pelullo's death, Tacconelli returned the dollar to Pelullo's parents. They told him he should keep it, and since that day, it has hung in a frame on the wall of his pizza parlor.*

*Pelullo was an altar boy at Mother of Divine Grace Roman Catholic Church, a 1963 graduate of Northeast Catholic High School, active in Port Richmond baseball and basketball leagues, and worked for a lumber company before entering the Army in October 1965. The twenty-one-year-old Private First Class was a machine gunner in Alpha Company, 5th Battalion, 7th Cavalry, 1st Cavalry Division. Pelullo was killed during a Viet Cong assault on their company command post north of Bong Son in Binh Dinh Province on February 13th 1967.*

At first light, they surveyed the aftermath. Barrow noticed that his extra-long radio antenna had been shot up. It was bent over and in pieces, held together only by its inner nylon cord. Then it hit him—this is what had caused all those sparks to rain down on him during the attack. He found two bullets lodged in the extra battery pack for their radios. CPT Wise's sleeping mat had gone flat due to two other bullets. Just outside their perimeter, Barrow found a Viet Cong who'd been killed by a hand grenade. The young Vietnamese man was in pieces.

Their four dead were wrapped in ponchos and laid out in a neat row. 1SG Potter and the other wounded sat nearby, solemnly smoking cigarettes. Two medevac choppers descended to collect them. Then they flew away as the rest marched back out into the Bong Son to commence Operation Pershing.

The first day of the operation goes like this, according to the battalion's daily staff journal. Just after 6:00 AM, a sniper kills one of Bravo Company's men. 8:50—Charlie Company finds a stockpile of rice and kills two Viet Cong. 9:00—

Charlie Company picks up a nurse with a Red Cross card and medical supplies. 9:15—Custer 9 captures two Viet Cong when they smoke them out of a cave. 9:17—Delta Company finds nine hundred pounds of rice. 9:18—Bravo Company finds a pair of sandals near a blood trail and footprints leading north. 9:30—Delta Company captures two Viet Cong prisoners in a hut. 9:35—Charlie Company finds two thousand pounds of rice in a storage bin. 11:05—Bravo Company calls a medevac for a young village girl with a bleeding tumor.

11:30—Alpha Company captures three Viet Cong hiding in a village hut. 1:56 PM—Captures three more in another village. 2:11—3rd Platoon captures two more prisoners in a hamlet along a river while 2nd Platoon removes two from an underground bunker at gunpoint.

4:15—Bravo Company requests a medevac for a wounded civilian woman shot in the hip. 4:36—Viet Cong prisoner claims soldiers took two thousand Vietnamese dong from him.

*4:45 PM—Bravo Company to TOC: Could you get a ship to come out to pick up the money that belongs to the POW? My 3rd Platoon has it. They said they found it in the bushes where they picked him up.*

As its companies scoured the Bong Son, the battalion's forward command post finally arrived at LZ Santana that afternoon while sky cranes lowered howitzers from the artillery unit. Alpha Company returned to the base of the hill where they had started that morning. They bivouacked here again, where they had just been attacked the night before, ending an especially long first day of Operation Pershing.

The next morning, Alpha Company lifted three miles north, air assaulting onto a plateau area of the mountains along the northern reaches of the Bong Son plain. The other companies assaulted onto another plateau just southwest of Alpha Company. They marched back down into the plains to search more villages while scout ships flew above. At 6:05 PM, Bravo Company's 2nd Platoon became pinned down by snipers while crossing a rice paddy. One of Alpha Company's platoons was picked up and assaulted onto the high ground where the enemy fire came from, but no further contact was made. The men trudged on through the Bong Son for the next two days.

At 4:51 PM on February 16th, Charlie Company's 2nd Platoon started taking machine gun fire from a village three miles east of LZ Santana. Their platoon leader was killed immediately. Delta Company troops were dispatched from LZ Santana, followed by LTC Charles Canham in the battalion command chopper. Attempting to reach Charlie Company, LTC Canham and nine Delta Company men were hit by an errant rocket strike from one of the gunships. Canham's leg was ripped apart. They tried to evacuate on the command chopper but were shot down just after lift-off. Fighting raged into the night. Many attempts were made to medevac the wounded but failed as the dustoffs were taken under heavy fire whenever they approached. At 7:32, the battalion commander and other wounded were finally airlifted to the field hospital at LZ English.

At 7:55, the 1/8th Cav's Bravo Company was dropped into the area to assist. They marched overland for thirty minutes before reaching Charlie Company. When it was over, four of Charlie Company's men were dead, and four were wounded. Delta Company counted one dead, eight wounded, and one of their medics missing. The next day, LTC Andrew Gatsis would replace LTC Canham as battalion commander.

Alpha Company returned to LZ Santana that night to guard the firebase. In the wee morning hours, three grenades exploded within the perimeter. Machine gunners opened fire as the sky filled with flares. Men scrambled out of their bunkers, half-dazed, blinking, and shooting into the dark. No muzzle flashes or green tracer rounds could be seen, however. The enemy had simply thrown their grenades and melted back into the darkness.

As the flares burned out and shooting quieted, cries of pain could be heard from various corners of the firebase. One was from a trooper whose machine gun emplacement had been hit. The glow of red-lense flashlights bounced in the darkness as medics and others treated the wounded. SSG Robert Matulac called for a dustoff. Soon its distant thumping could be heard, becoming louder until the chopper landed to collect the four wounded. Then it thumped back into the night, leaving them again in silence. The grenade that hit the machine gun emplacement had also knocked the M-60 down the hill, and no one wanted to go down to search for it in the dark.

Found lying near one of the bunkers at daybreak was another grenade that had been thrown into the firebase. It was of the ChiCom variety and turned out to be a dud. Searching the area below the machine gun emplacement, it was apparent that the enemy had made off with the missing M-60.

### *17 February '67 – 22 weeks left*

*Been over a week, so I better write again. Those steel pots—well, we're wearing them again. We moved from LZ Hump to this rock and scrub brush hill, Santana, five miles from the sea. This area is nothing but bad news. I just talked with this guy in Rod's company yesterday at supper, and he got killed later last night. A good friend of Rod, too. Our Colonel was with them and got hit in the leg. Probably heard about us by now on the news. I heard Rod's company made it back on our hill, and Quinn says he saw Rod. So I'll see what he has to say about the bad news. This should be our last operation. I guess it'll last until June or July. I don't know, and neither do the generals. It depends on what we run into. Don't know what it is, but us guys haven't been getting along so good with our new sergeant.*

*Been taking a few pictures. One of me with over a week's growth of beard, the artillery guns, and all the fellows here. I'll get them developed and sent home when I'm in Hong Kong. Say, I got a Valentine from Mrs. Henning. It was sweet smelling, too. Woo, woo! So long,*

*Will*

## 17 February '67 – 22 weeks left

*Dear Hop-a-long,*

*Been an awful lot of action going on. Bravo, Charlie, Delta, and our company ran into a lot of shit last night and this morning. I took a few pictures of where we've been fighting. Less than a mile away from our big hill. Huey gunships, Chinook gunships, two jets, and two old-type fighter planes—plus artillery, and us guys with our mortars—leveling everything in sight. Last night about 8:00, seen some green tracer rounds from a V.C. shooting at a gunship. Man, that chopper whipped around and shot at the V.C. Good gravy, did he ever bring smoke. He turned on that machine gun, and it looked like a red snake. That V.C. didn't shoot back anymore. I hate those choppers too. Every time they blow our tent down, our gear flies away, and dirt gets all over our food. After they did our V.C. in, I'm not saying a bad word against them. They just might hear me.*

*Yes, I remember old Paula Marie. Never had her for any subjects. Did you have Sister Jean d'Arc? I had her for biology—do you like that subject? You're taking out Donna Bohl? My goodness, puppy love, haha! What do Ma and Dad think of this? That's worse than fighting a war sometimes! Tell me, what's it like? Do you walk around starry-eyed? I can see you two in school now, yeah, yeah!*

*I'll let you go now, so I can write another letter before chow gets here. Last night, we had all the hot dogs and cake and ice cream we could eat. Ain't that unbelievable news? Okay, lover boy. Next time, I'll just drop a line.*

*Camera Man,*

*Will*

On February 18th, Bravo Company was to conduct a recon-in-force mission in a large palm tree-laden village known as Tuy An, where an enemy command post was suspected. Nearby village chiefs and surrendering Chieu Hoi soldiers had reported "boo-coo" VC from the mountains moving into the village. A battalion after action report described what happened.

*Approaching the area at 4:01 PM, Bravo Company came under intense small arms and automatic weapons fire from within the fortified hamlet. They established a base of fire covering the platoon in contact, called for supporting fires, and attempted to maneuver other platoons to the flanks of the hamlet. The company command post took mortar fire until the enemy position was put out of* action by a recoilless rifle round. Charlie and Delta Companies were assaulted into the area along with the 1/7th Cav's Delta Company in an effort to encircle the enemy force of an estimated hundred men inside the well-fortified hamlet. Due to intense enemy fire across the open paddy and quickly arriving darkness, the elements failed to link up. Artillery and ARA fires were employed all night within the hamlet.

As the sun set on the 18th, six Bravo Company men lay dead just outside the village, along with one from Charlie and another from Delta. Meanwhile, Alpha Company's 4th Platoon received sniper fire at 5:20 PM atop LZ Santana. Fire was returned, killing one Viet Cong.

The next morning, Alpha Company was air assaulted into the rice paddies on the southwest side of Tuy An, where the other companies had fought the day before. Hundreds of civilians had already evacuated the hamlet at daybreak. Airstrikes had pummeled enemy positions throughout the village just minutes before Alpha Company's arrival. Along with Charlie and Delta, they formed a cordon and swept through. Many dead Viet Cong were found among the smoking huts, and more were taken prisoner. Sporadic firefights broke out during their search. One Charlie Company trooper hit a booby trap that killed him and mangled three others. Later that afternoon, two soldiers of Delta Company were wounded by an enemy grenade. After searching every hut, bunker, tunnel, and water well in the village, the companies fanned out from Tuy An and continued searching and destroying in the area for the next two days.

SSG Robert Matulac was responsible for calling in the helicopters and for giving the proper direction, or azimuth, from which to approach the landing zone. Once the chopper was in the area, smoke grenades were set off to show their exact location. Matulac would guide the pilot in with hand signals. Once the nose of the chopper was nearly touching his chest, he would lower his arms to his sides, signaling the pilot to touch down.

On the morning of February 22nd, Matulac was guiding in a log ship. "I gave the pilot the azimuth to land and told him to ignore what appeared to be the proper approach," he recalled. "All of a sudden, the bird disappeared. Then I heard the chopper coming in behind me. As he attempted to land, he hit a hidden rock crop that ripped off the tail section. A team came out to assess the damage. 'I told him to come in on this azimuth,' I said to the Major in charge. 'But he decided I didn't know what I was doing, and he came in the wrong way.' I was told it was pilot error. I was very relieved."

One of 1LT Barry Gallagher's men feared becoming the target of friendly fire. Many blamed Rocco Valentino for the night attack that had killed four on February 13th. Gallagher had him pulled from the field for his own safety.

*Leonard Pelullo — Carl Mueller*

*Donnie Ward — James Ulrich*

# 21
# HUNTER-KILLERS

*If they made a Top Gun movie about gunship pilots,*
*he'd have been cast in the lead role.*

Forward observer 2LT George Kalergis arrived in February to replace Alpha Company's 1LT James Ulrich, who had been killed on the 13th. He'd been in Vietnam for about a month, initially assigned to the 1st Air Cavalry Division's 1/9th Cav. "I knew I should have studied harder in college," he said of his first mission. "It seemed like just yesterday I was opening the letter from Uncle Sam. The next thing I knew, I had volunteered for Officer Candidate School at Fort Sill, Oklahoma. After six grueling months, I graduated as a Second Lieutenant, a commissioned officer in the field artillery. Now it's January 1967, the sun is setting, and I'm sitting in a GP Medium tent at LZ Pony."

Sweating in the heat amid the smell of hot canvas, 2LT Kalergis and the 1/9th pilots awaited the squadron commander. The new lieutenant was filled with nervous excitement. This was his first real mission. But the only live artillery he'd ever called in was at Fort Sill's training range—three rounds in all—while sitting comfortably on a folding chair perched atop a hill overlooking the impact area.

Everyone rose to attention as the 1/9th's commander entered the tent. "At ease, men," he said as he picked up a pointer and motioned to a map of An Lao.

Describing the commander as confident and fit, Kalergis remarked, "If they made a *Top Gun* movie about gunship pilots, he'd have been cast in the lead role."

There may not be a *Top Gun* movie about helicopter pilots. Still, there is that scene in *Apocalypse Now* where Robert Duvall plays LTC Bill "I love the smell of Napalm in the morning" Kilgore, a 1/9th commander who blasts *Ride of the Valkyries* on loudspeakers attached to his gunship while attacking a village—then goes surfing in the South China Sea afterward. Though not realistic, the famous scene speaks to the crazy, fearless reputation of the 1/9th Cavalry.

"This is our new forward observer, Lieutenant Kalergis," the commander began. "Charlie Troop, he will be flying with you tomorrow and will take the place of a door gunner with one of your Red teams. He will be available to call in artillery and air strikes. Welcome to Nam, Kalergis. Do you have your radio and maps ready?"

The 1/9th aviators flew in teams. The White Team scouts flew lightly armed, bubble-shaped H-13 scout ships, searching for the enemy. The Red Team hunter-killers did the same in heavily armed Huey gunships, attacking with mounted grenade launchers, rockets, M-60s, and miniguns. Following the Red Team's aerial assault, the Blue Team Hueys would drop in and unload their infantrymen to pursue the enemy on foot. Responsible for calling in artillery, Kalergis was also tasked on his first mission to "fill in" for one of the Red Team's door gunners. He had never fired an M-60 before, so the other door gunner gave him a crash course just before take-off.

Kalergis described his first flight on a gunship as a roller coaster ride on steroids—the chopper laboring up over the mountains north of LZ Pony, then plunging wildly down the other side and into the An Lao Valley. "Holy shit," he thought, "I've never been on a gunship before, and here I am flying into combat and manning a machine gun I have never fired."

They followed the scout ship through the valley for about an hour. Kalergis became comfortable with the chopper's movement and started enjoying the ride. He noticed the beauty of An Lao, how the valley floor appeared as an emerald carpet that became terraced as it approached the surrounding mountains. A wide river known as the Song An Lao meandered through the valley. So low was their flight that he could see dozens of fish swimming in the clear water. Scattered about were many burned-out villages and others that just looked deserted.

Making a sharp turn, their gunship started following a ravine up a steep mountainside. Kalergis noticed a small group of Viet Cong running up a trail below. The pilot came over the intercom, "Fighter Red, rolling in hot!" He felt the aircraft lurch upward briefly before nosediving, firing a rapid stream of 40mm grenades at the fleeing enemy. He watched the men fall violently as if struck by some invisible force—then only patches of blood where the soldiers once stood. The other door gunner had opened fire. Kalergis followed suit but was told to hold off as friendlies were in the area.

His heart was still pounding when they moved farther up the valley. A lone middle-aged man was working in the field near an abandoned village. The area had been evacuated and was considered a free-fire zone, but the man didn't look like a soldier. Another helicopter descended toward the nervous-looking farmer as Kalergis and the gunship crew hovered above. A door gunner from the chopper below jumped into the dried-up rice paddy with his pistol, preparing to take the man in for questioning. Dirt suddenly erupted all around the helicopter below. For a moment, Kalergis was confused as he couldn't hear the gunfire beneath the thumping of the chopper. As the door gunner fell face-first into the paddy, he realized they were taking machine gun fire from the village. The chopper below strained upward, leaving the door gunner to die in the paddy. Kalergis felt his stomach drop as his gunship lurched forward, unleashing a volley of rockets on the village. Like giant Roman candles, they launched from the sides of the gunship, engulfing him in a torrent of red sparks swirling through the chopper's open doors. "Why aren't you shooting?" yelled the pilot over the intercom.

"You just told me not to!"

"Just shoot, God damn it!"

Kalergis unleashed a six hundred-round-per-minute stream of lead on the enemy. The gunship banked to the left and made another run. A bullet tore through the floor of the chopper next to his boot, then exited through the wall near his head, leaving him dazed for a moment.

After several more runs, the Blue Team arrived to drop infantrymen into the paddy surrounding the village. Kalergis described the men jumping from the chopper, "like popcorn jumping wildly from beneath the lid of a popcorn popper." He was relieved to see the other chopper's door gunner, who he'd thought had been killed, running toward the troopers.

As the gunships ran low on ammunition, the pilot told Kalergis to call in artillery. He got on his radio. In successive volleys, he called in over two hundred 105mm high-explosive rounds. "Watching it rain down on that village seemed unreal," he recalled. "The incandescent flashes, the billows of black smoke, the shock waves that followed. It was more artillery than I'd ever called. Hell, it was more than I'd ever seen."

Kalergis went out with the H-13 scout ship the next day, calling in even more rounds. In the middle of their attack, the pilot was shot in the neck, yet he continued the mission. Eventually, he grew weak, and they returned to LZ Pony.

Now in late February, Kalergis found himself on a helicopter full of food containers and mail bound for Alpha Company, 5/7th Cavalry. In the whirling dust of the chopper's downdraft, a squinting CPT Wise greeted him as he jumped off. He introduced Kalergis to his new radio operator. "I hope you last longer than Lieutenant Ulrich, sir," said Danny Garrity, shaking his hand. And so began his life as a ground pounder with Alpha Company.

*An Lao Valley, source unknown*

# 22
# RUMORS

*I will not use my grade or position to attain pleasure, profit, or personal safety. — Creed of the Noncommissioned Officer*

On February 22nd, the 5/7th Cav was designated the 1st Air Cavalry's Ready Reaction Force. The companies were split up and sent to different firebases throughout the division's area of operations. When needed, the nearest company would be called to assist a unit in contact. The battalion command and Delta Company flew to LZ Two Bits. Alpha Company would move to LZ Pony, Bravo to LZ English, and Charlie to LZ Dog. But first, Alpha Company was dropped at LZ English for a chance to get cleaned up. Will ran into some old buddies here and met a little monkey looking for handouts. Then they flew to LZ Pony. The firebase sat on a short wide hill mass in the Kim Son Valley, flanked by rice paddies and surrounded by distant mountains. It was accessible by a dirt road that led to a nearby village. They were five miles east of where LZ Bird had been nearly overrun in December. Two days later, 3rd Brigade commander Colonel (COL) Jonathan Burton came to present Air Medals earned for performing over twenty-five air assaults.

### 24 February '67

Dear Folks,

*Sorry about the dirty paper, but beggars can't be choosey. We left Santana and went to LZ English. Met old Figueroa, Leona, and Big King—they're with the 1/7th now. We had some time, so we went to the village and had a beer and a bunch of bananas. Later, we came to LZ Pony. Ain't too bad here, right next to another village. Taking all kinds of pictures. When we first got here, Doc and I were standing around, and a full Colonel came up to us. He whipped out his knife and made some sketches in the dirt—had a nice little chat and gave us the scoop on what's happening. The 25th Division is just a little ways from us. The rest is pretty much confidential. You know how it is when important people discuss tactics. Yeah, got to keep a tight lip. Anyway, got a kick out of it. Everyone else was sitting and watching us. I had my shirt off—maybe he thought I was a lieutenant.*

*We're getting our Air Medals. This is for twenty-five air assaults. I'm going to throw out the medal with my C.I.B. if them damn cooks and clerks get one.*

*The guys in Rod's company like their new C.O., Captain Swain. They say they're in good hands. I hear we're losing Captain Wise. Hate to see him go.*

*Say, I am going on R&R on March 21st. Closed up for now. Mosquitoes are getting so bad you need a blood transfusion every morning. And it's starting to get hot, hot, hot. And also getting dark.*

*So long,*

*Will*

Sitting on sandbag bunkers at LZ Pony, Marvin Bierschbach told Will about a rumor he'd heard. Apparently, one of the Vietnamese barbers at An Khe had been a Viet Cong informant. Also, someone in supply had been selling their stuff to the locals.

In *On The Tiger's Back*, Bernard Grady tells of how he caught the soldier in charge of the 5/7th's supply shop in a scheme to line his pockets by selling poncho liners and other supplies to a Vietnamese laundry in An Khe. CPT Grady had been transferred from Charlie Company to the battalion's rear headquarters. He was now the Battalion Adjutant in charge of personnel administration.

The poncho liners were lightweight, semi-waterproof, and dried out quickly—a vast improvement on the old wool blankets that were heavier, readily soaked up water, and never dried out. In damp conditions, they were far superior in dryness, comfort, warmth, and weight. They were also prized by the Vietnamese, who would sew them into jackets. Plenty of old wool blankets lay around the 5/7th supply shop, but no poncho liners. According to the man in charge, there was a severe shortage of poncho liners throughout the division. This was his excuse for why replacement soldiers were sent to the field with the old wool blankets. In reality, they would unwittingly sign for the new poncho liners, and he would later write them off as field losses or lost in combat. He was also selling Lifeline packs and uniforms. I wondered if this had anything to do with the disagreement Donald Duncan had with his boss—before volunteering for field duty and then getting killed on Thanksgiving Day.

The soldier in charge of supply was eventually caught red-handed by MPs who had been tipped off by Grady. Thinking that he and Grady were friends, he seemed surprised. He asked Grady why he did it. He replied, "For the good of the men. For the guys out in the boonies with a wet blanket. You wouldn't know because you've been back here in relative comfort and safety. They're the reason. Good Lord, man, we've shipped fifty or sixty good soldiers home in boxes already. Don't you think they deserve some comfort before they're zipped into a body bag?"

*Will Bowe with monkey at LZ English*

*Wilson (left) and Rodney Henning (right) at LZ English, photo by Will Bowe*

*Chinook delivering howitzer and ammunition to LZ Pony, photo by Will Bowe*

*Fire mission at LZ Pony, photo by Robert Matulac*

# 23
# R&R

*This is a Pan Am aircraft, which means you are now on American soil!*

As Will and Martin Quinn shared some C-Rations at LZ Pony, the Beach Boys could be heard harmonizing on one of the artilleryman's transistor radios, *"Straight to Hawaii, do you wanna come along with me..."* The AFVN disc jockey chimed in, "There's no doubt that Hawaii is the surf and sun capital of the world, and a great place for a five-day vacation, and a great place to meet your own 'Honolulu Lulu.' So say aloha to the islanders, and say hello to your R&R officer, and *'go to Hawaii...'"* Will's R&R was coming up at the end of March. Just like Royce Barrow, Al Patrillo, and Martin Quinn, he chose Hong Kong.

On March 1st, the 5/7th Cav was released as the division's reserve force and returned to the Bong Son region. At 9:35 AM, the first of Alpha Company's choppers touched down on LZ Geronimo, a firebase secured by Delta Company. The battalion command would arrive later in the day. Bravo and Charlie Companies were dropped into different landing zones in the same area that morning. Returning to the Bong Son, they captured twelve Viet Cong on their first day back. The next day, they captured three and killed four.

### 4 March '67 – 21 weeks left

*Dear Folks,*

*Best start this letter before it gets dark. We humped with the company the other day. Those rice paddies sure haven't changed. Now we're on this hill, Geronimo. We came to guard an artillery unit, but we're moving back out tomorrow.*

*Well, happy birthday, Ma. Wish I could send something, but the best I can do is my thoughts in a letter. I got a letter from the Simons the other day, and they said Allen's coming home on the 12th—said he had third-degree burns. Say, I got Joanne's flag. I wanted to put it in the mess hall, but it's closed. So I'll put it in the barracks when I leave for R&R. I am going to send a surprise home when I'm on R&R.*

*Will*

After patrolling around LZ Geronimo for four days, Alpha Company flew west on March 5th, dropping into the mountains between An Lao and Bong Son at 9:21 AM. They marched south. The next night, one of their ambushes spotted a group of Viet Cong moving in from the high ground to their east. They called in artillery. Searching the blast area, they found three killed. Another had been wounded but escaped, leaving a blood trail through the jungle. Another ambush team reported movement at 11:05 PM, and artillery was again called in. This time they found only packs and no bodies while spotting one man running away with a flashlight.

On March 7th, the men of Delta Company discovered a cave suspected of housing Viet Cong. A former intelligence officer, CPT Walt Swain valued information over dead bodies. Rather than throwing in heavy explosives, he placed a grenade outside the cave's tiny entrance and pulled the pin. Following the blast, six enemy fighters emerged through the smoke to surrender. Then, instead of sending in one of his men to search the tunnel as most officers would have done, he stripped off his gear and crawled in with his pistol and flashlight. Minutes later, he emerged with a dirty smile and five enemy rifles.

That same day, Alpha Company was picked up and dropped into a small river valley in the mountains. They reported finding ten water buffalo in a pen. Battalion told them to move on and leave the water buffalo alone. They also found many hastily dug graves. The enemy lacked medevac helicopters and typically buried their dead wherever they died. The men would dig up each of these graves as they found them and search the decomposing bodies for papers and maps. After bivouacking on March 8th, a scout ship reported three individuals observing the company from atop a hill across the valley at 8:35 PM.

They patrolled through the small river valley for two more days. On March 10th, Alpha Company flew back to LZ Pony with the battalion command to serve as the reserve force for 3rd Brigade. Meanwhile, Charlie Company was flown to a bridge that spanned the Bong Son River near the town of Bong Son. Bridges were prime enemy targets, so one company always pulled security at the Bong Son Bridge.

One of the more established firebases, LZ Pony had outhouses. They were ramshackle affairs, made of plywood with a shad-type roof and a screen along the top. Inside was a bench and two toilet seats. Beneath each seat was one half of a fifty-gallon metal drum, with handles attached to the sides.

When the buckets were full and teeming with flies, they would be replaced with empty ones, but something had to be done with the waste. "Everyone had shit-burning detail at least once or twice, but I got it all the time," Arnott Graham recalled. "Sergeant Jesus DeLeon was a stocky Puerto Rican in his forties. I told him I was done burning shit. We argued, and he punched me in the chest. Then I pushed him up against the outhouse with my bayonet."

Each bucket held about two hundred pounds of waste, so two men were required to lift it out through a hinged door in the back. To avoid discouraging its continued use, the buckets were dragged about thirty feet away from the outhouse before burning. If they were full—and they were always full—the waste would slosh and splash the men as they lugged the buckets over rough terrain. They poured diesel fuel on the waste and set it on fire. The smoke was profuse, thick and black, completely opaque, and they immediately knew which way the breeze was blowing. Amid the stench, they would take tent poles and "stir it like you're mixing a cake," Graham explained. The buckets had to be stirred every few minutes, and more diesel fuel added whenever the flames dwindled.

After several hours, the buckets would be empty, save for a crusty black residue at the bottom. The stench would remain on the workers for the rest of the day, even after showering and changing fatigues. The job's only benefit was that officers and NCOs would all keep their distance while the work was performed.

SSG Robert Matulac often took up mail call duty. For some time, SFC Thomas Meek had been looking for a package whenever a log ship came in. Two bags of mail arrived one day, one filled with letters—the other mostly empty, but for a damaged box at the bottom. The much-anticipated box was for SFC Meek. "Sorry about that," Matulac said, handing him the box with his crushed birthday cake. A bit disappointed, he took the box and sat down to eat the crumbs.

Graham had also gotten a birthday cake from his mother, spoiled by the time he received it. SSG Bobby Hayslip had approached him once, shortly after mail call. "Graham, I know you'll understand," he began, explaining how he couldn't read very well. And so it was that Graham would read Hayslip's letters for him—some from his mother, but most from the girl he'd married just before shipping out to Vietnam.

During some free time at LZ Pony, Will took his camera to the nearby village with Graham, Willie Harris, Kazimierz Slomiany, and a few others. One of the villagers Will made friends with was Ten Ninh, a boy who tended his family's cows in the valley.

### 14 March '67 – 19 weeks left

*Dear Folks,*

*I better start writing, for it's been a while. We started humping the hills, and wouldn't you know, it rained from the very first day to the last. Now we're back at LZ Pony. Went to Mass last Sunday. Didn't know it was Passion Sunday already. Easter will be on my R&R. Only three more days, and I'll be cutting out of the field. This is for sure, no more Army after August 1st—hot dog! But I have to be in Viet Nam at least until July 25th. I have to order a car sometime between now and the end of April if I want one to drive home. I was looking at this Charger or maybe a GT.*

*I got a good Vietnamese friend, about twelve years old. He has five cows he tends every day. His name is Ten Ninh. Nice little kid.*

*Had a hard time staying up on guard*

At 11:40 AM on March 14th, the brigade commander's helicopter was shot down near the banks of the Song Con, four miles into the mountains west of the Kim Son Valley. Forty-five minutes later, Alpha Company's troopers descended to secure the chopper. After a ninety-minute wait, a Chinook arrived to carry off the command chopper, and they returned to LZ Pony.

The next day, Alpha Company's 1st and 3rd Platoons air assaulted into a small valley where enemy activity had been spotted in the mountains to the east. No contact was made, but they kept searching until the following day. On the 16th, 3rd Platoon came upon three recently occupied huts, finding bloody identification cards and bandoliers filled with rice. 1st Platoon discovered two more huts on their own patrol that afternoon. They burned the huts to the ground and returned to LZ Pony at dusk.

## 16 March '67

*Dear Folks,*

*I didn't sign that last one because we were rushing to rescue a downed chopper. Yes, I got your package. But so small, my goodness. Send me a big box of those walnut cookies, some instant cocoa, and some Kool-Aid. Cocoa goes good with guard duty and Kool-Aid for this bad water. Yes, I know General Norton. Doc was going to take a picture of me yesterday while I shook his hand, but he never showed up.*

*Will*

## Early 17 March '67

*All excited and ready to take off. So I won't be writing for a while. Well, I best pack up. Don't want to miss the flight to LZ English—then to An Khe, then to Cam Ranh Bay, and then to Hong Kong. So be ready for a pleasant surprise in about three weeks, okay?*

*Rip-Roaring R&R,*

*Will*

On March 17th, Will took a series of helicopter flights until arriving at Cam Ranh Bay's airfield. On the tarmac, a gleaming white commercial jet with a blue Pan Am logo on its tail sat waiting. Boarding the plane, the men were greeted by smiling Pan Am stewardesses—the most glamorous in the world with their baby blue caps and white gloves. They immediately advised them, "This is a Pan Am aircraft, which means you are now on American soil!" Spirits were high, and the cabin was noisy. Unless they had spent time in a military hospital, most had not seen a round-eyed American woman since arriving in Vietnam. Many took their chance to flirt with stewardesses, and some flirted back. They all cheered as the plane lifted. On their way to Hong Kong, they were served a first-class meal of filet mignon and ice cream.

Several airlines contracted to fly servicemen to and from Vietnam, along with military cargo and remains of the dead, but only Pan Am ran R&R flights.

The program started in March 1966 and functioned like its own mini airline. Pan Am charged the government one dollar per month for the R&R program's first four months, costing the company nearly three million dollars, after which it operated at cost.

In the 1960s, Pan Am's stewardesses were required to have twenty-twenty vision, at least two years of college, fluency in a foreign language, and could not be married or pregnant. Adhering to a strict code of dress and appearance, they also maintained height and weight standards. The mandatory retirement age was thirty-five. Routinely flying in and out of the war zone, Pan Am's R&R crews were all volunteers, receiving no special training or extra pay.

Several former stewardesses were interviewed for the story *Pan Am in Vietnam* by Business Insider reporters Charlie Herman, Julia Press, and Sarah Wyman. They told of how they would make the R&R flights fun and the boys feel at home by doing pretend fashion shows in the aisle and baking chocolate chip cookies. They all spoke of how young the men looked—many still teenagers, reading comic books—and how some had never flown in an airplane. One recalled exchanging letters with some of the young men she met on her flights and how each was eventually killed in action.

Will stayed in a cheap Hong Kong hotel with some of the guys he met on the plane. They went out drinking every night and slept in each morning. For fifty cents, rickshaws would take them anywhere in the city. Will went to church once during his visit, but when the service started, he realized they were Presbyterians. While downtown, he bought a Beatles album, a reel-to-reel tape recorder, and a silk jacket with a map of Vietnam embroidered on the back.

The 5/7th Cav recorded the following radio transmissions on March 17th.

*10:06 AM—Delta Company to TOC: Found decomposed body in a cave entrance and two NVA packs. Tried to remove the body but only removed portions of it.*

*12:30 PM—Alpha Company to TOC: 3rd Platoon burning huts at BR 791-832.*

Later that night, in the sweltering command post tent at LZ Pony, CPT A.J. Wise dictated a letter to Mr. and Mrs. Salvatore Pelullo. The letter told of the respect and admiration that all the officers and enlisted men had for their son Leonard—how his death was a shock to all who knew him—how Chaplain Thomas Widdel held a memorial service for him attended by all the men in the company—how they'd been attacked, and how their son was successful in defending their position yet mortally wounded in the battle—and how he was not subject to any undue suffering. It was one of many such letters he'd already sent.

The next morning, medevac was called for a man who had shot himself in the hand with his pistol. An hour later, Alpha Company was flown from LZ Pony to take over the security mission at Bong Son Bridge.

*March 19th*

*4:50 AM—Bunkers 8, 9, 10, 11, and 12 were inspected by CPT Frey with no discrepancies. Charlie Company commander was notified of the lack of Claymores. Bunker 12 was alert and answered questions without hesitation.*

*March 20th*

*5:06 PM—Alpha Company to TOC: ARVN advisor reports that a woman was killed by a mine, as reported by village chief of Lang Quang. People will carry the body down to the river at BR 809-959 to bury the body.*

Civilians were everywhere as the men secured the Bong Son Bridge and patrolled the area. Bill Purdy spoke of a rare time when their platoon leader got really pissed at them. They were on a hilltop near the bridge. There usually wasn't much action here, but they had been taking sporadic sniper fire. One of the "Coca-Cola girls" was climbing up, trying to reach the thirsty soldiers holding out dollar bills atop the hill. 1LT James Harmon was livid and chewed them all out for putting the girl at risk.

The other time was when their platoon sergeant, SFC James Bonner, went around checking their guard positions one night in April to find absolutely none of them awake. "Lieutenant Harmon was really disappointed in us that night," Purdy said, noting how no one meant to fall asleep on watch but that it was inevitable when they were so sleep-deprived.

Most of the battalion's areas of operation were under evacuation orders, meaning no one was supposed to be there unless productively engaged in the war. Many villagers were relocated to New Life hamlets established by the South Vietnamese government. Radio transmissions recorded in the battalion's staff journal show just how many civilians inhabited the battlefield during this time.

*March 21st*

*8:38 AM—Custer 1 to TOC: Picked up three young kids around twelve years old and two old ladies driving cattle. Delta Company commander requested we pick them up. What should we do with them?*

*TOC to Custer 1: Move them towards LZ Pistol, then release them. Just get them out of the area.*

*March 22nd*

*7:22 AM—Delta Company to TOC: 3rd Platoon picked up nine male Vietnamese in white uniforms, ages twenty to thirty. 7:30—We now have fifty detainees. There are ARVN forces at my 3rd Platoon location protesting against them picking up these individuals of military age. Two ARVN men with BARs have gotten down into position and made threatening gestures. 8:30—Individuals turned out to be farmers getting hay for their cattle.*

*11:13*—Alpha Troop 1/9th Cav to TOC: Inserting Blue Team to search villages.

*11:45*—As soon as we started our prep, the whole valley started to move out. People moving northwest carrying belongings and herding cattle.

*12:45 PM*—Delta Company to TOC: 3rd Platoon picked up seven Viet Cong suspects. One dressed in gray garb, Buddhist type, herding cattle. He says he is a Buddhist yet knows nothing of Buddhism. Found this out after interpreter questioned him. He also believes suspect is Viet Cong. Remainder of Viet Cong suspects, age twenty-five to thirty, dressed in black pajama shorts. *2:50*—3rd Platoon found some huts with writing, "American G.I. go home." In Vietnamese, writing says the people like the VC and the VC will win the war.

*2:50*—Alpha Company to TOC: Some ARVNs came up to my 3rd Platoon and said four Viet Cong were moving east at BR 885-953. 3rd Platoon is pursuing them. Artillery was called in.

*2:55*—TOC to Brigade: Request scout ship to check out area where ARVN spotted four Viet Cong.

*4:45*—Alpha Company to TOC: Reference four Viet Cong spotted earlier by ARVN. 3rd Platoon spotted three Viet Cong suspects getting into a boat on the river at 889-958. Scout ship called in, observed three suspects in the boat smiling and waving at scout ship. No weapons sighted.

*March 23rd*

*11:38 AM*—Scout Ship to TOC: We spotted several people at 865-865. Looks like they are moving out. Several military-age personnel working in rice paddies.

*12:01 PM*—Delta Company to TOC: Between 10:00 and 11:00 AM, we picked up twenty-five Viet Cong suspects moving across rice paddies. Wearing pajamas and straw hats, all males. They are being returned to LZ Pistol.

*12:06*—Scout Ship to TOC: Haven't seen anything significant in the area, except there are about eighty percent fewer people than when I arrived.

*4:41*—Delta Company to TOC: Request medevac for four wounded in action from a booby trap at 785-885. Made from butterfly bomblet. Point man tripped what appeared to be vines stretched across the trail. Blast covered sixty meters.

*5:06*—Charlie Company to TOC: Found booby trap at 784-868. Was U.S. hand grenade with pin pulled and safety pin inserted. We destroyed it.

*5:45*—Bravo Company to TOC: 1st Platoon spotted five Viet Cong at 852-886. Believed they had weapons. Fired at them, and they fled, and one woman was killed in action. 1st Platoon pursued, pushing them into 3rd Platoon's blocking position. Woman had khaki shirt and black bottoms. Three in black pajamas. Fifth had light blue trousers and black shirt, also had weapon.

*10:00 PM—The barrier at LZ Pony was inspected by CPT Frey. All personnel questioned were very alert and responsive. Mosquito nets have been ordered but have not yet arrived.*

*March 24th*

*10:25 AM—Delta Company to TOC: Reference booby trap that went off last night. Point man says it was a grenade inside of a coconut.*

*12:10 PM—Alpha Company to TOC: While reconning, 2nd Platoon received two sniper rounds, then two or three more while on ground. Spotted unknown size force in rice paddy. Artillery and armed Chinooks called in. Chinooks also took sniper fire.*

*1:20—Scout Ship to TOC: In restricted area near LZ Pony on southwest side of river, about twenty male children and females herding buffalo moving north.*

*1:35—Alpha Company to TOC: Request medevac for two hit by booby trap—one seriously wounded. Booby trap believed to be a grenade with tripwire.*

On March 26th, all companies of the 5/7th Cav were relieved in place by those of the 1/5th and 2/12th Cavs as the battalion prepared for a contingency mission in the An Lao Valley with the Vietnamese Marine Corps. Alpha Company's lift-off was set for 10:15 the next morning. Bob Matulac described their previous eleven days at the Bong Son Bridge.

*We provided security for the Bong Son Bridge area. The NVA had attempted to destroy the bridge as it was the main thoroughfare. All day, people brought things to sell at the markets—animals, pigs, chickens, ducks, foodstuffs, and even furniture. Army vehicles also used the bridge. It gave us a break, and we washed our uniforms and bathed in the river. Guarding the bridge was boring. We had a checkpoint to ensure the VC weren't infiltrating. We sent patrols to different areas, and 4th Platoon provided mortar fire when requested.*

*One day, the Donut Dollies, who were Special Service volunteers, came down to entertain us and give us donuts and candy. Well, they were accompanied by some officers from our battalion, and they decided to take a swim. Of course, the enlisted were not invited to the soiree. While the officers and dollies were cavorting, I noticed some "logs" floating by, coming from some houses further upstream. These were not wooden logs but rather brown logs of defecation. When I pointed this out, the swimmers evacuated the river really fast! The speed with which the party broke up was enjoyed by the troops.*

*When we got our traveling orders back to An Lao, the battalion priest came and gave mass as helicopters landed on the pickup zone.*

Following Father Tom's sermon on the sandy riverbanks, Alpha Company loaded its choppers and headed back to An Lao. At 10:38 AM on March 27th, they dropped onto LZ Beaver in the mountains west of the valley. To their south, Charlie Company was flown to LZ Buffalo, while to their north, Delta Company was flown to LZ Bear. Bravo Company secured the battalion command post at LZ Sandra, a high mountaintop overlooking the valley. Winding through the two-mile-wide valley was the Song An Lao, with many large villages along its banks.

The men of Alpha, Charlie, and Delta Companies moved through thick jungles and down steep mountainsides to take up blocking positions while the Vietnamese Marines pushed through the valley. Each company encountered recently used enemy huts and burned them all to the ground. The sun was relentless in the early afternoon, and several passed out from heat stroke. One Delta Company soldier was wounded by a punji stake on their initial assault, as were four others that afternoon. A couple hours later, they took fire from enemy snipers, but no one was hurt.

Charlie Company suffered two wounded by punji stakes on their initial assault and three more while hacking through the jungle. A dustoff hovered above and lowered its hoist to collect the first of their wounded but was taken under fire and forced to abort the rescue. The chopper had taken four hits but made it back to LZ English. At 2:12 PM, snipers killed one of Charlie Company's men and wounded two. At 5:00 PM, two more were wounded by an artillery round that fell short of its target. Killed by the sniper fire was SFC Thomas Meek, the one Matulac recalled eating his crushed birthday cake. He'd recently been transferred from Alpha to Charlie Company. From Grand Rapids, Michigan, he was twenty-nine years old.

That same day, Will was headed back from R&R. Unlike their flight to Hong Kong, their return flight was utterly subdued. After landing at Cam Rahn Bay, Will traveled by military transport to An Khe, then to LZ English, where he ran into Arnott Graham, and they visited the town of Bong Son together.

### 27 March '67 – 17 weeks left

*Dear Folks,*

*Back at LZ English, hanging out in the clubhouse. I hope you received your package. I sent it Air Mail. I sent another by boat with my sports jacket and four rolls of film. I can't wait for you to get that first package. A lieutenant at Cam Ranh Bay offered me fifty dollars to delay my R&R two days. "Sorry about that," I said. I seen Rod today as I left An Khe, on his way to R&R in Taipei.*

*Your son,*

*Will*

*Thomas Meek*

*Vietnamese civilians, photo by Marvin Bierschbach*

*Ten Ninh standing in front of other village children, photos by Will Bowe*

*Willie Harris and village kids near LZ Pony*

*Kazimierz Slomiany (middle) and buddies, photos by Will Bowe*

*Bill Purdy near Bong Son Bridge*

*Left–right: Al Patrillo, Doc, Martin Quinn, John Fulford, Marvin Bierschbach, Gerald Anderson, and Paul Lussier*

*4th Platoon firing mortars at Bong Son Bridge*

*Father Tom Widdel conducting mass*

*SFC James Bonner coordinating lift-off, photos by Robert Matulac*

## 24
# BEAUTIFUL THINGS

*They all call me "Bow-E," ha! What a time we all have.*

Flying out on the next morning's resupply, Will and Graham returned to Alpha Company in the An Lao Valley. That afternoon, the company reported finding women and children washing rice along a stream near a cave, one military-age male among them. A half-hour later, they spotted three Viet Cong with weapons walking along the same stream and called in artillery strikes. Meanwhile, Charlie Company suffered six more wounded from punji stakes and one who tripped a crossbow-type booby trap, resulting in an arrow shot through his pack. Hoists were used to sling-load their casualties out the next morning.

On March 30th, Charlie Company was flown to LZ Sandra while Alpha and Delta were flown to the northernmost reaches of the valley. They found signs of recent enemy activity and many more encampments. At 2:36 PM, they took sniper fire amid the crackling and popping and smoke of burning huts—but the enemy proved elusive. When dark came, they performed a fake extraction to draw the enemy into the area but with no success. They marched on the next day, finding more recently used huts, bunkers, and tunnels. Another soldier was evacuated with heat exhaustion, along with others suffering punji stake wounds.

Later that afternoon, Alpha Company's platoons were split up and moving on their own. 1LT James Harmon's 2nd Platoon was searching along a small tributary stream of the Song An Lao, where a narrow offshoot of the valley jutted into the mountains. Marty Scull was walking point, followed by his buddy A.G. Hensley with his M-79 grenade launcher. Just behind was their machine gunner Bill Purdy and assistant gunner Ed Raciborski. Scully recalled how 1LT Harmon had ordered them to go through this clearing and across a wide-open rice paddy. It looked like the perfect spot to get ambushed, and Scully argued against it. But Harmon was getting orders directly from battalion command, and there seemed to be no choice. The following is Purdy's account of what happened.

*Following the stream, the going was tough in the thick of the jungle, and we were moving slow. Lieutenant Harmon was on the radio with the battalion command chopper as a result of the slow movement. Following a heated exchange with the command chopper, our platoon was ordered to cross the stream and move on to a parallel trail. Normally, we avoided trails whenever possible due to ambushes. Before moving out along the trail, we took a five-minute smoke break where John Kruetzkamp, Ed Raciborski, and A.G. Hensley and I shared some C-Ration cheese crackers and a canteen of "iodine Kool-Aid."*

*I can still picture it in my mind as if it were yesterday. When we moved out along the trail, we started across a clearing. Hensley was carrying his M-79 grenade launcher and approximately ten feet in front of me. Immediately ambushed; upon entering the clearing, Hensley was shot and killed, and another soldier was wounded. Lieutenant Harmon was instrumental in recovering Hensley's body while we returned fire on the enemy's suspected position. When it was over, Hensley's body and the wounded were flown to LZ English.*

Purdy thought that if Hensley had just gotten down and waited for the machine gun to be employed rather than immediately returning fire, his life might have been spared. In the ensuing firefight, he just kept firing his machine gun while others tried to get Hensley's body along with the wounded. Raciborski loaded the ammo chains as Purdy fired, bringing up two more cans of ammunition as they ran low. Then he ran down to the stream and filled his helmet with water to cool off the barrel. When it was over, Purdy's barrel was overheated, and its rifling worn out.

Scully told of how he had started across that same clearing Purdy spoke of with Hensley close behind, how they began crossing the rice paddy, how he was shot in the helmet and knocked into the water, how the ringing in his ears was louder than the gunfire, and how their radio operator had also been shot in the back. He faded in and out of consciousness during this time, so his memories are somewhat intermittent. Yet he remembers crawling back to Hensley through the rice paddy, seeing him lying in the water with his neck bleeding, and thinking he looked peaceful. He remembers looking up and seeing others sloshing toward them through the muck, then someone carrying him amid the sounds of yelling and radio traffic—then hearing someone say, "They killed A.G."

SP/4 Arthur G. Hensley was from Limestone, Tennessee. He was twenty-one years old.

On April 1st, the platoons were flown further into the mountains, just north of where Hensley was killed the day before, and phantom snipers followed. Gunships were called in after taking more sniper fire on April 2nd.

*12:20 PM—Alpha Company to TOC: Letting gunships go. Would like to get another one. We are checking the area with negative results. CO believes it's the same two snipers that have been harassing us the past couple of days.*

Alpha Company lifted off again and returned to the Kim Son Valley later that afternoon. 2nd and 4th Platoons secured a firebase at Hoai An while 1st and 3rd marched through the main trunk of the valley. They came upon many civilians and moved them out but did not encounter the enemy.

## 6 April '67 – 15 weeks left

Dear Folks,

Me and Graham went to the town of Bong Son last week. People there are not as friendly as at An Khe. They even have a Shell station and machine shop, but the place has such a bad odor.

Now we're taking it easy, guarding an artillery battery. We'll move out again in a few days. We're having a lot of fun with these people in the village. I get along with them better than most 'cause I can talk their language a bit. They are really dinky dau (crazy). I think the children are the most precious things. They are so happy, innocent, and cute. I wish I could take some home. And there are so many of them, wow. They are not really starving. I haven't ever seen a skinny one, but they always say, "Give baby son, chop, chop!" They all call me "Bow-E," ha! What a time we all have. About the only nice thing over here is the people. These other units, like the engineers and artillery, burn my ass when they try and show how bad they are by kicking these people around. Man, I hate them when they show off.

Artillery had a fire mission a little while ago. This is when someone spotted some V.C., and they're blowing them up with six 105mm guns. When they're not shooting at V.C., they're shooting at the hills for the hell of it. All that banging really gets sickening, and those crazy choppers flying around. I am really weary and fed up with this war. Been here eight months and still don't know why. If we'd only fight this war with everything we got. Yeah, if I were President, I'd bring smoke.

You guys exaggerate. I meant it as a joke, saying the shorter my time gets, the deeper my foxhole. It's the same as saying the less time I have over here, the more scared I get. We all feel more cautious than when we first started. You said that I don't mention everything in my letters. Now I don't say any more to anyone than I do to you. Of course, I won't write the same type of letter to you as I would to the Schindlers or Geisslers. Sometimes we do have a little fight, but nothing to speak of. So cool your heels. You do more worrying than the whole company. I hope you got my packages by now. Can't wait to hear what you'll say. I got your package last week and an Easter package from Mrs. Henning. She's always thinking of me. I wrote her a letter today.

It's getting so hot here now that I don't care much for eating. When I went on R&R, it was the first time I tasted some good whole milk in eight months. And you guys are dumping milk, good grief! I was reading about the N.F.O. and listening about it on the radio. You might have lost money dumping your milk Dad, but you gained a lot of respect and pride from me and a lot of other people. Trying to make farming better for the next generation.

*That Mike better be good in English. I wasn't, and it sure shows in my letters. I don't feel too bad 'cause a lot of guys are worse than me. Yes, school is very important. I only wish I had made more of it. So Mike, don't ever let sports deprive you of your education. Hop along when Ma says that most hateful word, "S-T-U-D-Y."*

*Right now, I am in my bunker with a flashlight, and it's 12:30. It's pretty secure around here, so a light is okay. Ten more minutes, and I go off guard.*

*3:20 AM now. An hour left of guard duty, then I can sleep until nine. That R&R was a funny thing. Sleeping in a nice soft bed, watching T.V., walking the streets, and hitting the bars. Seems so natural, as if I was doing the same thing only yesterday. You just completely forget about the war. It was so wonderful. And then the day you come back to this ugly place and sergeants telling you to do this and that. What a rotten day that was. And for those who re-up, for God's sake, I don't know why. Yeah, that R&R was just a big tease. But it was something I looked forward to ever since I got here. Rod is probably back from Taipei by now. He should have went to Hong Kong. It's morning now, and I hope to get this letter off when the log ship comes in.*

*Em' a w on'*

*Will*

The following message was relayed from 3rd Brigade on April 8th.

*8:40 AM—Brigade to TOC: Brigade desires to have—as many as possible—individual pictures or negatives of dead Viet Cong or atrocities committed by Viet Cong taken by individuals while on search and destroy missions. Individual pictures or negatives should have date and location if possible. This request is from division psychological warfare department. Any film or negatives will be replaced.*

    On April 9th, Alpha Company was lifted to LZ Pony to replace Delta as the security force. Arnott Graham was keeping watch in one of the sandbag bunkers. SSG Harry Coit called over the radio, telling him to move to another bunker. Graham argued that no one else was at his position, but Coit insisted. In the darkness, Graham collected his M-16 and rucksack and walked up to the next bunker. As he approached, he could make out the tall thin figure of Martin Quinn. "Hey Graham," he started.

    "You're relieved, Quinn," said Coit, seeming to appear out of nowhere along with SFC James Bonner. What followed was an altercation between Graham and Bonner that led to a fistfight and eventually resulted in a wrestling match of sorts.

    When it was over, they stood outside the commander's tent. "I didn't see a damn thing," said Coit. Out of spite, Graham punched Bonner in the nose and knocked him to the ground. Both now bloody and scuffed up, they were warned that this could go no further. Nothing more came of it, but a permanent scar remained on Graham's forehead.

Alpha Company stayed at LZ Pony until April 12th, when they set out on foot, crossing the Kim Son River. They marched north through the valley and returned two days later.

On the 14th, they airlifted to an area just south of the Song Ba, touching down on LZ Hatch at 4:53 PM. This is where they had patrolled following their first air assault in September during Operation Golden Bee. For six days, they searched for the enemy in the jungle and river areas. They found thousands of punji stakes, smoldering fires, dozens of huts, tunnels, bunkers, and elephant tracks, but no Viet Cong.

On the 19th, the battalion returned to An Khe for a three-day standdown. On the morning of the 22nd, they held a ceremony to honor their fallen and present awards to the living.

Flying out to An Lao the next day, the battalion command post set up at LZ Hump while Alpha Company was dropped a half-mile northwest onto the same mountain ridge. Over the next ten days, they made numerous air assaults as the battalion swept through the area. Scout ships and gunships circled above as they marched through the valley and into the mountains, finding enemy huts to burn, rice caches, equipment, and dead bodies left by the enemy. Contact was light, and for the first few days, there were only two calls for medevac, one for a heat stroke, the other for a snake bite.

In the last week of April, Alpha Company's 2nd Platoon was getting picked up in a rice paddy. As the chopper hovered just above the dikes, Bill Purdy threw his M-60 and pack aboard and climbed on. Lifting off, he saw John Kruetzkamp was still stuck in the muck below. He yelled at the crew chief, then jumped from the chopper to help Kruetzkamp, twisting and injuring his knee. Purdy's knee would require surgery, and he ended up at a hospital in Okinawa.

On April 26th, Delta Company was in a blocking position in the An Lao Valley as Charlie Company swept through a village. Their commander, CPT Walt Swain, had removed his helmet in the stifling heat. A round fired from one of the tanks supporting them ricocheted off a tree, and when it burst, a shell fragment struck CPT Swain in the head. Another fragment hit one of his men, and they were both critically wounded.

In his book, Bernard Grady recalls finding his friend lying alone and barely alive in a medical tent at LZ English. The docs had already given up on him, moving on to those in adjacent tents who they could actually save. The tent smelled like hot canvas and antiseptic. It was eerily dark and quiet as he lamented, "They finally got Walt Swain."

On April 27th, SSG Robert Matulac wrote another letter to Mrs. Rankin.

*Dear Mrs. Rankin,*

*I received your letter this evening, and it was a very pleasant surprise. It's funny, I was thinking of you the other day. You see, I'm always catching myself thinking that Donald would have liked to have seen this or that. For Donald loved beautiful things. A beautiful flower, a beautiful baby, and scenery, etc.*

*I know it must be hard for you to lose such a loving son. He mentioned you often, and he spoke of his home all the time. I hope you don't mind, but I showed your letter to some of the boys from Kentucky and to the boys in the section. As I said before, your loss is great, and it is the eternal cross that mothers everywhere must bear.*

*I guess, when you are doing your housework or have a free minute, you may come across some memento Donald may have left, or memories of his childhood may enter your thoughts. Those childhood days are the happy days of your helpless baby becoming strong and inquisitive. Strong enough to stand on his own two legs and finally totter around. Later, he grows more bold and sure of himself. He asks questions like, 'Why is there a moon? Why is the grass green?' or things like that. Later he grows up and starts school, and still later, he goes to college. And after a few years of manhood, he is struck down suddenly, and you ask yourself why—why was it my son?*

*All of us here are living with death by our side every day. It is terrible, but we just go on doing our jobs, hoping the next one is not for us. Yesterday, a company commander was killed. Walt Swain, a man who was a dedicated soldier. We old-timers, those who knew him well, all felt bad and depressed. Not one of us can explain death, although we are familiar with it.*

*I guess people must die, but why is it always the good ones? I guess only God has the answer. Whenever I think of Donald as that broken soldier lying in the rice paddy—I push these thoughts from my mind and think of the days when he was happy, smiling, and concerned about what he wanted to do in life. This helps me very much. And when I look at the men in my section, I tell myself it is my duty to bring them home safe, and I must try harder to keep them alive. It is very difficult for me to write to a mother and tell her of the death of her son. Before I wrote to you, I stared at the blank paper for three days, trying to think of what to say.*

*I have been in the Army for fourteen years now, and I have seen my home in San Francisco very little. I guess you can say I'm the eternal traveler. Being the mother of servicemen, I guess you know how my mother feels about me being here in Viet Nam. It's ironic, but did you notice on the back of the clippings you* sent to me is the story of An Khe being attacked? Several men were killed in that action.

Right now, we are in the same area, not far from where Donald was killed. I keep hoping I meet the VCs that killed him, for I vowed to myself before that I would kill ten VCs for each man that is hurt in my section. I know it sounds cruel, but that is what I'm here for.

We have done a lot in the past nine months. I just hope that in the next three months, everyone will be able to make it home safe and sound. I will remain here, but not with the 1st Cavalry. I cannot stand to see any more boys hurt. I'll be going to Ving Tau, where the transportation units are.

I hope that someday soon, we can both find peace.

Sincerely,

Roberto Matulac

  On April 30th, Alpha Company would conduct a night raid on Hung Long, a large village in the center of the valley, near the banks of the Song An Lao. Arnott Graham recalled a sense of dread as they splashed into the rice paddies from choppers surrounding the village, where a large enemy force was suspected. Pigs, chickens, and other animals started a terrible racket as they approached in the dark. He was relieved to find only frightened women and children.

  4th Platoon medic Tom Monnier had been transferred to the 1/7th Cav in April. His R&R came up at the end of the month. While stopping at base camp, he found all his civilian clothes had been lost when others had moved their stuff from the old battalion tents to the new wooden barracks. So he flew out with only his dress uniform. He spent his first afternoon in Hawaii shopping for clothes and wearing them straight out of the store. He was happy to find that his buddy and fellow medic, Mike Walker, was also in Hawaii for his R&R.

  A replacement soldier from New York named Kenny Jensen arrived at the end of April. "Jensen was from Jamaica Queens. He had a hard life," Martin Quinn recalled. Jensen had a girl back home named Dolly. He showed the guys her picture. "A real blonde bombshell," remarked Quinn. One day, Jensen got a letter from Dolly asking if he had any friends her girlfriend could write to. He wrote back and suggested his buddy Quinn.

  After mail call one night, Jensen asked Quinn if he'd gotten a letter.

  "Yeah," Quinn replied, "some broad named Georgina."

  "Well, you're welcome."

  "Gee, thanks, Jensen. Wait a minute, what does she look like?"

That same night, Will received a Red Cross message from home. His dad was having surgery for complications resulting from a tractor accident. Millie had sent a request to bring him back home. He would stay with the company through the end of April and fly home the first week in May.

*Dear Folks,*

*I received your letter yesterday. Captain Grady is typing up papers for me to take back to An Khe. I am with the company, and tomorrow we hump the hills or paddies again. But we should be going in for a while at the end of this month. It is hard to believe that I'll be home soon. Wish only that Rod could come with me. This is all going too fast. It needs time to sink in. I don't know how long it will take for them to let me go. At least I'll be home soon.*

*In a daze,*

*Will*

A.G. Hensley

*Left–right: Marty Scull, A.G. Hensley, and Buford Bennett*

*John Kruetzkamp (left) and James Harmon (right), photos by Bill Purdy*

*Scenes from An Lao, photos by Robert Matulac*

# 25
# UNUSUAL LOAD

*I thought for sure I would have gotten a medal for this...*

For the daily danger they faced, the infantrymen had great respect for the pilots and flight crews that supported them in the field. In 1967, my uncle Dave was a Chinook crew chief and door gunner in the 196th ASHC, resupplying units of the 1st Air Cavalry and ROK in the Central Highlands. He recalled how many were glad to see them when being evacuated from dangerous spots. He also recalled getting flipped off as his Chinook blew down their tents and made a mess of their outposts, once sucking someone's poncho into one of its engines.

While attempting to resupply a Special Forces unit in Pleiku Province near the Laotian border, Dave Mason's crew came under fire from enemy ground forces. A .30 caliber round smashed a heater transformer between him and the pilot. The pilot banked left and hauled ass down the mountain pass as pieces of the transformer and the spent round rolled about the floor of the aircraft. Coming out of the mountains, torrential rain forced them to land in an open area in the wilderness. They found two forward rotor blades had also been hit. One round had pierced the leading edge of the blade, after which it had been flung to the end of the blade's tip cap, where it remained lodged. The pilot and copilot kept the enemy bullets as souvenirs.

A far worse forced landing occurred for Dave's crew while flying ROK troops who were dropping barrels of tear gas on a landing zone. The barrels were fitted with small TNT charges that would explode on a delay of about ten seconds from when the charge pins were pulled. The Korean soldiers would pull the pins, then push the giant barrels of tear gas out the back of the flying Chinook. With three left, they pulled the pins from one of the barrels. But during turbulence, it tipped over and rolled back toward the cockpit. Ten seconds was not enough time to get the barrel out. It exploded inside the cabin, instantly killing one of the Korean troops. Chaos and panic ensued as tear gas filled the Chinook. Fortunately, the pilots had been wearing gas masks and activated the fire suppression and autorotation systems. Desperate for air, several troops used their heads to smash through the portal windows. Engulfed in flames, the Chinook was expertly landed on a Korean outpost in the valley.

Dave told of his most unusual load in his own words.

*A Special Forces Major oversaw this loading. While loading the first cow, two Hmong soldiers held the cow with slings on the left and right. Being a brave farm boy, I held the sling leading the cow onto the aircraft. About halfway up the ramp, the cow went crazy! The Hmongs let go, and that cow charged me full force! It knocked off my glasses as I grabbed onto its horns, and it carried me all the way to the companionway of the cockpit!*

*I could only hold on to those horns for dear life and thought that cow would surely put me through the ceiling! The Hmongs returned to pull the cow back and tied it down in the cabin. I moved down the steps on the starboard side and cocked a round in my .45mm pistol. The Special Forces Major noticed this and said, "What are you going to do?"*

*"I am going to shoot that son of a bitch if they let it go again!" I replied.*

*"That's right, son," he said. "You shoot it!"*

*Then I calmed down and realized he thought I was about to shoot his Hmong troops. I don't know how many times that cow smashed me to the ceiling of the companionway, but it sure was plenty. She knocked the wind out of me! I thought I would have gotten a medal for this, but I guess there are none awarded to those attacked by mean cows? In the photo, you will note the plastic put down to keep the cow shit off the floor. During the flight, I do not think any of these cows hit it once!*

Joseph Galloway, co-author of *We Were Soldiers Once... And Young*, once remarked of the aviation pilots and crews, "No matter how bad things were, if we called, you came. Down through the green tracers and other signs of a real bad day, off to a real bad start. To us, you seemed to be beyond brave and fearless—that you would come to us in the middle of battle in those flimsy, thin-skinned crates. And in the storm of fire, you'd sit up there behind the thin plexiglass, seeming so patient, and so calm, and so vulnerable. Waiting for the off-loading and the on-loading. We thought you were God's own lunatics, and we loved you—still do."

*Hmong cows aboard Dave Mason's Chinook*

*Korean soldiers dropping barrels of tear gas*

*Korean troops boarding Chinook for air assault mission*

*Dave Mason (left) and crew*

# 26
# HEART OF DARKNESS

*I take it no one told you yet.*

Heading home on emergency leave, Will was walking through the San Francisco airport en route to his connecting flight to Minneapolis. He saw throngs of reporters gathering further up the concourse and wondered what all the fuss was about. He pushed his way through the crowd and captured a somewhat blurry photo of Senator Robert F. Kennedy holding a press conference.

Millie was happy to see her boy Willie when he made it home that night. Returning to the farm seemed strange, especially knowing that he would soon go back to Vietnam. Eddie's surgery went as planned. While he recovered in the hospital, Will worked the farm with his little brother Mike. He appreciated the home-cooked meals, soft bed, and clean water that didn't taste like iodine tablets. His friend Larry Geissler stopped by to visit, and while Millie cooked supper, they swapped tales over the kitchen table. Will told of the things he'd seen in the last year and found much of it hard to explain. As he fed and milked the cows each morning and night, he thought about his Army buddies and what they could be doing this very minute.

Eight thousand miles away, the mission continued in An Lao. On May 2nd, Alpha Company lifted to firebase LZ Sandra, where they pulled security for six days. On the 7th, they assaulted onto LZ Hump, no longer a firebase. They marched down into the valley to find the enemy had mostly disappeared, but refugees were everywhere—large groups plodding through the valley toward resettlement camps with whatever they could carry.

*11:42 AM—Alpha Company to TOC: Picked up thirteen women refugees, one child, and five Viet Cong suspects in black pajamas.*

*12:26 PM—Now eleven women, eight children, and two Viet Cong suspects.*

*1:11—Requesting medevac for Vietnamese child who is very sick at BR 775-960.*

*2:26—Disregard the medevac for the sick child. He has died.*

Early in the month, Bobby Hansen and his buddy Jim Hirschuber were sent to other units. Only three original members were left in Hansen's squad when he was transferred, SSG Kenneth Gregory, Phil Jones, and Guy McNay. On May 11th, McNay wrote to his sister Annette Sebastian, who had raised him and knew him as Juggy. He wrote of how he'd almost been shot again but had been saved by his sergeant—and that he would soon make Specialist-Four.

That same day, a resupply chopper landed with more fresh meat—nineteen-year-old Caesar Pinto. From New Bedford, Massachusetts, he was of Portuguese descent and wore thick glasses. He was what might have been called a "change of life" baby in those days—his mother deceased, his two sisters over twenty years his senior. Pinto had struggled through basic training. His bunkmate Paul Plaine had taken Pinto under his wing and helped him along. After each day of training, they would go over what they had learned. Assigned to different units, they would go their separate ways after training. As they said goodbye at Penn Station, Paul reminded Pinto to pay close attention to his sergeants and to ask for help when he needed it—and to be careful. Paul had a foreboding feeling as he watched Pinto board his train.

Around this time, a Cuban exile named Jose Dorta replaced A.J. Wise as Alpha Company's commander. He'd been a Major in the pre-Castro Cuban Army and was considered an expert in jungle warfare. Tall and tough, he wore a white shock of hair and smoked cigars. English was not his first language, however. He spoke rapidly when excited, and no one could understand his words. Fortunately, one of their new replacements spoke Spanish and served as an interpreter.

George Kalergis, their forward observer who'd joined the company in February, recalled the day CPT Dorta showed up in the field. "He brought an excessive amount of gear," Kalergis remarked. "Everything but the kitchen sink, and I had to help him carry it all as we set off on our first patrol together."

On May 15th, they found themselves deep in the mountains, two miles northeast of LZ Sandra. Arnott Graham was digging in atop a hill at the end of their day's hump. A new lieutenant had just arrived the week before. He showed a map to Graham and his squad leader, SSG Jennige. "A great soldier, smart, with a lot of grit and a raspy voice," Graham said of Jennige, "but he looked too old to be in the Army." The lieutenant pointed out where they were to set up that night's ambush. This six-man ambush patrol would include Graham and his friend Jesse James. Alpha Company would act as a blocking force as the 1/9th Cav swept the area to their west. The company would send out six ambush patrols. Theirs would be patrol #1, and they expected contact.

Charlie was always watching, so they typically waited until dark to head out to their ambush spots. Graham argued with the lieutenant when he ordered them to move out in the waning daylight but couldn't convince him to wait. As Graham started out with the others, SSG Jennige called him back and sent someone else in his place. He watched as his buddy James, the lieutenant, and the four others trudged down the trail. Later, he could see where they had set up along a saddle area between theirs and an adjacent hill. He figured Charlie could see them as well. At 6:00 PM, all six ambush patrols were in place, and Alpha Company reported their locations to battalion.

All was quiet until about 4:00 AM when the sound of gunfire erupted from where patrol #1 had set up—then grenades exploded. Graham could see the muzzle flashes, green tracer rounds, and red tracer rounds in the distance. Radio contact was lost with the patrol during the firefight. Then, after a few minutes, all went suddenly silent—still no radio contact. 4th Platoon fired illumination rounds over the area. They could see movement but couldn't discern enemy from friendly. Ambush patrol #3 tried to find them but couldn't in the darkness, with communications lost. About forty-five minutes later, the company started taking machine gun fire. They returned fire but didn't attempt to move. They waited for sunrise to search for the lost patrol.

Graham feared what they might find as they set out at daybreak. He found his friend James alive but with a hole shot through his hand—a million-dollar wound. They found four more wounded and one killed, Corporal (CPL) James Ray from Spruce Pine, North Carolina. Twenty-five years old and married, he'd joined the company as a replacement in February.

A friend of John Kruetzkamp was in that same patrol. He told of how they were getting overrun and how he played dead while the Viet Cong came through. They took his rifle, then took the boots right off his feet before slipping back into the jungle.

The men moved down off the hill the next morning. They humped through the valley and returned to the same area. When dark came, it was Kruetzkamp's turn to go out on ambush. Late in the night, a large group of Viet Cong approached. Kruetzkamp tried to radio the company, but the radio operator was asleep. They felt outnumbered and wanted to get back to the company—but without radio contact, they would risk being shot by their own men. Having no choice, they set a tripwire on one of their Claymores and retreated. Running back in, Kruetzkamp wounded his leg on jagged remnants of bamboo that had been cut down just outside the perimeter. He asked who had been manning the radio as the medic bandaged his leg, but no one would tell him.

During this time in May, SSG Robert Matulac was searching for fourteen men who'd gone AWOL. Soldiers were often sent back to An Khe for medical treatment or R&R and would sometimes disappear. Matulac visited nearly every field hospital in Vietnam in search of his lost sheep. He would ask when they were discharged, then search the surrounding camps, G.I. bars, and brothels. The bartenders and madams offered little help. He put the word out that they could be charged with desertion and sentenced to death under the UCMJ, the Uniform Code of Military Justice. Not that this ever actually happened—he just wanted them to know he meant business.

Eventually, Matulac found a group of these wayward troops hanging out in the company area at An Khe. "We heard you were looking for us, sergeant," one said sheepishly. Matulac ordered them to get on the next chopper going out to the company.

Marijuana was illegal under the UCMJ, but a blind eye was often turned as a practical matter. This one soldier had returned to the field from R&R with a large stash of premium Bangkok dope. He was warned to only smoke it at night but not on guard duty. Matulac heard a loud clang in the middle of the night. It came from the other side of the perimeter where 1st Platoon was bivouacked. Moving around at night was dangerous, so he waited until daylight to investigate. Apparently, this soldier had gotten high and passed out while on guard duty, and his squad leader had knocked him over his helmet with an entrenching tool.

While setting up in the field the next night, Matulac checked to confirm that each platoon had accounted for their men. 1st Platoon was missing one. The last time anyone remembered seeing him was during their last smoke break while marching through the bush. He'd gotten high and fallen asleep, and they had accidentally left him. It was getting dark as Matulac prepared to report the incident to battalion. Just then, a lone figure resembling a soldier came walking up the trail. "I can't believe they left me," he said, "out there in Indian country."

On the morning of May 19th, Gerald Anderson and Kurt Elmer left together for R&R in Tokyo. Anderson had some recent letters and photos from a girl back home and left them with his buddy, SGT John Fulford. This *Cavalair* story tells of what happened later that day.

### Sergeant Saved By Alert Dog
*By SP/4 Marc Davies*

*"I'd rather have been shot than that dog. She saved my life twice that day," said Staff Sergeant Harry Coit of the 1st Air Cav's 5th Battalion, 7th Cavalry. He made the statement with deep serenity about a scout dog named Krim. Coit, of Long Beach, Mississippi, had doubts about the scout dog working with his platoon during Operation Pershing. He claimed it lacked drive and had passed several booby traps without giving an alert. Coit was thinking of having the dog sent back for more training. But SP/4 Michael Lister, the dog's handler, and Krim showed their value and left no doubt in Coit's mind that they were indeed a valuable team in search of the elusive enemy.*

*Alpha Company was moving cautiously along a trail deep in the jungle when Krim gave her first alert. The troopers found fresh enemy positions. In the next thirty minutes, the dog and handler alerted them eight more times. Then Krim gave two strong alerts, and Lister pointed them out. Just then, the enemy opened fire from one position and hurled a grenade from another. Seeing the grenade coming through the air, Lister took the enemy under fire, killing one as the rest withdrew. After evacuating a wounded squad leader, they went in pursuit. After chasing the enemy for about an hour, Krim gave another strong alert but did not wait for her handler to inform the infantrymen. She jumped into a bush where three waited in ambush, fighting the enemy until one shot* her. Medic PFC Gerald Robinson of Adams, Massachusetts came up and gave the dog first aid. Krim had been shot through the nose but calmly let Robinson treat her wounds. The men improvised a stretcher and gave her water from their canteens. They knew that a lot of them were still alive because of the dog's alertness and courage.

Later, the men drafted a letter to Mrs. Betty Rowe of Midland, Michigan, who donated Krim, thanking her for sending the dog. Lister of San Antonio, Texas and Krim were both put in for Bronze Stars with "V" device for valor in combat.

The article did not mention what befell Alpha Company next.

It was the first week in June, and Will was back at An Khe—checking in at the 5/7th's rear battalion headquarters where CPT Bernard Grady now held court as Battalion Adjutant. "We need more guys like you out here," Grady remarked, "guys with experience."

From An Khe, Will flew to LZ English, where he ran into Rodney Henning. The camp's ammunition dump had been struck by enemy mortars the night before. The resulting fire and explosions lit up the sky, wreaking havoc through the night. Two soldiers were killed, and nearly forty were wounded by falling debris. The camp's medical tent and over sixty civilian homes were destroyed in the resulting fires that also killed one child. Explosions were still going off the next morning, with debris landing dangerously close to the mess tent as cooks prepared breakfast.

From LZ English, Will flew in a Huey with Alpha Company's dinner. Looking down at the rivers and valleys, the now familiar landscape was serene and picturesque from above. He knew all too well its dark side. With each leg of the journey, a knot of despair grew in the pit of his stomach. But then he thought about how good it would be to catch up with his friends. They were closer to him than any before his life in the Army. "Only two more months and this will all be over," he told himself. Descending again into the heart of darkness, he could see the light at the end of the tunnel growing brighter.

Will grabbed a mail bag and jumped off while others swarmed the chopper to unload the hot chow. The company was encamped on the valley floor of An Lao. The sun was setting as the men ate their food and set up their hooches. Will also needed to set up and dig in before dark, and he was starving after a long day of traveling. But all that would wait as he squinted through the swirling dust of the chopper's downdraft, looking for his friends. There were so many new guys now—he barely recognized his own platoon. Thinking he should check in with his sergeants, he looked around for Fulford and Hayslip. He saw Martin Quinn standing by his hooch, shoveling in food from a paper plate. He walked over, ready to hear of the latest shenanigans. A pleasantly surprised look appeared on Quinn's face as he looked up. Then it disappeared.

"I take it no one told you yet," he said grimly. He pulled out two Marlboros, handed one to Will, then delivered the news. Fulford and Patrillo were dead, and so was Hayslip. They had been killed two weeks ago in a battle that took seven of their men.

It took a while to sink in. Will walked off and sat on a dead tree that lay near the company's perimeter. The knot of despair returned, and his eyes ached. Fulford and Patrillo were good buddies—and he hadn't been there on their last day. He wondered about their final moments. The "what if" questions filled him with regret. He pictured Patrillo with his camouflage fedora, reading the comics and smoking his Pall Malls. Just minutes before, he'd envisioned that light at the end of the tunnel. That light was gone now.

A few days earlier, Quinn had written a letter to tell Will about what had happened. Will was already on his way back to Vietnam when the letter arrived and never read it—but Millie did. Fifty years later, I would find it mixed in with my dad's letters home that she had collected.

*May 29th 1967*

*Hi Wilbur,*

*Sorry for not writing sooner but Will, it's been hellish here. I have some sad news to tell you. On May 19th, we got into a terrible firefight, and many fellows were killed and wounded. From our platoon, Sergeant Hayslip, Fulford, and Patrillo were killed. I tell you, it was terrible. If I told you everything, I would have to write at least twenty pages.*

*But now everyone is working together. There have been many changes in the platoon. We now have Sergeant Lyons as platoon leader, Lussier as platoon sergeant, and Elmer and me are sergeants. And we are squad leaders. Andy is section chief. Everyone else has been transferred to other units. Bierschbach was transferred, and Bronson was too. We all wish they were back. We have many new replacements in the company and platoon. Well, enough sadness.*

*How are the folks doing? Fine, I hope. I am doing a-okay with sixty-two days to go. I hope all works out for us. Well, I hope you don't come back here. We all want to see you, but not back here. Well, you sure were my best buddy here, and of course, you still are. I hope to make it to the farm one of these days. I bet you're boozing and flying every day and night. Knowing you, you're fat catting it, but you sure deserve it. Right now, we are at LZ Sandra, but tomorrow we are making an air assault. I don't want to go, but that's the breaks. Well Wilbur, I will write again, and the guys are always thinking and talking about you. Regards to the family. Take care and keep out of trouble.*

*Sgt. Quinn*
*Ha! Ha!*

*James Ray*

*Senator Robert Kennedy at San Francisco Airport, photo by Will Bowe*

*Kurt Elmer (left), scout dog and handler (right), photo by Robert Matulac*

*LZ English, photo by Dave Mason*

*LZ English, morning after ammo dump explosion, photo by Will Bowe*

# 27
# MAY 19TH

*You're a damn good soldier.*

The battle had taken place four miles north of LZ Sandra. Aside from a bloody poncho left on a trail, they had found nothing of the enemy the day before. But on the morning of May 19th—as Kurt Elmer and Gerald Anderson left for R&R—Alpha Company's men found an abandoned tunnel system and several bunkers. George Kalergis, Martin Quinn, and Arnott Graham told of what happened.

"Ninety men strung out single file for a hundred meters along the side of a jungle-covered mountain," Kalergis recalled. "The ground we walked was at such a steep incline, I was constantly leaning left and thought, 'This is what it must feel like to wear one high-heeled shoe and one flat.' We could only see about ten meters up the trail as the vegetation was so thick. The light was restricted, making for an eerie kind of semi-twilight, and the jungle noises were strangely subdued." Kalergis's radio operator Danny Garrity was out with malaria, and now John Curtis walked beside him with the radio.

At 11:40 AM, a small group of Viet Cong attacked the lead platoon with grenades and rifle fire. As Graham recalled, SSG Jesus DeLeon was shot in the leg. A dustoff came in but had nowhere to land. A hoist dropped from the chopper, and they strapped him in. Kalergis recalled the sight of the man spinning around and bouncing off tree trunks while ascending through the branches of the jungle canopy.

2LT Kalergis marched along next to their new commander and 4th Platoon's mortars in the middle of the company. "Sir, I better move up," he said. "We're strung out so far—I won't be able to call artillery without hitting our own men." CPT Jose Dorta agreed, and Kalergis ran ahead with his radio operator.

The lead squad was following their scout dog as Kalergis and Curtis caught up. She had passed several places where the Viet Cong had been cooking and failed to alert her handler. "She was mangy and seemed rather docile," Kalergis recalled. "I wondered, 'Is she really cut out for this fighting stuff?' She earned her dog food that day, though. She suddenly runs and leaps with a fierce growl into the jungle to grab a Viet Cong with a machine gun who was about to fire on us. Curtis and I dive off the trail, and a flurry of gunfire is exchanged. When the dust clears, enemy soldiers are dragging one of their wounded down the trail. Man, I had sure misjudged that dog! She had taken a bullet to save our lives." Graham helped the handler and medic carry their wounded scout dog back to the rear on a stretcher improvised with bamboo stalks and a poncho.

Kalergis radioed CPT Dorta, who told them to pursue the fleeing Viet Cong. Kalergis argued that they should stop so he could call in artillery, but to no avail. "Captain Wise would've never sent us running down a trail like this," he complained to Curtis. "We'll stay near the front but not so close to the lead squad. I'm pretty sure there's more VC, and we're in a perfect position to be ambushed."

The lead squad was following the blood trail of the wounded Viet Cong about fifty yards ahead of Kalergis and Curtis. Kalergis feared they were moving too fast as they disappeared into a deep ravine. Then a barrage of machine gun fire was unleashed from bunkers hidden in the hillside above. Kalergis and Curtis watched several men in front of them fall to the ground with helmets sent flying in the initial blast. They jumped off the trail and crouched behind a small tree. Kalergis grabbed the handset from Curtis and radioed for artillery.

The command group and 4th Platoon lagged over a hundred yards behind those in front. Martin Quinn was serving as SSG Bobby Hayslip's radio operator and following him closely through jungle brush. Al Patrillo followed close behind Quinn, along with SGT John Fulford, Marvin Bierschbach, and John Bronson. Patrillo was in good spirits, telling Quinn how his brother was getting out of Korea that day.

Then bullets started cracking through the leaves and bouncing from trees about their heads. "It started with just a few shots," said Quinn. "Then the jungle exploded, and everyone went crazy. We were lying on the ground, Hayslip only a couple feet away. He shouted something about snipers in the trees. 'No, they're just over that ridge!' I yelled back."

Just over that ridge near the top of the hill lay the fortified machine gun bunkers that had ambushed the lead platoons. Housing a large force of Viet Cong, the bunkers were staggered about thirty yards apart, up and down the craggy hillside. They were also firing from trees, spider holes, and caves.

Graham was also in the rear after carrying back their scout dog. He heard the raspy voice of SSG Jennige yelling at him to bring up ammunition for the machine gunners. Lugging ammo cans and with extra belts of M-60 bullets draped around his neck, he started up to the front. "Graham, don't go up there!" Quinn yelled.

Graham kept running up in the open until he reached Romanov Gunner with the ammunition. Romanov laid a base of fire with his M-60 that allowed many who were pinned down to get to safety. "I thought for sure he was going to get shot," said Graham. "Romanov just stayed on that gun and kept firing until the barrel turned red. He should have gotten a medal for that."

With the two lead platoons pinned down and separated, CPT Dorta ordered 4th Platoon to the top of the hill to secure a landing zone. "I'll show these gooks," said Hayslip, rising from the ground. As they fought their way up the hill, Hayslip was shot in the head, and then Fulford was shot in the neck. To Quinn, it was all just a blur of screaming, smoke, and machine gun fire. Lying beside Hayslip in the thick brush, he thought he'd also been hit. He felt around for holes in his chest and realized his Miraculous Medal was gone.

Then a torrent of Viet Cong descended from the high ground. Patrillo moved up while firing grenades from his M-79. His aim was accurate, but they were already within thirty meters and too close for his grenades' detonators to activate. Still, his unexploded rounds knocked down three or four enemy fighters. Along with Hayslip and Fulford, he would also die trying to take the hill. He would be awarded the Silver Star for his actions.

*The President of the United States of America takes pride in presenting the Silver Star (Posthumously) to Specialist Four Albert John Patrillo, United States Army, for gallantry in action. Specialist Four Patrillo distinguished himself by exceptionally valorous action on 19 May 1967 while serving with Company A, 5th Battalion, 7th Cavalry during a search and destroy mission in Quang Ngai Province, Republic of Vietnam.*

*Specialist Patrillo's company was following the trail of a wounded Viet Cong sniper when two platoons became pinned down by intense automatic weapons fire. Specialist Patrillo's platoon was sent up a hill with another element with instructions to secure a landing zone at the top. Upon approaching the summit, the platoon was fired upon by Viet Cong in treetops and camouflaged bunkers. Recognizing the danger to his comrades if the enemy proved successful in halting their advance, Specialist Patrillo left his cover and moved against a heavily fortified bunker complex. Firing his weapon continuously, Specialist Patrillo pressed his determined attack until he was struck and mortally wounded by hostile fire.*

*His gallant action contributed to the ultimate success of the company in securing the landing zone and evacuating the wounded. Specialist Patrillo's display of personal bravery and devotion to duty was in keeping with the highest traditions of the military service, and reflects great credit upon himself, his unit, and the United States Army.*

Meanwhile, Kalergis had called for artillery, but his initial round had flown clear over the hill where the Viet Cong were holed up. He radioed, "Drop two hundred," to bring the fire closer. The second round landed behind him. Unable to adjust the fire accurately, he feared killing his own men. "We have to get closer to the front," he yelled. "I can't see our guys or where the rounds are landing!"

"You gotta be shitting me, sir!" Curtis yelled back as he followed Kalergis, running up the trail under fire for another thirty yards to where many lay wounded and dying.

"It was like watching a movie in slow-motion as we ran up the trail," Kalergis said. "I was scared much of the time moving through the jungle. But during the ambush, I was almost emotionless, full of adrenaline, and everything seemed crystal clear. I would later be scared shitless thinking back on it."

Now even closer to the bunkers, Kalergis managed to bring gunships on station. He popped a red smoke grenade to signal their location, but the smoke drifted and weaved under the jungle canopy, emerging from the treetops far from their actual location. As a result, the first volley of rockets came in nearly on top of them. "Check fire!" he radioed.

Kalergis spoke of the visions that still haunt him. "One of our dead being dragged back by his feet, his limp head bouncing on the ground each time he hits a bump in the trail. Two young soldiers were friends and had joined the company together just a few weeks before—one had been killed in the ambush, and I see the other curled up and moaning next to his dead friend."

During the battle, machine gun fire sent splintered tree fragments into Graham's neck, and he briefly thought he'd been shot. He spotted his nemesis, SSG Harry Coit, off to his right and farther up. During a lull in the gunfire, he saw two soldiers just up the hill from his position. "One was lying dead on the ground," he recalled, "and the other with his leg all shot up. He was leaning against a tree, unconscious and losing blood. I'm standing over him, thinking about how to get him down. Sam Underwood yells up at me, 'Hey blood, get outa' there!' so I go back. Then a medic and two others go up there, and they all get zapped right where I'd been standing just a minute before."

Taking the hilltop and bunkers would prove impossible. By 6:30 PM, they had managed to break contact. Graham helped recover two of their dead. He recalled how one young soldier took his last breath as he carried him. "I remember the blood," he said. "We were soaked in it. I remember it squishing and oozing out of my boots as we carried the bodies down off the hill." SGT Vernon Garrett, known to his buddies as "Roy," also recovered some of the dead and wounded that day and would be awarded the Silver Star for his actions.

*For gallantry in action: Sergeant Vernon Garrett distinguished himself by exceptionally valorous action on 19 May 1967 while serving as a squad leader with Company A, 5th Battalion, 7th Cavalry during a search and destroy mission in Quang Ngai Province, Republic of Vietnam.*

*On this date, the company was pursuing a wounded enemy sniper when it came under intense hostile fire. Sergeant Garrett was directed to join his squad with a platoon and move up a hill to secure a hilltop landing zone. While advancing up the hill, both elements were taken under heavy automatic weapons fire from treetops, trenches, and fortified bunkers. Due to the intensity of the fire, Sergeant Garrett's squad was instructed to withdraw to the base of the hill, leaving behind the bodies of three mortally wounded members of the platoon, their weapons, and equipment. Sergeant Garrett, with his squad covering him, moved up toward the bodies. Attacking two bunkers, he killed one enemy soldier and wounded another. With complete disregard for his own safety, Sergeant Garrett fought his way to the position and recovered the soldiers and their equipment. When he was sure that his mission had been successfully completed, he covered his squad's withdrawal to the base of the hill and finally withdrew himself.*

*Sergeant Garrett's gallant action is in keeping with the highest traditions of the military service, and reflects great credit upon himself, his unit, and the United States Army.*

Despite their efforts, they could not recover all their dead and wounded before dark. With the enemy still dug in and no landing zone for the medevac, they would have to wait until morning. Under sporadic fire, they pulled back and regrouped near a dirt road farther down the hill. "I remember my fatigues—all our fatigues—stiff and hard from all the dried blood," Graham recalled. "I can still smell that blood—etched in my mind, I'll never forget it. And the wounded we left out there, I could hear them calling out for help through the night."

Kalergis called in the airstrikes as darkness fell. The first was an AC-130 Spooky gunship. The giant airplane circled in the night sky. Its guns made a foghorn-like sound while spraying the hilltop with a steady red-glowing stream of 20mm rounds. The gunship continued its pummeling until forced to refuel. Next came the bombers, just before daybreak. Martin Quinn recalled the drone of their engines growing louder as they approached, the walls of napalm fire erupting on the hilltop, the radiating blasts of heat, and the earth shaking beneath them. Everything before them was burning—the hill, the trees, the bunkers, even the rocks seemed to be burning—and they were engulfed in a choking black haze.

As the first rays of sunlight filtered through the trees, two more had succumbed to their wounds, bringing the death toll to seven. Caked in dirt and blood, the exhausted troops advanced up the hill to find a hellscape of sorts where they had fought. What had been an enormous bunker complex was now a smoking black heap, with bodies and parts scattered about.

Though most had escaped, some surviving enemy fighters had taken refuge in the caves. The men entered those caves to pull out both the dead and the living. An ARVN interpreter commenced intense interrogations as they tied up the prisoners. Among them were a handful of women who carried weapons but were actually members of a traveling propaganda troupe, or "Bob Hope show for VC." Kalergis recalled how one young woman was wounded by shrapnel yet putting up a vicious fight, and how the men finally carried her off tied to a pole like a tiger. The site had been used as an ammunition depot and training camp.

Once the area was deemed secure, Graham helped to clear a landing zone on the hilltop, blowing up trees with pipe bombs and C-4. Meanwhile, Quinn helped search for the few remaining dead who had been left on the hill. Only by his blond hair could he identify Patrillo. He and a few others carried him to the hilltop. He took one last look as they laid him beside the others. Then he turned to see four others carrying Guy McNay. As his body passed before him, McNay's eyes opened as if he had just awakened and was looking right at Quinn. Another one of those visions that stick in your mind.

After the wounded were flown away, more choppers arrived with hot food, cold beer, and fresh uniforms. Graham and some others walked down to a nearby river to wash up. Minutes later, they returned to the hilltop in their new fatigues. They threw their old bloody clothing in a pile and set it ablaze with the help of some gasoline.

"I'll never forget seeing those bodies," Graham remarked. "All in a neat row, wrapped up with their black jungle boots sticking out from beneath their olive-drab ponchos, their dog tags attached to their boots."

They were still waiting for another chopper to pick up the dead when the men started cracking beers. Some took the opportunity to do a little weed. Graham recalled how the guys were smoking and joking and how their dead buddies were still lying on the ground only a few feet away. "I got angry and freaked out for a bit," he said. "But then again, I may have been a little high at the time."

A dustoff finally arrived to collect its grim payload. Squinting through the blowing dirt of the downdraft, Graham watched the dead being loaded on.

"Hey, Graham!" He turned around to see SSG Coit marching up to him. He squeezed Graham's shoulder and said, "You're a damn good soldier."

A few days later, on Sunday evening, Al Patrillo's friend Tom Ivey was working on a college lab report in his family's kitchen. The Patrillos' home was directly across the street. Sensing some movement outside the window, he looked up from his report. He saw two soldiers in dress uniform ascending the steps to the Patrillos' front door, along with their priest. His heart stopped as he realized he would never see Al again. All their years of childhood misadventures flashed before him, from riding their tricycles together to riding around in Al's pride and joy convertible—and to their last conversation, the day before he left.

Survived by his parents, Millie and Cy, and his two brothers, Tony and Vincent, Albert Patrillo was laid to rest with military honors in his hometown of Susquehanna, Pennsylvania on Memorial Day 1967. Nearly the entire town turned out to see him buried. His older brother Vincent had just been honorably discharged on the day he was killed. His younger brother Tony would later volunteer for service in Vietnam.

CPT Jose Dorta had also fought bravely during the battle, even after being shot in the back. He would survive his wounds and be replaced by CPT C.W.

Creech. A week later, Alpha Company would air assault onto a landing zone named LZ Dorta in his honor.

Guy McNay would be awarded the Army Commendation Medal, the Vietnam Military Merit Medal, the Vietnam Gallantry Cross with Palm, and the Silver Star.

*For gallantry in action: Specialist Four Guy McNay distinguished himself by exceptionally valorous action on 19 May 1967 while serving as a grenadier with Company A, 5th Battalion, 7th Cavalry during a search and destroy mission in Quang Ngai Province, Republic of Vietnam.*

*Specialist McNay's platoon was leading the company in pursuit of a wounded Viet Cong sniper when the enemy opened fire with automatic weapons. Despite the concentrated enemy fire, Specialist McNay moved forward and neutralized an enemy machine gun emplacement singlehandedly with his grenade launcher. Although wounded during his daring attack, he continued to fire his grenade launcher in an attempt to cover his comrades as they moved to evacuate the wounded. In order to pinpoint the concealed and camouflaged enemy positions, Specialist McNay repeatedly exposed himself to attract hostile fire. As a direct result of his heroic action, several casualties were inflicted on the enemy force. Although asked to withdraw when wounded a second time, he remained in the battle, utilizing his position to direct reinforcements moving toward him. Exposed to the intense hostile fire, he was struck a third time and mortally wounded.*

*Specialist McNay's courageous and aggressive action was in keeping with the highest traditions of the military service, and reflects great credit upon himself, his unit, and the United States Army.*

In addition to McNay, Patrillo, Fulford, and Hayslip, among the dead were PFCs James Eldridge from Nickerson, Kansas, Juan Gonzalez from Uvalde, Texas, and SP/4 Anton Bornstein from Bellingham, Washington. I believe Gonzalez and Bornstein were the two young soldiers George Kalergis spoke of, as they had both arrived in Vietnam less than three weeks before being killed. Bornstein would be awarded the Silver Star.

*The President of the United States of America takes pride in presenting the Silver Star (Posthumously) to Specialist Four Anton Thomas Bornstein, United States Army, for gallantry in action. Specialist Bornstein distinguished himself by exceptionally valorous action on 19 May 1967 while serving with Company A, 5th Battalion, 7th Cavalry Regiment, 1st Cavalry Division (Airmobile), during a search and destroy mission in Quang Ngai Province, Republic of Vietnam.*

*Specialist Bornstein's company was in pursuit of a Viet Cong sniper when two platoons became pinned down by heavy automatic weapons fire. The two remaining platoons were also taken under heavy enemy fire while attempting to secure a hilltop landing zone. Seeing a fellow soldier fall to the ground with wounds in both legs, Specialist Bornstein voluntarily left his position of cover and exposed himself to the enemy in order to pull the man to safety. After removing his comrade to a reasonably secure position, he called for medical aid, placing a suppressive fire on the enemy positions to enable the Aidman to reach his location. After killing two of the Viet Cong, Specialist Bornstein began seeking a better position, but he was mortally wounded before he could reach his objective.*

*His courageous and aggressive action was in keeping with the highest traditions of military service and reflects great credit upon himself, his unit, and the United States Army.*

Kim was a friend who knew Anton Bornstein as "Andy" and had graduated high school with him in 1965. On the Wall of Faces, she recalled working as a telephone operator at Pacific Northwestern Bell and hearing the toll of the nearby church bells during his funeral as she grieved quietly at her station.

"Kurt Elmer and I were in an Army and Air Force-sponsored club in Tokyo," recalled Gerald Anderson. "A soldier from another platoon in our company saw us. He told us what had happened the day before. I was devastated. John and Bobby and I were very close friends and had served together since Fort Carson. I was so upset that I wanted to leave and go back to the platoon. Kurt talked with me, and we decided there was nothing we could do that couldn't wait until we returned from R&R. We also decided that we were going to survive this and make it home. We had a little over two months left."

On Sunday, May 21st, SGT Charles Thornell stood in dress uniform at the doorstep of Annette Sebastian at 17 Division Street in Erlanger, Kentucky. In his hand, he held a telegram. Its message was painfully brief. Her brother Guy McNay—Juggy—had been killed two days earlier. She had just received his letter written on the 11th, telling of how he would soon be promoted to Specialist-Four.

On that same day, Alpha Company's men found themselves searching the area where the battle had taken place on the 19th. Meanwhile, Charlie Company searched the area where Alpha Company's ambush patrol had been overrun in the dark morning hours of the 16th when CPL James Ray was killed.

*1:45 PM—Charlie Company to TOC: Follow up on May 16th area of contact. Found one more Viet Cong killed in action—head completely blown off—unable to tell his age. He was wearing a khaki shirt and black pajama shorts. Also found five steel helmets, one set of field gear, and two rucksacks with equip-*

ment. All of this belonged to Alpha Company, 5/7th Cav. Found one M-79 grenade launcher SN 3627, possibly the one Alpha Company lost about four days ago.

*4:40—Alpha Company to TOC: Follow up on May 19th area of contact. Found one Viet Cong body in a grave, shot in chest, in khaki pants and black pajama shirt. Found over three hundred pounds of rice and a hundred pounds of potatoes, seventeen well-fortified natural rock formation bunkers, many caves and tunnel complexes—accommodated up to fifty persons. There was a lot of bamboo scattered in this area. Found one clip with ten rounds of 7.62mm ammo. Also found four helmets belonging to Alpha Company that were lost in the initial contact. Found another helmet that appeared to have been worn by a Viet Cong. Also found two packs belonging to Alpha Company that were also lost in the initial contact. This area was worked over well by aerial rockets and artillery strikes. A lot of flesh, blood, and hair found in the area. Appears there were many Viet Cong killed and wounded that were dragged away.*

"It's sad. I think about it every day," Martin Quinn reflected. "Like certain things will cross my mind, and I think of how this guy or that guy isn't here—never had a chance to get married or have children—how Bobby Hayslip had just gotten married before coming to Vietnam."

*Albert Patrillo funeral, photo courtesy of Patrillo family*

*CPT Jose Dorta, photo by Robert Matulac*

*Left–right: Patrillo, Fulford, Evans, and Quinn investigate dead body on trail, photo by Marvin Bierschbach*

*Helicopter sling-loading casualty and bombing run over hilltop, photos by Marvin Bierschbach*

*Albert Patrillo — John Fulford — Guy McNay*

*James Eldridge — Juan Gonzalez — Anton Bornstein*

*Bobby Hayslip*

# 28
# AMONG FRIENDS AND STRANGERS

*This isn't my company. You're dropping me at the wrong place.*

From May 1st to July 31st 1967, the 1st Air Cavalry's nineteen thousand soldiers suffered 160 killed and 885 wounded in action, 640 non-combat injuries, and 2,504 diseases of various type, including 412 cases of malaria. The division also counted twenty-nine cases of hookworm, thirty-two psychiatric cases, sixty-five heat strokes, thirty-four animal bites, and a hundred punji stake wounds.

### *8 June '67 – 7 weeks left*

*Dear Folks,*

*Well, I finally made it back to the field. Seen Rod today. He and I were going to do some serious drinking tonight at English, but the First Sergeant says, "Out to the field with you!" Quinn says hello to you all. Made E-5 Sergeant, ha! I finally made E-4. Gee, am I excited. At least it's good to be back with the guys. Only four of the old regulars left in my platoon. Just about all the originals got transferred. Bierschbach got transferred, but I'll probably see him when I get home. The company is really up to strength now, but so many new guys that don't know anything. Have this one new guy—no matter what we say, he did or has something better. Oh boy. Well, I guess I'll go and set up for the night. Get Sergeant Quinn to dig my foxhole, ha! He's my squad leader now.*

*Will*

On June 12th, Alpha Company was picked up near the sandy banks of the Song An Lao and flown eight miles north—the deepest they had ventured into the highlands—air assaulting onto LZ Jay at 1:44 PM. Some platoons were sent out to search the jungle below, and within two hours, they had killed the first of the enemy in their new area. LZ Jay was to become another firebase, so the rest started clearing the ground for the artillery.

### *15 June '67 – 6 weeks left*

*Dear Folks,*

*Right now, we're at LZ Jay for a little rest. We captured five V.C.s, eight tons of rice, and two weapons. Plus, no injuries. What did Joanne name the baby?*

*Counting my days,*

*Will*

Mid-June brought a severe heat wave, and on the 16th, one of the company's troopers was medevaced with heatstroke. On the 18th, the battalion command and artillery battery were lifted from LZ Sandra to LZ Jay while Alpha Company pulled security. At 8:30 the next morning, a platoon was air assaulted onto a nearby mountaintop dubbed LZ Fang. Forty minutes later, a medevac was called in for a trooper bitten by a bamboo viper.

### 19 June '67 – 6 weeks left

*Dear Folks,*

*Been at LZ Jay for a week and moving out today to do some humping. The guys told me what a great C.O. they had when I was home. It was this Cuban who could hardly speak English. He would work right with the guys and wasn't afraid to speak against any officer higher ranking than he. He got seriously wounded in May but is in good shape now. Even then, he refused to be evacuated until his company was in control and safe. He is being awarded the Silver Star or even the Flying Cross. Everyone said he was the best commander they'd ever had. Guess I'd missed something good.*

*We've got a lot of new guys in our platoon. In a way, I'd hate to be close friends 'cause I'll be leaving them behind in such a horrible place. It sure feels good when no one has less time left than you. When we got here, some of the guys would razz us by saying they got five days left or a week or two. Well, now it's my turn. And man, I am letting the guys know how short I am.*

*My turn,*

*Will*

Alpha Company sent the following reports on June 19th.

*10:45 AM—1st Platoon found two butchered cows and three sets of footprints leading off to the south, about three days old. Found and destroyed one hut. In the hut was a campfire, also about three days old. About a hundred meters from the hut was a stream where someone had washed off some meat.*

*1:40 PM—Found two NVA canteen covers, pair of sandals, Viet Cong jungle boots, and two empty M-16 magazines. This area had once been occupied by U.S. forces due to the fact there were C-Rations and beer cans on the ground.*

Later that month, the men learned of the death of a good friend—the Polish immigrant who'd hoped to earn citizenship for his Army service—SSG Robert Matulac's skiing buddy, Kazimierz Slomiany. He'd been transferred to Bravo Company, 2/5th Cav and had only been with them a few days. On June 19th, he spotted a Chinese Claymore hanging on a palm tree while walking point. Sensing an ambush, he opened fire and was wounded in the resulting firefight that killed four others. Slomiany was put on an armored personnel carrier to be evacuated. It hit a hole and threw him off, after which he was run over and crushed. From Wallington, New Jersey, he was twenty-two years old.

On June 20th, Alpha Company marched southwest from LZ Jay, about halfway down the mountainside toward the narrow valley below. Contact was briefly made with a small group of Viet Cong during the night. Illumination was called in, but the enemy slipped away. They sent this report the next morning.

*7:05 AM—Found one Viet Cong body in black pajamas. Had been dead for ten to fifteen days. Also found some baskets with C-Ration cans. One cave with fresh straw inside. There were footprints and blood all around this cave. Prints heading south. Estimate two to three Viet Cong wounded. Also found thirty-five hogs feeding off a dead water buffalo.*

They marched down into the valley and around the mountain, and medevac was called for another heat stroke at 9:28 AM. They started up a draw on the other side and found an abandoned encampment with over twenty huts, thirty bunkers, and over twenty spider holes. The bunkers were searched, then destroyed with explosives. They burned the huts and marched on.

On June 22nd, they were picked up and assaulted onto another mountain two miles east. The men continued hacking through the jungle until the 23rd, when another victim of the heat was medevaced at 11:30 AM. About a half-hour later, they lifted back to LZ Jay. Then the entire battalion airlifted in Chinooks to LZ English, marking the end of their participation in Operation Pershing.

From their days at Fort Carson, Alpha Company had remained relatively intact until the transfers started in December 1966. During that time, Will had known everyone in his platoon. But everything was different now. Their leaders, CPT A.J. Wise and 1SG John Potter, were no longer at the helm—and they were now on their third company commander. With most of its original members killed, wounded, sick, or transferred, the company was now mainly composed of replacements. And now, after losing two of his best friends, even within his own platoon, Will felt he was largely among strangers.

John Kruetzkamp also returned to the company in June. He had just recovered from his wounds inflicted while running over that thicket of cut bamboo in May. He didn't recognize anyone as the chopper landed. "This isn't my company," he told the pilot. "You're dropping me at the wrong place." He remarked of the new guys, "After our patrol was done for the day, they weren't digging foxholes or clearing fields of fire like we'd been trained. They just wanted to eat their C-Rations and listen to their transistor radios."

"The only good thing about being a squad leader was that I didn't have to pull KP duty anymore when the food came in," said Martin Quinn. "The bad part was that now I had to be the first to jump out of the helicopter whenever we flew into a landing zone, and I was afraid of getting shot by our own door gunners."

By mid-June, only five of the original thirty-some men remained in 4th Platoon, Will Bowe, Martin Quinn, Kurt Elmer, Gerald Anderson, and Paul Lussier. With John Fulford dead and John Bronson and Marvin Bierschbach transferred, Will was the only one left of his original four-man team.

The remaining five "originals" of the platoon had all been drafted in 1965. They had been yelled at by their drill sergeants and endured many of their collective punishments together. They had trained together, gotten drunk together, and broken the rules together. They had set out on their first patrol, made their first air assault, and survived their first firefight together. They had suffered together and grieved together. They would now rely on each other for whatever time they had left, hoping they could all go home together.

*Kazimierz Slomiany*

*Pickup in An Lao Valley, photo by Robert Matulac*

*Left–right: Reynosa, Fox, and Spaur, photos by Will Bowe*

*Artillerymen at LZ Sandra, photos by Will Bowe*

*Will Bowe carrying mortar tube*

*Front–back: Knight, Spaur, Fox, and Elmer, photo by Will Bowe*

*Patrolling through jungle and evacuating heat stroke, photos by Will Bowe*

*Mortar platoon soldiers*
*Back left–right: Williams, Billy Smith, P.J. Rainy, Wilkerson, unknown*
*Front: Bill Knight, unknown*
*Photo by Will Bowe*

# 29
# THE FINAL PATROL
## (Operation Greeley)

*It was really neat. Just like in the movies.*

On June 24th 1967, the men of the 5/7th Cav loaded onto C-130 cargo planes and flew to a Special Forces base in the westernmost province of Kon Tum. As the 1st Air Cavalry Division continued with Operation Pershing, their battalion, along with the entire 3rd Brigade, was put under the command of the 4th Infantry Division to assist in Operation Greeley. In the northwesternmost reaches of II Corps, the bamboo-covered mountains of Kon Tum were the highest of the highlands, near the Laotian and Cambodian borders where thousands of NVA soldiers crossed into South Vietnam each month.

### 24 June '67 – 5 weeks left

Dear Folks,

I hear we are moving west of An Khe. Maybe it's cooler over there. It sure is hot here. Three guys had heat stroke the past few days. My feet are cleared up from ringworm and athlete's foot. Elmer says he'll come home with me. Wants to know if there's any planes leaving Eau Claire to Chicago daily. No sweat, I'll make it. Only twenty-five days left. If I get bumped off over here or while crossing the road to get the newspaper, doesn't make a difference. When your number is up, ain't much you can do.

Will

With virtually no rice paddies and little farmable land, Kon Tum was sparsely populated, mainly by native tribesmen known as Montagnards, French for "people of the mountain." Wearing little more than loincloths, the Montagnards were semi-nomadic hunter-gatherers, clearing small plots of land to grow corn, yams, and other crops, moving on when the soil was no longer farmable.

The Montagnard people had been driven out of southern China hundreds of years ago, migrating to the coastal plains of Indochina. Later, when the Vietnamese people were also driven from China and into those same coastal plains, they drove the Montagnards into the uninhabited highlands. Their lifestyle relatively unchanged since the Bronze Age, they were considered savages by the Vietnamese. The Montagnards distrusted the Vietnamese but especially hated the communists and readily fought alongside both the French and the Americans. In the early years of American involvement—in the era of advisors—Special Forces units had trained and armed hundreds of tough Montagnard fighters, and they were considered excellent warriors.

At the Kon Tum base, they received two clean-shaven replacements with freshly starched uniforms. They looked like they belonged in high school rather than a war zone. "These two guys came into our squad," Martin Quinn recalled. "This tall black guy says, 'Sarge, whatever you want me to do, I'll do.' I told him, 'I don't want you to do anything 'cause I'm not giving anyone any orders.'"

On June 27th, Alpha Company followed Bravo, dropping onto a mountain known as LZ Top at 4:09 PM. After the battalion command post and artillery arrived, they marched out into the jungle led by CPT C.W. Creech.

This would be the most punishing phase of their tour as the terrain here was more rugged, the mountains higher, and the jungle impenetrably clogged with bamboo. Gunship and artillery support would be difficult should they encounter a large enemy force. With their new commander leading so many inexperienced troops over this unfamiliar terrain, the old-timers had doubts.

Continuing through the mountains the next morning, their scout dogs picked up a trail but could not find the enemy. They moved out again at daybreak on the third day of their patrol. In a line formation, they hacked through thick vegetation down a craggy mountainside. Progress was halted several times, and every so often, another platoon rotated to the front to share the burden of the hacking. The jungle was dark, and each could only see as far as the man before him. Will followed Quinn while looking back to check on the two new guys. They both looked scared.

Still moving downhill, the first two platoons had entered an open area as 4th Platoon approached the same clearing. As they descended a steep downward slope, moving out into the light, they watched one of the men in the clearing collapse. A split second later, they heard the pounding of machine gun fire. Troopers jumped down the slope and ran for cover. The firefight went on for some time, and when it became apparent that no one was shooting back, the commander yelled, "Cease fire!" Everything fell silent except for the radio, crackling with beeps and voices from a distant outpost. Two men lay wounded, and their scout dog handler had fractured his leg while negotiating the rocky slope as the firefight broke out.

The attack had come from the tree line across the clearing at enough distance that artillery could be called in from LZ Top. The ground shook as they watched the earth erupt and trees explode. Then gunships descended to spray lead into the area, and a dustoff collected their wounded.

They cautiously moved across the clearing and into the forest to search the area. They found the bodies of three enemy soldiers, and parts of them, scattered about in craters among the shattered stumps and bamboo. With ripped fatigues covered in dirt, the two new guys had just survived their first firefight.

They moved out again the next morning, ending the day's patrol near a mountaintop over three thousand feet above sea level.

### 29 June '67 – 5 weeks left

*Dear Folks,*

*The whole battalion is operating out of Kon Tum, not far from the Cambodian border. Not nearly as many rice paddies here. I saw Rod the other day. You know what? He applied for Officer Candidate School and is thinking about re-enlisting. Can you believe that? Sending back these nice pictures that Mike took of us. Showed them to the guys. As you can see, they're a bit sticky. Received those doughnuts, but they were all moldy. Can't hardly see. Too dark.*

*Will*

After marching through the mountains and valleys for another two days, late in the afternoon of July 1st, Alpha Company was flown to LZ Top to pull security. On their first day back, the firebase was attacked by snipers. They were quickly repelled, but the men on the perimeter were still on edge as dusk fell. Silhouetted by the setting sun, three figures could be seen approaching. As the men trained their weapons, the figures waved their hands above their heads while one shouted, "No VC!" Emerging from the wilderness was a man, woman, and child, a small family of Montagnards trying to escape the bombardment of artillery in the hills.

### 2 July '67 – 4 weeks left

*We got sniped at yesterday. All I remember is a few shots zipping over my head. Don't even remember running to the foxhole. Just like old times. No one got hurt too bad. I tore my hand a little bit while breaking some bamboo. That's why I can't write too well. I really got a kick out of these new guys after the little fire-fight. Big-eyed and thought it was really something. They're digging deeper next time, ha! Me too. We're on LZ Top now. Figure to stay here a while and maybe do some humping just once more before we're done. Twelve days left in the field, I am fairly sure of. They say we'll go in on the 15th. So the gooks got one more chance to get me, and I am shaking in my boots. It's really nerve-wracking. Rod and his company were on this hill until we came and kicked them off. Now they are out humping, ha! I got the guys to open my C-Ration for me 'cause of my sore hand, ha! Darn Chinook blew our tent down. I'll be so happy to get away from them. Twelve and a half days and counting,*

*Will*

On the evening of July 3rd, Delta Company returned to LZ Top to take over security. As the last of their Chinooks descended, they were taken under fire by snipers. Alpha Company was still at the firebase the next morning when they took more sniper fire at 11:25 AM. They responded with machine guns and mortars and called in the gunships.

## 4 July '67 – 4 weeks left

*Dear Folks,*

*Got sniped at again. But the V.C. is sorry now 'cause we threw everything at him but the kitchen sink. One of our guys got shot in the neck by our own men. Guess he's okay. Going to LZ Hasty today. Tomorrow we make an air assault. You won't find any of these LZs on the map 'cause they're tiny places and only temporary. Bad news again, don't know when we're going in. General what's-his-face wants us back in the An Lao Valley 'cause all the V.C.s came back and are partying it up. Our C.O. is trying to get us old-timers out of the field, but he knows darn well the Colonel won't approve. A rumor came down yesterday saying all sergeants may be extended if necessary. Quinn and Elmer are worried, haha! A couple of us guys had moustaches, but the C.O. made us shave them off. The Cuban C.O. we had before wanted everyone to have a moustache. That's all the news from the Peanut Gallery.*

*Will*

    Later that afternoon, Alpha Company was flown about eight miles north to establish another firebase near Dak To. As the first lift departed, they again took fire from the snipers surrounding LZ Top. Shortly thereafter, airstrikes were called in on the enemy that had been harassing them. Later that evening, the battalion command post and artillery battery joined Alpha Company on the new firebase known as LZ Hasty.

    Alpha Company set off by foot the next morning. For those who had arrived in Vietnam aboard the USNS Gaffey, it marked the beginning of the end, as this was to be their last search and destroy mission. They marched down the mountain and into a narrow valley through which ran the Dak Akoi River. That night, they found a hidden complex of twenty bunkers and caves that had recently been occupied and an NVA helmet that had been left behind. With grenades and C-4, they destroyed everything and encamped in the same area.

    A downpour started the next morning, and the ground became increasingly muddy and slippery. While hacking up the mountain slopes, their feet often gave way, soaking their fatigues in mud and making their slow progress even more demoralizing. Later that day, they moved back down and started following the river through the valley.

    As the rain continued on the 7th, the men searched the draws leading up the hills along the river, finding more enemy huts, clothing, spider holes, and punji stakes. As they marched through the valley that afternoon, movement was detected to the right of the formation, and artillery was called in. They continued through the valley the next morning and secured a river crossing for Charlie Company.

*Charlie Company patrolling mountains, photo by John Goodpaster*

The rain lifted on July 9th. Continuing their search through the Dak Akoi Valley, the men found a hidden pit filled with punji stakes at 8:17 AM. Ten minutes later, they found two empty bunkers with overhead covers dug into the hillside along the river. They appeared to be about two months old. Later that morning, a soldier detected a grenade-type booby trap. Shortly thereafter, in the same area, the men discovered an encampment that seemed to have been occupied only two or three days before. More recently used dug-in positions were found at 12:41 PM. By mid-afternoon, the sun was scorching, and a medevac was called in for a soldier with a temperature of 103 degrees who was heaving blood. At 3:10 PM, Alpha Company reported finding tracks of twelve to twenty personnel moving southwest through the valley. The tracks were less than a day old, mostly from VC sandals, but included at least one set of boots. Later that afternoon, another downpour started and continued through the next day.

### 10 July '67 – 3 weeks left

Dear Folks,

Only a short letter, getting dark and it's been raining and raining. Been humping for the past six days. It's hard to say when I'll get home. At least I'm out of the field no later than July 24th. I doubt now if Elmer or Quinn will make it home the same time as me. Got a letter from Joanne. Sounds like a lot of rain back home.

So long,

Will

Drizzling rain persisted through the evening of the 10th. In the middle of the night, one of Alpha Company's men was struck by a violent epileptic seizure, and another was bitten while trying to restrain him. A medevac was called in for both the next morning.

Now on the seventh day of their patrol, the men had not fired their weapons in some time, and so they all test-fired their rifles and M-60s before moving out. At 11:28, they were ordered to locate a pickup zone. CPT Creech was told that the company would be picked up and assaulted into another area where scout ships had spotted a group of NVA moving along a trail. From the depths of the valley, it took about ninety minutes to climb up to a suitable area. After reporting their location for pickup and waiting several hours, the mission was canceled.

## 11 July '67 – 3 weeks left

*Dear Darrell, Joanne, and Gang,*

*I hope everyone is making out okay, especially the baby. Ma says he looks like Scotty. Just been humping our legs off and getting wet. I know it can't be raining more back home than it is here. Seen very little of the sun since we moved to the Cambodian border. I'll be as white as a sheet when I come back. It's all I ever think about, if I can just make it thirteen more days. Guess I better dig a hole before it gets too dark. Can't afford not to. Getting too short, you know. Really get a kick out of these new guys. I remind them every morning of how short I am, haha! By the way, don't call me SP/4. "Mr." will be fine.*

*A short-timer,*

*Will*

Rain continued on the 12th as the men marched back down into the valley, crossing the river around noon and finding nearly impenetrable bamboo thickets. Two hours later, a dustoff was called for a soldier who had suffered severe lacerations from jagged remnants of the stalks they'd been hacking through.

They crossed the river again the next morning and proceeded along the other side. They found smoldering campfires near the river before crossing again. At 5:50 PM, medevac was called for a soldier who had shot himself in the foot with his M-79. The grenade did not explode, but the impact fractured his foot. He was lifted out of the jungle in a hoist.

At 10:26 AM on July 14th, the company was picked up and assaulted onto a mountaintop one mile east of LZ Hasty. Within ten minutes, they had found ten enemy huts. They burned them to the ground.

### 14 July '67 – 2 weeks left

Dear Folks,

*It's been our tenth straight day of humping. Never humped so hard before. This C.O. sure doesn't know what he's doing. Just ten more days at the very most. I bet it rains at least two inches every day now. Miserable, holy smoke. Itch, scratch, what a mess we're in.*

*A hobo,*

*Will*

Resuming the search the next day, the men discovered another enemy camp on a forested hillside. Instead of destroying it, CPT Creech left a small team as overwatch, hoping to catch the enemy returning that night. The enemy never returned, and the huts were burned at daybreak. They continued moving northeast, and at 1:45 PM, medevac was called for a punji stake wound. They had resumed their march for only forty-five minutes when another was called for a second punji stake wound, this time requiring a hoist.

### 16 July '67 – 2 weeks left

Dear Folks,

*Everything is going as usual. Nobody knows what they're doing. Right now, we're on the highest hill in Viet Nam. These hills don't have a top to them. At least it is very cool. Rain, rain, that's all it's been doing. But yesterday and today, we're getting a little sunshine. Just ate some C-Rations and started to move out, and a guy just stepped on a punji stake. So I thought I'd drop a few lines while waiting for the medevac chopper. What grabs me is that he just got here yesterday. Rod and Delta Company are back at LZ Hasty again. When I wonder, are they going to take this fool company in? Well, I am hoping to get out of the field on July 21st. I hope the 24th for sure. Come hell or high water, I am going. Can't hack this humping much longer.*

*So Long,*

*Will*

On July 17th, having marched for nearly two straight weeks, the men continued north into the mountains northeast of LZ Hasty, now moving even closer to the Cambodian border. It was still raining, and nature seemed resolved to break them as they hacked their way through the jungle in ankle-deep mud. They could see only a few feet in front of them, and most hoped desperately not to find the enemy they were searching for.

They marched doggedly, starting up a steep rise late in the afternoon, and a hard rain fell. Will thought back to how it all began. How he and Rodney Henning had tried to go airborne, this famous cavalry regiment with their bush hats and camouflage scarves—esprit de corps. The anticipation of being sent to where the action was and how he couldn't wait to make his folks proud.

And now he had lived the reality of this war, its unrelenting drudgery and despair—nothing like John Wayne's movies. They were told that they were winning as generals spoke of impressive kill ratios. Ten or more Viet Cong bodies for each of their dead friends was considered a good ratio. Despite their many killed in action, even on their worst days, they had never so much as lost a battle. And yet they would always return to the same valleys and villages and hills, chasing the phantom Charlie as if chasing ghosts.

The sun appeared briefly as they ended the day's march near the top of a mountain that towered nearly four thousand feet above the valleys. Will pulled out his pack of Camels—only one left. He saved it for his guard shift.

He awoke in the middle of the night to someone nudging his shoulder. "Your turn, buddy," said Quinn. It had rained again but had recently stopped. It was still dripping from the trees, and off the edge of the ponchos stretched over their foxhole. Quinn lay down in the dampness while Will rose to a crouch. Staring into the darkness, he commenced his watch. Against a chorus of jungle insects, he strained his ears for the sounds of soldiers shuffling through the brush or the "shunk" of enemy mortars. They'd been attacked at night before, twice in February in the Bong Son. Now much deeper into the depths of the deepest dark forest—Indian country—with signs of the enemy's presence everywhere, it seemed destined to happen again. It was hard to stay awake, real hard. He lit his last cigarette, keeping it just beneath the edge of their hole. With a small amount of moonlight shining through the parting clouds, he could discern the outline of some bushes and trees.

They seemed to come out of nowhere—images that once again flashed through his mind. Unlike before, these were from a more recent time. The running man, running for his life through the valley, and Tall Lee Roy, standing there on the dike getting shot at, and their radio operator, wrapped in a poncho flapping violently from the chopper's downdraft, and a blonde Hollywood actress hopping out of a helicopter, and Burtis standing there with his newspaper, smoking and joking just moments before getting shot, and the dustoff chopper disappearing into the sky, and laughing Vietnamese kids, and bodies pulled from a tunnel, Viet Cong bodies in piles, those of their friends in neat rows, and the last time he saw Patrillo—the letter sitting on the kitchen table.

Again, he concentrated on the shapes of the bushes and trees before him. He checked the illuminated dials on his watch. It had been only twenty minutes.

Will awoke to the usual sounds—shuffling, clanking, muttering, and cursing. Everything was damp and covered in dew. A dense fog lay in the valley below where they had patrolled the day before, making it seem like they were above the clouds. They would soon descend back into that fog. Will's feet ached, and the first few steps each morning were always the worst. He shook the water off his poncho, packed it up, and prepared to move out again. He considered brushing his teeth. Then Quinn bummed him a smoke. "Don't worry," he said. "We ain't going anywhere yet. We're waiting for a chopper to come in or something. Hey, if we ever get out of here, maybe I'll get to meet this girl." Quinn showed him a photo of Georgina, the girl Kenny Jensen had set him up with.

The distant thumping of an inbound chopper could be heard as their cigarettes dwindled. "Maybe they're bringing hot chow," Will suggested, rare as that would be for a morning resupply. Instead, leaping out of the chopper were soldiers of Bravo Company as more choppers descended onto the landing zone. They had been sent to relieve them in place. It was over.

### 19 July '67

*Dear Folks,*

*I am making this my last letter 'cause by the time you receive this I should be on my way home. We finally got out of the field yesterday. We are pulling security on LZ Hasty. Tomorrow we should be going to An Khe and should leave Viet Nam between the 28th and the 1st. I hope I leave on the 1st 'cause I'll get sixty-five bucks more in combat pay. The Colonel gave out awards today. It was really neat. Just like in the movies.*

*Got Mike's cookies today. I was wondering what happened to them chocolate-covered cherries. And a box full of cookie crumbs instead? Ha! And Ma, you're telling me not to re-enlist, haha! What a laugh. Good grief.*

*You know, I can hardly believe it is really the end. No more Army or Viet Nam. Finally, I am finished. No other day can be finer than the day I leave the Army. I know that is a fact. Right now, I have a hard time sleeping at night, and I don't care much for eating. I am so happy and so proud. What a feeling. I have just one deep sadness, and that is two of my buddies didn't make it. That's the worst experience you can have. Nothing more to write about. Every day gets more exciting. It's getting so that I forget to breathe. I can dangle my feet off the edge of this letter, I am so short. Well, this is it. The beginning of the end. I am finished—through. Just sitting in my bunker nervously smoking one cigarette after another. Walking in a daze. Telling everybody how short I am. Yeah, this is finally it. The living end. Think I am going to crack up.*

*Happy,*

*Will*

*Five "originals" of mortar platoon after final patrol at LZ Hasty
Back left–right: Will Bowe, Gerald Anderson, Kurt Elmer, Martin Quinn, and Paul Lussier in front*

# 30
# FOR WHAT IT WAS

The war strategy dramatically changed when General Creighton Abrams replaced General William Westmoreland as commander of MACV in 1968. Abrams shifted from fighting a war of attrition and body count to that of winning hearts and minds, protecting the population from guerrilla attacks, and rehabilitating the South Vietnamese military. The new approach held promise, but support for the war was already deeply eroded, as were the experienced ranks and morale of the American military. It's impossible to know whether this strategy could have succeeded if adopted from the start, but it may have cost fewer American lives.

The agreement signed between the United States and North Vietnam in 1973 allowed our forces to leave with honor, our POWs to return home, and our allies to be defeated in our absence. In 1975, with the republic on the verge of collapse, President Gerald Ford pleaded with Congress to continue supporting South Vietnam with money and weapons. Had they done so, the South could have delayed the communist takeover. But whether the South's unpopular government could have kept the country free with only our material support is unclear. The North had weapons supplied by the Chinese and Soviets, and as a communist state, public support for their war was not a concern. Most of all, they were far more committed to their cause and willing to die—or send others to die—in far larger numbers than the South Vietnamese.

The book that best describes the challenge of fighting the communists in Vietnam was actually written years before the United States went to war there. Published in 1961, war correspondent Bernard Fall's *Street Without Joy: The French Debacle in Indochina* tells of the decade-long struggle of the French military and their Foreign Legion to hold on to their former colony from the end of World War II to 1954. While providing a glimpse into the misery suffered by French troops in Southeast Asia, he explained how the communists in Vietnam were fighting a different kind of war. Different, not because it was a guerilla war—many guerrilla wars had already been fought all over the world—but because they were waging a genuinely ideological war.

Fall noted how the Viet Minh were far better than the French at propaganda, intelligence gathering, and terrorism. Also, how they would subject French prisoners to indoctrination, brainwashing, forced confessions of war crimes, what communists call reeducation—all militarily pointless but demonstrating their sincere fanaticism. He wrote of propaganda troupes traveling the country with their costumes, instruments, and props, performing revolutionary-themed plays and songs for the villagers. While the French pursued a military strategy, the Viet Minh, through propaganda and terror, were after hearts and minds.

He observed how the violence of the Viet Minh, and later the Viet Cong, was targeted, accurate, and reliable. Anyone opposing them could count on swift and brutal retaliation. The same could never be said of the French or Americans, who possessed superior firepower but inferior intelligence. Howitzer shells and bombs dropped from planes could not distinguish friend from foe. American violence was big, clumsy, and often killed the wrong people—ultimately unreliable in the minds of those caught in the middle. While supporting efforts to keep South Vietnam free of communism, Bernard Fall predicted failure if war planners did not learn from the French experience.

Many accused President Johnson of getting the country into a war he never intended to win. True or not, he was never willing to do what was necessary to win. But an invasion of North Vietnam would have likely drawn China into the war, and its planners did not want a repeat of the Korean disaster. And yet, more Americans would die in Vietnam before it was over. And so, the country found itself mired in what was called "limited warfare," characterized by half-measures and contradictions. The most glaring of these was the president's shocking refusal to mobilize the National Guard and other reserve forces. Mobilizing would have signaled an actual war rather than just a conflict, and that was not the message he wanted to send. Nothing could have done more to damage the reputation of the National Guard. That reputation would not be restored until National Guard units were sent to wars in Iraq and Afghanistan.

Expanding the draft while trying not to upset those with the most social and political clout, the government exempted not only the National Guard, but also large swaths of the male population. If you were in college, had political connections or any kind of connections, or were otherwise privileged, you could likely obtain some sort of exemption.

Many well-to-do young men served bravely in Vietnam. Despite his misgivings, Alan Weisman—said to have come from money—ultimately did his duty at the cost of his life. But he seems more the exception than the rule. I think of Donald Rankin from Kentucky, Elvin Wideman from Saint Louis, Thomas Erickson from Saint Paul's east side, and Arnott Graham, who immigrated to New York from Trinidad—all from impoverished backgrounds. Most of Alpha Company's men grew up either dirt poor, working class, or farmers like my dad. They typically didn't have connections with congressmen who could get them into the National Guard or high-ranking military officers who could get them assigned to some rear-echelon duty station. Nor did they have doctors who were "friends of the family" to request medical exemptions on their behalf. Mostly though, dodging the draft is something that just wouldn't have occurred to them.

I attended a book signing where Mark Bowden, author of *Blackhawk Down* and *Hue 1968*, was speaking at a Barnes & Noble in Edina, Minnesota. He noted how in the past, there had always been two well-defined opposing sides on the subject of Vietnam, pro-war and anti-war, with no significant middle ground. He spoke further of how today—while there is still no universally accepted view—there is at least an understanding of sorts, and everyone is allowed to hold their own opinion. His words visibly resonated with the small crowd of sixty-five to seventy-five-year-olds, many of them veterans.

*"...still the man, he hears what he wants to hear and disregards the rest."* From Simon & Garfunkel's *The Boxer*, it speaks to how we all believe what we want to believe. I think it's important to at least try to remember Vietnam, not for what we want it to be, but rather for what it was—unsatisfying as that is. While their government may have never been worth saving, I believe the people of South Vietnam were—a noble cause that simply wasn't meant to be. Then again, maybe that's just what I want to believe. In the end, it was a monumental tragedy that tore our country apart.

Over fifty-eight thousand Americans and millions of Vietnamese died defending the republic. Hundreds of thousands were simply killed in the crossfire as collateral damage. Millions more died in the aftermath while fleeing the communists or in reeducation camps—but, to borrow a line from Bob Dylan, *"...you don't count the dead when God's on your side."*

Following Saigon, Laos also fell to the communists, resulting in hundreds of thousands of additional Hmong refugees. Many resettled in Saint Paul, Minnesota, and many of their children and grandchildren now serve in our military. An officer of Hmong descent swore me in when I enlisted, and I've served alongside many Hmong soldiers in the Minnesota National Guard. It's hard to imagine anything good coming from this war. Still, I would look to the millions of Vietnamese and Hmong people who are Americans today. Not to suggest that they are better off after losing their countries, but that we are better with them among us.

Regardless of how we view the war, there is something I hope everyone can acknowledge. The men who fought this war did not choose this war. They had no say in its conduct or strategy. In service to their country, they fought as bravely as any generation of American servicemen. Sent into the jungle to confront the brutality of guerrilla warfare against a vicious and competent enemy, their humanity would be challenged in ways that no man could be prepared for. They deserve our respect and gratitude.

# 31
# HOMECOMING

*Oh, where have you been, my blue-eyed son?*

It was the first week in August 1967. Will stood in line once again, this time at the 5/7th Cav's rear battalion headquarters at An Khe with what was left of the original Alpha Company, each man clutching his precious discharge papers as if they were a million dollars. Since their arrival in August of the previous year, thirty-one men had given their lives while serving with the company.

Martin Quinn recalled how the night before, after cleaning and turning in their weapons, they had all gone into town to get haircuts for a dollar, then came back and got stoned at the clubhouse. Many were hungover as they packed their bags. Then they stood around in their dress uniforms, waiting to board a military transport plane that would take them to the Pleiku Air Base, from where they would depart Vietnam.

Amid the heavy smell of engine fumes, they began loading on. Will recalled how he had first seen the words "An Khe" near a dot on a map during his time at Fort Carson, how obscure and far away it had seemed. Climbing aboard the plane, he took one last look around as the band played *Garryowen*.

A hard rain fell as they landed in Pleiku. Their hearts sank when they were told they would not make it out that day because of the rain. They were sent to some empty barracks to await further instruction. Now they needed beer, and fortunately, someone was willing to brave the monsoon to go out and find the PX. Waiting out the storm, they spent one last night in Vietnam smoking, drinking, and playing cards until they fell asleep in their dress uniforms.

Despite staying up late, everyone was too anxious to sleep in and got up before dawn. As the sun rose, Will and Quinn stepped out of the barracks to a beautiful clear blue sky. Before long, they were all milling about near the airstrip, smoking and joking as soldiers do. They recalled a few war stories but mostly talked of what they would do upon their return to The World. After what seemed an eternity, a behemoth commercial-style jet airplane known as the "freedom bird" taxied toward them along the runway. A few cigarettes later, they were finally given the go-ahead and piled on.

As Will felt the plane's wheels leave the ground, an incredible sense of relief washed over him. At first, the men sat subdued, many contemplating what had just happened. They were still young and had just endured a lifetime of ordeals compressed into a single year. Some cried. Minutes later, the pilot announced they had just left Vietnamese airspace, and everyone cheered.

They stopped to refuel in the Philippines, then flew to California for out-processing. Their Army careers ended much like they had started, with lines and paperwork. That night, however, they were all treated to a steak dinner where Will, Quinn, Elmer, Anderson, and Lussier would share one last meal.

Their year in Vietnam had changed them. The country they fought for had also changed since that day in August 1966 when the people of San Francisco showered them with flowers as they sailed off to war beneath the Golden Gate Bridge. Young men were burning draft cards in the streets, and major cities were burning in race riots, the worst having erupted in Detroit that summer. Within a year of their return, Reverend Martin Luther King, Jr. and Senator Robert F. Kennedy would be assassinated. And in the wake of the bloody Tet Offensive, President Lyndon Johnson would make the shocking announcement that he would not seek reelection. They returned to a country coming apart at the seams, that knew little of what they had been through and seemed to care even less.

That fall, Will and Rodney Henning would use the G.I. Bill to attend the University of Wisconsin in Stevens Point for one semester. Then they traveled to Washington State to work a construction job for about a month. Later, Will used his benefits to attend Dunwoody Technical Institute in Minneapolis and became an electrician.

Will's little brother Mike still lives on the farm. In 1969, he married Donna Bohl, the high school sweetheart he'd started dating in February 1967. They ran the farm for many years and raised four of their own children there.

In the spring of 1971, Will found himself driving to a club known as the Belmont-A-Go-Go in Minneapolis. His friend Dan was meeting a girl there named June and needed a ride. Walking into the bar, Will saw another girl sitting beside June at the table. Her name was Carol, and he was immediately struck by her dark, long-flowing hair and smile. She gave him her number, and they were married in October. They would have two sons, me and my brother Nicholas.

In 2011, after much prodding from my wife and me—and armed with a week's supply of Dramamine—my dad finally agreed to embark on his second voyage on the high seas, this time on the Norwegian Epic.

Upon out-processing in California, Martin Quinn took a red-eye flight to New York. Then he rode the subway, hailed a cab, and arrived at his parent's home in the predawn darkness. His arms and hands still carried remnants of jungle rot. His mother wanted to take him to the doctor. He told her the Army doctors had already given him medicine for it, but she didn't think they knew what they were doing. A few days later, his dad asked him when he was going to get a job. So he went out and found one the next Wednesday. He never caught up with Georgina, the girl he'd been exchanging letters with—nor did he get around to visiting the farm, but he and Will exchanged Christmas cards every year. Will visited him on a family vacation to New York in 1993. Then they lost touch for about twenty-seven years.

Quinn worked for decades as a purchasing administrator for a large hospital downtown. He remembers a beautiful September morning, walking through a skyway between the two hospital buildings. He noticed billows of black smoke rising from distant buildings. He stopped as he realized the smoke was coming from one of the World Trade Center towers. Others started gathering. Moments later, they watched as a commercial jet slammed into the other tower. Then they watched the first tower collapse. Many casualties were brought to the hospital that day, and everyone worked through the night. One of only a few mementos he kept from his time in Vietnam, he still has his green patrol cap.

Marvin Bierschbach would marry his girlfriend Jane about a year after returning home. They reside in their home in the country, alongside a county road near Saint Cloud, Minnesota. He and Will have kept in touch over the years. Now retired, Marvin raises chickens and makes spearfishing lures that he sells to local sportsmen.

Jim Hirschuber returned home to his bride and five-month-old daughter. He came in through Fort Lewis, Washington, then through a crowd of protesters throwing things at their bus on their way to the airport. Taking a train from Minneapolis on the last leg of his journey, he rode with a group of about a dozen brand-new soldiers. When their sergeant climbed aboard, he made them all move up to the front of the car, warning them not to speak to the soldier who sat in his dress uniform in the rear. He returned to his job at a screw factory in Rockford, Illinois. He had only worked there briefly before being drafted and knew only one other guy working there when he returned. On his first day back, he was advised not to mention to his coworkers where he had been for the last two years.

Hirschuber's buddy Bobby Hansen returned to his job at a newspaper in New Jersey. He would buy that '68 Plymouth with the Hemi engine he had talked about with Alan Weisman.

After being transferred in December, Robert Figueroa had been shot in the stomach while on a mission with the 1/7th Cav. He laughed while being loaded onto the dustoff, knowing the war was over for him.

Fred Brodosi had also been transferred and finished his tour with the 1/12th Cav. He did a lot of partying and drugs after the war and was a roadie for a rock band for a few years. Then he quit the drugs and worked in the restaurant business for twenty-five years. He married at the age of thirty-eight and has two sons. Now divorced, he lives in his home state of Florida.

For years, Bill Boyce continued making payments of exactly one dollar per month for the weapon he'd lost after being shot on November 19th 1966. The Army eventually gave up on trying to collect the debt.

Killed on Thanksgiving Day, CPT Wise's radio operator Donald Rankin had willed all his possessions, including part of his life insurance benefit, to his church in rural Kentucky. The proceeds were used to build an addition to the Silas Baptist Church, dedicated in his memory in 1967.

To send his family sixty dollars seemed trite. For decades, Royce Barrow contemplated how to repay the R&R money he'd borrowed from Rankin before he died. In 2010, he donated two hundred and fifty dollars to Rankin's church in his honor. He had also named his son Donald.

Lou Lupo was a neighborhood friend of Leonard Pelullo. Back in their high school days, Lou pulled duty as a crossing guard in the mornings before school. Every day, Lenny would wave to him from atop the front steps of the Pelullos' home in the Port Richmond neighborhood of Philadelphia. Lenny was a few years older, and Lou looked up to him like an older brother. Lou joined the Army in March 1967, a month after Lenny was killed, and went to the war in November. Lou would see Lenny's parents at veterans' memorial events over the years. He wanted to say something to them but never had the heart to. He and fellow veterans erected a memorial stone in a neighborhood park in 2015. Beneath the stone, Lou placed a card from Lenny's funeral along with his photo. He hoped to see Lenny's parents at the memorial's dedication. Regretfully, he did not.

Alpha Company, the 5/7th Cav, and the 1st Air Cavalry Division would continue their mission in Vietnam. One of many left behind to carry on that mission was Caesar Pinto, the one who had struggled through basic training and came to Alpha Company as a replacement in May. Paul Plaine, who'd helped him along in their training, always had a foreboding feeling about Pinto's fate since they said their goodbyes at Penn Station. Decades later, he journeyed to The Wall, hoping not to find his name. PFC Caesar A. Pinto, killed in action on August 9th 1967. Paul cried for him. He would continue to return to The Wall on every tenth anniversary of Pinto's death.

Alpha Company's forward observer George Kalergis would remain in Vietnam for several months. In October 1967, he was the fire direction officer for Charlie Battery, 1/21st Field Artillery. They had recently moved north into I Corps, establishing the 5/7th Cav's forward command post and firebase at LZ Colt. They had run out of both trip flares and Claymore mines. They were supposed to receive more from 3rd Brigade, but monsoon rains kept the supply ships grounded. They were also short on concertina wire, with only one roll surrounding their perimeter rather than the usual three. Severely undermanned and in a poor defensive position—a small rise amid vast fields of rice paddies and jungle—Kalergis felt they were vulnerable. He voiced his concern to the 5/7th's battalion commander, LTC John Wickham. Kalergis was told that there was nothing they could do and then dismissed.

In the early morning darkness of October 10th 1967, Kalergis was lying on his cot in the Fire Direction Center tent and listening to the World Series on the AFVN radio station. He was rooting for the Boston Red Sox, and Jim Lonborg was pitching a no-hitter when he heard the explosions. Mortars were raining down on LZ Colt, one destroying part of the tent he'd been resting in. He ran out to see where the enemy mortars were coming from. He spotted the flashes of mortar tubes on a small hill mass about seven hundred yards away.

Hands shaking with adrenaline, Kalergis plotted the enemy's position on his map and called in an adjusting round. An adjusting round is used to gauge and adjust artillery fire onto the target. It landed just beyond the enemy mortars. Into the radio, he yelled, "Drop five-zero, fire for effect!" This told the battery to bring their rounds fifty meters closer and to fire all their guns at once. He could hear the sports announcer's voice emanating from his transistor radio while waiting for his rounds to impact. Then he was told that LTC Wickham had just called in artillery directly on their own position. "Hell no, don't fire on us! Everything's under control," Kalergis radioed back. He continued to call in artillery until the enemy mortars fell silent. "End mission," he radioed.

Their mortars were destroyed, but three sapper squads had already breached their perimeter during the initial mortar barrage—running straight to the command post tent, throwing in grenades, and killing everyone inside. They had also thrown a satchel charge into the battalion commander's tent, killing one of his officers and gravely wounding LTC Wickham. Thinking they'd been completely overrun, he had attempted to bring artillery on their own position.

The enemy intended to overrun LZ Colt, but the sappers had only targeted the command post. A larger force was positioned to attack from the surrounding jungle, but the continuous rain of artillery and gunships kept them at bay while the defenders managed to kill or run off the infiltrators.

With seven Americans dead, Kalergis and Wickham were among a small number of the battalion's officers to survive the attack. President Ronald Reagan would appoint John Wickham as Chief of Staff of the Army in 1983. George Kalergis would retire as a Lieutenant Colonel.

Along with those visions of his dead fellow soldiers on May 19th, he would also remain haunted by those of the poor Vietnamese peasants. He can still see their grim faces looking through him, carrying all their possessions on their backs, forced to leave their homes because the government had declared their region an evacuation area. He reflected on how he could feel his humanity leaving him "like the smoke rising from the villages we were burning."

Rather than going home with the rest of the original battalion, Father Tom Widdel chose to stay for another year, preaching to the living, comforting the wounded, and positively identifying the dead.

Ron Wideman remembers the last time he saw his older brother Elvin before he was killed on November 19th 1966. He had returned to Saint Louis to say goodbye to his family just before leaving for Vietnam. Ron still has the photo of Elvin that was taken that day.

In 1971, Ron's number came up in the draft. He remembered how Elvin had threatened to kick his ass if he ever joined the Army, so he enlisted in the Air Force. After training as an Aircraft Maintenance Specialist on the B-52 Stratofortress, he was sent to Andersen Air Force Base in Guam, where they launched over 140 bombing runs per day during Operation Linebacker in 1972. From Guam, he was sent to the U-Tapao base in Thailand, where bombing runs were launched until the very end of American involvement in the war. He recalled how the entire flight line fell eerily silent after the last bomber took off on August 15th 1973. He was at U-Tapao again in April 1975 when over a hundred South Vietnamese military aircraft filled with thousands of refugees began landing at the airfield during the fall of Saigon.

Chinook crew chief Dave Mason was still in-country when the Tet Offensive started on January 30th 1968. Virtually every major city and military base in South Vietnam was under attack. The NVA had taken part of the city of Qui Nhon. Dave's crew was sent to pick up Korean troops from a small island nearby used for R&R. They assaulted them onto the airfield at Qui Nhon to take back the city.

As attacks continued deep in the highlands on the Dak To base, Dave and his crew spent twelve hours a day in flight, carrying supplies from Pleiku to Dak To and returning with dozens of dead and wounded. They ended their missions at dusk each night but would still have to perform hours of maintenance, then have the aircraft ready an hour before take-off at dawn. With only a few hours left for rest, he just slept on the chopper. At the end of his tour, he flew into Fort Hood in the dead of night. As he found out later, it had been planned this way to avoid protesters.

SSG Robert Matulac stayed with Alpha Company until September, then extended for four additional tours in Vietnam. He said he felt like he belonged there. Each time he extended, he was given a forty-five-day pass to spend anywhere in the world. His theory was that if the Army thought you actually wanted to stay there, they would pull you out.

He would not remain in the infantry, however. Returning to Vietnam from his forty-five-day pass late in 1967, he was assigned to an engineer unit building a road from Pleiku to Laos. In January 1968, he was to go to Saigon to pick up some classified documents. Complaining that Matulac always got to go on "field trips," one of their sergeants asked if he could go instead. He had the proper security clearance, and Matulac owed him a favor, so he agreed.

It was later that night when Matulac heard the explosions. Unlike the usual distant thumping of artillery, mortars were raining down on their Pleiku base camp. Seconds later, sirens sounded. It was the initial wave of the Tet Offensive. A handful of soldiers were huddled behind the door of their barracks. Matulac ordered them out to their bunkers to defend the base camp. The engineers could locate their distant targets only by their tracer rounds, and some mistakenly fired at friendlies outside the perimeter. "Shoot at the green tracers, not the red!" Matulac yelled.

The attack was short-lived and turned out to be either a diversion or a mistake. The big attack would be launched a few hours later on Saigon, Hue, and dozens of other major cities and bases throughout the country. While walking to the PX for smokes the next morning, Matulac passed by a general talking to reporters about the recent action. Nearby was a pile of enemy dead about ten feet high, and they were still piling them up.

Over a week had passed since Matulac sent that sergeant to Saigon for those classified documents. The sergeant walked into their barracks, unshaven and wearing filthy, tattered fatigues. He told of how he'd been in bed with a girl in Saigon when the attacks started. MPs came into his room and dragged him out to an armored personnel carrier. He spent the next week gathering the dead and wounded from the streets of Saigon as fighting continued. "Don't do me any more favors," he said, handing Matulac the documents.

Matulac's theory was eventually proven correct in 1971 when he was told he could no longer extend his tour. He was on the last leg of his journey home to his parents' house in California. Duffel bag in tow, he wore a dress uniform decorated with medals from five combat tours. He'd heard of others being welcomed home with protest signs and eggs. His parents lived in the heart of hippie country, and he expected the worst—yet he encountered no protesters at the airport or bus terminal, only a kind lady who offered him her seat on the bus. He arrived to find his parents out, and the door locked. He went around the corner to the neighborhood bar and ordered a beer. The bartender set down ten ice-cold Budweisers in front of him. "I only ordered one," Matulac said.

"Well, I hope you're thirsty," said the bartender, nodding to a group of men in the back. "They're from those guys over there."

After returning to his stateside post, Matulac was visited by two agents from the Army's Criminal Investigation Department. They asked him about black marketeering in Vietnam. He said he had no idea what was happening in the supply room as he was in the field the whole time. He could only say that they never seemed to get the supplies he ordered.

Matulac moved around a lot while in the Army and kept a lot of his stuff at his parents' house. Eventually, his dad got sick of it taking up space and threw most of it out. The only thing he regretted losing was that journal he had kept in his rucksack while in Vietnam.

After twenty-seven years in the United States Army, Robert Matulac retired as a Sergeant First Class. He had been offered a promotion to First Sergeant but would have been sent to Korea had he accepted. With a wife and two young daughters at home, he told his commander to "keep the stripe." He would go on to work in admissions and coach track at Monterey Peninsula College.

Matulac spoke of one of his last memories with Alpha Company in August 1967. He was at An Khe, again rounding up soldiers that had gone missing. "One of the young men begged me not to send him back to the field," he reflected. "He was crying, but I marched him to the helicopter and ordered him aboard. The next day, I called the first sergeant and told him I was coming back out to the field. He told me to go to Long Binh first. I asked why, and he said one of our men had been killed that morning. I had to go to Graves Registration to identify his body. I could still see the tears coming from behind his glasses as he begged me not to send him back out there. I identified PFC Caesar Pinto lying there, cut open from the autopsy. I'll never forget that scene. It haunts me even today."

*Caesar Pinto*

*Remaining Alpha Company soldiers with discharge papers at An Khe*

*Left–right: Martin Quinn, Donald Burtis, and Gerald Anderson*

*Paul Lussier (left) and Kurt Elmer (right), photos by Will Bowe*

*1st Air Cavalry Band playing for departing soldiers, photo by Will Bowe*

*Refueling in Philippines en route to United States, photo by Will Bowe*

*President Lyndon Johnson presenting Silver Star to LTC Trevor Swett*

In 1968, the 5/7th Cav was sent north to help take back the city of Hue after it had fallen to the communists, taking part in the deadliest battle of the Tet Offensive. The 1st Air Cav lost over a hundred helicopters in the fight to take back Hue. In 1970, President Richard Nixon sent the battalion deep into the jungles of Cambodia. After weeks of bloody fighting against the NVA, they uncovered an enormous underground stockpile of weapons.

1st Platoon leader Barry Gallagher would be awarded the Silver Star for his actions on Thanksgiving 1966. He is still married to his high school sweetheart Margie who he'd married during his basic training. Over the years, he has worked as a high school English teacher and Human Resources professional. Recalling how he'd lost Charles Bradford in the mangrove swamps on October 4th 1966, then Michael Stoflet and medic Bill Garcia on November 1st, he remarked, "I was a functional alcoholic for thirty years, self-medicating to overcome the ghosts of the men I lost in Vietnam." He remembers the bravery of LTC Trevor Swett and the love he had for his men, recalling how he landed his command chopper under heavy fire while trying to save Garcia that day.

A sophomore in high school when his uncle Mike Stoflet was killed, Steve Hubbard was drafted into the Marines in 1970. His older brother Dan had dropped out of college and enlisted in the Army. Because Dan was already serving in Vietnam when Steve finished his initial training, Steve was sent to Germany. After Dan returned, Steve realized his brother had enlisted only to keep him from being sent to the war.

On the wall in a high school in Elkhorn, Wisconsin, hangs a plaque dedicated by the graduating class of 1963, honoring their classmate Michael Stoflet, known to them as "Herbie." Terry Riesen—one of Donna's daughters that Mike used to drive to the candy store—still has the handwritten poem she wrote in grade school about her uncle's death. "For years, I dreamt there had been a mistake, and he came home," remarked Sally Stoflet. In 2011, she traveled to Vietnam with her daughter to visit the country where her uncle gave his life.

Among the newspaper clippings, award citations, and photographs kept by Mike's family is a collection of letters received after his death. One is from President Johnson, another from the governor of Wisconsin, and others from the Secretary of the Army, MACV Commander General Westmoreland, Division Commander General Norton, CPT A.J. Wise, and many others. They all spoke of how their son had died a hero, and all the other things one would expect them to say. There were also a couple of handwritten letters from LTC Swett. He spoke of how he and Father Tom Widdel had visited each company bivouac area that November to hold services for each of their fallen, and how he would have CPT Wise check with his men for any photographs they may have of their son.

The 5/7th Cav's original battalion commander, Trevor Swett, was eventually promoted to Colonel. Personally presented with the Silver Star for gallantry in action by President Johnson, he accepted the award on behalf of his men. In the film *Shakey's Hill* by CBS journalist Norman Lloyd about the 5/7th's 1970 incursion into Cambodia, he spoke of a time after he had returned from the war. He had been invited to speak at his son's graduation ceremony at the same prep school he'd graduated from. As he began to speak, many of the professors and students seated in the front two rows got up and left. "I realized just how unpopular the Vietnam War was when that happened," he said. He would remain haunted by the death of Alan Weisman, the young Jewish soldier he had persuaded to do his duty while at Fort Carson in 1966.

CPT A.J. Wise was talking to Weisman on the radio at the moment he was killed on November 19th 1966. Wise returned to Vietnam in 1972 as an advisor to ARVN regiments in the An Loc region of III Corps. He was sent there to replace an officer killed in action the day before. His helicopter was shot down while flying into An Loc. After twenty-four years of service, a veteran of both Korea and Vietnam, he retired as a Major in 1976. He would spend several years as a high school teacher and then work on an offshore oil exploration rig until he fully retired to his hometown of Blountstown, Florida.

When I first received a phone call from A.J. Wise, I sensed I was speaking with a true southern gentleman. He expressed great admiration for each of the men he led for what they had accomplished and endured during their time together. He felt that he had been given the best group of NCOs and officers he could have asked for as a company commander. He noted how so many of the company's draftees had become very successful after leaving the Army and how the 5/7th Cav's veterans' association was founded not by officers and senior NCOs but rather by a handful of their lower enlisted men. "They were not your average group of Vietnam veterans—if there is such a thing," he remarked. "I tried to bring them all back, but I couldn't."

1LT James Harmon was lying by Alan Weisman's side at the moment he was killed. After leaving the Army, he became a prosecutor and served as Assistant District Attorney in New York City. He would also provide free legal assistance to fellow veterans, helping them obtain the benefits they'd earned for their service in Vietnam.

As his stint in Long Binh Jail didn't count as good time, Arnott Graham would spend another three months in Vietnam. He recalled how Donnie Ward's mother kept sending baked goods to the company, even after he was killed on February 13th 1966. The last time he saw SSG Harry Coit was after the battle on May 19th 1967, when Coit called him a damn good soldier. In the movie version of this, they would have hugged and become best of friends. But in real life, that's all that was said. "My father died when I was four years old," Graham said, reflecting on his old commander, "but Captain Wise was like a father to me. He vouched for me and always saw the good in me."

Graham joined the local elevator mechanics union in 1971. Blacks were previously not allowed in this union, but he got in because he was a veteran. It was dangerous work but paid well, and soon he was working on the elevators at the World Trade Center. That same year, he was reminded of his time at Long Binh Jail as he watched news coverage of the Attica prison riot in upstate New York. The Attica riot ended with helicopters dropping tear gas into the prison yard as police opened fire, shooting over a hundred men, killing thirty-three inmates and ten guards.

For a few years, Graham stayed in touch with his buddy Robert O'Brien, who became a New York City police officer. Angel Reynosa had a baby girl in 1975 and asked Graham to be the godfather. John Bronson became a corrections officer. Graham recalled seeing him and Robert Figueroa occasionally in Brooklyn and how someone mentioned that Willie Harris had re-enlisted. In 1987, Graham would take two of his sons to The Wall to find the names of his friends Alan Weisman, Leonard Pelullo, and Donnie Ward.

Graham still blames himself for what happened on February 13th 1967. My dad still feels regret over the day Burtis was shot. Tom Ivey regrets not writing to his childhood friend Al Patrillo before he was killed on May 19th 1967. Tom Monnier thinks about that village woman who was in labor and how he couldn't help her. He wonders if she and her baby survived.

After recovering from his wounds from when he was blown up by a grenade but before he became a police officer, Joe Sanchez was working as a delivery driver in Manhattan. He was somewhere near Wall Street when he saw his old buddy Rocco Valentino crossing the street. He pulled over and called out to him, but he just disappeared into the crowd. Years later, Sanchez would reach out to the parents of his friend Leonard Pelullo, and each Mother's Day thereafter, he would send flowers to Lenny's mom.

Malcolm Brouhard was the young replacement who'd gotten married just before leaving for Vietnam and had been with Alpha Company for only a month when he was killed on Thanksgiving Day 1966. On the Wall of Faces, his wife's niece recalled visiting The Wall with her children. They found Malcolm's name and left roses in his honor. She took photos of the statues and names. "The one that still haunts me," she wrote, "is the photo I took of an elderly woman and her granddaughter. They were looking for her son on The Wall. She had Alzheimer's and had to be reminded of who they were looking for and why. She had a moment of clarity and started crying. She said, 'I remember you, my son.' I could not help but cry. I gave her one of the roses and asked if I could take her picture."

Beside a flag pole in Wallington, New Jersey stands a plaque that reads "Kazimierz H. Slomiany Memorial Bridge," honoring the young Polish immigrant and friend to many in Alpha Company, who was killed in action on June 19th 1967.

In 2023, the Tennessee legislature voted to dedicate a bridge in honor of A.G. Hensley, killed in action on March 31st 1967, in his hometown of Limestone. His friends Marty Scull, Bill Purdy, John Kruetzkamp, and Bill Hardenburgh each spoke at the dedication on a beautiful July 8th morning. I asked his brother Dallas about A.G.'s Corvette that he had told Scully about at Fort Carson. "I don't remember anything about a Corvette. Perhaps he was wishing he had a car like that back home," he speculated.

Camp Radcliff remained in use by the Army until 1971. Today, Hon Cong Mountain is just another mountain in the highlands, overlooking only wilderness and farmland. Almost nothing remains to suggest that thousands of Americans once inhabited this place they called An Khe.

After being bombed twice by war protesters, the government center at 39 Whitehall Street was shut down in 1969. The building had been used as a recruiting center since 1884, inducting nearly three million Americans into the military, including Joe Sanchez, Arnott Graham, Martin Quinn, and all the other guys from New York City.

The USNS Gaffey continued transporting thousands of troops to Vietnam until she was put into reserve in 1968. The rusting troop carrier remained docked and was used for several years as a barracks ship for the crews of vessels undergoing major overhaul. She was still afloat in 2000 when the Navy decided to use her for target practice during a training event near the Hawaiian Islands. The Gaffey and two other ships slated for sinking were bombed by Australian and United States Air Force jets, followed by two days of bombardment by naval gunfire. While the other ships sank, the old Gaffey refused. Divers with explosives were eventually sent down.

Now a mere ghost ship lying on the ocean floor, the Gaffey remains a symbol of a great turning point in the lives of thousands of once-young men. The 5/7th's voyage upon her in 1966, during the massive build-up of forces in Vietnam, would also come to symbolize a great turning point for the country.

In *Better Times Than These*, Winston Groom—author of *Forrest Gump*— tells of a fictional 4th Battalion, 7th Cavalry, sailing to Vietnam aboard the USNS Gaffey in the summer of 1966. Inspired by his own real-life voyage aboard the Gaffey with the nonfictional 5th Battalion, 7th Cavalry, his novel relates their many sea-faring shenanigans, misfortunes, and incidents, including the life vest fiasco and boxing matches. "In the boxing matches, my cabinmate Phil Collins got his front teeth bashed in," he mentioned in our correspondence. "The doc said that if he could stay in Okinawa for a week, he could wire him up and save them. But the asshole colonel said no, so they pulled them."

In his story, I found many parallels to the actual events, places, and men of the 5/7th Cav during this time. On the inside cover is a hand-drawn map of the Central Highlands, depicting a base camp known as Monkey Mountain, a hill known as The Tit, the Valley of The Tit, and the Village of the Running Man. Also, the Village of the Banana Cat, where a young soldier buys a small animal from a villager to keep as a pet. They called it a banana cat, described as something like a small monkey. I wanted to see what a banana cat looked like, so I googled it. I found a photo of a soldier in Vietnam, holding what looked more like a large snarling rodent than a cat or monkey. The photo was posted on a website belonging to Joe Sanchez, and this is how I found Joe.

Lumbering ashore from the Navy ship Albion, SP/4 Brutus T. Bear—the original battalion's mascot from Fort Carson—arrived in Da Nang Harbor with the 1/11th Mechanized Infantry in September 1968, tipping the scales at over three hundred pounds. She never faced the enemy, but Brutus would die of natural causes, officially pneumonia. Her diet of canned dog food, soda, and beer may have been contributing factors.

Armed Forces Vietnam continued broadcasting from Saigon until March 1973, when the American Radio Service took over the station. The final broadcast was made on April 29th 1975, playing Irving Berlin's *White Christmas* to signal the final evacuation of Saigon had begun.

Chris Noel continued visiting troops in the war zone and making her radio program *A Date With Chris* until 1969, when a Green Beret officer proposed to her while riding in a helicopter. They married in January, but suffering from the psychological effects of several combat tours, her husband took his own life in December of the same year. In 1981, veterans at the Los Angeles Veterans Hospital commenced a hunger strike demanding better treatment. The Reagan Administration reached out to Noel for help. With her assistance, a deal was negotiated for better treatment, ending the hunger strike. In 1993, she opened Vetsville Cease Fire House, a shelter for homeless veterans. She has received many awards from veterans' organizations and continues supporting Vietnam veterans at events nationwide.

Journalist and author Bernard Fall continued covering the war in Vietnam. On February 21st 1967, he was on a patrol with a company of Marines in Thua Thien Province, in the area the French had dubbed the proverbial Street Without Joy. Into his tape recorder, he spoke, "We've reached one of our phase lines after the firefight, and it smells bad—meaning it's a little bit suspicious. Could be an amb—" as he stepped on the Bouncing Betty that killed him.

Just before Saigon fell to the communists in April 1975, the United States launched Operation Babylift to evacuate over three thousand orphans of the war. Filled with mostly children, the first military aircraft to lift off was a giant C-5 Galaxy. It crashed in a rice paddy shortly after take-off, killing nearly half of its three hundred passengers. The next day, a Pan Am jet and its crew were sent to the airport in Saigon to evacuate the survivors, plus as many additional babies as would fit. They flew to San Francisco with over four hundred babies on board.

The members of these all-volunteer flight crews, many of whom spent years flying in and out of the war zone, never received any official recognition for their contribution to the war effort.

Among those sent back early was Bill Purdy. He had injured his knee in April jumping from a helicopter to keep John Kruetzkamp from being left behind in a rice paddy. Upon their return to the states, draftees with more than ninety days remaining were kept on duty for the remainder of their two-year Selected Reserve service term. After recovering from his injury, Purdy was sent to Fort Knox to serve his remaining time. He was assigned to a platoon of men who had also just returned from the war and were serving out their final months. Their job was to help train new soldiers headed to Vietnam. He recalled how some of them were also sent to quell the riots in Detroit that summer.

Returning to his ironworkers job, Purdy was confronted by an older coworker known as Red. "So what do you think about all that baby killing over there?" Red probed. "You were a part of all that—right, Purdy?" He had made a point of asking this in front of everyone in the break room.

"You don't know what you're talking about," Purdy replied.

Then Red spit on him. Faced with the prospect of fighting an old man, Purdy just walked away. His coworkers asked why he didn't take him down. He said it wasn't worth losing his job over. Maybe after everything he'd been through, he didn't feel the need to prove anything. In the following years, eight of his coworkers would also be drafted. He still has occasional nightmares from his time in Vietnam.

In 1992, Purdy got together with fellow 5/7th Cav troopers from the other companies, including Jasper Catanzaro and Don Shipley. They formed the 5/7th Cav Association and held their first reunion that August. Every two years thereafter, they would gather to remember their time together and their fallen friends. Their only rule, that they leave their politics, religion, and rank at the door.

While finishing this book, I asked my dad if there was anything he wanted to add. "Although our mortar platoon was often in mortal danger," he said, "it was minor compared to that of the rifle platoon soldiers who were the first to take a bullet and be killed. They are the crazy brave soldiers that deserve all the credit."

I'd like to know what happened to Ten Ninh, his little friend who tended cows in the Kim Son Valley. As only a privileged few of his country's young men could avoid service in the war, he would have been forced to choose sides as he came of age. His fate would be uncertain, given that the war would rage on for another eight years and all the brutal reprisals that followed the fall of Saigon. I'd like to think that he survived all of this and is still alive today. If so, he is now over sixty years old. Who knows, just maybe he still remembers a young American soldier named "Bow-E" who showed him kindness.

In August 2018, Dad and I flew to Pittsburgh to attend his first 5/7th Cav reunion. I had just printed the first two hundred copies of this book, and many had already been delivered to veterans of Alpha Company. One was Joe Williams, who greeted us in the hotel lobby and made us feel welcome. "It's sort of strange reading something that's written about you and your friends," he said. We met Gene Cross, whose helmet my dad recalled with the hole shot in it on October 4th 1966. He showed me the scar left on his scalp.

"Krazy" Karl Haartz spoke to the group as we ate dinner in one of the hotel's banquet rooms. I learned that Karl had earned his nickname by stealing the Charlie Company First Sergeant's car and taking it for a joy ride while at Fort Carson. Then he mentioned how he had recently met up with someone he remembered from their advanced mortar training at Fort Carson, Wilbur Bowe. I looked over at my dad. He looked nervous as tiny sweat beads formed on his forehead. Karl asked him to come up on stage. Karl gave him a big hug, and everyone applauded.

"Man, I was scared there for a minute," Dad said after returning to our table. I asked why, and he replied, "I thought he was going to ask me to speak!"

We were sitting around late one night in the hotel. Bobby Hansen recalled their first big battle in the mangrove swamps. In animated fashion, he was reenacting how one of their platoon sergeants would run from one spider hole to the next, killing NVA troops. "I got the little bastard!" he exclaimed. Chester Millay remarked how all he could remember from that day was a bunch of noise, screaming, and chaos, amazed at how Bobby could remember everything so vividly. "Like it was yesterday," as he put it. Then it struck me. Despite their outward appearance, they weren't old men to me—they were the same nineteen and twenty-year-old kids they were over fifty years ago.

Dad and I attended a second reunion a year later, and Mom joined us. This was a smaller affair just for Alpha Company, hosted by Jack Fleming in Albuquerque, New Mexico. While working on the book's original publication, we'd not had a chance to speak with Martin Quinn as he and Dad had lost touch since their last visit in 1993. Just before the reunion, he called my dad out of the blue and said he would join us in Albuquerque. He'd lost his wife the year before, so his cousin Dennis and wife Bobbie would accompany him.

After a few hours of reminiscing at the reunion, we pulled out a copy of the book. Quinn turned to the page that featured the letter he had written to Will in May of 1967, telling of the deaths of their friends Al Patrillo, John Fulford, and Bobby Hayslip. It was good to see two old friends reunited after twenty-seven years. We also met their old commander, A.J. Wise—the first time for me and the first in fifty-some years for my dad and Quinn.

Those who have faced real combat will typically speak more of their own comical mishaps and misdeeds than they will of actual warfare. Regarding the battles and firefights, they often just say how scared they were. I never knew that

A.J. Wise had been awarded a Silver Star for his actions during the rescue of that pilot and his gunner. He never mentioned it in our conversations. It was Royce Barrow who told me of this. It was Vernon Garrett's wife who sent me a copy of his own Silver Star citation for his actions on May 19th 1967, saying that he doesn't really like to speak of it. Most have mixed feelings about such awards when many of their friends faced the same circumstances and never received one. Awards depended on many things unrelated to a soldier's actual bravery, such as his leaders taking the time to write him up, their ability to write, and his reputation among the brass, who would ultimately have to approve such an award. But to me, these citations are important pieces of history, describing what they all experienced during their company's most harrowing moments.

Today, many anti-war activists have realized how some of their excesses only denigrated the service of those who fought in Vietnam with the best intentions. I would like to think that most who had accused our troops of war crimes or sympathized with North Vietnam's brutal regime now regret the worst of what they said and did in those days.

It would be an understatement to say that today's servicemen enjoy much better treatment from society than those of my dad's era. Public gratitude is so pervasive that it's hard not to take it for granted. Over the years, I've attended the homecomings of many deployed units of the Minnesota Army National Guard. They typically arrive at their hometown armory or airfield in a caravan of buses amid the roar of Harley engines. They are escorted by throngs of leather-clad men and women on motorcycles as families wait to be reunited with their soldiers. Most of these riders are twice the age of the soldiers they welcome home, and many are Vietnam veterans. One such rider is one of Alpha Company's former combat medics, Michael Handley. Known as the Patriot Guard, they ensure that no soldier is made to feel the way they felt when they returned home from an unpopular war.

I enlisted in the Army National Guard in July 2007. I was thirty-three years old and married, with four children at home. My wife Misty wasn't thrilled but was supportive anyway. My mom didn't think it was fair to my family, and it wasn't. The unit I'd joined was just then returning from a nearly two-year mobilization, sixteen months of which were spent in places like Fallujah and Tikrit. I figured my dad would be against it but was surprised at the fierceness of his opposition. At the time, I didn't understand why he was so adamant.

While enlisting at Fort Snelling, Misty found out from my recruiter—our next-door neighbor—that I had signed up to be an infantryman. I thought it offered the best chance to kick in some doors. She called my dad, who in turn dialed my cell phone. He very forcefully insisted that I choose something else. "My God," he said, "if there's one thing you don't want to be in, it's the infantry." I already felt bad about going against his wishes, so I relented and signed up to be a forward observer instead.

On August 4th 1967, SP/4 Wilbur E. Bowe was out-processed and discharged from the Army in Oakland, California. On his chest, he wore the National Defense Service Medal, Vietnam Campaign Medal, Vietnam Service Medal, Air Medal, Bronze Star, Expert Rifle Badge, and Combat Infantryman Badge. From here, he took his final flight to Minneapolis.

"*Oh, where have you been, my blue-eyed son?*" Whenever I hear Bob Dylan's *A Hard Rain's A-Gonna Fall*, I imagine what my grandpa Eddie might have said to his own blue-eyed son when he returned home from the war. Then I think of my own blue-eyed son, now almost the same age as my dad was when he went to the war. Now in college, he also plays football and has the same sense of humor and disregard for rules as my dad at that age.

While Martin Quinn returned home in a dingy subway car, Will traveled home along a dusty county road. As they passed farmhouses, cattle, and cornfields, Millie spoke of what she knew of the other boys who had been sent to the war. The ones who were still there, those who had made it back, and those who never would. As it was for most, Will's homecoming was uneventful. Life had gone on without him. Despite the scenes of social upheaval on the evening news, little had changed in rural Wisconsin.

And what to do with the rest of his life. Before he could think about that, he needed to do something. He took his dad's Oldsmobile into town. He passed the post office where he had first met Rodney Henning. It was hard to believe that less than two years had passed since that chilly October morning in 1965. He drove on to the corner drugstore, picked up the photos from his last roll of film, and bought a small photo album.

Sitting at the kitchen table, he arranged his photos. He looked at them for a while—and then the one of Patrillo. He placed the album in a cardboard box with his medals, newspaper clippings, and discharge papers. Then he put the box on the shelf in the back corner of his closet. He took one last look at his dress uniform before zipping the garment bag and hanging it up, never to wear it again.

Everyone has regrets. If there's one thing I could wish for my dad and his friends, it would be to let go of any lingering regrets from that year spent in Vietnam. At an age when many young men would be attending college, going to parties, and chasing girls, you were sent to fight in the jungles of a foreign land. You witnessed and endured things that most of us could never comprehend. At a time when so many would turn their backs on their country, you showed up, did your duty, carried out your orders every day until the very last day, and somehow you survived. In this war, that's as good as it gets. There's nothing to regret. And by the way, welcome home.

Garryowen

# ACKNOWLEDGMENTS

To all who have posted reviews on Amazon, Goodreads, and elsewhere, thank you for making *The Ground You Stand Upon* a popular choice among readers of Vietnam memoirs and biographies. It is always heartwarming to read the comments of those touched by our story. I would also like to thank the following people for their contributions.

Carol Bowe, my mom, for accompanying us on our journey to the National Archives, spending long days scanning documents, and each night at College Park, Maryland's finest Super 8. Also, for proofreading several drafts. I had aspired to be an author when I was a kid, and she had always wanted me to write a book. Thank you, Mom, for supporting me and my brother Nick through everything in our lives.

Dave Mason, my uncle, Vietnam veteran, and Chinook crew chief, for sharing photos and memories of his most remarkable missions.

Kathleen Perez and Cynthia French, Sam Daily's daughters, for providing background of their father, photographs of their young family, and additional information about the battle where he gave his life on October 4th 1966.

Patty Perkins and Vivian Deaton, Charles Bradford's nieces, for sharing background, memories, and a wedding photo of their uncle Charlie, killed in action on October 4th 1966.

Annette Sebastian, for sharing news clippings, memories, and photos of her younger brother, Guy McNay, Jr. (Juggy), killed in action on May 19th 1967.

Walter Sebastian, Annette's son, for sharing memories of his uncle Guy McNay, who was really more like a brother.

Lea Ann Bird, a family member of Guy McNay, for finding additional information and putting me in contact with his sister Annette.

Wayne and Tony Rankin, for sharing Donald Rankin's letters and the photo of him carrying a Vietnamese child. Wayne is Donald's younger brother. His son Tony was born the year before Donald went to Vietnam.

MAJ A.J. Wise (Ret), original Alpha Company commander, for speaking with me about his experience and memories of those he led into battle.

Robert Wagner, fellow Alpha Company soldier, for sharing memories of October 4th, November 19th, and Thanksgiving Day, and documentation of Purple Hearts awarded for October 4th 1966.

Marty Scull, fellow Alpha Company soldier, for sharing his own memories of A.G. and the day he was killed.

Dallas Hensley, fellow Veteran, for sharing memories and photos of his younger brother A.G.

John Kruetzkamp, fellow Alpha Company soldier, for sharing memories of their most harrowing and most comical moments.

Chester Millay, fellow Alpha Company soldier, for sharing memories of Vietnam and training at Fort Carson.

Bill Purdy, fellow Alpha Company soldier, for putting me in touch with Bobby Hansen and sharing photos and memories, including those of his last moments with A.G. Hensley, killed on March 31st 1967.

Bobby Hansen, fellow Alpha Company soldier, for sharing memories of Donald Smith and Alan Weisman, killed on October 4th and November 19th, respectively, and of Thanksgiving Day 1966.

Jim Hirschuber, fellow Alpha Company soldier, for sharing memories of their voyage on the Gaffey, November 19th 1966, and his own homecoming.

SFC Robert Matulac (Ret), fellow Alpha Company soldier, for sharing memories and photos and putting me in touch with Bill Purdy and Jim Hirschuber.

Mo Dhania, Joe Sanchez's friend, for proofreading several drafts of this book.

Joe Sanchez, fellow Alpha Company soldier, for sharing photos and memories of Alan Weisman and Leonard Pelullo, killed in action on November 19th 1966 and February 13th 1967, respectively, and for putting me in touch with Robert Matulac and Robert Wagner.

James Harmon, fellow Alpha Company soldier, for suggesting *Better Times Than These*. Without reading that book, I would have never found Joe Sanchez.

Don Shipley, fellow 5/7th Cav soldier in Charlie Company, now Vice President of Membership for their veterans' association, for putting me in touch with James Harmon and suggesting *On The Tiger's Back*. "So why hasn't Will been to any of our reunions?" was his first question for me. Like a shepherd searching for his lost sheep, he's brought many skytroopers back into the fold.

Gene Cross, fellow Alpha Company soldier, for sharing memories of October 4th 1966 and Donald Duncan, killed on Thanksgiving Day 1966.

Michael Handley, fellow Alpha Company soldier and medic, for sharing his memories of October 4th 1966.

Tom Monnier, fellow 4th Platoon soldier and medic, for sharing memories of October 4th 1966, and many other experiences.

Marvin Bierschbach, fellow mortar team member, for meeting with my dad and me in June 2017 to share memories and photos of Vietnam.

Gerald Anderson, fellow 4th Platoon soldier, for sharing memories of Fort Carson, An Khe, R&R in Tokyo, and New Year's Eve on the outpost.

Fred Brodosi, fellow 4th Platoon soldier, for sharing memories of October 4th and November 19th 1966.

Arnott Graham, fellow Alpha Company soldier, for sharing very colorful memories of Fort Carson, Vietnam, and my dad.

Jack and Josephine Fleming, fellow Alpha Company soldier and wife, for hosting Alpha Company's reunion in Albuquerque in August 2019, allowing my dad to reunite with Martin Quinn after twenty-seven years.

Martin Quinn, fellow 4th Platoon soldier, for meeting us at the reunion and sharing memories of my dad and their friendship.

Dennis and Bobbie Sheppard, Martin's cousin and his wife, for encouraging him to attend and accompanying him to the reunion.

Royce Barrow, fellow Alpha Company soldier and radio operator, for sharing memories of October 4th and Thanksgiving Day 1966 and February 13th 1967.

Barry Gallagher, Alpha Company's 1st Platoon leader, for sharing memories of October 4th, October 27th, and November 1st 1966.

Paul Plaine, fellow Army veteran, for sharing memories of his basic training friend Caesar Pinto, killed in action on August 9th 1967.

Lou Lupo, fellow Vietnam veteran and hometown friend from Philadelphia, for sharing memories of Leonard Pelullo, killed in action on February 13th 1967.

Steve Hubbard, fellow veteran, for sharing memories of his uncle Michael Stoflet, killed in action on November 1st 1966.

Karen Gramenz, Michael Stoflet's high school friend, for putting me in contact with his nephew Steve Hubbard.

Donna and Jim Newhouse, Michael Stoflet's older sister and husband, for sharing memories of Mike before he went to the war.

Priscilla Stoflet, for sharing memories, photos, and excerpts of letters from her brother-in-law Mike.

Terry and Paul Riesen, Donna's daughter and grandson, for sending articles, photos, and a journal of his military service kept by Mike's sister Nancy.

Sally Stoflet, for sharing childhood memories, photos, and newspaper articles of her uncle Mike.

Nick Lian, fellow Alpha Company soldier, for sharing memories of Vietnam and my dad during their time there.

LTC George Kalergis (Ret), Alpha Company's forward observer from February to June 1967, for sharing memories of his first missions with the 1/9th Cav and with Alpha Company 5/7th Cav during the battle of May 19th 1967.

John Goodpaster, fellow 5/7th Cav soldier in Charlie Company, for sharing memories of the Gaffey and a photo of Charlie Company on patrol in the jungle.

Tom Ivey, friend and neighbor of Albert Patrillo, for sharing memories of Al, from childhood to the day he watched soldiers in dress uniform approaching the Patrillos' family home in May of 1967.

John Benson, schoolteacher in Albert Patrillo's hometown. He'd written an article for their local paper in 2017 honoring the 50th anniversary of Patrillo's death. In 2018, a friend told John how he'd come across Albert Patrillo's name while reading this book. Then John called me and sent his article about Al's life growing up in Susquehanna, Pennsylvania, and photos from Al's family. He also put me in touch with Al's childhood friend Tom Ivey.

Ron Wideman, fellow veteran, for sharing memories of his older brother Elvin, killed in action on November 19th 1966.

Vernon and Linda Garrett, fellow Alpha Company soldier and his wife, for sharing photos and a copy of his Silver Star citation for actions on May 19th 1967.

Keneth Miller, for sharing information about his cousin Malcolm Brouhard, killed in action on Thanksgiving Day 1966.

Harald Hendrichsen, fellow Vietnam veteran of the 604th Transportation Company. An aerial photo of the Mang Yang Pass originally appeared in this book attributed as "source unknown." In 2019, Harald emailed me to say he was the one who took that photo at the age of nineteen in 1969. He sent me a copy with landmarks labeled, including the French cemetery, which is now included in the book. Harald has documented his own company's experience in Vietnam on his website: www.604th.com

The Staff of the National Archives in College Park, Maryland, for helping in our search for records of the 5/7th Cavalry in Vietnam. One especially helpful staff member was a fellow Vietnam veteran named Stanley Fanaras. This story would not be what it is today without them.

# BATTLE MAPS

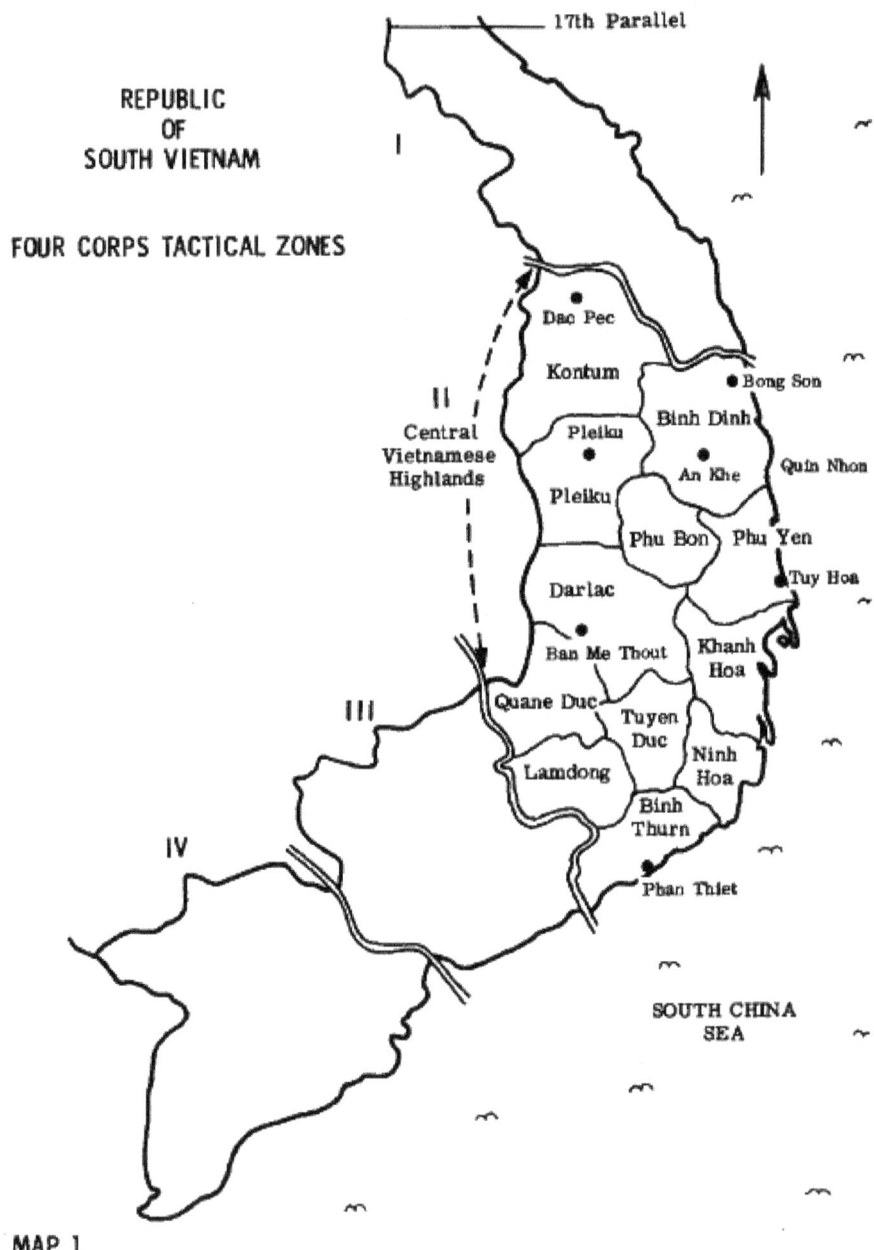

MAP 1

*II Corps, Republic of Vietnam*

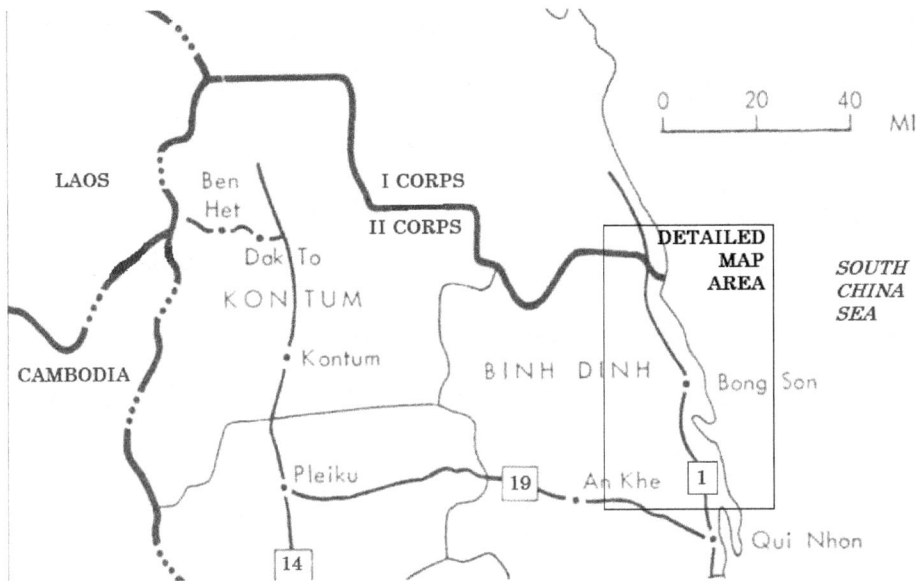

*Binh Dinh, Pleiku, and Kon Tum Provinces (detailed map on next page)*

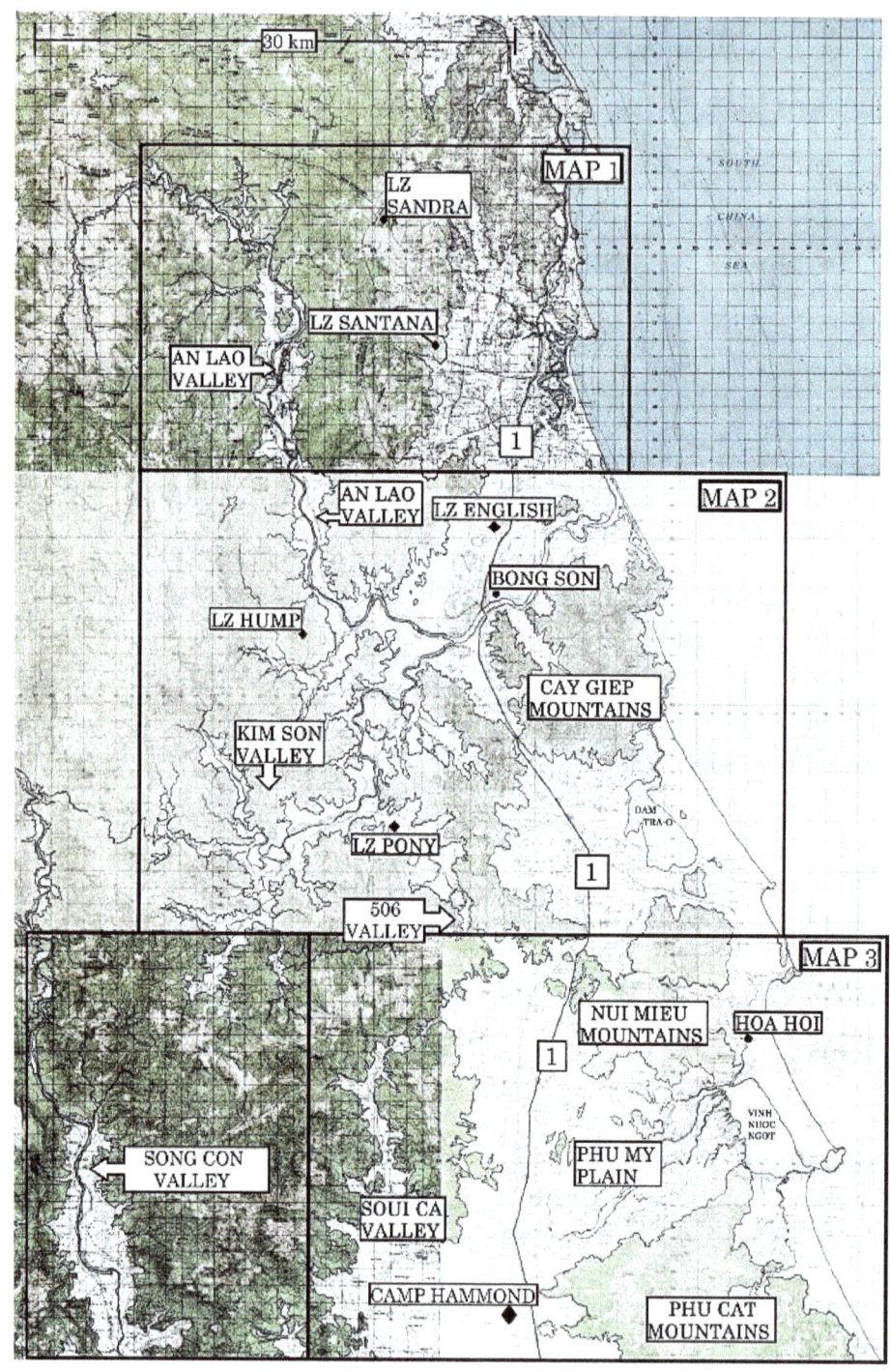

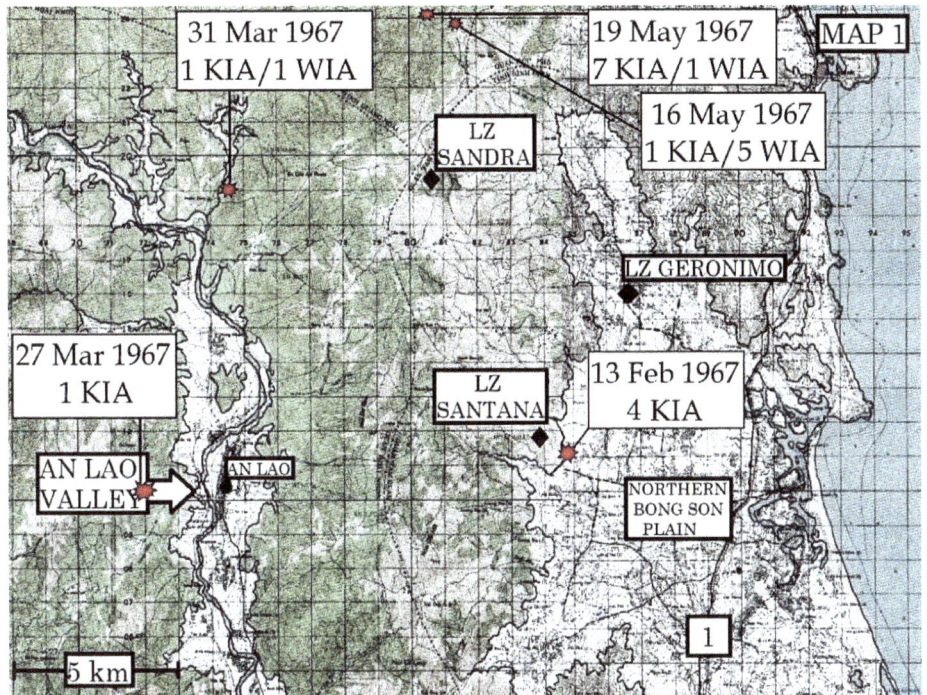

*Map 1: Northern An Lao Valley and Bong Son plain*

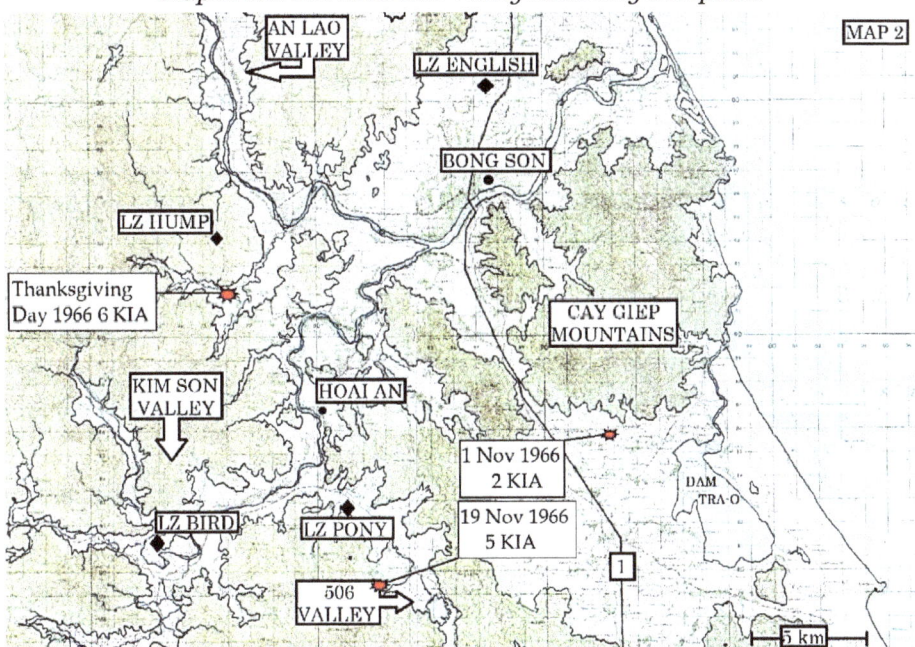

*Map 2: Southern An Lao Valley, Bong Son, Kim Son Valley, and Valley 506*

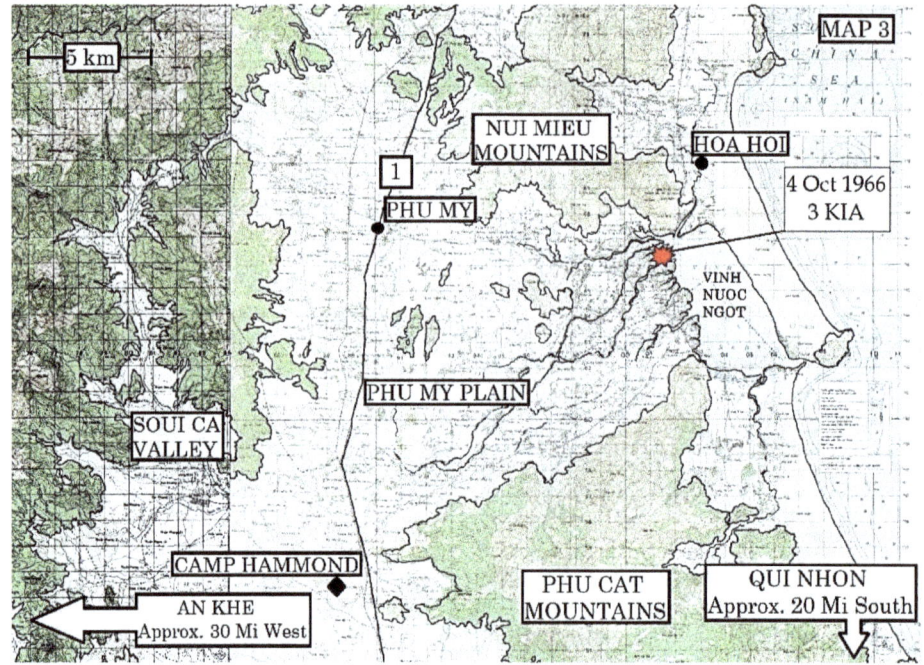

*Map 3: Soui Ca Valley and Phu My plain*

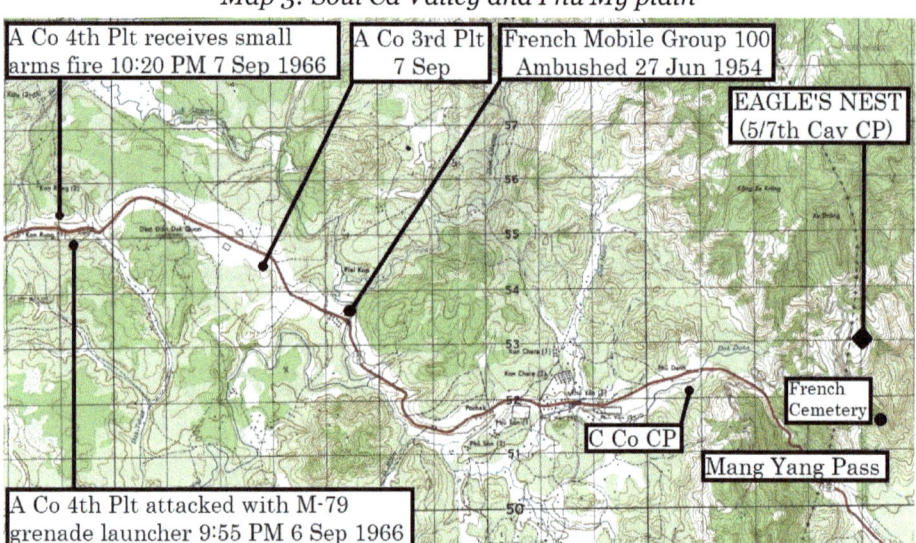

*Highway 19 from Pleiku to An Khe*

# About the Authors

Joshua Bowe lives in Chaska, Minnesota with his wife Misty. Two of their four children are in college, and two have families of their own. He served twelve years in the Minnesota National Guard and continues to work full-time for the National Guard as a civilian. You can follow his blog and post reviews on his Amazon and Goodreads author pages. Check out his YouTube channel to view a book trailer and slideshow featuring photos taken by his dad and fellow soldiers during their time in Vietnam.

Wilbur Bowe lives in Cameron, Wisconsin with his wife Carol, where they raised their two sons, Joshua and Nicholas. Born and raised on his family's dairy farm in Tilden, Wisconsin, drafted in 1965 and sent to Vietnam, he returned as a combat veteran in 1967. Since then, he has spent most of his life as a maintenance electrician. Now retired, he spends much time building and fixing things for his friends, neighbors, and local Catholic church. Along with others in his infantry company, he contributed greatly to *The Ground You Stand Upon*, much of it written over fifty years ago in the jungles of a foreign land.

*Wilbur Bowe — Joshua Bowe*
www.thegroundyoustandupon.org
www.youtube.com/@joshuabowe1424
www.facebook.com/thegroundyoustandupon.org

# BIBLIOGRAPHY

ON THE TIGER'S BACK—1994, by CPT Bernard E. Grady (Ret), Bravo Company, 5/7th Cav's Executive Officer, then Commander of Charlie Company during the battalion's initial tour of duty from August 1966 to August 1967.

1966 THE YEAR OF THE HORSE—2009, by Robert K. Powers, an infantryman in Bravo Company's mortar platoon. Drafted in January 1966 and sent to Vietnam in October, he was wounded in action on May 18th 1967.

TRUE BLUE, A Tale of the Enemy Within—2007, by Joe Sanchez, an infantryman in Alpha Company. His book tells of his experiences as a New York City cop and his fight to expose corruption but also relates his memories of Fort Carson and Vietnam, where he was wounded in action in January 1967.

BETTER TIMES THAN THESE—1978, by Winston Groom, a fellow Vietnam veteran who also wrote *Forrest Gump*. His novel follows the fictional Bravo Company, 4th Battalion, 7th Cavalry, sent to Vietnam in August 1966.

THE 1ST CAV IN VIETNAM, Anatomy of a Division—1987, by CPT Shelby L. Stanton (Ret), who served in the 82nd Airborne Division in Southeast Asia and was wounded in action. The book tells of the 1st Air Cavalry Division's development of the Airmobile concept in Vietnam.

THE RISE AND FALL OF AN AMERICAN ARMY, U.S. Ground Forces in Vietnam, 1965 to 1973—1985, by CPT Shelby L. Stanton (Ret). An assessment of the toll the Vietnam War took on the U.S. military, along with the government's refusal to mobilize the National Guard and other reserve forces.

STREET WITHOUT JOY: The French Debacle in Indochina—1961, by Bernard B. Fall. Tells of the French military's struggle to regain control of Vietnam from the end of World War II until their defeat by the Viet Minh in 1954.

DEAR AMERICA: Letters Home From Vietnam—1985, edited by Bernard Edelman. A collection of letters home from servicemen and women serving in Vietnam. The book was also made into an HBO documentary. Both the book and film include the letter written by Alpha Company's Richard Cantale about the death of his friend Donald Rankin.

A WALK AMONG THE BRAVE—2011, by Tina Susedik. A collection of veterans' experiences with profiles of Rodney Henning, Wilbur Bowe, his brother Darrell Bowe, and others from the Chippewa Falls area.

HEROES: A Year in Vietnam With the First Air Cavalry Division—2008, by Mike Larson. Memoir of a combat journalist writing for the *Cavalair* newspaper.

THE FACES BEHIND THE NAMES: The Vietnam War—1996, by Don Ward. Profiles of Minnesotans who gave their lives in Vietnam.

PAN AM IN VIETNAM—2020, by Business Insider reporters Charlie Herman, Julia Press, and Sarah Wyman. Features interviews with Pan Am stewardesses who flew servicemen in and out of the war zone.

1ST CAVALRY DIVISION, Memoirs of the First Team, Vietnam, August 1965 to December 1969—1970, edited by J.D. Coleman.

BUYING TIME 1965 to 1966—2015, by Frank L. Jones.

COMBAT OPERATIONS: Stemming the Tide, May 1965 to October 1966—2000, by John M. Carland.

COMBAT OPERATIONS: Taking the Offensive, October 1966 to October 1967—1998, by George L. MacGarrigle.

AFTER ACTION REPORT (September 3rd 1966 attack on Camp Radcliff)—September 17th 1966, 1st Cavalry Division (Airmobile) Headquarters.

BATTALION DAILY SITUATION REPORTS, September 1st 1966 to March 12th 1967—5/7th Cavalry, 1st Cavalry Division (Airmobile), from National Archives.

BATTALION DAILY STAFF JOURNALS, January 1st to August 9th 1967—5/7th Cavalry, 1st Cavalry Division (Airmobile), from National Archives.

PRESIDENTIAL UNIT CITATION for the period September 30th 1966 to March 30th 1967, Supporting Documentation—5/7th Cavalry, 1st Cavalry Division (Airmobile), from National Archives.

TOPOGRAPHIC MILITARY MAPS OF VIETNAM—University of Texas Libraries website.

VIETNAM VETERANS MEMORIAL FUND WALL OF FACES—Memorial website by the organization that built The Wall.

THE COFFELT DATABASE (National Archives Online)—Lists all servicemen killed in the Vietnam War with date of birth, date of death, home of record, branch of service, unit, rank, MOS, and enlistment status.

SHAKEY'S HILL (Documentary)—2007, by Norman Lloyd, a CBS journalist embedded with Bravo Company, 5/7th Cav during their incursion into Cambodia in May 1970. Film features footage taken as they fought the NVA. Named for the young soldier, Chris Keffalos, nicknamed "Shakey," who was killed atop a hill shortly after discovering a massive underground stockpile of weapons. While producing the film decades later, Lloyd reunited many Bravo Company men who served during the mission.

# Glossary

Agent Orange: An herbicide-defoliant chemical sprayed in large quantities over jungle areas to deny concealment to guerrilla forces.

Airborne: Soldiers who jump out of airplanes.

Airmobile: Soldiers who jump out of helicopters.

AIT: Advance Individual Training, specific to a soldier's MOS.

Ambush: Position taken to catch the enemy by surprise, typically a handful of soldiers in darkness, just outside a company patrol base or outpost.

ARA: Aerial Rocket Artillery, rockets fired from helicopter gunships.

Article 15: A low-level official military disciplinary action.

ARVN: Army of the Republic of Vietnam, main South Vietnamese forces.

Base Camp: Large military installation with some permanent structures and airfields, surrounded by perimeter wire and guard towers.

Bivouac: Small, improvised, temporary military encampment or patrol base.

Bouncing Betty: Small anti-personnel mine that, when activated by stepping on its prongs, is propelled upward three to four feet before exploding.

Brass: Military slang for high-ranking officers and important people.

Buck Sergeant: A junior NCO in the rank of Sergeant (SGT), E-5.

C-4: Plastic explosive used in varying quantities and molded into desired shape, only exploding by a detonator or blasting cap. Used for blowing up trees and clearing landing zones.

Caribou: De Havilland C-7A and B, large, fixed-wing military transport aircraft.

Chinook: Boeing CH-47, large twin-propeller helicopter used for troop transport, air assault, and supply.

Claymore: Directional anti-personnel mine placed around patrol base or other defensive position, activated by an operator using a detonator attached by wire.

Cobra: Bell AH-1, heavily armed attack helicopter.

C-Rations: Canned military food for soldiers in the field.

Deuce-and-a-half: Slang for two-and-a-half-ton truck.

Dustoff: Informal term for medevac helicopter.

ETS: Expiration Term of Service, a soldier's last day in the Army

Fields of Fire: Areas beyond defensive positions, cleared of vegetation to provide visibility over potential avenues of approach.

Firebase: Military outpost with artillery, located in range to support infantry.

Forward Observer: An artillery soldier typically attached to an infantry company, responsible for calling artillery fire.

Galaxy: Lockheed C-5, one of the largest military transport planes in the world, capable of carrying other aircraft and tanks within its airframe.

Garryowen: Derived from the Gaelic, *Eóin* (an Irish form of John), and the word for garden, *garrai*, meaning "John's Garden" in Gaelic. John's Garden was that of a church founded by the Knights Templar and dedicated to John the Baptist in Limerick, Ireland. This garden, known as "Garryowen," was the subject of a popular Irish drinking song in the late eighteenth century that was eventually adopted as the marching tune of the 5th Irish Royal Lancers. A century later, this song that was popular among the Irish immigrants of the U.S. 7th Cavalry was adopted as their marching tune.

Grenadier: Soldier whose primary weapon is the M-79 grenade launcher.

Gunship: Helicopter armed with machine guns and aerial rocket artillery.

Hamlet: Small village.

Hercules: Lockheed C-130, large military transport airplane. A heavily armed modified version was also used as a "Spooky" gunship.

Howitzer: Modern artillery gun with rifled bore, capable of shooting explosive shells for several miles.

Huey: Bell UH-1 Iroquois, helicopter used as troop transport, air assault, supply, and gunship.

KP: Kitchen patrol or duty.

Lifeline Packs: Boxed kits for soldiers in the field with candy, gum, cigarettes, shaving kits, and letter-writing materials.

Log Ship: Helicopter used for resupply.

LRRP: Long-Range Reconnaissance Patrol, a small unit sent on extended missions to report enemy locations.

LZ: Landing Zone, a place to land a helicopter or drop troops into combat, also may refer to an outpost or firebase.

M-16: Standard rifle issued to soldiers in Vietnam beginning in 1965, replacing the M-14.

M-60: Most commonly used machine gun by infantry and helicopters in Vietnam.

M-72 LAW: Light Anti-tank Weapon, rocket launcher used to destroy bunkers.

M-79: Shotgun-style grenade launcher used by infantrymen called grenadiers.

MACV: Military Assistance Command, Vietnam, highest level of command over all services in Vietnam, responsible for running the war.

Malingering: Faking a medical condition to avoid duty.

Minigun: Gatling gun-style weapon mounted to attack helicopters, firing over six thousand 7.62mm rounds per minute.

MP: Military Police.

Mortar: 81mm system consisted of a base plate, bipod, and barrel, used to lob explosive rounds at enemy.

MOS: Military Occupational Specialty, the specific job of a soldier, such as infantryman, artilleryman, or combat medic.

NVA: North Vietnamese Army, main-force communist soldiers from North Vietnam, often wearing khaki uniforms and helmets.

Patrol Base: Improvised temporary encampment or bivouac, usually that of a company-size unit or smaller.

Poncho: Large plastic sheet with a hole and hood, could be used as a raincoat or buttoned to another to make a tent or hooch.

Poncho Liner: Lightweight blanket issued to soldiers that resisted soaking and dried out more quickly than the standard wool blanket.

PRC-25: Standard radiotelephone that could be carried on operator's back.

Profile: Issued by an Army doctor, limiting a soldier's duty due to injury or medical condition.

PX: Post Exchange, the military's version of a convenience store.

PZ: Pickup zone, place for a helicopter to pick up troops, typically marked with smoke grenades.

Rear-Echelon: Refers to those working primarily in base camp or headquarters.

Recoilless Rifle: A large, man-portable anti-tank rifle that fires explosive shells for destroying bunkers.

ROK: Allied Republic of Korea forces.

Sappers: Soldiers who sabotage firebases and base camps at night to destroy command posts, communications equipment, aircraft, and vehicles.

Scout Ship: Small observation helicopter used for reconnaissance.

Sky Crane: Sikorsky CH-54 Tarhe, heavy-lift helicopter, hauling equipment, other aircraft, and tanks.

Skytrooper: Airmobile infantrymen who jump out of helicopters.

Sorry About That: interj. sorry; whoops; a gross understatement, said more as a self-deprecating joke than as an apology; most often an ironic understatement, as when one has been responsible for making a big mistake; popularized in the 1960s TV program *Get Smart*.

Spooky Gunship: Douglas AC-47, large military airplane armed with miniguns and other armaments, capable of dropping five-hundred-pound bombs and illuminating vast areas of terrain, also known as "Puff the Magic Dragon." In 1967, the Lockheed C-130 Hercules replaced the AC-47 in this role.

Stratofortress: Boeing B-52, large long-range strategic bomber airplane.

The World: Military slang for any place that wasn't Vietnam.

Top: Informal name for a company First Sergeant.

Trip Flare: Illuminating flare propelled into the sky when its tripwire is pulled, typically used around firebases and patrol bases.

USO: United Service Organizations, a nonprofit corporation providing live entertainment, social facilities, and other programs to service members worldwide since 1941.

VC: Viet Cong, communist guerrilla forces in South Vietnam, typically wearing black pajamas and no helmets.

VNMC: Marine Corps of the Republic of Vietnam.

# Army Ranks

Enlisted Ranks

Private: PVT, Pay Grade E-1, entry-level enlisted soldier, no rank insignia.

Private 2: PV2, Pay Grade E-2, entry-level enlisted soldier with one stripe.

Private First Class: PFC, Pay Grade E-3, enlisted soldier with one stripe, one rocker, and some experience.

Specialist or Specialist-Four: SPC or SP/4, Pay Grade E-4, enlisted soldier with more experience.

Corporal: CPL, Pay Grade E-4, junior noncommissioned officer or NCO, typically in charge of a team of three to four lower enlisted soldiers.

Sergeant (buck sergeant): SGT, Pay Grade E-5, junior NCO, typically in charge of a team of three to four lower enlisted soldiers.

Staff Sergeant: SSG, Pay Grade E-6, NCO typically in charge of a squad comprising two teams (6 to 8 soldiers).

Sergeant First Class: SFC, Pay Grade E-7, senior NCO typically in charge of a platoon comprising four squads (24 to 32 soldiers).

Master Sergeant: MSG, Pay Grade E-8, senior NCO typically battalion staff or acting First Sergeant.

First Sergeant: 1SG, Pay Grade E-9, senior NCO typically in charge of a company comprising four platoons (90 to 175 soldiers).

Sergeant Major: SGM, Pay Grade E-9, senior NCO typically in charge of a battalion composed of four to six companies.

Command Sergeant Major: CSM, Pay Grade E-9, senior NCO typically in charge of a Brigade comprising several battalions or a division comprising several brigades.

Officer Ranks

Second Lieutenant: 2LT, Pay Grade O-1, junior officer, typically commanding a platoon

First Lieutenant: 1LT, Pay Grade O-2, junior officer with some experience, typically commanding a platoon or on battalion staff.

Captain: CPT, Pay Grade O-3, officer with more experience, typically commanding a company or on battalion staff.

Major: MAJ, Pay Grade O-4, field grade officer, typically commanding a battalion or on battalion staff.

Lieutenant Colonel (light colonel): LTC, Pay Grade O-5, field grade officer typically commanding a battalion.

Colonel (full bird): COL, Pay Grade O-6, field grade officer typically commanding a brigade.

Brigadier General: BG, Pay Grade O-7, general officer, typically assistant division commander, one-star insignia.

Major General: MG, Pay Grade O-8, general officer typically commanding a division, two-star insignia.

Lieutenant General: LTG, Pay Grade O-9, general officer typically commanding a field force (several divisions), three-star insignia.

General: GEN, Pay Grade O-10, general officer commanding MACV (Military Assistance Command, Vietnam), that is to say, the entire war, four-star insignia.

Warrant Officer: WO1 to CW5, Pay Grades W-1 to W-5, officers with highly specialized skills, but who do not command large units of soldiers as commissioned officers do. Most Army helicopter pilots are Warrant Officers.

# UNITS OF THE 1ST AIR CAVALRY DIVISION
(not a complete listing)

**1st Brigade**
1st Battalion (Airborne), 8th Cavalry
2nd Battalion (Airborne), 8th Cavalry
1st Battalion, 12th Cavalry

**2nd Brigade**
1st Battalion, 5th Cavalry
2nd Battalion, 5th Cavalry
2nd Battalion, 12th Cavalry

**3rd Brigade (Garryowen Brigade)**
1st Battalion, 7th Cavalry
2nd Battalion, 7th Cavalry
5th Battalion, 7th Cavalry

**Division Artillery**
2nd Battalion, 19th Artillery
2nd Battalion, 20th Artillery (Aerial Rocket Artillery)
1st Battalion, 21st Artillery
1st Battalion, 30th Artillery
1st Battalion, 77th Artillery

**Support Command**
8th Engineer Battalion
13th Signal Battalion
15th Medical Battalion
15th Supply & Service Battalion
15th Transportation Battalion
27th Maintenance Battalion
15th Administrative Company
15th Supply & Service Battalion Aerial Equipment Support Company (Airborne)
545th Military Police Company
191st Military Intelligence Detachment
371st Army Security Agency Company

**11th Aviation Group (Airmobile)**
227th Assault Helicopter Battalion
228th Assault Support Helicopter Battalion
229th Assault Helicopter Battalion
1st Squadron, 9th Cavalry

www.ingramcontent.com/pod-product-compliance
Lightning Source LLC
Chambersburg PA
CBHW070342010526
44107CB00004B/598